deviance, reality, and change

Consulting Editor
Peter I. Rose
Smith College

 RANDOM HOUSE   NEW YORK

deviance, reality, and change

H. TAYLOR BUCKNER

Sir George Williams University

UR SAY

GUARD YOUR

FREEDOM

ALL THE

PHOTO CREDITS

Photos for the cover and for pages 3,
43, 73, 115, 163, 209, 253, 275, 315, 361,
399, and 413, George Gardner.
Photo for page 381, Wide World Photos.

Library of Congress Catalog
Card Number: 72–121071

ISBN: 0–394–31002–0
Manufactured in the United States
of America. Composed by Cherry Hill
Composition, Inc., Pennsauken, N.J.
Printed and bound by The Kingsport
Press, Kingsport, Tenn.

First Edition
98765432
Design by Jack Ribik

TO FRANK M. VICROY,
TEACHER

preface

I wrote this book because I couldn't find a good text on deviance for my students. Some of the books were listings of everything that had ever been written about deviance—collections of facts without much order. Others were good but particular studies which treated one deviance without regard for others. I've tried in this book to assemble the most relevant parts of a number of these good studies within a coherent theoretical framework.

The adaptations in the book could be looked upon as long quotations interspersed with my comments. I see a great deal of convergence among students of deviance from many fields and I have tried to make this more apparent by translating the various terms used in different specialties into a common language.

My theoretical perspective has been developed largely from Peter Berger and Thomas Luckmann's book *The Social Construction of Reality*. I first read it in 1967 at the suggestion of Sherri Cavan at San Francisco State College. As I read it literally hundreds of my own observations and thoughts found their relationship to one another within the framework of Berger and Luckmann's theory. I first found it useful in my doctoral dissertation which was based on a participant observation study of the police. (One article taken from the dissertation has been published, "Transformations of Reality in the Legal Process," *Social Research,* Vol 37, No. 1, Spring, 1970, pp. 88–101.) I thought about this theory for a couple of years and finally saw that with a few modifications it could give a comprehensive organization to the study of deviance. The terms "bad habits" and "counter-institutions," and the concept of the "reality flaw" are my own additions to Berger and Luckmann's schema.

I don't read very much—I watch and think a lot. There are undoubtedly gaps and oversights in this book that come from not having read everything. I hope, however, that you will find my thinking straight and clearly explained.

I would appreciate it if you would drop me a line when you find an error in the book, a point with which you disagree, or when you find in your own research and observations some aspect of deviance which either fits into or invalidates my framework. You can write to me at the Department of Sociology, Sir George Williams University, Montreal 107, Quebec, Canada. I'll probably learn something from your letter, and if there is another edition of the book, everybody who reads it will benefit.

Erica Wiener made sense out of passages that were nonsense, took care of all the correspondence necessary for getting permissions to reprint the adaptations, provided me with the wisdom of her keen and observant mind, and went with me for Chinese food many a morning at four A.M. when we finished working. A good head is hard to find.

I really hope that the book is clear. I hope that you will be able to see with the perspective I have developed. Whether you like it or detest it, accept it or reject it is your choice—but so, of course, is everything.

H. Taylor Buckner
Montreal
Summer, 1970

contents

x □ CONTENTS

Flashes

A bisexual is very much attracted to another boy at a party, but doesn't ask him to dance because he fears the reaction of the heterosexuals around him.

A waitress, dealing with a customer who didn't speak English, needed to know if the customer wanted a chicken leg or breast. She said "leg" and pointed to her leg. Then she said "breast" and pointed to her arm.

On a first visit to a couple's home, a student observed a single leather chair and a long sofa in the living room. Though she would rather have sat in the chair, she felt it might have been the "favorite" chair of the man in the house, and to avoid even minor dislocation she sat on the sofa.

The traffic division of a police department is a riot squad keeping busy until a riot breaks out.

One young man reached across the back of another, and momentarily his arm rested across his shoulders. The second young man jumped up, laughing, dropped his wrist, and said, "be careful—you know I'm not that kind."

A teenager realizes that if he keeps on stripping cars he will get caught, and suddenly becomes more involved with a conventional friend.

A number of students were treated to an episode of irrational behavior at a party where they were smoking marijuana, most of them for the first time. Several went home that night vowing never to touch the evil weed again.

A student, knowing that the telephone company doesn't trust students and requires a large deposit before installing a phone for them, told them that he was a visiting professor from India and that his name was Hare Krishna. He got the phone with no mention of a deposit.

In Kentucky it is often rumored that bootleggers discreetly contribute money to fundamentalist ministers who wish to prohibit the legal sale of liquor in their towns by local option elections. The payoff is that Kentucky towns are known to "vote dry, and drink wet," which provides a nice profit for the bootlegger. Abstract morality made into rules whose systematic violation by the public provides an open field for criminals to exploit at little risk is the basic support for both the Cosa Nostra and the small town bootlegger.

The prostitute may feel that she is performing a useful social service, taking care of the handicapped, the lonesome, and the strange ones who might otherwise be on the streets undoing innocent girls. The marijuana smoker may have an almost missionary zeal for spreading this beautiful way of seeing the world. The marijuana smoker might feel shame and embarrassment if company drops over and he has no grass to offer.

In conventional reality one might "talk about the sit-in at the college," while in hip reality one "raps about the pig administrators." In conventional reality it's a "Negro riot," in hip it's "urban guerrilla warfare." In conventional, drugs are an "escape from reality," in hip they are "part of reality." In conventional it's "the government, the schools, business, the club, the police, liberals and conservatives, law and order, morality, propriety, freedom, justice, investment, marriage, home ownership, and chastity," in hip it's "the system."

deviance, reality, and change

The area of sociological studies now called "deviance" has had a long history in sociology. Early sociologists were often very interested in social reform. Some of them were ministers before they became sociologists, some were ministers' sons. When they focused their attention on the unfortunates of society—the poor, the destitute, the immoral, the promiscuous, the perverted, or the lazy—they were concerned with the breakdown of social organization that "caused" such behavior. In many cases they were motivated by sympathy or outrage to attempt to change the conditions they thought brought about social disorganization. These sociologists had an idea of society that was very much like Hobbes's *Leviathan;* that is, that society is a huge body composed of interdependent organs, which could get sick. So they called the study of people who broke the rules "social pathology." C. Wright Mills has pointed out in "The Professional Ideology of Social Pathologists"[1] that many if not all of the social pathology textbook

[1] *American Journal of Sociology,* September 1942, Vol. 49, pp. 165–180.

DEVIANCE
AND REALITY

writers were affirming the values of the protestant, middle-class, neighborly small towns from which most of them came. Their view of society as an ordered, homogeneous, stable, predictable set of relationships caused them to consider anything that disturbed this view of the world as an indication of disorganization and pathology. When they wrote about social pathology they thought of the afflicted individuals as "unhappy creatures," leading lives of vice, sin, crime, and corruption. In other words, they were taking society's point of view when they studied people who broke its rules.

As sociologists became more concerned with following the "scientific method" these value concerns became embarrassing to them, and in the late 1940s and early 1950s the term "deviance" began to be substituted for "social pathology." Introducing a supposedly value-free word with a more general definition broadened the area of interest, since now all behavior that deviated from the social norm could be studied. "Deviance" may consist of almost any "rule-breaking" activity. Students may be interested in deviance from professional rules and norms, deviance from expected interaction patterns, and deviance from expected style of dress and demeanor, as well as in the traditional areas of deviance: crime, alcoholism, mental illness, homosexuality, and prostitution.

At the University of Chicago in the twenties and thirties several changes in the study of deviance began happening. George Herbert Mead and Herbert Blumer proposed the symbolic interactionist approach for the study of society. Within this new framework, some sociologists went out in the field to do participant observation of people as they actually behaved. They began looking at the world through the eyes of the deviant, and understanding what the deviant saw.

Becoming involved in the perspective of the deviant led to a certain sympathy for his position, and a certain skepticism about the morality of society. In the sixties, a number of people, including John Kitsuse, Kai Erikson, and Howard S. Becker, suggested that the focus of study be shifted away from the "deviant" and toward the social process that labels him "deviant."

Indeed, Howard Becker notes in *The Other Side*[2] that sympathy for the deviant is less likely to result in error than the widespread sympathy for conventional society: any sympathy for the deviant is likely to be challenged.

Regardless of the tradition followed—looking at the deviant as a defective person, or looking at the process through which he came to be called deviant—the word itself is negative. Would you like to marry

[2] Howard S. Becker, ed. *The Other Side* (New York: Macmillan, 1964).

a deviant? Would you feel comfortable eating lunch with a deviant? The word denotes a person who has varied from the normal, and connotes that this is bad. To call someone deviant is to call him abnormal and bad, whether we are sociologists or laymen. I think that it makes our lives much more difficult to use words like "deviance" and "deviant" because we must keep reminding ourselves that it only means that some people think that what some other people are doing is not right.

At the same time as the first social pathologists were writing in the United States Émile Durkheim produced his classic study *Suicide*,[3] in France. In this study he suggested that disorders in the relation of the individual to society could be produced by a malintegration of society itself. This theory, which suggested that *anomie* or rulelessness was a source of deviance, was carried forward by Robert Merton, Richard Cloward, and others. This theoretical tradition explained many different forms of deviant behavior within an analytic framework.

There have also been attempts at genetic and biological explanations of deviance, from Lombroso's evolutionary throwbacks to Sheldon's somatotypes, which have been largely discredited by decades of research that show that criminals are not biologically distinctive. There is always the possibility that someday some biological factor will be found that invariably (or often) leads to deviance, but generally social factors seem to be more influential.

The perspective that has been missing most in the study of deviant behavior is an overall view that takes the perspective of neither society nor of the deviant as its starting point, that does not assume that society is right and the deviant wrong, or that the deviant is right and society wrong. In order to gain this perspective it is necessary to understand where judgments of value come from, and how these definitions of reality came to be held. Such a perspective may be assumed by following the work of Alfred Schutz on the commonsense world of everyday life as it was elaborated into a theory of *The Social Construction of Reality* by Peter L. Berger and Thomas Luckmann.[4]

I will use their theory to attempt to provide an integrated view of deviance by examining the production, influence, and change of social reality. Using this framework, I find that there is a great deal of unity among the various traditional ways in which deviance has been studied —a unity that has been hidden by the lack of a uniform language to describe behavior, and by the lack of an overall theory of human behavior that applies to both the "normal" and the "deviant."

[3] Émile Durkheim, *Suicide* (New York: Macmillan, 1951).

[4] P. L. Berger and T. Luckmann, *The Social Construction of Reality* (New York: Doubleday and Company Inc.,1966).

In the following pages I will try to demonstrate this underlying unity by creating a theoretical framework and by examining the works of a number of authors to show how they fit into this framework. I have been forced to use a certain number of "jargon" words or technically defined terms, for several reasons. First and most important, the technical terms that I define and use may be used in a precise way without the ambiguity of everyday language. Secondly, they are free of the value implications of everyday language. I have tried to avoid the word "deviance" whenever possible, and when it is used it is simply short-hand. Third, using a uniform language allows us to "translate" the works of authors who use many different terms for the same observations. I will try to define each technical term the first time it is used, and always try to use it in exactly the same sense thereafter.

In adapting the works of various authors I will insert my comments in their texts within brackets, to provide a common language for the entire book and to point out the significance of some of the authors' points. I hope in this way to pull together theories and observations from different traditions and to create an overall model of the social construction of reality, the social construction of "deviance," and the ways in which "deviance" can lead to changes in social reality.

If you follow the logical argument I develop I think you will see that "deviance" is a very normal social process, one that is often useful to society, and a process that is not strange or impelled by the forces of darkness but very similar to your own ordinary everyday behavior. I ask only that you test everything I say against your own experience before you accept it as true. I will try to provide examples to aid you, but you can only convince yourself of the truth of these theories by finding that this is a useful way to look at the world, and this will never happen until you try to use it.

THE CREATION OF SOCIAL REALITY

I believe that a useful view of deviance may be gained by looking at the way people put their social worlds together, the way they come to do and believe in what they do, and the way they construct what is real for them. Two key processes in the creation of human behavior are the development of institutions and the development of legitimations which explain these institutions.

BIOLOGY AND SOCIAL ORDER

Biological evolution takes place over unimaginable spans of time; cultural evolution now takes place with increasing rapidity. Imagine attempting to travel to the moon by biological evolution. The world record for high jumping is a little over seven feet, five inches. The longest a trained person can hold his breath is around six minutes. Suppose that we took all of the world's best jumpers and breath holders and scientifically mated them to one another for the next thirty generations, that is, the next 900 years. Do you suppose that the ultimate hybrid could jump high enough, or hold his breath long enough, to go to the moon and return? Not likely. From the beginning of life on earth, organisms developed random biological variations, some of which proved useful for species survival, most of which did not. With the advent of man, biological evolution became an increasingly obsolete strategy for coping with changes in the environment. In fact, it is through social cooperation that soon it will be possible for biologically unremarkable men to visit the other planets. The relative efficiency of biological evolution and social cooperation for getting to the moon may be gauged from the times involved—900 years for a failure, seventy years from the first powered flight for a success. Individual biological variation has lost most of its impact on human activity because of the ways man has shaped the environment. A person need not be particularly resistant to cold to live in the northern climates; he makes heat and shelter. A person whose bad eyesight would lead him to starvation in a hunting economy wears glasses. Babies' birth defects can often be corrected surgically. Very few forms of unusual social behavior can be convincingly linked to heredity—men make their own social worlds.

Man has few and trivial instincts; they are not sufficient for forming a social order. He is not bound to specific environments because he can form his environment to order. His biological urges can be satisfied in many different ways. He can eat an amazing variety of things. He can sleep in the day or the night. He can ingest drugs that alter his perception and thus his subjective reality. His sexual drives can be completely divorced from simple biological reproduction. Think of some of the fantastic ways in which men gain sexual gratification: homosexuality, fetishism, necrophilia, paedophilia, masturbation, oral intercourse, anal intercourse, oral-genital and oral-anal intercourse, bestiality, heterosexuality, voyeurism, exhibitionism, clusterfucks, masochism, and sadism, to name only the more direct methods. Somewhere in some human group each of these practices is either the accepted order of doing things, or a variation that causes little concern. Entire cultures, such as the classical Greeks, created sexual patterns in which biological reproduction was the less favored form of sexuality. Animals, which exist in close and dependent contact with their environments, have biological natures structured by instincts. Given a stable environment, these instincts propel them into patterns of species survival. Such is not the case with men. If men were left at the mercy of their almost nonexistent instincts, thousands of patterns would arise and the species would die from the resulting chaos. Instead of inborn instincts, the human child encounters a social order that limits and guides his development, tastes, desires, and thoughts into the patterns common to the group in which he grows up.

Human social order is produced by human activity, not by biology or by the demands of the environment. Environment and biology set only outside constraints, but leave open a multitude of possible cultural patterns. Man's biological instability requires social limitation in order for man to survive. This social limitation is created and transmitted by his living group.

CREATING INSTITUTIONS

In the ordinary round of your daily activities you help create and sustain the institutions that will shape and limit human children to come. You participate in patterned activities created by others, thereby making them real for yourself and those around you. You create new patterns of activities when you solve problems for yourself, and if your solutions work well you may pass them on to your own children, or to other people who have the same problem. Imagine what the world would be like if you did not have these patterns of personal habits to guide you through the day. Think of a day in which you did everything you did today for the very first time. You stumble out of bed and try to figure out how to turn off the alarm clock. Find the bathroom (assuming you have been toilet trained—that took a long time) and a strange looking stick with bristles on the end with which, after poking yourself in the face a few times, you brush your teeth, sideways. It took a long time, when you were first learning, to learn to brush up and down. You find a clothes closet and try to pick out some clothes. You don't know what matches what, you don't know what other people will be wearing when you get to school, and there are a thousand possible permutations and combinations of slacks, shirts, coats, ties, and shoes, or skirts, blouses, hose, belts, and shoes that you could try on. Slipping into a rakish combination of purple shoes, brown slacks, and a fuchsia shirt, you carefully knot a regimental striped tie around your waist and wander off to the kitchen to prepare breakfast. The chaos at breakfast is imaginable. You find a cookbook (assuming you know how to read— that took time too) and try to cook an egg. You try to eat with a fork, spilling egg on your clothes, burn the toast, and hunt through every cabinet trying to find soap and the wastebasket. Four hours late, you set off for school (since you have never done it before you find a map and plan out your route). You find the owner's manual of the car so that you can learn how to start it. Then you drive. Remember when you were first learning to drive? Clutch, shift, clutch, shift, clutch, shift, brake, clutch, shift, clutch, shift, signal, clutch, shift, brake, look at the map; so far you have gone two blocks. You get to school. You get a map of the school so that you can find the classes. You meet someone in the hall and don't know the routine greetings, "May peace be upon you," you fumble in response to his "hi." You go to the cafeteria for a sandwich, forgetting that you did not *consciously think* to put money in your pocket. Assuming that you have made it so far without being bagged for psychiatric observation let's think about how you would ordinarily manage such a day. You would get up, shut off the alarm, brush your teeth, slip into one of your "outfits," fix one of your standard breakfasts, get into the car, and drive to school. About halfway there you might wake up and think your first completely conscious thought of the day. You do not create your activity anew every day. Anything you do routinely you habitualize, you narrow your choices, and eventually the conscious portion of your mind is hardly involved at all in your daily routine. You create routines, and subroutines, and your ordinary daily round of activities is a lot of routines all strung together, pretty much the same every working day. As you carry out these automatic routines, or habits, your conscious mind is free for daydreaming, or for planning and dealing with the few aspects of your experience that are not routine, or those that you choose for special attention. You create these habitualizations because it makes a complex life possible. They speed you through the day at the cost of making you something of a zombie. You may almost forget that you ever made choices. Your habits in some senses will *become* "you," and you will root some of your self-concept in the things you have habitualized in your daily routine: "I'm a sharp dresser," "I'm good in bed," "I'm punctual," "I'm a good cook," etc.

Just as you come to depend on your habits, the people who routinely interact with you come to depend on your habits as well. They see you doing the same thing time after time, and they make the assumption that it is typical of you. You, conversely, assume that their habits are typical of them. You meet your friend every day for lunch at a certain table in the cafeteria. This is your habit, and this is his habit. He thinks that it is typical of you, and you think that it is typical of him. This reciprocal typification of habitualized action then becomes an incipient "institution" between you and your friend. If you don't show up for lunch one day, the next time he sees you he will ask what happened, or you may offer the explanation that you had a dentist appointment before he asks, because you will want to explain this deviance from the coordination you established. You have many such coordinations with the people you see frequently, coordinations that you and they have created together. You don't deal with everyone you meet in a personal way, however. Some people you deal with as "types," in which case any individual could handle the transaction as well as any other. Ticket-takers, telephone operators, repairmen, and policemen are routinely "types" of actors for most of us.

We assume that "types" of actors will engage in habitual patterns of action just as we assume that our friend will meet us for lunch. Policemen will act like policemen, repairmen will act like repairmen. You assume that the other drivers on the streets will engage in typical actions, that they will habitually obey or bend certain of the rules of the road; that they will usually drive on the right and stop for red lights. They assume that you will do the same thing. Without these reciprocal typifications among anonymous persons, driving would indeed be more of an adventure.

Each reciprocal typification is a product of its own history, it has been built up by many people, each potentially adding his own style; and what you encounter is a product of this process. In California, drivers tend to run through amber lights that are turning red; in Montreal, drivers frequently jump the green light by a few seconds. A driver who learned the coordinations of driving in California is likely to be halfway through a Montreal intersection on amber when a cab starts into it. The laws that regulate behavior at red lights are the same, but the coordinations built from the driver's habits differ.

Each reciprocal typification in which you are involved has developed through this process. Your special relationship with each member of your family is a coordination that has grown over time, one to which both you and they contributed. The same is true for the patterns you have established, or participate in, with your co-workers, your co-drivers, your friends, your enemies. The explanation of "why" a reciprocal typification is as it is, why it contains certain elements and not others, is not to be found in a master plan drawn up by a social engineer, but in the history of its own development.

These coordinations you are involved in, the ones you helped establish, and the ones you joined, control your conduct by setting up predefined patterns of conduct for "types" of people. You feel some obligation to get to lunch with your friend, this exerts some control over your behavior, and you feel an obligation to explain why you didn't make it if you don't get there. If you fall into a "type," for example a driver, either you conform to the institutions of motoring as they are practiced or you have accidents. It is not as much the fear of getting a ticket that keeps you from driving on the left-hand side of the road and running red lights, as it is the fear of an accident. You gain the benefits of the coordination when you do what is expected of your type of person. As a motorist you get where you are going without much difficulty if you follow the coordinations of driving. A businessman does not wear sandals with his navy blue business suit because he fears that by violating the coordinations of dress his business will be more difficult to transact. People are generally honest for the same reasons, not as much from fear of the penalties for dishonesty as for the benefits of the cooperation that others will give.

Coordinations are incipient in every continuing social situation; as soon as an action is repeated a reciprocal typification of behavior has the possibility of arising. Married couples institutionalize levels of passion —"Darling, today is Thursday"; dinner hours—"My wife expects me at six"; activities—"It's Sunday, go pick up mother for dinner"; and patterns of conflict—"We've got to cut down expenses . . ." Work groups coordinate the level of output expected—ratebusting and chiseling are the deviances; modes of dress—"This is a very popular pin stripe suit this year, sir, all the bankers are wearing them"; forms of deference— "Yes sir, J. B."; and various informal "arrangements" which speed or impede work—"If you will work a little late tonight to get these letters done I'll take you out to dinner." Neighbors coordinate patterns of sharing—"Hey Bill, can I borrow your saber saw?"; gossip—"Did you see what Erica and her boyfriend were doing in the car last night?"; and appropriate behavior. Many of these patterns are common to numbers of people, some are the property of only a few. They all influence behavior.

All people who work or play together develop a language to refer to their common activities. By using this specialized language they communicate very efficiently with others with whom they are interacting. Married couples often communicate telegraphically, with the merest gesture or tone of voice having the most intense meaning. In other scenes these phrases are common: "Tin and Lead futures closed quiet. No Sales," "A Lazy Daisy cake is a hot milk sponge with a broiled-on topping of coconut and brown sugar," "Oh, you're a Capricorn," "A's Win and Lose, Trail Twins by 3½," "Licorice Papers and Panama Red," "It has twin carbs and a ¾ race cam," "An obvious Oedipal resolution." Each of these statements, jargon to the outsider, is part of the pattern of communication of a particular kind of behavior. The routinization of communications is important for any coordination. Communications are the reality-defining agent for the participants; without communications only the most basic cooperation is possible.

Although there are many continuing social situations that *could* provide a basis for coordination, most of them can be gathered into four categories which can be found in all human groups. Labor and leisure, economics and work relations provide the first category of continuing social situations. Patterns of sex, the family, and kinship form the second. Patterns of territory, interpersonal space, neighbors, cities, and nations form the third, and patterns of communications and symbol systems the fourth. Every person is involved in coordinations in all of these areas, and they all tend to control his behavior. Everyone is involved in a unique pattern of coordinations, some of which he helped establish, some of which existed before he began following them.

Picture yourself flying in a light plane across North America. As you fly, you pass over farms, villages, small towns, suburbs, cities and more farms, villages, small towns, suburbs, and cities. You pass over thousands of people, thousands of buildings. And each building has a history. There are people who live and work in it. These people make up some sort of family group, and each family group has members who are also involved with others in other buildings. Within each building the occupants have built up habit patterns that allow them to communicate with one another quickly and telegraphically rather than slowly and formally. They have built up habits based on the different affairs in which the different occupants are involved. In each house the various people are involved in different kinds of labor—going out to a job, working around the home, exchanging services with relatives and neighbors. The members all depend on one another to continue doing what they are doing, or to change (only in predictable ways and with appropriate warning). The family members have established sexual coordinations—patterns of appropriate behavior with members of the opposite sex, relations with their parents and with their children, relations with their brothers and sisters, and patterns of sexual approach or avoidance with friends and neighbors. Each family has ways in which it takes care of its house, modes of decorating that they consider "right"; they are involved with others in concern over city government, in problems of access to shopping areas, in worrying about the quality of their schools and the increases in their taxes. In every single house these patterns are different.

What looks like similarity—so many Baptists, so many middle class, so many retired, etc.—really tells us little about the behavior that actually goes on. Each person, in each house, in the entire country, has a unique combination of habits, a unique pattern for dealing with the problems of labor, sex, territory, and communications. Each household has a complex network of connections between these individual habits and coordinations; this network forms an "institution," an institution with a history, an institution that trains children and has a logic that tends to control the behavior of its members. Each household is involved in connections with myriad other institutions, other households, working places, governments, swimming pools, taverns and public utilities, churches, markets, and Sunday afternoons at the drag strip. All of these variations between patterns of institutions exist even within a single country. In any geographical political division in which language and the environment differ, the patterns of institutionalization of labor, sex, territory, and communications will also be different.

INSTITUTIONS AND SOCIAL CONTROL

The fact that people have made "institutions" out of their relationships provides *the* basis for social, or group, control over their behavior. The institutions provide the basis for social control whether the behavior is conventional or unconventional, whether it is "straight" or "deviant" according to some conception of what behavior "should be." Thus the institutions of behavior that have developed in a street-corner gang control the behavior of a member of that gang just as the institutions of behavior that have developed in a business office control a clerk in the office. The institutions of behavior that have developed in drug culture control the users just as the institutions that have developed in tavern culture control the drinkers. The institutions that have developed around prostitution control the prostitute just as the institutions of the family control the wife. In each of these pairs the institutions are *different,* and the behavior that is controlled is *different,* but the fact of the institution controlling the behavior is the *same.* In each case, if the participant wants to gain the benefits of the institution he must behave as the others in the institution who interact with him expect him to behave. The social control that arises from institutions I call "the social control of relations." The people who enforce conformity to the institution are the other participants in the institution. If the behavior of a participant is as expected, he benefits from the institution and the other participants welcome him. If his behavior departs from the expected, he will not benefit from the institution and the others will punish him by excluding him or taking other steps to "correct" his behavior. Lest this be too abstract, remember the motorist. If he drives correctly he is welcome on the street; if he drives incorrectly people will blow their horns at him, curse him, and possibly collide with him.

As a person grows up he becomes involved in many different reciprocal typifications and institutions. As he interacts with others and is rewarded for doing the expected thing, he comes to think of himself as the sort of person who does the expected thing. Since he develops his idea of what he is like by watching the responses of others to him— you get the idea that you are bright or dull by watching your parents' or teachers' responses, that you are pretty or plain by watching your dates' behavior—he soon comes to the feeling that he *is* a certain sort of person from whom a certain sort of behavior is expected, in all matters of dress, performance, taste, style, etc. This is his *self-concept,* largely constructed by attending to the responses of others who are participating in the same institutions of behavior with him. Thus a person's self-concept is derived from his participations in behavioral institutions, and it reflects the nature of his participation. Once a person has established an idea in his mind of what he is like, this idea tends to control his behavior. It does this both specifically—the businessman thinks of himself in a business suit and would recoil from going to work in a sweater—and generally; when he encounters a new situation he has all of these ideas of what he is like that direct his presentation and response to the new situation. This is his *self-control.* Since a person is involved in a great many institutions, not all of which are in complete harmony with one another, he has a very complex idea of what he is like, and one part or another of this self-concept may be relevant to any given situation. The businessman may have a reputation as a "great man with the ladies" among the people he meets at his annual convention. This part of his self-concept tends to control his behavior at conventions, but not when he is home with his wife. The way in which his self-concept controls his behavior is relatively simple. When he encounters a situation he thinks back over what has happened in similar situations in the past, and he thinks about the consequences of various possible lines of action. If he then acts in accord with his self-concept he will probably feel good, satisfied, and happy. If he violates his self-concept he will probably feel doubtful, ashamed, and guilty. At least this is what he expects will happen, and his expectation usually controls his conduct. In the ordinary situation a person is acting repeatedly in the same coordinations and institutions with the same others, and their controls reinforce his own self-controls. This is the social control of the relationship with others that I call "relational control." In other words, relational control and self-control usually work toward the same behavior. There are exceptions in which the two forms of control work at cross-purposes; for example, a college student's self-control may tell him that smoking marijuana is wrong—he learned this from his parents and from the media—and his relational controls may tell him that it is right —all of his friends smoke. There may be different outcomes. Most often, however, if a person continues to interact in a certain way with others, he gradually takes this behavior into himself as part of his self-concept. It follows that institutions and reciprocal typifications are the first and most important source of social control.

In addition to self and relational controls, there is a third kind of social control: *formal social control.* Very briefly (because it will be expanded upon later), formal social controls are the "official" laws, regulations, and understandings that are supposed to encompass all of the members of a group or a society. Formal social control also comes from the institutions of behavior that have existed in a society. Institutions are not planned logically; they arise out of the behavior of the individuals involved in them. Because the relational and self-controls of the participants in an institution lead them to think of their behavior as "right," and the behavior of others who do not follow the same pattern of behavior as "wrong," the people who are involved in the most popular or the most powerful institutions of a kind in a society may attempt to make *everyone* follow their patterns of behavior. Obviously, this is an oversimplification. There are many political issues and much contention as to which way of doing some particular thing will become *the* correct way. In any event, *some* institutions in a society gain predominance and the machinery of formal enforcement. Through formal enforcement of this institution other possible ways of behaving are stigmatized, declared illegal, immoral, or unreal. In other words, in any society, the "straight" people have written their notion of what constitutes proper sex relationships into law, their notion of what constitutes good property ownership principles into contracts, their notion of ideal work habits into company rules, and their notion of correct ways of seeing reality into their demonology or psychology. Usually through "government" they have hired agents—policemen, judges, psychiatrists, and social workers—to enforce all the behavior required by these predominant institutions. To be a homosexual, to plant a "Peoples Park" on unused private property, to try to get a job with long hair, or to believe that these alternatives may be better than what is, invites these formal control agents to reassert the predominance of the institutional order through fines, firing, imprisonment, therapy, and, ultimately, death. The institutional order, that is, the "legitimate" collection of predominant institutions of behavior in the areas of labor, sex, territory, and communications within a society, has these powers of formal control at its disposal. Institutions of behavior that exist outside this institutional order do not share the legitimations of the institutional order and do not have the "right" to exercise formal social control. I call them "counter-institutions."

Both the predominant institutions and the counter-institutions of behavior have relational social control at their disposal. Both predominant and counter-institutions reward the people who follow their expectations of proper behavior. Both predominant and counter-institutions become part of their participants' self-concept, and thus exert self-control, through happiness and guilt. But only the institutional order has formal controls and agents who attempt to enforce their pattern of behavior and definition of reality *on the entire society.*

Table 1 summarizes the source of each of these types of social control, the agent(s) who or that enforce it, and the rewards and punishments that are used to ensure performance to expectations.

INSTITUTIONS AND KNOWLEDGE

Many coordinations of behavior exist only between two people. These are often spontaneous—meeting your friend for lunch, temporary—if

TABLE 1 SOCIAL CONTROL SUMMARY TABLE

Level	Source	Agent	Sanctions
Relational Controls	Interactive institutions that come from reciprocal typifications and expectations around sex, labor, territory, and communications.	Alters involved with ego, or for whom ego's behavior is important.	*Positive:* acceptance, survival, friendship, love, emotional support, and employment. *Negative:* ostracism, hatred, exclusion from activities, emotional withdrawal.
Self-Controls	Socialization of ego by ego and alter so that ego fits into the institutions (or counter-institutions) in which ego is involved.	Intra-active self that examines prospective and retrospective consequences of decisions and acts.	*Positive:* feeling good, pride, satisfaction with self and world. *Negative:* guilt, shame, doubt, uncertainty.
Formal Controls	Predominant institutions in society that enact laws and other abstract regulations supporting themselves.	"Legally" authorized agents. Police, mental hospitals, social workers, administrators.	*Positive:* "awards," citations of merit. *Negative:* fines, imprisonment, death, therapy, treatment, and excommunication.

you have a class next term at lunchtime the lunch date may cease to exist and provide benefits only within the context of that particular relationship. Such coordinations are constantly in the process of being changed to suit the desires and needs of the particular people involved. Other living problems are more generally experienced, particularly those involving labor, sex, territory, and communications. The reciprocal typifications that have been developed to coordinate the behavior of the participants must be passed on to new participants; either children growing up into jobs, families, and communities, or recruits who become participants through social or physical mobility. In order for these children or recruits to understand the pattern of behavior being passed on, it must be explained to them. This means that what had been simply a coordination of behavior, possibly one that had been worked out without much conscious reflection, now must be made into a set of instructions for the child or recruit to learn. In the process of stating what had before been simply understood, the coordination becomes solidified, formalized, and less open to change. If a third person, a recruit, were going to join you for lunch, you would have to explain to him the time and place at which you would meet. In the process of explaining this, and because a third person is now depending on you and your friend being there, your informal luncheon has become more formal; it has become a "thing" in the minds of all three of you. To change it now to another time or place would be more difficult than it was before. The luncheon coordinates the activity of its independent receiver as well as the activities of its creators. It has become an institution of behavior—a way of doing something that can be transmitted to others.

As he grows into the thousands of institutions of behavior established by his parents and peers, and the myriad of institutions that they did not establish but learned themselves, a child becomes a social being, capable of participating in social activities. The child, unlike the recruit, has no knowledge of other possible institutions of behavior. As a result the child grows up in (or out of) the institutional order thinking that the ways he has learned are right, and, in fact, are the only possible ways of behaving. His self-concept is also developed from his participation in these institutions, so to him behaving in accord with them is moral. Only in rare instances is a young child likely to see contradictions among the institutionalized behaviors he learns from various sources. Immigrant children, whose family institutions conflict with institutions transmitted by their schools, and the children of parents deeply and visibly involved in a counter-institution, are two possible exceptions.

Since institutions of behavior grow from *specific* persons involved in *specific* coordinations with *specific* others for *specific* ends, and not from any general plan, each institution has an existence independent of other institutions. Since the same people are involved in many different institutions, crosscutting their work, family, and community, they tend to "make sense" out of these various activities in which they are involved. They make some sense out of the relations between institutions; they see the connections between their jobs, supporting their families, and participating in their communities, and they see these connections within the wider context of the understandings common to these institutions in their society. The institutions themselves, however, are not *necessarily* or logically integrated with one another in any sort of functional pattern. The monogamous family can exist in a capitalist or socialist system of labor. Ideas of community, and community institutions, can exist without private property. Alcohol or marijuana use can be the predominant method for altering consciousness without altering the pattern of courtship in a society. Some things can change, new relationships can exist between these institutions, but what *is* is not necessarily the only way in which people can order their lives.

People think about the institutions of behavior around them and make up verbal explanations for why they are as they are. It is important to note, however, that these explanations are quite distinct from the process of institution formation. A large part of the information transmitted to the young in a culture, in their schools or other training, consists of such ideas and explanations about why institutions are as they are. As a result, most people usually do not question the patterns of institutions that constitute their institutional order. Sociologists have made sense of the institutional patterns they saw around them, much as everyone else does but with more emphasis on the necessity, functionality, and logic of these relationships. In this regard they have been among the maintaining theoreticians of the institutional order, explaining the order and explaining why it is necessary. It is from this second-order operation, reflecting on patterns of institutions, that the idea of society-as-an-organism grew. And from this analogy to organisms grew the idea that behavioral institutions that did not fit into the institutional order were "pathological," problematical, or deviant. If we examine the process of institution formation, however, keeping quite clearly in mind that ideas of a "social organism" are an abstract theoretical construct, we can see that institutions are institutions, and that judgments of an institution being "deviant" come from the "logic" imposed on the institutional order by reflective consciousness, not from anything inherent in the behavior.

If we want to understand how members of society come to think of some institutions as bad or deviant we must look at the "knowledge" that they have about the institutional order. Of course, at the simplest level, most people are convinced that the way they do things is right and the best way to do them. But at a more complex level, they have learned through all the force of their education that the way in which things are done is right, and that other ways are wrong, for such and such good reasons. These "good reasons" are part of the "legitimations" of the institutional order.

The term "counter-institutions," then, refers to those institutions of behavior that have not *at the moment* been given a place in the institutional order of society by the logic of reflective consciousness of social theoreticians and popular understanding. Obviously there are many reciprocal typifications that fit into the institutional order that do not themselves have the possibility of using formal sanctions, such as meeting your friends for lunch. Just as obviously, there are counter-institutions of behavior that have not had formal sanctions used against them, usually because they have not yet come to the attention of anyone who would be upset with them, for example, chewing Hawaiian Wood Rose seeds to get high. Even though formal sanctions have not been used, the generally held *knowledge* of what is correct and incorrect in terms of the institutional order is a fairly reliable guide to whether or not a behavioral institution is within the general definition of correctness. Advice columnists such as "Dear Abby" are constantly providing this "knowledge" to people who write to them asking whether institutions in which they are involved are right or wrong.

It is very important to keep in mind that the institutional order is *constantly changing,* and that it is *only one way* out of an infinity of possible ways of applying reflective consciousness to the behavioral institutions in which people are involved. Its moral suasion is powerful, its control over knowledge, institutions, and self-concept makes it seem monolithic, but it *is* constantly changing and it is always, in theory at least, problematical. For example, in Greek society at the time of Socrates, the institutional order had an honorable place for homosexual love between men and boys. It was considered the normal and most pure form of love, and sexual love between men and women was considered a necessary but somewhat inferior form of relationship. This later ceased to be the case.

As we progress through the book it will become clear how present normalcies are often past counter-institutions, and many present counter-institutions are future normalcies. What is "deviant" today may be the orthodoxy of tomorrow, and to fail to see this is the greatest oversight a student of society could make. To look at "deviance" only from the perspective of our own current institutional order is to see no further than ethnocentrism allows.

Each institution of behavior carries with it recipe knowledge that defines correct behavior. Since all of the people involved in an institution think and agree that the recipe knowledge they have is a body of generally valid truths about "reality," any departure from this recipe knowledge appears to them a departure from "reality." The institutional order as a whole defines a complex reality, based on the recipe knowledge of its component institutions, and thus participation in a counter-institution may be considered a manifestation of depravity, mental illness, or ignorance. Most generally, people will say that they do the things they do because they consider them enjoyable and worthwhile, but they are unwilling to grant these reasons to others who do different things, preferring to find some motivation such as being "duped by outside agitators," being "mentally disturbed" or "insecure," or being affected by a "bad environment."

The knowledge of institutions that most people have tends to be a rather simple formula they have been taught, that they call upon to explain why it is that they are doing what they are doing. People have learned explanations of why they work—have to make money, marry—in love, live in the best country of all—biggest, strongest, most just, etc., walk on the street side of a lady—various explanations, follow Kosher laws—early sanitary regulations, explanations that they generally don't think about, but will parrot if asked. Actually, they are probably doing what they are doing because they drifted into it and only learned the "reason" for the institution later. These explanations for institutions are as diverse as the institutions themselves. They are put together into a seemingly logical whole through the legitimations of the institutional order.

Not all institutions are important enough to require that the "meaning" of the institution be transmitted to the participants. The "meaning" of meeting your friends for lunch is probably never explicitly developed and passed on. Before the "meaning" is passed on the institution must be seen as a relatively permanent way of dealing with a problem of coordination that arises repeatedly. We have health classes in school that teach children about the seven basic foods, which provides the knowledge and legitimation for eating what is considered a "balanced" diet. Australian aborigines show their children how to dig for grubs for the same reason.

It should be clear from what has been said that it is possible for a counter-institution to grow in complexity and popularity until it is the way in which so many people are behaving that it may become part of the institutional order. When this happens, what had been a "deviance" became an "orthodoxy" and it gradually will take on the ability to defend itself through legitimated formal social controls. Institutions of today, the nuclear family, for example, were counter-institutions in the four-teenth century; counter-institutions of today, such as recreational drug use, may make themselves a place in the institutional order of tomorrow —legitimated into the logic of the institutional order by interested theo-reticians.

LEGITIMATIONS

A legitimation is a "second-order" objectivation of meaning. It is a statement *about* a behavioral institution or collection of institutions that in some sense explains and justifies it.

Almost every act in which people engage has some sort of subjective meaning for them. These subjective meanings may not be cause for much reflection; they may be momentary feelings usually associated with the act. There are a great many things that we do each day, or do sometimes, that have little more than random and general meaning for us. The way in which we customarily handle our eye behavior, for example, is not something we think much about. Yet we were taught not to stare, and to look people directly in the eye when talking to them. We only notice eye behavior if someone else violates the rules, or if we realize from their reaction that we are violating them. We may suddenly realize that a person of the opposite sex is staring at us, and then this little gesture begins to take on some meaning. Similarly we do not pay much attention to our small body movements, such as readjusting in a chair, or to the short, inconsequential encounters we have with those we pass on the street. Although it is possible to do so, generally we have not made any special meaning for most of these acts; we have not made them into separate social objects in our world of social objects. They are not usually matters one bothers to discuss with others, or even to think about himself; so many acts even lack names. Try, for example, to describe in words all of the small body movements that you have made in the last two minutes. You will probably not know a very descriptive set of words. You might say that you squirmed around, or that you moved your hands around, but if you wanted to be more precise you would have to say things like: "I moved my right hand up and to the right curling my fingers around the edge of the book." In other words, instead of having a word to describe your act you would have to use a lot of words that would refer to directions, parts of the body, and possible subjective reasons, some of which may not have been conscious, for making the gestures. There are other acts, little different from these random ones, that we do have words for, and that, by naming, we separate out as objects in the world. "Waving good-bye" is one example, "knitting your brow," is another, "shrugging your shoulders," is a third. By giving them names we make social objects of their meanings for us, meanings that can be transmitted to others in the group.

The meanings we attach to each discrete action, including actions such as meeting your friend for lunch, are "first-order" meanings. Everything that we separate out as a discrete act has a first-order meaning for us. Most of our social acts, the actions we carry out in institutions of behavior, also have a "second-order" meaning attached to them in the form of legitimations.

Legitimation, as a process, produces new meanings that are intended to "make sense" out of the first-order meanings attached to discrete behavioral institutions. "Legitimations" make these meanings available as plausible explanations. Thus, waving good-bye may be seen as an obligatory part of social etiquette signifying friendly leave-taking, and it is legitimated as part of the way in which we end interactions with others. Knitting the brow may be an expression of worry or perplexity, which stands as a request for elaboration. Meeting your friend for lunch may be legitimated as a time for relaxation, exchanging information, or for enjoying a conversation. In these cases the *level* of legitimation is quite low. These are not actions that we feel are required by God, Science, or societal necessity; they do not need such high levels of legitimation. More complex institutions, however, do require high levels of legitimation.

In general, legitimations answer the question "why?": "Why do we drive on the right-hand side of the road?" "Why do teachers give examinations?" "Why should I eat healthful foods?" "Why should I fight in a war?" As long as a pattern is in its early stage of formation, just an agreement, a reciprocal typification between two people on how to go about something, high levels of legitimation are unnecessary. When the institution is passed on to children or recruits, however, it will probably be necessary to explain why such an institution arose, because this may

not be self-evident to the people who are newly following it. Legitimation is, thus, the process of explaining and justifying important elements
of an institutional tradition.

Legitimations explain the institutional order to the people who participate in it. The standard answers to questions such as "Why are some
people rich and others poor?" "Why is prostitution illegal?" "Why
should I bathe daily?" "Why should I go to school?" "Why do physicians
make so much money?" and so forth, are legitimations. Although the
legitimations for one institution, such as the family, may conflict with the
legitimations for another institution, such as owning a Ferrari, the people
involved generally do not notice this conflict, or if they do they appeal
to a higher level of legitimation that orders both the family and sports
cars in terms of priorities and values. These higher legitimations give
the participants the comfortable feeling that their own activity and the
activities of others around them fit together in a total pattern that is both
logical and necessary. Counter-institutions, which do not fit into the
legitimations of the institutional order, are thus seen as illogical, unnecessary, immoral, and wrong. For example, when people say, "I don't
understand why these students are demonstrating, they should take their
grievances up through proper channels," they are saying that the
institutional order, as far as they know or assume, *has* a legitimate
method for resolving differences and the fact that the students don't see
this is beyond their understanding—that is, the reasons are outside of
their stock of knowledge. Most people feel that the institutional order
can eventually resolve all problems, particularly if they don't know how
problems are actually resolved, so failures to resolve problems are not
"understandable" to them.

The legitimations of the various behavioral institutions in the institutional order also explain the steps in an individual's life—in his biography. They give him reason to expect that certain rights and duties
will fall to him at certain stages of his life. They give him the expectation
of an ordered career from birth to death. In this way, childhood, adolescence, adulthood, and old age, with their consequent shifts in institutional participation, are seen as preordained, logical, necessary, and
moral progressions. At each stage in the life cycle "reasons" are available to explain why one should do some things, and should not do
other things. Thus, "children should be seen and not heard," "teenagers
should not go steady because it might lead to pregnancy," "you should
finish college so you can get a good job," "it's a man's duty to support
his family," "a woman's place is home, church, and children," "life
begins at forty," "age should be respected," and "it was a blessing that
she died," are some of the legitimations that guide a person through
life. Each of these legitimations supports activities that fit into the
institutional order, and implicitly or explicitly condemn participation in

counter-institutions. The legitimations of each institution attempt to prove to a person, and to make it subjectively plausible, that his present age and activities are the best and most correct, as long as he does what he is supposed to.

Similarly, legitimations are available for work careers—successful ones, mediocre ones, and unsuccessful ones—that attempt to make the individual happy with his position. "I'd rather be poor and happy than rich and unhappy," "I'm an honest working man who didn't get ahead because I didn't have the connections," "there are things in life more important than getting ahead in a job," all legitimate a lack of success in a career.

In small societies that have few specialized occupations, where the division of labor is largely along sex lines, the legitimations are pervasive and are easily organized into a "rational" whole. This is the case because each person has participated or will participate in most of the institutions of behavior appropriate to his sex. Thus his biography is much the same as everyone else's, and his own career spans much of the institutional order of his society. Making sense of the entire institutional order is not hard for him because he will probably live through all of it, or almost all of it.

In complex societies, which have minute divisions of labor, more legitimations are necessary, because each institution of behavior requires a reason, or legitimation. The individual living in a complex society experiences only a fraction of all of the behavioral institutions around him, and thus, on his own, would find a great deal of difficulty in understanding the totality of the institutional order; thus, a new group has arisen, "specialists" in legitimation, people who attempt to explain the way in which the entire institutional order hangs together. Whether they be priests, philosophers, politicians, or social scientists, they try to reflect on the institutional order, and, within their frame of reference, to explain it. Many of the older explanations thought up by these theoreticians have become widely diffused as popular "commonsense" knowledge. Some of the newer explanations are still in the books of the theoreticians, though the mass media spread them with astonishing rapidity. Legitimations from many different perspectives are available, all competing for predominance, each trying to define and legitimate the institutional order. Individuals may pick from among these legitimations to find the ones that suit them best. Thus they may explain the family in terms of natural law, and their jobs in terms of economic philosophy.

Counter-institutions also require legitimations to make them plausible and to help their members integrate their subjective biographies. People in counter-institutions attempt to show that they are "really" part of the institutional order, and therefore should not be suppressed, and so may propose legitimations designed to demonstrate that they are "no different" from others in some similar institution in the institutional order. The confidence man says, "you can't cheat an honest man," the marijuana smoker points out that grass is less of a health hazard than alcohol, the prostitute calls herself a "working girl," the gambler, bootlegger, and drug dealer point out that they are just providing a service their customers desire, and anyway, "what's wrong with it?" These counter-institutional legitimations are more difficult to maintain than are straight legitimations because they are the legitimations of an isolated behavioral institution, and they are not usually integrated with, or supported by, a more abstract legitimation that would give them a place in the institutional order. Thus there are no specialists in integrating the legitimations of the entire collection of institutions outside the institutional order. (Comprehensive legitimation does take place in alternate realities, as we will see later.) There are no theoreticians, for example, of crime in general, except the negative theoreticians of the institutional order who are against it. There *are* alternate realities that propose an entirely different way of integrating an institutional order, but they in turn will exclude some institutions from their pattern of legitimation. As we go through the various counter-institutions mentioned in the adaptations I will attempt to point out their legitimations.

Maintaining biographical legitimations is often quite difficult for those involved in counter-institutions. Unless they live a life so distant from the institutional order that they rarely contact it, their biographical legitimations are constantly being called into question. A prostitute, for ·example, may find no problem in her working environment, but she will have some difficulty when she visits her parents. Much of the force of biographical legitimation comes from the fairly universal integration of the institutional order, and counter-institutions do not have this support. Thus, biographical legitimations in many counter-institutions are fairly ad hoc. In counter-institutions with low levels of legitimation the individual is likely to try to excuse his participation. One of the most common forms of excuse is the medical-psychiatric "cop-out." These legitimations relieve the participant of psychic responsibility for his actions. Some examples are, "alcoholism is a disease," "I was born a homosexual," "I'm addicted," "I was suffering from temporary insanity," "I grew up in a bad neighborhood," "I had a bad home environment," "I never had a chance because I was discriminated against," and "It's a compulsion."

Counter-institutions with a higher level of legitimation provide biographical legitimations such as: "homosexuality is the most pure form of love," "it's a gay life," and "it's where it's at." These legitimations are characteristic of counter-institutions that are becoming popular or powerful, and have a chance of becoming a new part of the institutional order.

They make following the counter-institution a logical and praiseworthy step, rather than something to be ashamed of. We will try to follow the development of these biographical legitimations in the course of the book.

As behavioral patterns grow from coordinations to widespread institutions of behavior, the legitimations they require and develop grow in generality as well. Berger and Luckmann implicitly distinguished four levels of institution growth, and four levels of legitimation generality. In Table 2, I have tried to suggest in what way each level of increasing institutionalization requires a higher level of legitimation. This chart applies to both institutions and counter-institutions.

When a person establishes a habit he may or may not think consciously to himself, "this is how I do it." If two people coordinate their actions it will be necessary for them to think "this is the way we do it" about whatever they are doing. When they pass it on to a new person, or when it becomes a matter for formal instruction, obviously the most basic data that must be transmitted are the mechanics of participating in this institution of behavior: "How to do it." There are some habits you think about consciously, and others which seem so trivial you don't even know that they are habits. You have countless thousands of habits that have never occurred to you as habits: the way you drive to school; the way you get up; the particular gait you have; the fact that you run your hand over your hair when you are talking with a boy you like; the way you settle arguments in your family—or the way you cause them. About *these habits* you don't even say "this is how I do it" to yourself. But the habits you have thought "what to do" about you have a name for. Like "typing." Like "smoking." Like "dating." Like "waving good-bye." The fact that you have a name for it means that you can tell someone else "how you do it." You can explain the mechanics of the behavior. This means that you can "linguistically transmit" the habit. There are some "personal" habituations, like posturing in "strange ways" and "staring" and talking "nonsense" that don't have names—but they make other people uncomfortable—they are outside of the legitimated patterns of "habits" and since they make people who "behave as they are supposed to" up tight, these habitually straight people often dispose of the

TABLE 2 THE RELATION BETWEEN INSTITUTIONALIZATION AND LEGITIMATION

Levels of Institutional Development	How is it done?	Why is it done?	Why are all the things like this done this way?	What is the universal plan of human life?
	Levels of Legitimation—Answers These Questions			
Habituation (individual)	Possible			
Coordination	Necessary	Possible		
Recruitment of outsider	Necessary	Necessary	Possible	
Formal instruction in institution for "all"	Necessary	Necessary	Necessary	Possible

problem by calling it "mental illness." That is, "I don't understand the way you think so you must not be normal, because I understand *normal* people, and if you are not normal you are sick." But since there are a large number of possible idiosyncratic habits there may be scarcely a dozen in a mental hospital who got there because of the same "bad habit."

If enough people have the same "habit," whether it is a "good" one or a "bad" one, somebody, sooner or later, is going to give a name to it. It may be somebody who likes it and thinks it is a good habit, or it may be somebody who doesn't like it and thinks other "decent" people wouldn't like it either. "Typing" didn't have a name until there were a number of people with the habit who all decided to call it by the same name. Men who like to dress in women's clothes, and women who like to dress in men's clothes, weren't given a "name" for their habit until Magnus Hirshfeld called it "transvestism" in 1910. Given a habit, the granting of a name begins to legitimate it. It separates it out, for good or ill, from all the random, unnamed behavior. It means that if it is acceptable within the bounds of the legitimated institutional order it is something that is all right, and if not, therapy will be provided for the people who do it. Granting a name also often tells much about the habit. Just as with a scientific taxonomy, or strategy for naming things, the name often indicates something of its relationship to other institutions. "Typing" is done in an "office," usually by "women" who are "typists." You see how much we have already learned about the other institutions of behavior "typing" is connected with? When we learn relationship with these people a "thing" that has certain "legitimate" words like "mother" and "father" and "friend" we also make our actions to be carried out, and certain "illegitimate" actions that would be a violation of the behavior institution. Some behavior, both legitimate and illegitimate, goes to higher levels of legitimation, and some never goes beyond being given a name. "Alcoholism," "transvestism," and "masturbation" are habits that a lot of people have but for which there isn't really any "good" reason "why." That is, they do not have a higher level legitimation. They are just "habits."

If your habit meshes with someone else's, either by design or accident, you reach the stage of "reciprocal typification" and coordination. At this level you have to have given your institution *some* conscious thought, because otherwise you wouldn't repeatedly mesh with another person who also does other things. So you have it separated out in your mind with a name, or something like a name. You may refer to it as "our thing," or as "lunch (with friend)." At any rate you *must* have thought "how to do it." So the level of coordinated actions always includes the "how to do it" level of legitimations. In addition you *might* also think up a reason "why" you are doing this thing. This may not be any complicated explanation "why," perhaps merely a slogan you have.

"A stitch in time saves nine" legitimates a lot of little precautionary actions. Other such slogans, from the institutional order and from counter-institutions, are: "love thy father and mother," "honesty is the best policy," "turn on, tune in, drop out," "an honest day's work for an honest day's pay," "marriage is sent from heaven," "if it were not for prostitutes more marriages would fall apart." Now, not all of these slogans are for institutions which are *only* legitimated at the first two levels, but they *are* second-level legitimations. A great many institutions are legitimated at this level, but are not legitimated at the level of explaining just exactly how they fit in with all the other "good" institutions of the institutional order. In the institutions of prostitution, premarital sex, confidence games, and homosexual "home territory bars," the participants know "how to do" what they are doing, and they have a reason for "why they are doing" what they are doing, but they don't have an explicit theory of how it really is part of the institutional structure of society.

You begin to need a theory when you are instructing people in the institution who say "prove to me it's a good thing." In order to do so you have to show them how the institution fits in with everything else they think is good. So you show your labor institution as good by using the example of "free enterprise," or "socialism," depending on where you are. You show your system of marriage as necessary for children's mental health, you show your cutting down a forest as acceptable because it is on "private property." So when an institution begins to take in people who didn't help found it, either children or recruits, its members must come up with an explanation of how to do it, why one does it, and, possibly, how it fits in with other "good" institutions. When a counter-institution can explain how it fits into the institutional order, how it is positively related to other good institutions, it has begun the process of becoming a new part of the institutional order. Homosexuals and marijuana smokers are beginning to point out these "good" connections; the labor movement just succeeded in the last thirty years.

Once an institution becomes a part of the institutional order it will be passed along to the young and to recruits, but particularly the young, because it is now an "official" solution to the question "what is the right way to do it?" It has become part of the conventional wisdom, and something that children can be taught in school. But still, children are curious, and teachers are curious, and there is a great deal of concern that something taught to everyone should be the "best way." How does anyone prove that the sum total of his society is the "best way"? The answer is always that it is "beyond concrete demonstration" but that something "above" or "beyond" mere man, something that man can seek to know but can never totally understand, indicates, or says, or proves that this is the right way. This orientation to the unknown may be through an elaborate mythology that tells us how the gods did things, or through the unknowable God as revealed to us by prophets, or through the law of nature as revealed to us by philosophers, or through scientific principles of behavior as revealed to us by social and psychological scientists. The orientation toward the unknown encompasses *everything,* everything we know, do, feel, and everything we don't know. It explains why the institutional order is necessary and legitimate, in broad terms, and it can be made to explain every bit of our behavior, even our unconscious behavior. All that has to happen is that one of the "experts"—priest, philosopher, or psychoanalyst—has to "interpret" our behavior for us, to tell us how it really fits in with the theory of the unknown.

Suppose you have a dream that you are making love to someone. For some strange reason this disturbs you, so you ask your expert in the unknown what it means. If you live in a tribe and your expert is a shaman, he will say that it was either a spirit, or a warning from the gods, or a sign of the gods' approval of you, depending on his theory. If you live in a theological society you ask a priest, and he may tell you it was a temptation of the devil, that it was a succubus or an incubus you made love to, the devil who took a "familiar" form to deceive you. If you ask a Freudian psychoanalyst he will tell you it was an unconscious attempt to resolve your Oedipus conflict, or something similar.

Say you wonder about the worth of your institutional order. The mythologist may tell you that it is working toward the perfection of the gods. The theologist may tell you that it is the divine drama. The philosopher may tell you it's the "natural" order. The scientist may tell you that it is working toward the expansion of human knowledge. All of the reality of everyday life, all of the institutions, and counter-institutions, all of your individual biography, all of your sense of self-esteem, all of your sense that things are "rational" and "sane," is ultimately buttressed by the opinions of the experts in the unknowable. This entire orientation toward the unknowable is called the "symbolic universe." It contains, supposedly, reasons for "everything." It orders phases of individual biography, keeps subjective identity straight, makes death a legitimate part of life, legitimates the institutional order, sets the limits of social reality, even decides who are people and who are not; it orders history and the future in a meaningful totality, making them seem logical, integrates all discrete institutional realities, and defends the sense of reality from chaos. Since it organizes *everything,* an inhabitant cannot admit that there might be another organization of *everything.* Thus, when some other culture, or people within a culture, believe in such a "counter-universe," the reaction of the defenders of the symbolic universe is, first, to deny its reality and, finally, to fight this alternate reality. When religion was a counter-universe of mythology there was bloodshed until religion won out. When science began to succeed religion there was also conflict. Successful counter-universes have been historically infrequent, though alternate realities not as complete as a symbolic universe have frequently established themselves.

There may be a great many changes in the institutional order within a single symbolic universe, but a change of universes is anticipated by and results in a massive reorganization of the institutional order.

The symbolic universe and all of its connections with everything represents the abstract structure of a great many subjective reflections. It is actually quite complex, being made up of the efforts of different theoreticians who each "explained" something through the years. The ordinary person living within a symbolic universe, however, usually does not understand these theoretical complexities; he takes the symbolic universe on faith and for granted. He just assumes that God, nature, or science is watching, and lets it go at that. But since God, nature, or science legitimates the symbolic universe, he can transmit his institutions of behavior, within the institutional order, safe from disturbing questions about its ultimate validity.

When a heretic, who is an individual unbeliever, or an alternate reality, which proposes to reinterpret everything arises, the symbolic universe fights against them, making conventional belief sharper and more comprehensive in an attempt to undercut the heretics. When the heretics take over and propagate their new reality, the old universe continues a rear-guard action defending its claim to organize all of reality. Witness the tortured theologians of today.

We may look at the way in which the symbolic universe legitimates the institutional order as a series of steps. First of all, the connections between the symbolic universe and the major patterning of institutions is relatively well "explained" by theoreticians. Within the patterns of each institution, coordinations that do not do violence to the institutionalized way of doing things are legitimated by the institution. Within such legitimate coordinations individual habits that "fit in" are legitimate. Thus, indirectly, the symbolic universe legitimates all of our behavior. A counter-institution, on the other hand, is outside of this chain of legitimation, and very frequently, in order to foster institutional development, a theoretician of the counter-institution will propose a chain of legitimation that shows how it could fit into the symbolic universe. Given the habit, the coordination "should be." Given the reciprocal typification, the institutional order "should be arranged thusly." And all of these institutional changes "should" fit into the symbolic universe easily because of some past prophecy or value that has not been given "proper" interpretation.

THE INSTITUTIONAL ORDER

One of the intellectual problems of growing up in an institutional order, as we all did, is that we think we understand it. Yet most of us live naïvely in our world, and we take as unshakable wisdom most of the things that we have noticed around us or heard repeatedly. Yet we all grew up in a particular location, we all grew up in a particular family, and we all grew up with parents in different occupations. Because our individual exposure to the institutional order is very influential in the things we *can* know and think, we each have a somewhat different understanding of what is involved in the institutional order, about what our society is like. But when we are dealing with a subject such as "deviance" it is important to know what the behavior is deviating from. We could not build a theory that would be applicable to all cases if we went at it by assuming that everything different from the way we thought right was "deviant." That would be putting ourselves at the center of the universe and judging everything only as it related to our own particular, private experience. Likewise, we cannot build a good theory if we take into account only what people *say* the order of the world is, because they too speak from particular perspectives. This is true even if we take what an "expert" says about the world. After all, he is working within a particular *theoretical organization* of the world. All of us would not agree, for example, to accept the definitions of right and wrong that might be propounded by a minister, or a philosopher, or even a scientist. Yet, somehow, people do think that some behavior is right and other behavior is wrong, and this is what we are interested in studying. But if each individual has a different perspective, and each theoretician has a different perspective, how can we truly decide what is "normal" and what is "deviant"? The answer is, of course, that as investigators we don't decide. We study other people's decisions. The way to best go about this is to see what people think, and what institutions actually do. Since we all have our particular perspectives we can't just shoot from the hip; we have to go out and look closely at actual thought and behavior. Since institutions control, or influence, or determine the behavior of their followers, and since they create the sense of morality that their followers adopt, they create definitions of what is right, and, negatively, what is wrong. This is the way that the institutional order and the people who participate in it decide what is "deviant." It is not usually what some individual thinks, be he layman or theorist, but, rather, the behavior required by institutions, and the values defined by the symbolic universe, that define a "deviant" for society.

THE WAY THE INSTITUTIONAL ORDER "WORKS"

We examined the way in which institutions grew from habits, to coordinations, to transmitted institutions, and finally to predominance in the institutional order of society. We also examined the growth of legitimations, which is part of this institutional growth. But we saw very little of the workings of an institution of behavior in its relation to other institutions of behavior. In the following adaptation Norton Long describes the way in which one institution in a community is related to other institutions. While he writes only about institutions in local communities, the principles he develops are applicable to both patterns of coordination, say within a family, and to larger institutions, which would cover nations. Professor Long uses his own terminology in writing his article. Each of the authors of the other adaptations does the same—there is no standard terminology as yet for sociologists, anthropologists, psychiatrists, psychologists, and medical doctors. In order to keep these different terminologies from obscuring the underlying consensus among the authors, I have inserted my own comments in brackets within their texts to provide a common language for the entire book. In addition, I have commented on other points that seem to me to be of particular interest or value. In doing this I am attempting to do in a book what I would do in class: organize knowledge so that it is more coherent and understandable.

□ □ □

1
THE LOCAL COMMUNITY AS AN ECOLOGY OF GAMES

NORTON E. LONG

The local community, whether viewed as a polity, an economy, or a society, presents itself as an order in which expectations are met and functions performed. In some cases, as in a new, company-planned mining town, the order is the willed product of centralized control, but for the most part the order is the product of a history rather than the imposed effect of any central nervous system of the community. [*This is the institutional order.*] For historic reasons we readily conceive the massive task of feeding New York to be achieved through the unplanned, historically developed cooperation of thousands of actors largely unconscious of their collaboration to this individually unsought end. The efficiency of this system is attested to by the extraordinary difficulties of the War Production Board and Service of Supply in accomplishing similar logistical objectives through an explicit system of orders and directives. [*Thousands of individual institutions perform the many specialized tasks that would be difficult to attend to through a master plan.*] Insofar as conscious rationality plays a role, it is a function of the parts rather than the whole. Particular structures working for their own ends within the whole may provide their members with goals, strategies, and roles that support rational action. The results of the interaction of the rational strivings after particular ends are in part collectively functional if unplanned. All this is the well-worn doctrine of Adam Smith, though one need accept no more of the doctrine of beneficence than that an unplanned economy can function.

While such a view is accepted for the economy, it is generally rejected for the polity. [*Both the economy and the polity are aspects of the institutional order, though they have been separated out as distinct areas of expertise for theoreticians.*] Without a sovereign, Leviathan is generally supposed to disintegrate and fall apart. Even if Locke's more hopeful view of the naturalness of the social order is taken, the polity seems more of a contrived artifact than the economy. Furthermore, there is both the hangover of Austinian sovereignty and the Greek view of ethical primacy to make political institutions seem different in kind and ultimately inclusive in purpose and for this reason to give them an overall social directive end. [*These were older theoretical formulations that are still followed by some theoreticians.*] To see political

Adapted from *The American Journal of Sociology*, Vol. 44, No. 3, November 1958, pp. 251–261. Reprinted with permission of the author and the University of Chicago Press, publisher.

institutions as the same kind of thing as other institutions in society rather than as different, superior, and inclusive (both in the sense of being sovereign and ethically more significant) is a form of relativistic pluralism that is difficult to entertain [*because our minds have always worked within the categories provided by these theories within our symbolic universe*]. At the local level, however, it is easier to look at the municipal government, its departments, and the agencies of state and national government as so many institutions, resembling banks, newspapers, trade unions, chambers of commerce, churches, etc., occupying a territorial field and interacting with one another. [*It is easier to look at local government because it is concrete and not as closely connected to the abstract theoretical structure.*] This interaction can be conceptualized as a system without reducing the interacting institutions and individuals to membership in any single comprehensive group. It is psychologically tempting to envision the local territorial system as a group with a governing "they." This is certainly an existential possibility and one to be investigated. However, frequently, it seems likely, systems are confused with groups, and our primitive need to explain thunder with a theology or a demonology results in the hypostatizing of an angelic or demonic hierarchy. [*In other words, we often impose a logic through retrospective consciousness on a system that is not inherently organized.*] The executive committee of the bourgeoisie and the power elite make the world more comfortable for modern social scientists as the Olympians did for the ancients. [*Social scientists are the "experts" in interpreting the symbolic universe.*] At least the latter-day hypothesis, being terrestrial, is in principle researchable, though in practice its metaphysical statement may render it equally immune to mundane inquiry.

Observation of certain local communities makes it appear that inclusive over-all organization for many general purposes is weak or nonexistent. Much of what occurs seems to just happen with accidental trends becoming cumulative over time and producing results intended by nobody. A great deal of the communities' activities consist of undirected co-operation of particular social structures, each seeking particular goals and, in doing so, meshing with others. While much of this might be explained in Adam Smith's terms, much of it could not be explained with a rational, atomistic model of calculating individuals. For certain purposes the individual is a useful way of looking at people; for many others the role-playing member of a particular group is more helpful. Here we deal with the essence of predictability in social affairs. If we know the game being played is baseball and that X is a third baseman, by knowing his position and the game being played we can tell more about X's activities on the field than we could if we examined X as a psychologist or a psychiatrist. If such were not the case, X would belong in the mental ward rather than in a ball park. The behavior of X is not some disembodied rationality but, rather, behavior within an organized group activity that has goals, norms, strategies, and roles that give the very field and ground for rationality. Baseball structures the situation. [*That is, baseball is an institution whose rules must be followed in order to derive its benefits.*]

It is the contention of this paper that the structured group activities that coexist in a particular territorial system can be looked at as games. [*"Games" are particular institutions of behavior, or a collection of such institutions that people think of as being related to one another.*] These games provide the players with a set of goals that give them a sense of success or failure. They provide them with determinate roles and calculable strategies and tactics. In addition, they provide the players with an elite and general public that is in varying degrees able to tell the score. There is a good deal of evidence to be found in common parlance that many participants in contemporary group structures regard their occupations as at least analogous to games. And, at least in the American culture, and not only since Eisenhower, the conception of being on a "team" has been fairly widespread.

Unfortunately, the effectiveness of the term "game" for the purposes of this paper is vitiated by, first, the general sense that games are trivial occupations and, second, by the pre-emption of the term for the application of a calculus of probability to choice or design in a determinate game situation. Far from regarding games as trivial, the writer's position would be that man is both a game-playing and a game-creating animal, that his capacity to create and play games and take them deadly seriously is of the essence, and that it is through games or activities analogous to game-playing that he achieves a satisfactory sense of significance and a meaningful role.

While the calculability of the game situation is important, of equal or greater importance is the capacity of the game to provide a sense of purpose and a role. The organizations of society and polity produce satisfactions with both their products and their processes. The two are not unrelated, but, while the production of the product may in the larger sense enable players and onlookers to keep score, the satisfaction in the process is the satisfaction of playing the game and the sense in which any activity can be grasped as a game.

Looked at this way, in the territorial system there is a political game, a banking game, a contracting game, a newspaper game, a civic organization game, an ecclesiastical game, and many others. Within each game there is a well-established set of goals whose achievement indicates success or failure for the participants, a set of socialized roles making participant behavior highly predictable, a set of strategies and tactics handed down through experience and occasionally subject to improvement and change, an elite public whose approbation is appreciated, and, finally, a general public which has some appreciation for the standing of the players. Within the game the players can be rational in the varying degrees that the structure permits. At the very least, they know how to behave, and they know the score.

Individuals may play in a number of games, but, for the most part, their major preoccupation is with one, and their sense of major achievement is through success in one. Transfer from one game to another is, of course, possible, and the simultaneous playing of roles in two or more games is an important manner of linking separate games. [*A person integrates the institutions in which he is involved as a practical, personal, and logical necessity.*]

Sharing a common territorial field and collaborating for different and particular ends in the achievement of over-all social functions, the players in one game make use of the players in another and are, in turn, made use of by them. Thus the banker makes use of the newspaperman, the politician, the contractor, the ecclesiastic, the labor leader, the civic leader—all to further his success in the banking game—but, reciprocally, he is used to further the others' success in the newspaper, political, contracting, ecclesiastical, labor, and civic games. Each is a piece in the chess game of the other, sometimes a willing piece, but, to the extent that the games are different, with a different end in view.

Thus a particular highway grid may be the result of a bureaucratic department of public works game in which are combined, though separate, a professional highway engineer game with its purposes and critical elite onlookers; a departmental bureaucracy; a set of contending politicians seeking to use the highways for political capital, patronage, and the like; a banking game concerned with bonds, taxes, and the effect of the highways on real estate; newspapermen interested in headlines, scoops, and the effect of highways on the paper's circulation; contractors eager to make money by building roads; ecclesiastics concerned with the effect of highways on their parishes and on the fortunes of the contractors who support their churchly ambitions; labor leaders interested in union contracts and their status as community influentials with a right to be consulted; and civic leaders who must justify the contributions of their bureaus of municipal research or chambers of commerce to the social activity. Each game is in play in the complicated pulling and hauling of siting and constructing the highway grid. A wide variety of purposes is subserved by the activity, and no single over-all directive authority controls it. However, the interrelation of the groups in constructing a highway has been developed over time, and there are general expectations as to the interaction. There are also generalized expectations as to how politicians, contractors, newspapermen, bankers, and the like will utilize the highway situation in playing their particular games. In fact, the knowledge that a banker will play like a banker and a newspaperman like a newspaperman is an important part of what makes the situation calculable and permits the players to estimate its possibilities for their own action in their particular game. [*Each institution in the institutional order relies on the other institutions it has dealings with to act predictably.*]

While it might seem that the engineers of the department of public works were the appropriate protagonists for the highway grid, as a general activity it presents opportunities and threats to a wide range of other players who see in the situation consequences and possibilities undreamed of by the engineers. Some general public expectation of the limits of the conduct of the players and of a desirable outcome does provide bounds to the scramble. This public expectation is, of course, made active through the interested solicitation of newspapers, politicians, civic leaders, and others who see in it material for accomplishing their particular purposes and whose structured roles in fact require the mobilization of broad publics. In a sense the group struggle that Arthur Bentley described in his *Process of Government* is a drama that local publics have been taught to view with a not uncritical taste. The instruction of this taste has been the vocation and business of some of the contending parties. The existence of some kind of over-all public puts general restraints on gamesmanship beyond the norms of the particular games. However, for the players these are to all intents as much a part of the "facts of life" of the game as the sun and the wind.

. . .

The ecology of games in the local territorial system accomplishes unplanned but largely functional results. The games and their players mesh in their particular pursuits to bring about over-all results; the territorial system is fed and ordered. Its inhabitants are rational within limited areas and, pursuing the ends of these areas, accomplish socially functional ends.

While the historical development of largely unconscious co-operation between the special games in the territorial system gets certain routine, over-all functions performed, the problem of novelty and breakdown must be dealt with. Here it would seem that, as in the natural ecology, random adjustment and piecemeal innovation are the normal methods of response. The need or cramp in the system presents itself to the players of the games as an opportunity for them to exploit or a menace to be overcome. Thus a transportation crisis in, say, the threatened abandonment of commuter trains by a railroad will bring forth the players of a wide range of games who will see in the situation opportunity for gain or loss in the outcome. While over-all considerations will appear in the discussion, the frame of reference and the interpretation of the event will be largely determined by the game the interested parties are principally involved in. [*In other words, each institution looks out for its own interests, even though people think of them as part of a rationally ordered system.*] Thus a telephone executive who is president of the local chamber of commerce will be playing a civic association, general business game with concern for the principal dues-payers of the chamber but with a constant awareness of how his handling of this crisis will advance him in his particular league. The politicians, who might be expected to be protagonists of the general interest, may indeed be so, but the sphere of their activity and the glasses through which they see the problem will be determined in great part by the way they see the issue affecting their political game. The generality of this game is to a great extent that of the politician's calculus of votes and interests important to his and his side's success. To be sure, some of what Walter Lippmann has called "the public philosophy" affects both politicians and other game-players. This indicates the existence of roles and norms of a larger, vaguer game with a relevant audience that has some sense of cricket. [*These are the values of the symbolic universe, making some institutional arrangements right and others wrong.*]

This potentially mobilizable audience is not utterly without importance, but it provides no sure or adequate basis for support in the particular game that the politician or anyone else is playing. Instead of a set of norms to structure enduring role-playing, this audience provides a cross-pressure for momentary aberrancy from gamesmanship or constitutes just another hazard to be calculated in one's play.

In many cases the territorial system is impressive in the degree of intensity of its particular games, its banks, its newspapers, its downtown stores, its manufacturing companies, its contractors, its churches, its politicians, and its other differentiated, structured, goal-oriented activities. Games go on within the territory, occasionally extending beyond it, though centered in it. But, while the particular games show clarity of goals and intensity, few, if any, treat the territory as their proper object. The protagonists of things in particular are well organized and know what they are about; the protagonists of things in general are few, vague, and weak. [*That is, most of the real organization comes from the ongoing institutions.*]

．　　　．　　　．

The community needs to believe that there are spiritual fathers, bad or good, who can deal with the dark: in the Middle Ages the peasants combated a plague of locusts by a high Mass and a procession of the clergy who damned the grasshoppers with bell, book, and candle. The Hopi Indians do a rain dance to overcome a drought. The harassed citizens of the American city mobilize their influentials at a civic luncheon to perform the equivalent and exorcise slums, smog, or unemployment. We smile at the medievals and the Hopi, but our own practices may be equally magical. It is interesting to ask under what circumstances one resorts to DDT and irrigation and why. To some extent it is clear that the ancient and modern practice of civic magic ritual is functional—functional in the same sense as the medicinal placebo. Much of human illness is benign; if the sufferer will bide his time, it will pass. Much of civic ills also cure themselves if only people can be kept from tearing each other apart in the stress of their anxieties. The locusts and the drought will pass. They almost always have.

While ritual activities are tranquilizing anxieties, the process of experimentation and adaptation in the social ecology goes on. The piecemeal responses of the players and the games to the challenges presented by crises provide the social counterpart to the process of evolution and natural selection. However, unlike the random mutation of the animal kingdom, much of the behavior of the players responding within the perspectives of their games is self-conscious and rational, given their ends in view. It is from the over-all perspective of the unintended contribution of their actions to the forming of a new or the restoration of the old ecological balance of the social system that their actions appear almost as random and lacking in purposive plan as the adaptive behavior of the natural ecology.

Within the general area of unplanned, unconscious social process technological areas emerge that are so structured as to promote rational, goal-oriented behavior and meaningful experience rather than mere happenstance. [*These are institutions that are directly related to the scientific universe, and thus their rationality is more apparent to us than that of institutions related to older universes.*] In these areas group activity may result in cumulative knowledge and self-corrective behavior. Thus problem-solving in the field of public health and sanitation may be at a stage far removed from the older dependence on piecemeal adjustment and random functional innovation. In this sense there are areas in which society, as Julian Huxley suggests in his *The Meaning of Evolution,* has gone beyond evolution. However, these are as yet isolated areas in a world still swayed by magic and, for the most part, carried forward by the logic of unplanned, undirected historical process.

.   .   .

□ □ □

Long has suggested a number of important ideas about the way in which institutions relate to one another in a community. I think these ideas can be usefully applied to many different kinds of communities if we keep in mind the particular characteristics of each. Families are communities of a certain sort. Work groups are too. So are neighborhoods. Even nations can be looked on as communities in which many different kinds of institutions push and pull and shove, each for its own benefit. I think with slight modification Long's ideas can be stated in the language developed here. Here is a summary of the ideas in his article:

1. That the "order" of a territorial area is an outcome of many historical processes, not of planning—or only very slightly of planning.
2. That the goals and strategies that men spend most of their time working for and with come mostly from the particular institutions of behavior they follow, not from national commissions on goals.
3. There are diverse institutions within an area, which interact with one another. Their interaction governs the nature of the community, not in the formal sense of government as an institution, but as a body that organizes and regulates all of the possibilities for activity that exist in the community.
4. All of these institutions do not necessarily form a single, comprehensive, "organized" group. There may be many practical and theoretical bases of organization, each of which would include a different collection of institutions. Like dipping a net into a tropical fish tank, each "organization" nets a different collection of fish.
5. There is probably no single group of people who organizes everybody and directs everything. In some cases an elite organizes a larger portion of the behavior than others. The army versus a beach party, for example.
6. Most individual behavior in institutions comes from the expectations of the institution, not from individual psychology. We can predict most of anyone's behavior by knowing the institutions of behavior he spends most of his life in.
7. As they grow older, individuals switch institutions (from time to time, they also do so as adults). Also, people are involved in several institutions at the same time so that their behavior in one often affects their behavior in another. When their behavior is so affected the institutions influence one another. This linkage may be trivial or important to the institutions involved, depending, in part, on the importance of the person.
8. Any distinct multi-institutional activity is going to be affected by

the transactions and bargains of the institutions involved. Each institution makes its bargains while seeking to perpetuate itself and also to gain other ends.

9. "Public opinion" forms a background for these institutional activities. Public opinion, however, must be mobilized to be effective, so unless one of the institutions mobilizes it, it will play little part in any resulting outcome. The further the outcome is from some mobilizable public's ideas of what is right the more likely that some institution will try to mobilize it for its own ends.

10. The meshings of institutions bring about the over-all institutional order we see: part "good," part "bad," but essentially unplanned. Usually, since there are the same people involved in many overlapping institutions, most people feel that the outcomes of the institutional order are beneficial. The outcomes include getting people fed, housed, and clothed.

11. The values of the symbolic universe set outside limits for the outcomes of particular institutional arrangements. This happens because the institutions of behavior are, ultimately, legitimated within the symbolic universe, and because the public also operates within the values of the symbolic universe and can be mobilized to fight heresy, such as "Communist" water fluoridation plots.

12. When reality flaws caused by the institutional order arise, a great deal of what appears to be conscious effort to set things right is actually ritual chanting of legitimations and common knowledge. While this ritual chanting is going on the uncoordinated meshings of institutions, usually for other ends, and the creation of counter-institutions, will probably achieve an eventual solution.

Long's emphasis on the idea that no single group organizes everything should not obscure the fact that there are differences in power between differently situated individuals and groups. The leaders of organizations are far more powerful than are their followers, and some men are influential in several different organizations. Every community probably has a number of such multiple-organization leaders who routinely interact with one another and collectively influence the outcome of many community issues. This group could be called, in C. Wright Mill's terms, the power elite. Though they do not organize everything they do have power out of proportion to their numbers, and they undoubtedly use their power, when they can, in their own interests, and in the interest of furthering those institutions of behavior from which they benefit. In the process of pursuing these interests they act, to a certain extent, as reality-defining agents because they can lead, command, or coerce organizations and the individuals within them to behave in certain ways and not in other ways, and because they can in some cases influence the definitions of reality passed on in socialization. It is easy to underestimate or overestimate their power in specific cases or in general unless their influence has been concretely investigated.

To the extent, however, that a power elite influences the definition of social reality in their own interests and thereby produces experience–social reality conflicts for others, they tend to create or maintain the "reality flaws" within which "bad" habits and counter-institutions grow. At a minor level they may enforce definitions of "correct behavior" that some members of society are unable or unwilling to meet. At a major level they may advance their class or racial interests at the expense of many members of society and produce the conditions necessary for the development of an alternate reality. But this influence of power elites is not total, and there are numerous other sources of reality flaws on which they have little influence.

□ □ □
The institutions that exist within a society, which, taken together, constitute all of the "correct" ways of doing everything, and the symbolic universe within which these institutions of behavior are legitimated, attempt and are assumed to provide final definitions of reality, complete legitimations of individual careers, and a definitive ordering of institutions into an interdependent hierarchical structure. Obviously, since the institutions developed in particular circumstances, and since the symbolic universe is largely an abstracted statement based upon these particular institutional arrangements, the symbolic universe does not, and cannot, cover all of human experience. People who live their lives within the institutional order will probably never discover that there are human phenomena that their symbolic universe does not explain. But if we stand outside the particular conceptions of our own society and observe the possible varieties of human experience, it becomes clear that *any* symbolic universe in its construction of reality makes some activi-

REALITY FLAWS

ties legitimate and real and denies legitimacy or reality to others. For example, the idea of aborting and eating your own unborn baby, though legitimate in some Australian aboriginal tribes, is not really "thinkable" in our construction of reality. Our construction of reality simply does not include provision for that much "meat hunger." But it is a human experience, and one on which institutions are built. The main purpose of a symbolic universe is reality *construction,* making the world orderly, logical, and finite for its inhabitants. In the process of constructing a reality out of some, but not all, experiences there is a necessary reality *constriction.*

Symbolic universes founded upon the experiences and institutions of a small, homogeneous society may explain it all quite well, but will leave other experiences not found within the society in the realm of outer darkness—often categorized as the demonic behavior of nonhumans. The old map-makers used to draw in all of the known world and fill in the unknown parts with the legend "here there be beasties." A symbolic universe does about the same thing. When the Spaniards found Indians in the New World, they constructed elaborate theological arguments (so the Indians could be enslaved) which "proved" that the Indians could not have descended from Adam and were therefore not human.

Symbolic universes founded on the experiences and institutions of large, complicated societies tend to be extremely abstract. The more diverse the institutions of behavior that must be contained under the umbrella of legitimations, the more the umbrella must be divorced from the particular. Only in this way can the contradictions of discrete institutionalizations of behavior appear to be resolved within the symbolic structure. As institutions of behavior become more numerous, their connection with the symbolic universe may become less obvious, and the work of the theoretician attempting to explain why some way of doing something is "right" becomes more difficult.

In a heterogeneous society with many people creating institutions from their own experience it is entirely possible—indeed it is likely— that many institutions of behavior will arise, become established, recruit new members, and persist over a time without being specifically legitimated within the symbolic universe. If the reality constriction of a symbolic universe leaves the experiences of individuals and groups unaccounted for they will feel lost, or they will attempt to explain their way into the symbolic universe, or they will begin to create their own alternate reality. They are experiencing and reacting to a flaw in the construction of social reality.

In many cases a symbolic universe may legitimate two somewhat contradictory institutions of behavior (more properly, the individuals who follow these two patterns of behavior may find legitimation for both within the symbolic universe). For the individual in a position of choice between two "legitimate" but contradictory institutions, for example choosing between following the orders of his commanding officer, and following the Nuremberg requirement of individual responsibility, there is a conflict. Here too the individual may feel "lost."

When an individual has a conflict between his own experience and the socially defined reality he will be, to say the least, uncomfortable. Social reality becomes subjective reality in the socialization process, in many ways, both obvious and unnoticed. Experience is usually seen in terms of social reality since social reality provides the categories, names, ways, and reinforcements for interpreting experience. When an individual's experience does not fit within socially constructed reality he may very well refuse to recognize that there is a discrepancy because of his effective socialization. He may recognize that there is a conflict between his existential position and socially constructed reality, but not do anything about it because of his immersion in the ties of various legitimate institutions. Finally, he may act upon the basis of his experience in violation of social reality. Since the realities created by institutions, and the realities explained by the symbolic universe supposedly cover "everything," almost any concrete experience might possibly conflict with a social reality. There are many different resolutions to this conflict that we will explore for the remainder of the book; suffice it to say here that the individuals and groups whose experience conflicts with social reality are often the people called "deviant" by society.

There are two ways of examining the conflict between social reality and individual experience. My own preference is to examine the conflict as a developmental process in which the individual's experiences are taken as the starting point and the flaws in social reality are revealed by his conflict. The other method is to begin with an examination of the flaws in social reality and to determine which kinds of individuals will have conflicts as a result. Either starting point can be productive, although they tell us different things. With the first method the analysis develops up from the individual; in the second the analysis is structured down from reality. There is basic agreement between the two approaches as to the source of the conflict: social reality contradicting individual experience. I favor the first method because I believe that it can tell us more about the creation of counter-institutions and the creation of alternate realities because they are created by people with conflicts. The second method, however, is more deductive and "elegant" as a theoretical approach. Sociologists have used both approaches to study "deviant" behavior. In this chapter we will look at the second method, starting with the flaws of social reality and analyzing what kinds of individuals will experience conflicts. In later chapters we will follow the developmental process.

The French sociologist Émile Durkheim first suggested that an incongruence between social reality and individual experience could cause "deviant" behavior in his study of *Suicide,* published in 1897. In this pioneering study Durkheim did not make a distinction between the institutional order and the symbolic universe but referred to both together as "society." He theorized that a person might kill himself if he was too much involved with society, if he was too little involved with society, or if his experiences diverged too much from what society, social reality, had led him to expect.

Durkheim said that each of these problems of the individual's attachment to society caused an analytically different "kind" of suicide. The first, when the individual is too much involved with society, he called "altruistic" suicide. This occurs when the individual kills himself for his society. The best and most consistent example is military suicide. For such a suicide to take place the individual must be convinced that his society is the only possible place to live, and that all alternatives are unacceptable. The military, and entire nations in times of war, frequently demand of individuals that they knowingly go to their deaths in defense of the collectivity.

The second type of suicide, when the individual is too little involved with society, he called "egoistic." In this type of suicide the society makes too few conformity demands on the individual; he is a master of his own fate. According to Durkheim, education, which frees a person from adherence to tradition, Protestantism, which is less confining than Catholicism, and small families, which encourage individualism, all lead a person to consider his own goals more important than those of the society, and thus to stand or fall by himself.

Durkheim's third kind of suicide, when the individual's experiences diverged too far from what social reality had led him to expect, he called "anomic" suicide. He suggested that an individual became used to a certain level of personal prosperity and that in an economic boom, or crash, he would be overwhelmed by new possibilities, unable to carry on in his usual manner, and this discontinuity of experiences would lead to suicide. Another of his examples was the discontinuity in the pattern of expectations and obligations of a married person when he become divorced or widowed. A third was that a long-term decline in moral and political controls lead to a long-term rise in anomie. It seems that he was here suggesting that increasing moral and political pluralism, rapid social change, can also produce discontinuities between subjective and social reality.

Durkheim's anomie theory, pointing as it did to what I call reality flaws, was the first theoretical statement of the proposition that devi-

ance, in this case suicide, could be caused by a conflict between social reality and individual experience. In the following adaptation from *Suicide,* Durkheim discusses reality flaws centered on institutions of labor, but his theoretical structure is much more generally applicable.
☐ ☐ ☐

2
SUICIDE
ÉMILE DURKHEIM

No living being can be happy or even exist unless his needs are sufficiently proportioned to his means. In other words, if his needs require
more than can be granted, or even merely something of a different sort,
they will be under continual friction and can only function painfully.
[*In other words, if experience exceeds or varies from socially defined
reality the individual experiences discomfort.*] Movements incapable of
production without pain tend not to be reproduced. Unsatisfied tendencies atrophy, and as the impulse to live is merely the result of all the
rest, it is bound to weaken as the others relax [*leading, finally, to
suicide, but other forms of behavior are also possible*].

In the animal, at least in a normal condition, this equilibrium is
established with automatic spontaneity because the animal depends
on purely material conditions. All the organism needs is that the supplies of substance and energy constantly employed in the vital process
should be periodically renewed by equivalent quantities; that replacement be equivalent to use. When the void created by existence in its
own resources is filled, the animal, satisfied, asks nothing further.
Its power of reflection is not sufficiently developed to imagine other
ends than those implicit in its physical nature. On the other hand, as the
work demanded of each organ itself depends on the general state of
vital energy and the needs of organic equilibrium, use is regulated in
turn by replacement and the balance is automatic. The limits of one are
those of the other; both are fundamental to the constitution of the existence in question, which cannot exceed them.

This is not the case with man, because most of his needs are not
dependent on his body or not to the same degree. Strictly speaking,
we may consider that the quantity of material supplies necessary to the
physical maintenance of a human life is subject to computation, though
this be less exact than in the preceding case and a wider margin left
for the free combinations of the will; for beyond the indispensable minimum which satisfies nature when instinctive, a more awakened reflection suggests better conditions, seemingly desirable ends craving
fulfillment. Such appetites, however, admittedly sooner or later reach a
limit which they cannot pass. But how determine the quantity of well-
being, comfort or luxury legitimately to be craved by a human being?
Nothing appears in man's organic nor in his psychological constitution

Adapted from Émile Durkheim, *Suicide* (New York: Macmillan, 1961). Adapted with permission of the Macmillan Company.

which sets a limit to such tendencies. The functioning of individual life does not require them to cease at one point rather than at another; the proof being that they have constantly increased since the beginnings of history, receiving more and more complete satisfaction, yet with no weakening of average health. Above all, how establish their proper variation with different conditions of life, occupations, relative importance of services, etc.? In no society are they equally satisfied in the different stages of the social hierarchy. Yet human nature is substantially the same among all men, in its essential qualities. It is not human nature which can assign the variable limits necessary to our needs. They are thus unlimited so far as they depend on the individual alone. Irrespective of any external regulatory force, our capacity for feeling is in itself an insatiable and bottomless abyss.

But if nothing external can restrain this capacity, it can only be a source of torment to itself. Unlimited desires are insatiable by definition and insatiability is rightly considered a sign of morbidity. Being unlimited, they constantly and infinitely surpass the means at their command; they cannot be quenched. Inextinguishable thirst is constantly renewed torture. It has been claimed, indeed, that human activity naturally aspires beyond assignable limits and sets itself unattainable goals. But how can such an undetermined state be any more reconciled with the conditions of mental life than with the demands of physical life? All man's pleasure in acting, moving and exerting himself implies the sense that his efforts are not in vain and that by walking he has advanced. However, one does not advance when one walks toward no goal, or—which is the same thing—when his goal is infinity. Since the distance between us and it is always the same, whatever road we take, we might as well have made the motions without progress from the spot. Even our glances behind and our feeling of pride at the distance covered can cause only deceptive satisfaction, since the remaining distance is not proportionately reduced. To pursue a goal which is by definition unattainable is to condemn oneself to a state of perpetual unhappiness. Of course, man may hope contrary to all reason, and hope has its pleasures even when unreasonable. It may sustain him for a time; but it cannot survive the repeated disappointments of experience indefinitely. What more can the future offer him than the past, since he can never reach a tenable condition nor even approach the glimpsed ideal? Thus, the more one has, the more one wants, since satisfactions received only stimulate instead of filling needs. Shall action as such be considered agreeable? First, only on condition of blindness to its uselessness. Secondly, for this pleasure to be felt and to temper and half veil the accompanying painful unrest, such unending motion must at least always be easy and unhampered. If it is interfered with only restlessness is left, with the lack of ease which it, itself, entails. But it would be a miracle if no insurmountable obstacle were never encountered. Our thread of life on these conditions is pretty thin, breakable at any instant. [*In other words, man can aspire to anything, but without boundaries he has no sense of where he is.*]

To achieve any other result, the passions first must be limited. Only then can they be harmonized with the faculties and satisfied. But since the individual has no way of limiting them, this must be done by some force exterior to him. A regulative force must play the same role for moral needs which the organism plays for physical needs. This means that the force can only be moral. [*That is, "self-control" derived from the behavior required by institutions and the values of the symbolic universe.*] The awakening of conscience interrupted the state of equilibrium of the animal's dormant existence; only conscience, therefore, can furnish the means to re-establish it. Physical restraint would be ineffective; hearts cannot be touched by physio-chemical forces. So far as the appetites are not automatically restrained by physiological mechanisms, they can be halted only by a limit that they recognize as just. Men would never consent to restrict their desires if they felt justified in passing the assigned limit. But, for reasons given above, they cannot assign themselves this law of justice. So they must receive it from an authority which they respect, to which they yield spontaneously. Either directly and as a whole, or through the agency of one of its organs, society alone can play this moderating role; for it is the only moral power superior to the individual, the authority of which he accepts. [*That is, the individual accepts the social reality created by the institutional order and the symbolic universe, and thus accepts their limits.*] It alone has the power necessary to stipulate law and to set the point beyond which the passions must not go. Finally, it alone can estimate the reward to be prospectively offered to every class of human functionary, in the name of the common interest.

As a matter of fact, at every moment of history there is a dim perception, in the moral consciousness of societies, of the respective value of different social services, the relative reward due to each, and the consequent degree of comfort appropriate on the average to workers in each occupation. The different functions are graded in public opinion and a certain coefficient of well-being assigned to each, according to its place in the hierarchy. According to accepted ideas, for example, a certain way of living is considered the upper limit to which a workman may aspire in his efforts to improve his existence, and there is another limit below which he is not willingly permitted to fall unless he has seriously demeaned himself. [*In other words, the values of the symbolic universe rank the institutions in the institutional order, and, consequently, individuals are assigned status in society by virtue of their participation in the ordered institutions.*] Both differ for city and country workers, for the domestic servant and the day-laborer, for the business clerk and the official, etc. Likewise the man of wealth is reproved if he lives the life of a poor man, but also if he seeks the refinements of luxury overmuch. Economists may protest in vain; public feeling will always be scandalized if an individual spends too much wealth for wholly superfluous use, and it even seems that this severity relaxes only in times of moral disturbance [*that is, when reality flaws become obvious*]. A genuine regimen exists, therefore, although not always legally formulated, which fixes with relative precision the maximum degree of ease of living to which each social class may legitimately aspire. However, there is nothing immutable about such a scale. It changes with the increase or decrease of collective revenue and the changes occurring in the moral ideas of society. [*These are changes in what the institutional order permits and what the symbolic universe legitimates.*] Thus what appears luxury to one period no longer does so to another; and the well-being which for long periods was granted to a class only by exception and supererogation, finally appears necessary and equitable [*that is, it becomes institutionalized and legitimated, necessary and equitable*].

Under this pressure, each in his sphere vaguely realizes the extreme limit set to his ambitions and aspires to nothing beyond. At least if he respects regulations and is docile to collective authority, that is, has a wholesome moral constitution, he feels that it is not well to ask more. Thus, an end and goal are set to the passions. Truly, there is nothing rigid nor absolute about such determination. The economic ideal assigned each class of citizens is itself confined to certain limits, within which the desires have free range. But it is not infinite. [*That is, outside limits for institutional arrangements are provided by the values of the symbolic universe.*]

This relative limitation and the moderation it involves, make men contented with their lot while stimulating them moderately to improve it; and this average contentment causes the feeling of calm, active happiness, the pleasure in existing and living which characterizes health for societies as well as for individuals. Each person is then at least, generally speaking, in harmony with his condition, and desires only what he may legitimately hope for as the normal reward of his activity. Besides, this does not condemn man to a sort of immobility. He may seek to give beauty to his life; but his attempts in this direction may fail without causing him to despair. For, loving what he has and not fixing his desire solely on what he lacks, his wishes and hopes may fail of what he has happened to aspire to, without his being wholly destitute. He has the essentials. The equilibrium of his happiness is secure because it is defined, and a few mishaps cannot disconcert him.

But it would be of little use for everyone to recognize the justice of the hierarchy of functions established by public opinion, if he did not also consider the distribution of these functions just. The workman is not in harmony with his social position if he is not convinced that he has his deserts. If he feels justified in occupying another, what he has would not satisfy him. So it is not enough for the average level of needs for each social condition to be regulated by public opinion, but another, more precise rule, must fix the way in which these conditions are open to individuals. [*There must be institutionalized rules of access to status.*] There is no society in which such regulation does not exist. It varies with times and places. Once it regarded birth as the almost exclusive principle of social classification; today it recognizes no other inherent inequality than hereditary fortune and merit. But in all these various forms its object is unchanged. It is also only possible, everywhere, as a restriction upon individuals imposed by superior authority, that is, by collective authority. For it can be established only by requiring of one or another group of men, usually of all, sacrifices and concessions in the name of the public interest.

.   .   .

. . . this discipline can be useful only if considered just by the peoples subject to it. When it is maintained only by custom and force, peace and harmony are illusory; the spirit of unrest and discontent are latent; appetites superficially restrained are ready to revolt. [*That is, self-control must be congruent with relational and formal social control.*] This happened in Rome and Greece when the faiths underlying the old organization of the patricians and plebeians were shaken, and in our modern societies when aristocratic prejudices began to lose their old ascendancy. But this state of upheaval is exceptional; it occurs only when society is passing through some abnormal crisis. In normal conditions the collective order is regarded as just by the great majority of persons. [*A stable social reality does not produce massive reality flaws.*] Therefore, when we say that an authority is necessary to impose this order on individuals, we certainly do not mean that violence is the only means of establishing it. Since this regulation is meant to restrain individual passions, it must come from a power which dominates individuals; but this power must also be obeyed through respect, not fear.

It is not true, then, that human activity can be released from all restraint. Nothing in the world can enjoy such a privilege. All existence being a part of the universe is relative to the remainder; its nature and method of manifestation accordingly depend not only on itself but on other beings, who consequently restrain and regulate it. Here there are only differences of degree and form between the mineral realm and the thinking person. Man's characteristic privilege is that the bond he accepts is not physical but moral; that is, social. He is governed not by a material environment brutally imposed on him, but by a conscience superior to his own, the superiority of which he feels. Because the greater, better part of his existence transcends the body, he escapes the body's yoke, but is subject to that of society.

But when society is disturbed by some painful crisis or by beneficent but abrupt transitions, it is momentarily incapable of exercising this influence; thence come the sudden rises in the curve of suicides which we have pointed out above. [*The sudden transitions cause individual expectations to conflict with social reality. The resulting reality flaws will produce many forms of unlegitimated behavior including suicide.*]

☐ ☐ ☐

Durkheim's method of analysis, that is, treating social reality as an object and analyzing its influence on individual behavior, was a giant first step for sociology. After Durkheim, social factors could not be ignored. One of the most impressive elements in Durkheim's analysis was that he chose suicide, a solitary, individual act, and demonstrated that even here the reality of society was important. Starting as he did from social reality, he could not predict that one individual or another would commit suicide, but he could predict the overall suicide rates for a country, and his analysis isolated a number of factors that contributed to the rise or fall of these rates.

Durkheim's importance in sociology is hard to overstate; his methods have influenced much of the sociology that followed. In the study of deviant behavior his theory of "anomie" was the beginning of a theoretical tradition. Following Durkheim's lead, Robert Merton published a paper in 1938 on "Social Structure and Anomie." In this paper, a later version of which is adapted in the following pages, Merton elaborated Durkheim's analysis by introducing the proposition that reality flaws could originate with conflicts between the cultural goals and the institutional means for attaining them. In the language developed here, these would be conflicts between the values of the symbolic universe and the behavior appropriate for legitimate institutions in the institutional order. Merton's analysis is more sophisticated than Durkheim's; he associates the various possible conflicts between the symbolic universe and the institutional order with specific kinds of individual response to the strains that these reality flaws produce.

The idea that reality flaws can be produced in the normal process of legitimating the institutional order is important. It allows us to see that not all of the institutions in the institutional order are equally or completely legitimated by the values of the symbolic universe. Because the symbolic universe *orders* institutions on a scale of more or less value, the patterns of behavior of the lowly valued are not as completely legitimated by the values of the symbolic universe as are the patterns of behavior of those highly valued. As a consequence, the people who live lives of poverty in a rich society have a conflict between their daily experiences and social reality. They are constantly reminded that they should succeed, but they do not have the tools—enough education, "proper" work habits, "proper" dress and manners—to succeed in the way that is legitimated. This is probably not as complete a conflict as following a totally unlegitimated institution would provide, but it is a flaw that is produced within the social construction of reality itself.

While Merton's theory is much more generally applicable, he, like Durkheim, found his best examples of the conflict between social reality and individual experience in the institutions and legitimations of labor.
□ □ □

3

SOCIAL THEORY AND SOCIAL STRUCTURE

ROBERT K. MERTON

TYPES OF INDIVIDUAL ADAPTATION

Turning from these culture patterns, [*the symbolic universe has a value on wealth, but it does not have a similar emphasis on legitimate means for obtaining it through the institutional order*] we now examine types of adaptation by individuals within the culture-bearing society. Though our focus is still the cultural and social genesis of varying rates and types of deviant behavior, our perspective shifts from the plane of patterns of cultural values to the plane of types of adaptation to these values among those occupying different positions in the social structure.

We here consider five types of adaptation, as these are schematically set out in the following table, where (+) signifies "acceptance," (−) signifies "rejection," and (±) signifies "rejection of prevailing values and substitution of new values."

TABLE 1   A TYPOLOGY OF MODES OF INDIVIDUAL ADAPTATION

Modes of Adaptation	Values of the Symbolic Universe	Legitimate Pathways in the Institutional Order
	Culture Goals	Institutionalized Means
I. Conformity	+	+
II. Innovation	+	−
III. Ritualism	−	+
IV. Retreatism	−	−
V. Rebellion*	±	±

* This fifth alternative is on a plane clearly different from that of the others. It represents a transitional response seeking to institutionalize new goals and new procedures to be shared by other members of the society. It thus refers to efforts to change the existing cultural and social structure rather than to accommodate efforts within this structure.

Examination of how the social structure operates to exert pressure upon individuals for one or another of these alternative modes of behavior must be prefaced by the observation that people may shift from one alternative to another as they engage in different spheres of social activities. These categories refer to role behavior in specific types of situations, not to personality. They are types of more or less enduring response, not types of personality organization. To consider these types of adaptation in several spheres of conduct would introduce a complexity unmanageable within the confines of this chapter.

Adapted with permission of the author and the Macmillan Co. from *Social Theory and Social Structure*, by Robert K. Merton. Copyright © 1968 and 1967 by Robert K. Merton.

For this reason, we shall be primarily concerned with economic activity in the broad sense of "the production, exchange, distribution and consumption of goods and services" in our competitive society, where wealth has taken on a highly symbolic cast. [*This includes the institutions and values which have grown around labor.*]

I. CONFORMITY

To the extent that a society is stable, adaptation type I—conformity to both cultural goals and institutionalized means—is the most common and widely diffused. Were this not so, the stability and continuity of the society could not be maintained. The mesh of expectancies constituting every social order is sustained by the modal behavior of its members representing conformity to the established, though perhaps secularly changing, culture patterns. [*That is, people's ordinary behavior is within the legitimating values of the symbolic universe; even though the institutions may change somewhat, the values remain established.*]

It is, in fact, only because behavior is typically oriented toward the basic values of the society that we may speak of a human aggregate as comprising a society. Unless there is a deposit of values shared by interacting individuals, there exist social relations, if the disorderly interactions may be so called, but no society. It is thus that, at mid-century, one may refer to a Society of Nations primarily as a figure of speech or as an imagined objective, but not as a sociological reality.

Since our primary interest centers on the sources of *deviant* behavior, and since we have briefly examined the mechanisms making for conformity as the modal response in American society, little more need be said regarding this type of adaptation, at this point.

II. INNOVATION   [CREATING AND FOLLOWING COUNTER-INSTITUTIONS]

Great cultural emphasis upon the success-goal invites this mode of adaptation through the use of institutionally proscribed but often effective means of attaining at least the simulacrum of success—wealth and power. This response occurs when the individual has assimilated the cultural emphasis upon the goal without equally internalizing the institutional norms governing ways and means for its attainment.

From the standpoint of psychology, great emotional investment in an objective may be expected to produce a readiness to take risks, and this attitude many be adopted by people in all social strata. From the standpoint of sociology, the question arises, which features of our social structure predispose toward this type of adaptation, thus producing greater frequencies of deviant behavior in one social stratum than in another?

On the top economic levels, the pressure toward innovation not infrequently erases the distinction between business-like strivings this side of the mores and sharp practices beyond the mores. As Veblen observed, "It is not easy in any given case—indeed it is at times impossible until the courts have spoken—to say whether it is an instance of praiseworthy salesmanship or a penitentiary offense." The history of the great American fortunes is threaded with strains toward institutionally dubious innovation as is attested by many tributes to the Robber Barons. The reluctant admiration often expressed privately, and not seldom publicly, of these "shrewd, smart and successful" men is a product of a cultural structure in which the sacrosanct goal virtually consecrates the means. [*Actions of individuals and institutions that are at the top of the institutional order are often legitimated by the values of the symbolic universe, with a little stretching, pulling, and theorizing. This legitimation is not so easy for less predominant institutions to obtain, or create.*]

. . .

III. RITUALISM

The ritualistic type of adaptation can be readily identified. It involves the abandoning or scaling down of the lofty cultural goals of great pecuniary success and rapid social mobility to the point where one's aspirations can be satisfied. But though one rejects the cultural obligation to attempt "to get ahead in the world," though one draws in one's horizons, one continues to abide almost compulsively by institutional norms.

It is something of a terminological quibble to ask whether this represents genuinely deviant behavior. Since the adaptation is, in effect, an internal decision and since the overt behavior is institutionally permitted, though not culturally preferred, it is not generally considered to represent a social problem. Intimates of individuals making this adaptation may pass judgment in terms of prevailing cultural emphases and may "feel sorry for them," they may, in the individual case, feel that "old Jonesy is certainly in a rut." Whether this is described as deviant behavior or no, it clearly represents a departure from the cultural model in which men are obliged to strive actively, preferably through institutionalized procedures, to move onward and upward in the social hierarchy.

. . .

IV. RETREATISM [HABITUATIONS WITHOUT LEGITIMATIONS]

Just as Adaptation I (conformity) remains the most frequent, Adaptation IV (the rejection of cultural goals and institutional means) is probably the least common. People who adapt (or maladapt) in this fashion are, strictly speaking, *in* the society but not *of* it. Sociologically, these constitute the true aliens. Not sharing the common frame of values, they can be included as members of the *society* (in distinction from the *population*) only in a fictional sense.

In this category fall some of the adaptive activities of psychotics, autists, pariahs, outcasts, vagrants, vagabonds, tramps, chronic drunkards and drug addicts. They have relinquished culturally prescribed goals and their behavior does not accord with institutional norms. This is not to say that in some cases the source of their mode of adaptation is not the very social structure which they have in effect repudiated nor that their very existence within an area does not constitute a problem for members of the society.

From the standpoint of its sources in the social structure, this mode of adaptation is most likely to occur when *both* the culture goals and the institutional practices have been thoroughly assimilated by the individual and imbued with affect and high value, but accessible institutional avenues are not productive of success. There results a twofold conflict: the interiorized moral obligation for adopting institutional means conflicts with pressures to resort to illicit means (which may attain the goal) and the individual is cut off from means which are both legitimate and effective. The competitive order is maintained but the frustrated and handicapped individual who cannot cope with this order drops out. Defeatism, quietism and resignation are manifested in escape mechanisms which ultimately lead him to "escape" from the requirements of the society. It is thus an expedient which arises from continued failure to near the goal by legitimate measures and from an inability to use the illegitimate route because of internalized prohibitions, *this process occurring while the supreme value of the success-goal has not yet been renounced.* The conflict is resolved by abandoning *both* precipitating elements, the goals and the means. The escape is complete, the conflict is eliminated and the individual is asocialized.

.   .   .

V. REBELLION [THE CREATION OF A NEW SOCIAL REALITY]

This adaptation leads men outside the environing social structure to envisage and seek to bring into being a new, that is to say, a greatly modified social structure. It presupposes alienation from reigning goals and standards. These come to be regarded as purely arbitrary. And the arbitrary is precisely that which can neither exact allegiance nor possess legitimacy, for it might as well be otherwise. In our society, organized movements for rebellion apparently aim to introduce a social structure in which the cultural standards of success would be sharply modified and provision would be made for a closer correspondence between merit, effort and reward. [*That is, the values come from an alternate reality that also legitimates a different ordering of institutions.*]

. . .

When the institutional system is regarded as the barrier to the satisfaction of legitimized goals, the stage is set for rebellion as an adaptive response. To pass into organized political action, allegiance must not only be withdrawn from the prevailing social structure but must be transferred to new groups possessed of a new myth.* The dual function of the myth is to locate the source of large-scale frustrations in the social structure and to portray an alternative structure which would not, presumably, give rise to frustration of the deserving. [*In other words, the new symbolic universe should not have a conflict between social reality and the life experiences of those who are supporting it.*] It is a charter for action. In this context, the functions of the counter-myth of the conservatives—briefly sketched in an earlier section of this chapter—become further clarified: whatever the source of mass frustration, it is not to be found in the basic structure of the society. [*That is, those who benefit from a social reality think that observed flaws are universal, and not a consequence of their own social construction of reality.*] The conservative myth may thus assert that these frustrations are in the nature of things and would occur in *any* social system: "Periodic mass unemployment and business depressions can't be legislated out of existence; it's just like a person who feels good one day and bad the next."† Or, if not the doctrine of inevitability, then the doctrine of gradual and slight adjustment: "A few changes here and there, and we'll have things running as ship-shape as they can possibly be." Or, the doctrine which deflects hostility from the social structure onto the individual who is a "failure" since "every man really gets what's coming to him in this country."

The myths of rebellion and of conservatism both work toward a "monopoly of the imagination" seeking to define the situation in such

* George S. Pettee, *The Process of Revolution* (New York, 1938), 8–24; see particularly his account of "monopoly of the imagination."

† R. S. and H. M. Lynd, *Middletown in Transition* (New York, 1937), 408, for a series of cultural clichés exemplifying the conservative myth.

terms as to move the frustrate toward or away from Adaptation V. It is above all the renegade who, though himself successful, renounces the prevailing values that becomes the target of greatest hostility among those in rebellion. For he not only puts the values in question, as does the out-group, but he signifies that the unity of the group is broken. Yet, as has so often been noted, it is typically members of a rising class rather than the most depressed strata who organize the resentful and the rebellious into a revolutionary group.

□ □ □

Merton's extension of Durkheim's theory further specified the way in which flaws in reality could cause an individual to come loose from the social reality that is supposed to guide and support his activity. By examining the four possible combinations of behavior and values he arrived at four logical types of adaptation. Type "V," rebellion, does not fit into his formal structure. It should be clear from our knowledge of the way in which the institutional order comes into existence, and the way in which the symbolic universe legitimates it, that there will often be discrepancies between behavior and values; therefore, the isolation of these patterns of conflict provides us with an analytical tool for examining nonconforming behavior.

Merton's theory has several limitations. First of all, the theory implicitly assumes cultural isolation. Given the speed of communications and travel of modern Western society, many people can become involved in institutions of behavior that their social reality has neither recognized nor condemned. The early, legal use of LSD 25 is one example. There were essentially no values in the symbolic universe that made it a desirable or undesirable practice until these values were created.

Second, the theory implicitly assumes that the institutional order is relatively complete and stable. Behavior outside of "institutionalized means" is "innovative" and therefore deviant. But new institutions of behavior are constantly arising and the legitimacy or deviance of these new institutions may be a matter of debate until they have won or lost a place in the institutional order. The growing number of people living in communal families is an example.

A third limitation, which is the subject of the next adaptation, is the assumption that a person blocked in legitimate means would be able to adopt illegitimate means without difficulty.

A fourth limitation is that the theory only covers four types of "fit" between institutions and goals: conformity, innovation, ritualism, and retreatism. The fifth type, rebellion, brings into the theory an entirely new dimension, the possibility of there being another complete reality.

These limitations of Merton's theory are typical of the pitfalls facing a theorist attempting to explain behavior through a deductive theory. In constructing such a theory one must always be sure that it is complete, logical, and exhaustive of the range of behavior under study. In order to do this each term must be chosen with care, each relationship must be specified, each individual covered by the theory should fit into only one category, and it should be obvious which category.

Merton recognized that by examining a certain cultural goal and the appropriate institutionalized means for obtaining it, he was making an analytic statement about the behavior of a person only in relation to that particular goal and those particular means. Other goals and other means are also relevant to the individual. Everyone seeks many goals and is involved in many institutions. In order to characterize a *person, all* of these different interests and involvements would have to be taken into consideration and his type of adaptation to each goal and each means would have to be examined. Thus, as Merton stated, these types "refer to role behavior in specific types of situations, not to personality." This is important to remember because it is very easy to think of a person as an "innovator," when, in fact, he is only an innovator in a certain situation.

OPPORTUNITIES FOR ADAPTATION

The theoretical tradition started by Durkheim and elaborated by Merton was further specified by Richard Cloward when he introduced the idea that entrance to *any* institution depended on a number of factors; a person might be incapable of reaching the cultural goal by legitimate *or* illegitimate means.

A person's social location—the pattern of institutions of behavior which he is involved in and has learned about—tends to define his future involvements. The accident of his birth puts him in a certain type of family that is involved in certain things. His routine behavior makes some neighborhoods and parts of the city better known than others. His education in a slum school or a private school teaches him about some institutions and leaves him ignorant of others. Every occupation opens some possibilities and closes others. The friends he makes teach him some things, but don't know about other things. Think about your own experience. Do you know the bus routes around town? Doesn't your answer depend on whether you have to ride the bus? Do you know how to blow a safe? How to open a door with a piece of celluloid? How to hotwire a car? Do you know how to embezzle funds? Do you know how to deal with an unwanted pregnancy? Do you know how to fly an airplane? Do you have a contact where you can cop a kilo of grass? Doesn't your answer to each of these questions depend on your social location? Out of all the possible things there are to do in the world any individual has the opportunity for only a few, and these are usually related to the institutions of behavior the individual already follows. Since most people are involved mostly in legitimate institutions, their knowledge of illegitimate institutions tends to be quite limited. Thus, a person caught in a reality flaw in which there are no legitimate means to obtain a desired end may find that there are no illegitimate means accessible either.

One of the most important advances in Cloward's work is the recognition that illegitimate behavior is institutionalized as well as legitimate behavior. As a consequence he was able to point out that acquiring illegitimate behavior is often as hard as acquiring legitimate behavior.

☐ ☐ ☐

4

ILLEGITIMATE MEANS, ANOMIE, AND DEVIANT BEHAVIOR

RICHARD A. CLOWARD

This paper represents an attempt to consolidate two major sociological traditions of thought about the problem of deviant behavior. The first, exemplified by the work of Émile Durkheim and Robert K. Merton, may be called the anomie tradition. The second, illustrated principally by the studies of Clifford R. Shaw, Henry D. McKay, and Edwin H. Sutherland, may be called the "cultural transmission" and "differential association" tradition. Despite some reciprocal borrowing of ideas, these intellectual traditions developed more or less independently. By seeking to consolidate them, a more adequate theory of deviant behavior may be constructed.

DIFFERENTIALS IN AVAILABILITY OF LEGITIMATE MEANS: THE THEORY OF ANOMIE

The theory of anomie has undergone two major phases of development. Durkheim first used the concept to explain deviant behavior. He focused on the way in which various social conditions lead to "overweening ambition," and how, in turn, unlimited aspirations ultimately produce a breakdown in regulatory norms. Robert K. Merton has systematized and extended the theory, directing attention to patterns of disjunction between culturally prescribed goals and socially organized access to them by *legitimate* means. In this paper, a third phase is outlined. An additional variable is incorporated in the developing scheme of anomie, namely, the concept of *differentials in access to success-goals by illegitimate means.*

.   .   .

Phase III: The Concept of Illegitimate Means

Once processes generating differentials in pressures are identified, there is then the question of how these pressures are resolved, or how men respond to them. In this connection, Merton enumerates five basic

Adapted from Richard A. Cloward, "Illegitimate Means, Anomie, and Deviant Behavior," *American Sociological Review,* Vol. 24, No. 2, April 1959, pp. 164–176. Reprinted by permission of the author and the American Sociological Association, publisher.

categories of behavior or role adaptations which are likely to emerge: conformity, innovation, ritualism, retreatism, and rebellion. These adaptations differ depending on the individual's acceptance or rejection of cultural goals, and depending on his adherence to or violation of institutional norms. Furthermore, Merton sees the distribution of these adaptations principally as the consequence of two variables: the relative extent of pressure, and values, particularly "internalized prohibitions," governing the use of various illegitimate means.

It is a familiar sociological idea that values serve to order the choices of deviant (as well as conforming) adaptations which develop under conditions of stress. Comparative studies of ethnic groups, for example, have shown that some tend to engage in distinctive forms of deviance; thus Jews exhibit low rates of alcoholism and alcoholic psychoses. Various investigators have suggested that the emphasis on rationality, fear of expressing aggression, and other alleged components of the "Jewish" value system constrain modes of deviance which involve "loss of control" over behavior. In contrast, the Irish show a much higher rate of alcoholic deviance because, it has been argued, their cultural emphasis on masculinity encourages the excessive use of alcohol under conditions of strain.

Merton suggests that differing rates of ritualistic and innovating behavior in the middle and lower classes result from differential emphases in socialization. The "rule-oriented" accent in middle-class socialization presumably disposes persons to handle stress by engaging in ritualistic rather than innovating behavior. The lower-class person, contrastingly, having internalized less stringent norms, can violate conventions with less guilt and anxiety. Values, in other words, exercise a canalizing influence, limiting the choice of deviant adaptations for persons variously distributed throughout the social system.

Apart from both socially patterned pressures, which give rise to deviance, and from values, which determine choices of adaptations, a further variable should be taken into account: namely, *differentials in availability of illegitimate means.* For example, the notion that innovating behavior may result from unfulfilled aspirations and imperfect socialization with respect to conventional norms implies that illegitimate means are freely available—as if the individual, having decided that "you can't make it legitimately," then simply turns to illegitimate means which are readily at hand whatever his position in the social structure. However, these means may not be available. As noted above, the anomie theory assumes that conventional means are differentially distributed, that some individuals, because of their social position, enjoy certain advantages which are denied to others. Note, for example, variations in the degree to which members of various classes are fully exposed to and thus acquire the values, education, and skills which facilitate upward mobility. It should not be startling, therefore, to find similar variations in the availability of illegitimate means.

Several sociologists have alluded to such variations without explicitly incorporating this variable in a theory of deviant behavior. Sutherland, for example, writes that "an inclination to steal is not a sufficient explanation of the genesis of the professional thief."* Moreover, "the person must be appreciated by the professional thieves. He must be appraised as having an adequate equipment of wits, front, talking ability, honesty, reliability, nerve and determination." In short, "a person can be a professional thief only if he is recognized and received as such by other professional thieves." But recognition is not freely accorded: "Selection and tutelage are the two necessary elements in the process of acquiring recognition as a professional thief. . . . A person cannot acquire recognition as a professional thief, until he has had tutelage in professional theft, *and tutelage is given only to a few persons selected from the total population.*" [*In other words, the counter-institution selects its new members on rational rather than random principles.*]

Furthermore, the aspirant is judged by high standards of performance, for only "a very small percentage of those who start on this process ever reach the stage of professional theft." The burden of these remarks—dealing with the processes of selection, induction, and assumption of full status in the criminal group—is that motivations or pressures toward deviance do not fully account for deviant behavior. The "self-made" thief—lacking knowledge of the ways of securing immunity from prosecution and similar techniques of defense—"would quickly land in prison." Sutherland is in effect pointing to differentials in access to the role of professional thief. Although the criteria of selection are not altogether clear from his analysis, definite evaluative standards do appear to exist; depending on their content, certain categories of individuals would be placed at a disadvantage and others would be favored.

The availability of illegitimate means, then, is controlled by various criteria in the same manner that has long been ascribed to conventional means. Both systems of opportunity are (1) limited, rather than infinitely available, and (2) differentially available depending on the location of persons in the social structure. [*A consequence of participating in a certain pattern of institutions, or counter-institutions, is that some lines of activity are more likely, more visible, and more suited to one's biography than are others.*]

· · ·

* For this excerpt and those which follow immediately, see Sutherland, *The Professional Thief,* pp. 211–213.

Modes of Adaptation: The Case of Retreatism

By taking into account the conditions of access to legitimate *and* illegitimate means, we can further specify the circumstances under which various modes of deviant behavior arise. This may be illustrated by the case of retreatism.

As defined by Merton, retreatist adaptations include such categories of behavior as alcoholism, drug addiction, and psychotic withdrawal. These adaptations entail "escape" from the frustrations of unfulfilled aspirations by withdrawal from conventional social relationships. The processes leading to retreatism are described by Merton as follows: "[Retreatism] arises from continued failure to near the goal by legitimate measures and from an inability to use the illegitimate route because of internalized prohibitions, *this process occurring while the supreme value of the success-goal has not yet been renounced.* The conflict is resolved by abandoning *both* precipitating elements, the goals and means. The escape is complete, the conflict is eliminated and the individual is asocialized."

In this view, a crucial element encouraging retreatism is internalized constraint concerning the use of illegitimate means. But this element need not be present. Merton apparently assumed that such prohibitions are essential because, in their absence, the logic of his scheme would compel him to predict that innovating behavior would result. But the assumption that the individual uninhibited in the use of illegitimate means becomes an innovator presupposes that successful innovation is only a matter of motivation. Once the concept of differentials in access to illegitimate means is introduced, however, it becomes clear that retreatism is possible even in the absence of internalized prohibitions. For we may now ask how individuals respond when they fail in the use of *both* legitimate and illegitimate means. If illegitimate means are unavailable, if efforts at innovation fail, then retreatist adaptations may still be the consequence, and the "escape" mechanisms chosen by the defeated individual may perhaps be all the more deviant because of his "double failure."

This does not mean that retreatist adaptations cannot arise precisely as Merton suggests: namely, that the conversion from conformity to retreatism takes place in one step, without intervening adaptations. But this is only one route to retreatism. The conversion may at times entail intervening stages and intervening adaptations, particularly of an innovating type. [*Cloward is writing here as if the theory were a process model. The theory specifies kinds of adaptations, but there is no theoretical statement that would explain the processes by which a person would actually reach these adaptations.*] This possibility helps to account for the fact that certain categories of individuals cited as retreatists—for example, hobos—often show extensive histories of arrests and convictions for various illegal acts. It also helps to explain retreatist adaptations among individuals who have not necessarily internalized strong restraints on the use of illegitimate means. In short, retreatist adaptations may arise with considerable frequency among those who are failures in both worlds, conventional and illegitimate alike.

□ □ □

Cloward's theoretical advance was very important for the construction of an integrated theory, but it was also somewhat piecemeal. In introducing the idea of access to illegitimate means he was actually introducing an entirely new variable to Merton's theory, the idea that there could be counter-institutions of behavior. When we take this together with Merton's "rebellion" category, in which he alluded to different "cultural standards of success," we can see that there are actually *four* variables that must be used to describe the various possible kinds of conflict between individual experience and social reality.

The *first* variable is whether or not the individual seeks a value of the symbolic universe. The *second* variable is whether or not the individual behaves in accordance with a legitimated institution. The *third* variable is whether or not the individual behaves in accordance with an illegitimate, or counter-institution. The *fourth* variable is whether or not the individual seeks a value of a completely different social reality. By examining all of these variables at once we can make a much more complete analysis of the kinds of reality flaws which are actually found in the world. Durkheim, Merton, and Cloward all implicitly assumed the universality of the cultural goals, or values of the symbolic universe, within which they were attempting to explain deviant behavior. This assumption, though understandable, is neither necessary nor useful; it constricts the behavior covered by the theory, and leaves some forms of behavior to be explained by residual categories such as Merton's rebellion category.

In Table 1 all four variables are considered at once. Following in Merton's footsteps it must be pointed out that these are specific patterns of adaptation, and not personality types. A problem that was already apparent in Merton's typology—that there are logical types that are either empirically rare or do not correspond to any meaningful pattern of social behavior—becomes rampant with this typology. In fact, this exposes one of the key difficulties of this type of deductive theorizing. We start with a desire to explain some behavior that has been made a social object, such as deviance. We construct variables and cross-classify them, as Merton did, and we may have said something about deviance. But to be logical we have to look at *all* of the cross-classifications, and behold, we find some pattern of behavior that people have never before separated out as an object in the world, such as ritualism. Social reality is constructed on the base of partially independent institutions; it is *abstracted up* from behavior. Theories are constructed *down* from these *abstractions* to behavior. In the process of cross-classifying abstractions we are constantly finding possible kinds of behavior, logical kinds of behavior, that people have never practiced, or if they have they never verbalized them in terms similar to those of our categories, which means they are not socially meaningful categories of behavior. Think of the differences between a city that grew up over a long historical period, and a city laid out on a grid by a city planner working with his theories. Imagine trying to explain how the city that just grew got to be the way it is by putting a grid overlay on an aerial photograph of it. Some of the streets would be explained by the grid, some wouldn't. This is similar to what we are doing when we lay a logical grid (such as the following table) on actual human behavior.

Let us look at these sixteen types of experience-social reality conflict and see if we can find what kind of individual would have each. Three facts are immediately apparent. First, following one institution does not *necessarily* imply rejecting the corresponding counter-institution. A person can work during the day and steal at night. Second, symbolic universes define themselves as total organizations of reality, so believing in two realities will usually result in being thought mentally ill or demonically possessed by those who believe in either reality. Third, the degree to which behavior can be institutionalized varies from category to category. If a person follows neither a legitimate nor an illegitimate institution in some area he can accomplish the ends ordinarily served by institutions only through his own individual and idiosyncratic habits.

1. + + + +   A person who finds himself believing and acting in contradictory social realities. This would be a very uncomfortable position, and I imagine there would not be many people who could do it for long. A factory owner who works for socialism at night might be an example.

2. + + + −   A person who believes in contradictory values, but whose behavior is conventional. A factory owner who believes in socialism but doesn't do anything about it might be an example.

3. + + − +   A person who believes in conventional values but does both legitimate and illegitimate things. The man who works by day and steals by night.

Table 1 Expanded Typology of Individual Adaptation

Symbolic Universe	Legitimate Institution	Alternate Reality	Counter-Institution	Merton's type	Expanded types	Description
+	+	+	+		1.	Person who believes in contradictory values and is in contradictory institutions.
+	+	+	−		2.	Contradictory values, conforming behavior.
+	+	−	+		3.	Believes in symbolic universe, does legitimate and illegitimate things.
+	+	−	−	Conformity	4.	Conformity.
+	−	+	+		5.	Contradictory values, counter-institutions.
+	−	+	−		6.	Contradictory values, no institutions. Behavior at "habit" level.
+	−	−	+	Innovation	7.	Counter-institutional behavior.
+	−	−	−		8.	Residual rule breaker. Behavior at "habit" level.
−	+	+	+		9.	Pluralist evolutionary. Rejects only conventional values.
−	+	+	−		10.	Belief in new values for old institutions.
−	+	−	+		11.	No values, does legitimate and illegitimate things to get by.
−	+	−	−	Ritualism	12.	Ritualism.
−	−	+	+	Rebellion	13.	Revolutionary.
−	−	+	−		14.	Belief in new values, behavior at "habit" level.
−	−	−	+		15.	Asocial institution. Behavior that "just grows" outside of any reality.
−	−	−	−	Retreatism	16.	Believes nothing, does nothing. Cloward's "double failure." Behavior at "habit" level.

4. + + − − A conformist. A person who does not have a reality–experience conflict.

5. + − + + A person who is involved in an alternate reality and a counter-institution but still believes in an old and contradictory value. A socialist revolutionary who believes in free enterprise.

6. + − + − A person who believes in contradictory values but is involved in no institutionalizations of behavior. This sort of person might be socially defined as a catatonic schizophrenic, or possibly a mystic.

7. $+--+$ A person who achieves conventional goals through counter-institutional behavior. This is a very frequent adaptation and we will study many examples.

8. $+---$ A person who believes conventional things but who breaks various rules of behavior because he does not follow institutions of behavior, but only his own habits.

9. $-+++$ A person who does both legitimate and illegitimate things but rejects conventional values. For example, a hippie who would reorganize values but who drinks alcohol as well as smoking marijuana.

10. $-++-$ A person who behaves conventionally but who believes in a different organization of reality.

11. $-+-+$ A person without values who does legitimate and illegitimate things in order to get by. The "rounder" mentioned in Chapter 4 might be an example.

12. $-+--$ The ritualist, who does what he is supposed to but doesn't believe in anything. A person who just goes through the motions required by the institution of behavior.

13. $--++$ The classic revolutionary, one who wishes to sweep away the old institutions and values and substitute new institutions and values. A person living in an alternate reality.

14. $--+-$ A person who believes in the values of an alternate reality, but who does not participate in legitimate or illegitimate institutions, following only his own habits.

15. $---+$ Asocial institutionalization. A person who participates in an institution of behavior that is not explained by legitimate or illegitimate values. Such institutions will probably be defined, eventually, as either legitimate or illegitimate.

16. $----$ A person who does nothing and believes nothing. A person who has withdrawn entirely from some aspect of social reality. The ultimate withdrawal from society may be suicide or "voluntary death."

The adoption of many of these patterns would ordinarily be considered mental illness in our social reality. This is because they are infrequent, or not understandable within the structure of the symbolic universe. Indeed, some people might be tempted to classify every adaptation except conformity as mental illness but this would be a very narrow and culture-bound perspective. Many forms of behavior that might be so classified may be forerunners of future change not yet recognized within the symbolic universe.

There are both positive and negative consequences of constructing such a formal typology in the study of human behavior. On the negative side, it is an essentially static theory. It tells us what "types" of adaptations are, but it does not tell us how people come to have these adaptations. Counter-institutions and alternate realities must come from somewhere; they do not suddenly appear by magic. If we were to pursue the causes of these types of adaptations we would have to introduce more and more variables until we had an incredibly large and unmanageable matrix. The typology also doesn't tell us much about actual patterns of behavior. A person might fall into many different kinds of adaptation in the different spheres of his life, and these might well influence each other in specific combinations of situations. Thus a person might be a ritualist in his marriage, break residual rules with his transvestism, be a conformist in his work, and believe in the flying saucerian's "new-age" values, though it would be fair to assume that he might be somewhat confused. Another limitation of this formal approach is that it does not have the necessary ingredients to tell us whether the type of adaptation will be followed by few or many people. This too would require the introduction of more variables. Finally, some types of adaptation are likely to be much more influential in actually changing reality than are others, and the formal typology cannot tell us which these are because it does not contain a model of change. After pointing out all these limitations it is reasonable that one would wonder why I bothered to expand on this formal theoretical tradition. The answer is that it provides us also with a number of useful benefits.

On the positive side, it gives us a "map" of analytic types. Not all of these types are socially recognized, but some important types might not have been obvious without this logical cross-classification. Its greatest value is that it exhausts the *range* of nonconforming behavior and therefore defines the various kinds of adaptations that people might consider deviant. By doing this it provides us with a formulation of "deviance" that is much broader than those usually employed. Thus we know that in our process model we must consider mental illness as well as criminality, and voluntary death as well as alternate realities. In working out the process model in the following chapters we will see how people reach many of these kinds of adaptations to reality flaws, and some of the ways in which they move from one type of adaptation to another. It should be clear, then, that this was not merely an exercise in formal theory but a necessary complement to the process model.
☐ ☐ ☐

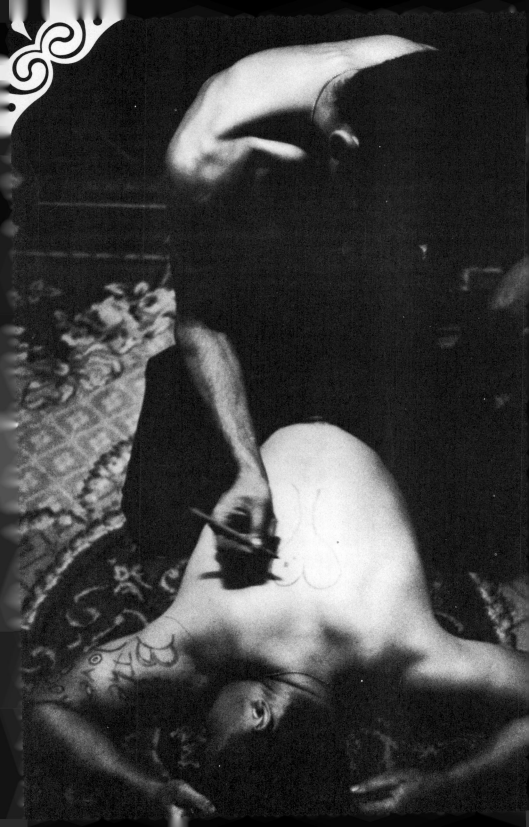

□ □ □
Habits are individual patterns of behavior. Every person has thousands of
habits, from the tunes he whistles
under his breath to the routes he takes
in driving around town; from the way
he holds his cigarette to the kind of
hashish he prefers; from the way he
smiles to the way he reads his newspaper. These habits may be quite individual—always wearing a leather wrist
strap, or quite general—smoking cigarettes. Habits are not themselves institutions of behavior, because they are
individual. Many habits form the *basis*
of institutions, such as offering cigarettes around; ultimately all institutions
of behavior depend on certain habits
and were long ago created from habits,
but habits themselves are performed
by the individual, not by the social
group. In the Expanded Typology of
Individual Adaptation (near the end
of Chapter 2) there are four forms of
adaptation that have no institutions of
behavior, or counter-institutions. These
adaptations, numbers 6, 8, 14, and 16,
all involve different patterns of belief in
realities, but no institutionalization of

BAD HABITS

behavior. Any behavior produced by a person faced with these reality flaws, therefore, is his own. It is habit, not institution.

Where did you get your habits? You may have made a very small number of them up for yourself, but probably far fewer than you think. Most of your habits you were taught by your parents, or in school, or learned from watching other people. Some probably came from television advertising or from the other mass media. As you go repeatedly through the routines of everyday life you will find that you pick up habits from others who are doing the same things that you are and make them your own. An act starts to become a habit about the second time it is done, because you think back to the way you did it before. Some of your habits are trivial and easily changed, others are rooted in personal style and require agonizing effort to modify, and this is true whether they are "good" approved-of habits, or "bad" disapproved-of habits.

In the process of learning habits you are receiving forms of behavior from a great cultural pool of available habits. Your social location will affect the ones you learn, so that it is often possible to tell a great deal about your social origins by seeing only a few of your habits. The cultural pool largely contains those that are indirectly legitimated by the symbolic universe. It also contains some habits that are generally disapproved of. The pattern of habits you get, and the habits you create, may thus be wholly conventional or somewhat unconventional. But even if you have conventional habits there is always the possibility that you didn't learn something crucial, or that you learned it "wrong." The fact that these possibilities exist means that your experience, some part of your everyday life and thus your subjective reality, may well conflict with some part of social reality. This conflict may be important to you and others, or unimportant and unnoticed. The conflict with social reality means that some of your habits may be characterized by others as "bad" ones—not conventionally appropriate to your age, time, geographical location, sex, race, or social class.

Let us look at some habits we learn and see how failing to learn them, or learning them wrong, or creating ones that don't fit, can cause trouble.

Take, for example, your face. According to a personal communication from Ray Birdwhistell, people with essentially similar bone structure wear their faces in quite different ways, ways assimilated while growing up in their social group. People who grew up in the same social group tend to wear their faces alike. In England, for example, the upper class tends to wear its eyebrows high, and the working class lowers them below the bony ridge. This is a matter of muscle tension that is learned in the process of socialization. With practice you can carry your eyebrows at a different level; it will greatly change your appearance. Canadian girls develop "laugh lines" at the corners of their mouths quite early because they smile from side to side rather than turning up the corners of their mouths. The lips are carried tightly closed by some groups, slackly open by others. In the southern United States one often sees people whose top lip is shoved entirely above their teeth. In certain areas in the northeastern states people habitually carry their lower lips over their upper teeth, giving them prominent chins. In some areas of the mountain states people carry their eyelids in a perpetual squint, in other areas, wide open. These are habits, learned and transmitted within the family and the peer group. Most people within broad social regions have facial habits not vastly different from others in the same region, except as it has been affected by migration. Thus, for regions and for the culture as a whole, there is an acceptable range of facial habits, ways of carrying the face which are considered "normal." Suppose that for some reason, perhaps having parents whose faces were always contorted, a person does not learn the proper facial habits for his group. Or, suppose that he creates an individual way of habitually wearing his face, a way possibly based on some peculiarity of muscle structure. His face is then not "normal," and from not "normal" to "abnormal" is an inference often made by people who assume that the way a person carries his face reflects his mental state. Lombroso felt that certain types of faces indicated hereditary criminality. The person with a distorted face constantly encounters an experience—social reality conflict in the responses and behavior reflected back to him by others. The implicit assumptions of these responses may, in fact, *create* an abnormal mental state. Experiment for the next day. Every time you go out in public or see anyone, and as much as you can at home, carry your eyebrows down low, your mouth half open, and your jaw twisted a little to the left. Watch the responses of the people you meet. The day after, resume your normal face and again watch the responses of people you meet. By doing this you will see the way a "bad" habit affects your subjective experience of social reality.

The way you groom your body is also a collection of habits. There are widespread patterns of expectations about grooming from which one abstains at his own risk. In addition to the patterns transmitted by parents, including the "cleanliness is next to godliness" legitimation, there is a whole host of expectations that have been created from profit motives by legitimate institutions. Watch the television advertisements, read the women's trade magazines, such as *Mademoiselle* and *Vogue,* and observe the grooming habits that various manufacturers are attempting to create. Starting apparently from the assumption that the human body in its natural state is something like a sewer, products are advertised and habits are created to turn people into plastic flowers.

Dandruff, earwax, mucus, bad breath, underarm odor, sweat, vaginal odor, and smelly feet can all be eliminated with the proper habits and products. The advertisements say, and sometimes it is true, that neglecting these habits will leave you offensive and unlovable.

The way in which a person communicates, verbally and nonverbally, is also a collection of habits. When you say something you generally also support your statement with your body and facial gestures. If your words are angry, you frown, you don't smile. If you are offering serious advice you don't giggle. If you are responding to a question with a "yes" answer you wag your head up and down. Try saying yes while nodding "no"; it's hard. These nonverbal gestures that support or disconfirm verbal communications vary from culture to culture, and, like language, they are learned. A person who habitually uses the wrong nonverbal habits in communicating is likely to be considered "insane" because his pattern of communication is incongruent with that sanctioned by social reality.

The ways in which you make sexual overtures and presentations to others is a collection of habits. Some people are extraordinarily successful with members of the opposite sex because they have the habits, learned habits, that are socially defined as appealing. Other people, without these habits, lead lonely lives of doubt and self-torture, reaching out, only to be rebuffed, until they reach out no longer. Their experience conflicts with socially defined reality. They may possibly, from frustration, reach out to others in the ways—sadism, masochism, rape—which become their habitual way of dealing with sexual drives. Others turn in on themselves and remain virginal even though married, spend their lives "peeping" at others, or become transvestites. More "bad" habits. Obviously, and as we shall see, there are more forces than a simple lack of sexually appealing habits that cause these patterns, but this lack is very often a precipitating event.

There are a large number of habits for dealing with money. Collectively, your bill-paying habits, your tendency to spend more than you have, and your repayment of loans are summarized in your credit rating. The consequences of "bad habits" in this area are known to us all.

The ways in which you react to other people's verbal cues are also habits. Apart from appropriateness, your reaction time is a key habitualization. In some parts of the country, people snap back answers, in others they think for a second or two and then drawl a response. If your reaction time falls outside of that defined as appropriate in our social reality, people will again begin making inferences about your mental condition. Try another experiment. In a conversation, when you are spoken to, remain silent and expressionless to a count of five. Do this for a few minutes, and if the speaker has not asked whether you are stoned, drunk, or sleepy (probably because he is tactful) ask him what he thought. A person who habitually answers slowly runs a very high risk of ᴗᴧciting police suspicion, because the police assume that the innocent answer directly, and the guilty pause, fumble, and contrive what they are going to say. The same habit of answering slowly will give a person a huge number of indicated "complexes" on a psychiatrist's word association test, because it too makes the social reality assumption that a delay in answering indicates that a psychological "problem" has been made salient by the question.

A person whose habits make him a "night person" is in constant, though not usually serious, conflict with social reality. First there is the reality embedded in the language. At four in the morning does he refer to the soon coming day as today or tomorrow? His pattern of participation in all the institutions of labor, sex, and territory will be quite odd; he may never be awake when offices and stores are open. The telephone will frequently disturb his sleep. His presence on the streets in the early hours of the morning make him a candidate for police suspicion. And, finally, the other night people he meets may be involved in counter-institutions such as prostitution, after-hours clubs, and pool hustling.

A final collection of habits, which by no means exhausts the list, revolves around a person's level of participation in society. Some people are constantly out in the world, constantly interacting socially. Recluses, the infirm, and the elderly, have often disengaged themselves from active participation in society. For a variety of causes a person may never develop the habits he "should" have for social participation, or he may have given them up. Social reality, and consequently the individual, has a definition of the amount of participation necessary for a person to function in society. If this level of activity is maintained the give and take of interaction with others keeps the individual a part of society. If, for whatever reason, a person gives up on society and withdraws into himself, these social supports are removed, and he sometimes will actually die from lack of will to live.

The reaction of other people to "bad habits" varies greatly with the habit concerned. Predictably, since they are by definition individual, many people with bad habits are considered mentally ill. Bad habits are sometimes profoundly disturbing to the habitually conforming people who encounter them. "Everybody" knows about theft and prostitution. These are counter-institutions often written up in newspapers, and the pattern of behavior is known to most of the public. No matter how outraged one might be at having something stolen, the knowledge is always there that the thief violated a law, and that it is not an uncommon happening. We carry around in our heads the knowledge that such things happen, might happen to us, and we buy insurance against it. Because stealing is a recognized counter-institution we are both physically and psychologically prepared for it. It may make us furious, but it doesn't astonish us. Bad habits, on the other hand, are extremely diverse; we never know what we will encounter. Furthermore, they often violate social reality in ways totally unanticipated. They violate assumptions that we never even knew we had. This is distressing. Imagine having it revealed after five years of marriage that your husband was a transvestite, and had been dressing up in women's clothing in secret, during and long before your marriage. Most people don't even *think* about the assumption that men will not dress in women's clothes. When the assumption is violated they may not be furious, but they will be astonished, and if the person is their husband, they will probably be distressed. Similarly, bad habits of communication may not violate a formal rule of which we are aware, but a person who frowns and glowers while saying "I love you" makes us very uncomfortable.

BAD HABITS—RESIDUAL RULE BREAKING

Bad habits may be picked up in many ways, adaptive responses to impossible situations in the family, adaptive responses to ongoing life problems, or simple failures to transmit information in socialization.

In the following adaptation Jay Haley analyzes schizophrenia as an adaptive response to reality flaws within a family. Since the family is the primary socializing agent, many habits are passed on there. The social reality that exists within a family may have flaws of its own, or it may simply reflect and transmit flaws that are part of the larger reality. In the generation of schizophrenia, Haley argues that a characteristic of schizophrenic families is to set rules but to deny that rules are being made. What this means is that family institutions of behavior exist, and behavior is governed by them, but no one in the family wishes to seem to take responsibility for their enforcement. As Haley clearly points out, this puts the child in the impossible position of not being able to respond to communications in a congruent way, for to do so would either violate a rule or imply that someone was making a rule. As a result he learns schizophrenic communications patterns, bad habits of communications. Learning these means that his behavior is often inappropriate for the larger social reality that has defined "proper" communications. There are undoubtedly other social situations that contain many of these elements, but the family is important because it is the child's whole world, especially when outside alliances are prohibited.

Since schizophrenia is an individual adaptation to a reality flaw existing within a particular family, it is a bad habit that isolates the individual from others—not only from people who communicate "properly," but also from other "schizophrenics." Analytically all the people with a certain sort of bad communications habit may be grouped together and called "schizophrenic," but each of them has a somewhat different bad habit of communications, and thus they cannot form the reciprocal typifications with others that would be necessary to establish a counter-institution of communications. This bad habit, and probably most that do not become institutionalized, has an element that *prevents* institutionalization. We shall see other examples as we examine other bad habits. Notice also that no attempt is made to legitimate, partially because legitimations would require communications congruence, but also because schizophrenics do not consciously get together to pass on their habit to others.

☐ ☐ ☐

5
THE FAMILY OF THE SCHIZOPHRENIC
A Model System
JAY HALEY

THE "DIFFERENT" BEHAVIOR OF THE SCHIZOPHRENIC

The inability of the schizophrenic to relate to people and his general withdrawal behavior seems understandable if he was raised in a learning situation where whatever he did was disqualified and if he was not allowed to relate to other people where he could learn to behave differently. Should he be reared in a situation where each attempt he made to gain a response from someone was met with an indication that he should behave in some other way, it would be possible for an individual to learn to avoid trying to relate to people by indicating that whatever he does is not done in relationship to anyone. He would then appear "autistic." However, the peculiar distortions of communication by the schizophrenic are not sufficiently explained by this description of his learning situation. If schizophrenic behavior is adaptive to a particular type of family, it is necessary to suggest the adaptive function involved when a person behaves in a clearly psychotic way.

The recovering schizophrenic patient, and perhaps the pre-psychotic schizophrenic, will qualify what he says in a way similar to that used by his parents. His behavior could be said to be "normal" for that family. However, during a psychotic episode the schizophrenic behaves in a rather unique manner. To suggest how such behavior might serve a function in the family, it is necessary both to describe schizophrenia in terms of behavior and to suggest the conditions under which such behavior might occur. To describe schizophrenic behavior, it is necessary to translate into behavioral terms such diagnostic concepts as delusions, hallucinations, concretistic thinking, and so on.

What appears unique about schizophrenic behavior is the incongruence of all levels of communication. [*This means that the recipient has the choice of which level to respond to, or just confusion regarding the meanings. When such ambiguity exists it is extremely difficult to coordinate behavior because reciprocal typifications cannot be made.*]

The patient's parents may say something and disqualify it, but they will affirm that disqualification. The schizophrenic will say something, deny saying it, but qualify his denial in an incongruent way. Schizo-

Adapted from: Jay Haley, "The Family of the Schizophrenic: A Model System," *Journal of Nervous and Mental Disease,* 129: 357–374, Copyright © 1959 The Williams & Wilkins Company. Reprinted by permission of the author and The Williams & Wilkins Co., publisher.

phrenic behavior described in this way . . . [is] . . . summarized briefly here.

Not only can a person manifest an incongruence between levels of total message, but also between elements of his messages. A message from one person to another can be formalized into the following statement: *I (source) am communicating (message) to you (receiver) in this context.*

By his body movement, vocal inflections, and verbal statements a person must affirm or disqualify each of the elements of this message. The symptoms of a schizophrenic can be summarized in terms of this schema.

1. *Source* A person may indicate that *he* isn't really the source of a message by indicating that he is only transmitting the idea of someone else. Therefore he says something but qualifies it with a denial that *he* is saying it. The schizophrenic may also qualify the source of the message in this way, but he will qualify his qualifications in an incongruent way. For example, a male schizophrenic patient reported that his name was Margaret Stalin. Thus he indicated that *he* wasn't really speaking, but by making his denial clearly fantastic he disqualified his denial that he was speaking. Similarly a patient may say that "voices" are making the statement.

. . .

2. *Message* A person may indicate in various ways that his words or action are not really a message. He may indicate, for example, that what he did was accidental if he blurts something out or if he steps on someone's foot. The schizophrenic may indicate that his statement isn't a message but merely a group of words, or he may speak in a random, or word salad, way, thus indicating that he isn't really communicating. Yet at the same time he manages to indicate some pertinent points in his word salad, thus disqualifying his denial that his message is a message.

. . .

3. *Receiver* A person may deny this element in a message in various ways, for example by indicating he isn't really talking to the particular person he is addressing, but rather to that person's status. The schizophrenic patient is likely to indicate that the doctor he is talking to isn't really a doctor, but, say, an FBI agent. Thereby he not only denies talking to the physician, but by labeling the receiver in a clearly fantastic way he disqualifies his denial. Paranoid delusionary statements of this sort become "obvious" by their self-negating quality.

4. *Context* A person may disqualify his statement by indicating that it applies to some other context than the one in which it is made. *Context* is defined broadly here as the situation in which people are communicating, including both the physical situation and the stated premises about what sort of situation it is. For example, a woman may be aggressively sexual in a public place where the context disqualifies her overtures. The typical statement that the schizophrenic is "withdrawn from reality" seems to be based to a great extent on the ways he qualifies what he says by mislabeling the context. He may say his hospital conversation is taking place in a palace, or in prison, and thereby disqualify his statements. Since his labels are clearly impossible, his disqualification is disqualified.

These multiple incongruent levels of communication differentiate the schizophrenic from his parents and from other people. If a person says something and then negates his statement we judge him by his other levels of message. When these too are incongruent so that he says something, indicates he didn't, then affirms one or the other, and then disqualifies his affirmation; there is a tendency to call such a person insane.

From the point of view offered here, schizophrenia is an intermittent type of behavior. The patient may be behaving in a schizophrenic way at one moment and in a way that is "normal" for this type of family at another moment. The important question is this: Under what circumstances does he behave in a psychotic way, defined here as qualifying incongruently all his levels of message?

. . .

It can be argued that psychotic behavior is a sequence of messages which infringe a set of prohibitions but which are qualified as not infringing them. The only way an individual can achieve this is by qualifying incongruently all levels of his communication.

The need to behave in a psychotic way would seem to occur when the patient infringes a family prohibition and thereby activates himself and his parents to behave in such a way that he either returns within the previous system of rules or indicates somehow that he is not infringing them. Should he successfully infringe the system of family rules and thereby set new rules, his parents may become "disturbed." [*This indicates that the family behavioral institution is being challenged, and relational social control is brought into play to reestablish the old institutions of behavior.*] This seems to occur rather often when the patient living at home "improves" with therapy. When improving in therapy he is not only infringing the family prohibitions against outside alliances but he may blame the mother in a reasonable way and affirm his statements or those of others. Such behavior on his part would shatter the family system unless the parents are also undergoing therapy. The omnipotent feelings of the schizophrenic patient may have some basis, since his family system is so rigid that he can create considerable repercussions by behaving differently.

A patient is faced with infringing family prohibitions when (1) two family prohibitions conflict with each other and he must respond to both, (2) when forces outside the family, or maturational forces within himself, require him to infringe them, or (3) when prohibitions special to him conflict with prohibitions applying to all family members. If he must infringe such prohibitions and at the same time not infringe them, he can only do so through psychotic behavior. [*This is the source of the reality flaw, and the individual's path of response.*]

Conflicting sets of prohibitions may occur when the individual is involved with both mother and therapist, involved with a therapist and administrator in a hospital setting, or when some shift within his own family brings prohibitions into conflict. This latter would seem the most likely bind the patient would find himself in when living at home, and an incident is offered here to describe psychotic behavior serving a function in the family.

A twenty-one-year-old schizophrenic daughter arrived home from the hospital for a trial visit and her parents promptly separated. The mother asked the girl to go with her, and when she arrived at their destination, the grandmother's home, the patient telephoned her father. Her mother asked her why she turned against her by calling the father, and the daughter said she called him to say goodbye and because she had looked at him with an "odd" look when they left. A typical symptom of this patient when overtly psychotic is her perception of "odd" looks, and the problem is how such a message is adaptive to the family pattern of interaction.

The incident could be described in this way. The mother separated from father but qualified her leaving incongruently by saying it was only temporary and telling him where she was going. The father objected to the mother's leaving, but made no attempt to restrain her or to persuade her to stay. The daughter had to respond to this situation in accord with the prohibitions set by this family system: she had to disqualify whatever she did, she had to disqualify what her mother and father did, she could not ally with either mother or father and acknowledge it, and she could not blame the mother in such a way that the mother would accept the blame.

The girl could not merely do nothing because this would mean remaining with father. However, by going with the mother she in effect formed an alliance and so infringed one of the prohibitions in the family system. The girl solved the problem by going with mother but telephoning her father, thus disqualifying her alliance with mother. However, her mother objected to the call, and the daughter said she only called him to say goodbye, thus disqualifying her alliance with father. Yet to leave it this way would mean allying with mother. She qualified her statement further by saying she called father because she gave him an "odd look" when she left him. By having an odd look, she could succeed in not siding with either parent or blaming mother. She also manifested schizophrenic behavior by qualifying incongruently all levels of message and thereby adapting to incongruent family prohibitions. Previously the girl could withdraw to her room to avoid the alliance problem, but when mother stopped staying home while saying she was going to leave, and left while saying she was not really leaving, the girl was threatened by a possible alliance whether she went with her mother or stayed at home. Her incongruent, schizophrenic behavior would seem necessary to remain within the prohibitions of the family at those times. If one is required to behave in a certain way and simultaneously required not to, he can only solve the problem by indicating that *he* is not behaving at all, or not with this particular person in this situation. [*This is an example of a reality flaw, and the way in which an individual can escape from its consequences.*] The girl might also have solved the problem by disqualifying her identity, indicating the context was really a secret plot, indicating that what she did was what voices told her to do, or speaking in a random or word salad way. In other words, she could both meet the prohibitions in the family and infringe them only by disqualifying the source of her messages, the nature of them, the recipient, or the context, and so behave in a psychotic fashion.

It is important to emphasize that schizophrenic behavior in the family is adaptive to an intricate and complicated family organization which is presented here in crude simplicity. The network of family prohibitions confronts the individual members with almost insoluble problems. This particular incident was later discussed with the parents of this girl, and the mother said her daughter could have solved the problem easily. She could have stayed with father and told him he was wrong in the quarrel which provoked the separation. This would seem to be the mother's usual way of dealing with this kind of situation—she stays with father while telling him he is wrong. However, the mother leaves herself out of this solution by ignoring the fact that she asked her daughter to go with her. This request was even more complicated—the mother asked the daughter to go with her during a period when the mother was saying the daughter must return to the hospital because she could not tolerate associating with her. When the parents reunited later that week, the girl was returned to the hospital because mother said she could not stand daughter in the room watching her, and she could not stand daughter out of the room thinking about her.

. . .

The family of the schizophrenic would seem to be not only establishing and following a system of rules, as other families do, but also following a prohibition on any acknowledgement that a family member is setting rules. Each refuses to concede that he is circumscribing the behavior of others, and each refuses to concede that any other family member is governing him. [*This feeling of the illegitimacy of the family institutions probably comes from the feeling that reciprocal typifications have been breached in the past, and that the other is therefore not to be relied upon to behave "typically."*]

Since communication inevitably occurs if people live together, and since whatever one communicates inevitably governs the behavior of others, the family members must each constantly disqualify the communications of one another. Should one affirm what he does or what another does, he risks conceding that he is governed by the other with all the consequences that follow being disappointed again by an untrustworthy person. Schizophrenic behavior can be seen as both a product and a parody of this kind of family system. By labeling everything he communicates as not communicated by him to this person in this place, the schizophrenic indicates that he is not governing anyone's behavior because he is not in a relationship with anyone. This would seem to be a necessary style of behavior at times in this type of family system, and it may become habitual behavior. [*This is the way the individual develops this bad habit.*] Yet even psychotic behavior does not free the individual from being governed or from governing others. The person who insists that he does not need anyone at all and is completely independent of them requires people to put him in a hospital and to force feed him. To live at all one must be involved with other people and so deal with the universal problem of who is going to circumscribe whose behavior. The more a person tries to avoid being governed or governing others, the more helpless he becomes and so governs others by forcing them to take care of him.

. . .

Although psychotic behavior may serve a function in a family system, a risk is also involved. The patient may need to be separated from the family by hospitalization and so break up the system, or he may enter therapy and change and so leave the system. Typically, the parents seem to welcome hospitalization only if the patient is still accessible to them, and they welcome therapy for the patient up to the point when he begins to change and infringe the rules of the family system while acknowledging that he is doing so. [*In other words, getting rid of the "bad habit," and communicating as required in the larger social reality, violates the pattern of behavior called for by family institutions. This threat to the status quo is then attacked by becoming hostile toward continued therapy. The family "fits in" with the bad habit.*]

□ □ □

While bad habits such as schizophrenia are usually created within the family, there may well be many other "causes" for all of the diverse behavior lumped together in the huge category with the name "schizophrenia." Haley's article is only about the schizophrenia that results in the pattern of communications he mentioned. Biochemical factors, working through as yet unexplored pathways, may also produce a person whose behavior has the same name.

Bad habits may also be produced by more general reality flaws. Obviously the reality flaw doesn't strike like lightning from the symbolic universe into the head of the individual. He learns about it. The family is still an important agent of transmission, which acts as an institution that educates the child in the ways of the culture. If a child's education at the hands of his family gives him the values of the culture, and it turns out that these cultural values are hard for him to attain, he will experience the conflict. This proper transmission of reality flaws may happen with almost any value of the symbolic universe: it seems to occur very frequently with the values and institutions involving sexual behavior. Perhaps this indicates that the social construction of sexual reality in North America is very narrow and hard to live up to; a great many people encounter various reality flaws and respond to them in different ways. In the following adaptation I have attempted to outline the steps a man follows in learning the "bad" habit of dressing in women's clothes.

□ □ □

6

THE TRANSVESTIC CAREER PATH

H. TAYLOR BUCKNER

The transvestite provides an interesting example of a socially induced "pathology" because he seems to have internalized part of a social relationship, and acts toward himself in a way that a normal person acts toward a sociosexually significant other.

From a survey of transvestites conduced by *Transvestia* magazine, which I coded, punched, and analyzed for my master's thesis, the following generalizations arise: The ordinary transvestite is a man. He is probably married (about two-thirds are); if he is married he probably has children (about two-thirds do). Almost all of these transvestites said they were *exclusively* heterosexual, more so, in fact, than the average for the entire male population. His transvestic behavior generally consists of privately dressing in the clothes of a woman, at home, in secret, though some go out in public dressed, and many more would like to, and some few live exclusively as women. (Possibly these are more transsexual than transvestic.) He generally does not run into trouble with the law. His cross-dressing causes difficulties for very few people besides himself and his wife. He tends to be fairly passive and secretive about his behavior. Conventional psychoanalytic opinion assigns the etiology of transvestism to latent homosexuality, an incorrect view in the opinion of many students of transvestism. With the exception of electric-shock aversion therapy which creates a mental block to dressing in women's clothes, there are no recorded cases in the medical or psychiatric literature of successful treatment of transvestism which caused the transvestic urge to disappear.

Transvestism is often confused with homosexuality because there is a certain amount of cross-dressing in the homosexual community usually for entertainment, drag shows, Halloween, or for prostitution, and people make the assumption that anyone who cross-dresses does so for primarily sexual reasons, as is the case with homosexuals. The two phenomena, transvestism and homosexuality, are analytically distinct, as noted by Kinsey and by Brown, though phenomenologically there is an overlap. Transvestism is often found in connection with other sexual patterns such as dominance, bondage, sadomasochism, and various forms of fetishism [*which may reflect a complex reality flaw*]. Pure transvestism is quite distinct from all these other patterns, however. It consists only of the desire to wear feminine clothing, and sexual gratification from the wearing of this clothing, by conventional definition. I will argue further, in this paper, that in addition to sexual gratification there is also a social gratification coming from the internalization and the internal enacting of a role relationship that is customarily enacted between two people.

Transsexualism is a related phenomenon in which participants are often cross-dressed. Transsexualism, however, consists of a complete psychic desire to become a woman, where often the male personality can be said to hardly exist at all. Transsexualists desire and obtain sex change operations, Christine Jorgensen being the most famous case.

There are several steps that must be taken before a person can become a transvestite. These may be preceded by biological conditions which lead to passivity, low libido, and the lack of a strong aggressive drive or, more likely, a socially conditioned passivity and lack of social drive. There is no evidence for a biologic etiology. In either event, the biological or socially induced passivity is not a necessary precursor to transvestism but is often found in conjunction with it. [*These factors may cause a subjective—social reality conflict that affects the quality of life experiences a person has.*]

In most cases, although not absolutely in all, the *first* step in becoming a transvestite comes from the association of some item of feminine wearing apparel with sexual gratification between the ages of about five and fourteen, usually through masturbation. [*The establishment of a habit.*] It may also come from what Stone calls *fantastic socialization* in which the child acts out roles that he can seldom be expected to adopt in later life, such as that of the parent of the opposite sex. It may also come from the child noticing a trait in himself more like his mother or sister than his father, putting on his mother's or sister's clothes and reinforcing this self-definition of femininity. Additionally, it may come from valuing the mother as she provides nearly all the rewards. This feminization may be encouraged by his mother. Whatever the source, this gratification usually comes before any heterosexual, or for that matter, homosexual, demands are made on the potential transvestite. Masturbation using some article of feminine apparel, or orgasm without direct masturbation again using some article of feminine apparel is not terribly unusual. It may be found in people who later grow up to establish normal heterosexual patterns of orientation. Its significance for the transvestite, however, is that it provides him with an already established pattern of sexual gratification which he can fall back upon when he encounters difficulties with his interpersonal sexual relations.

The *second* step in becoming a transvestite comes when he perceives some heterosexual difficulties, which may come from his low libidinal energy, if this is the case, or a lack of the stable sense of self-esteem needed to switch into heterosexual functioning. It should be noted at this point that the transvestite has, in fact, the same sociosexual goal as many young men, a goal of marriage and compatible family relationships. [*He has been "properly" socialized to symbolic universe values.*] For a variety of reasons, however, this goal may be for him unobtainable. His fear of inadequacy in the male role may come from one of several factors.

First, he may be a perfectionist, demanding a great deal of himself both in his personal and social relationships. [*Such perfectionism almost guarantees a subjective–social reality conflict.*] He may have obtained this perfectionism from his parents. No actual performance of which he is capable will measure up to the high ideals he holds. Second, he may have an exaggerated notion of the requirements of masculinity, from magazines or from the "male culture" in which he participates. Third, he may be engaged in actual roles which are too dominant for comfortable performance, given his weak constitution or commitment. At puberty these roles may be in the areas of sports, delinquency, or other activities demanded by his peers. Further on in life he may be engaged in roles that are difficult for him because they require a fair amount of masculinity, such as being a military or police officer (which may have been adopted because of his ambivalence). Fourth, he may have an exaggerated fear of the consequences of failure in male or heterosexual performance which keeps him from attempting these performances. Fifth, at puberty or later, he may fail at almost any activity, sports, occupation, or marriage that he feels (or may have been told) is an indication of inadequate masculinity. Sixth, he may have a low level of sexual interest or performance compared with true, or false, knowledge of what is normal or average. It does not matter in this case whether he is actually a low performer as long as he feels that he is.

Up to this point the preconditions of transvestism are similar to preconditions commonly associated with homosexuality in that they both alienate him from "normal" masculinity. With the possible exception of the ideal goal of marriage and heterosexual functioning of the transvestite, he has the same fears of inadequacy in the male role that are often associated with homosexuality. This may be one reason psychiatrists often confuse the two forms of behavior.

The *third* step in becoming a transvestite is the blockage of the homosexual outlet. There are two reasons why homosexuality may be an unacceptable response for someone with these preconditions. First, and most likely, he may have a socialized aversion to homosexuality as do many people within our culture. If this is the case he fits into Merton's category of the retreatist because innovation is blocked by socialization. [*In the expanded typology this would mean that the counter-institution of homosexuality is blocked by "self-control."*] The second reason that a transvestite may not turn to homosexuality is that he may lack an opportunity structure to learn the behavior appropriate to homosexuality. If this is the case, he is then a "double failure" in being unable to make it legitimately or illegitimately. [*The fact that he is committed to the values of the symbolic universe would mean that he is a residual rule breaker, type 8 in the expanded typology.*] This lack of availability of a homosexual outlet may come because he, though psychologically willing, either does not run into any homosexuals at the appropriate time, or may not be attractive enough for homosexual solicitation at this point in his life.

Being blocked in both homosexual and heterosexual directions, the transvestite goes back to the earlier pattern of gratification (which he may never have given up); using articles of feminine wearing apparel for masturbation [*his habit*]. Were he to stay with this pattern he would be considered a fetishist. However, since he is strongly committed to the goals of a normal heterosexual relationship including, but not limited to, a sexual relationship with the opposite sex, and also including a social relationship with the opposite sex, he begins to build in fantasy a more complete masturbation image than that provided by a single item of feminine wearing apparel. He does this through a process of identification and fantastic socialization in which he takes the gratificatory object into himself.

The *fourth* step in becoming a transvestite involves this elaboration of masturbation fantasies into the development of a feminine self. This may come from a variety of causes. At a biological level he may have, as a result of this regression to autoeroticism, a large amount of libidinal energy left over which he uses to complicate his gratificatory object, making it more complete. A second possible reason for the expansion of his activities is that he may come to learn that he is a "transvestite" and he may then discover what is appropriate for transvestites. Taking a feminine name is often associated with discovering that this is something transvestites do. [*Learning that others have the same habit, that it has other aspects, and that it is common enough to have the legitimacy of a name.*] Labeling theory is not generally relevant, however, because most transvestites apparently do not discover that there are other people who have this same pattern of behavior until well after they have elaborated it themselves. In those cases where labeling is relevant, the role of transvestic literature, which may be found on a newsstand, of meeting other transvestites socially, or of seeing a psychiatrist who informs him of transvestic patterns, may be an impetus for further elaboration of his transvestic activity. He will learn that he is not alone in the world. The legitimations proposed in *Transvestia* or

Turnabout magazines may make him feel more comfortable with his habit. The third reason that he may expand fetishistic interest into a more complete transvestism would be that he would have a Gestalt of his fantasy, a drive towards a completion or perfection—the same completion or perfection which he has been led to expect from social relationships, but which social relationships rarely provide. The seven transvestites interviewed for this paper have a very high orientation toward symbolic rather than biological gratification. Their masculine roles were largely involved with symbolic manipulation such as being a medical doctor engaged in research, a professor, a Ph.D. in research, an architect with a couple of professional degrees, a university student, an executive, and a minister. If Kinsey's data on the occurrence of masturbation fantasies among college men can be taken as relevant, and is an indication of the fantasizing power of the well educated, or if education can be taken as an indication of having higher symbolizing and thus fantasizing power, it may very well be that transvestites live a somewhat more complicated fantasy life than most people. Kinsey also suggests that transvestism depends on an individual's capability to be psychologically conditioned. The occupational levels of the 262 transvestites questioned by *Transvestia* magazine, which I analyzed in my master's thesis, were very high, and if the same association holds we might also suspect that their fantasizing powers are also very high. Some of the medical studies of transvestites have been carried out on prison populations, or on populations that have gone to psychiatrists for help. In these cases there is often a low level of education and yet complete transvestism, so the actual level of fantasizing power available must remain an open question. Most practicing transvestites appear to have enough, however. There are presumably a great many transvestites who are neither so disordered that they wind up in prison or with a psychiatrist, nor yet so comfortable in their transvestism that they are willing to join a transvestic organization, or respond to a letter to the editor in the newspaper. About these silent transvestites almost nothing is known.

It may well be that there are a number of people who get to this stage and elaborate their fantasies somewhat, but for one reason or another take up successful, satisfying heterosexual functioning, and give up transvestism before reaching the next stage, which makes transvestism a permanent part of their personality.

The *fifth* step in becoming a transvestite involves the fixing of the gratification pattern in the identity of the transvestite [*making the habit an integral part of his self-concept, giving reinforcing self-control that will protect his habit*]. Until this fifth step occurs we may not be able to speak of a person as having been a true transvestite, and he may have branched off into some other form of sexual patterning, or of normal functioning. The combination of the initial autoerotic retreat with the elaboration of the fetishistic interest into complete cross-dressing, and possibly the development of a feminine personality within the individual (78 percent feel themselves a different personality when dressed) as an alter to his male personality *provides a synthetic dyad within the individual,* which gives the individual the libidinal rewards of both narcissistic and dyadic regression. The narcissistic regression and the later elaboration into a synthetic dyad neatly slip in between the socialized controls of narcissism which make the individual dependent on others, and thus necessarily required to cathect these others, and the social controls appropriate to actual dyadic regression (such as the intrusion of society into all socially recognized forms of two-person relationships). A person who is autoerotic has no dependency needs on others for sexual gratification, and a person who has internalized his dyadic relationship with this autoerotic object has no fear of society stepping in between him and it (except possibly a psychiatrist). The transvestite thus internalizes and carries out within himself both the erotic and social aspects of what is ordinarily a social process which would link him to the social order.

Once the transvestite discovers that he has, in a sense, both male and female within himself, he can play out many of the culturally prescribed heterosexual patterns internally. He can, for example, give himself gifts of shoes and nightgowns. He can also provide many of the male-female complementarity expectations all by himself. After a hard day at the office he doesn't need to come home to a nurturant wife; he *becomes* a nurturant wife. Furthermore he has an undemanding gratification scheme. His feminine self is highly predictable, something like playing chess with himself, which fits in well with his fear of failure or his passivity. "Connie (a transvestite's femme name) isn't bossy, she isn't demanding, she doesn't fly into jealous rages. She exists only for me, and she knows I'm her lord and master. I like it that way," a transvestite writes about himself.* He can also cathect the female role by dressing and acting it out, and have sexuality by masturbating at the same time, without the inconvenience of dealing with a real woman who might provide him with a failure or with some disconfirmation of his masculine identity. These points may be illustrated with this quotation from a transvestite talking about his two personalities:

> Keeping her lovely is a full-time job. *It literally takes several hours a day—but when I look into the mirror and see what we have made, it's worth every bit of the hard work and discomfort involved.* When we walk down the street, our feet flying in their tight patent leather

* Larry Maddock, *Sex Life of a Transvestite,* Hollywood: K. D. S. Publishing Co., 1964, p. 120.

pumps because Connie's skirts are so narrow at the knees, our heels clicking in precise feminine rhythm. It's a great feeling to know that heads are turning. The women look, and they envy Connie her wardrobe; the men look and they envy whoever she belongs to, and maybe they think she doesn't belong to anybody, but they're wrong. *She belongs to me. I'm the man whose hands run over her body, the man who touches her where only a lover is allowed to touch.*

Yes, quite frankly, I get great pleasure from her body. It's more than just sex, I know that now. *It takes the place of sex.* It's a tingle that I feel through me. It's how I suppose sex feels to a woman.*

Because of the passive and undemanding nature of the female role which most transvestites adopt—a form of the female role, by the way, which may be becoming far less common in our complex society—the transvestite can escape from real life problems by going home and dressing. He combines social retreat, sexual gratification, in the context of the fantasy reenactment of the old cultural norm of the aggressive providing male complemented by the passive nurturant affectionate wife. He enacts this role toward himself, obtaining the same tension release that the most vital marital relationship could provide. Transvestites don't give up on transvestism for some of the same reasons that happily married couples don't get divorced.

After this pattern of gratification [*the "bad" habit*] becomes fixed in the transvestite's identity, usually by the age of 18 to 20, though in some instances later in life (when it possibly arose from a discomforting contact with an early marriage, or some other setback in the masculine role) it is entirely possible, in fact likely, that the transvestite will go on to get married in reality. He still has, remember, the ideal of the successfully functioning male heterosexual adult, and he assumes that transvestism is only a sexual release, which will become unnecessary when he is getting regular sex in marriage. By making this assumption he overlooks the social aspects of the gratification. For example, the fact that he is used to getting a libidinal cathexis from directly enacting a counterrole to his beleaguered male self.

The transvestite will often find that his actual marriage is not as satisfying for tension release as his internal marriage. The transvestite assumes marriage will be better, and often it is for a time, and while this is the case transvestic activities stay buried. As the real life relationship loses some of its power to gratify, either because of interpersonal problems or boredom, the transvestite's internal wife steps in to once again provide direct, uncomplicated, gratification. He finds again, as he did earlier, that it is more gratifying than social relationships,

id., pp. 120–121. Emphasis added.

because it directly, and without the problems of an other, gives release from the tensions of his everyday life through his own passivity and sexuality. Compared with this *direct* release the indirect process of getting release through taking the role of an other, a wife, seems very circuitous to him, and transvestic behavior becomes firmly fixed as part of his behavior pattern. In some cases a transvestite will get divorced from his real wife rather than give up his internal wife.

Many transvestites keep their transvestism secret from their wives throughout their marriage. In other cases, however, they introduce their wives to their femme selves (or are discovered) with variable results. Some very few wives are reasonably enthusiastic and cooperative (they may have problems themselves). In other instances the wife goes along because she is dependent upon her husband and doesn't want to strike out alone in the world simply over this. In other instances she puts her foot down and tells him to stop it, with or without consulting a psychiatrist. However, just as when a wife puts her foot down and tells her husband to stop seeing a mistress, the results can be disastrous, not terribly effective, or alienating. The transvestite can see his internal wife anytime he is alone. In extreme cases the transvestite attempts to induce his wife into accepting his femme self and acting with "her"; for example, by going out in public, going on shopping trips as girls, or by making love while the transvestite is wearing feminine clothes. The mere fact that the transvestite resumed his transvestic activities indicates that the marriage relationship is not a terribly vital one for him. It may also be that it is not terribly vital for his wife, and therefore they may continue without getting a divorce, in a utilitarian marital relationship. The relationship, however, has many of the aspects of the eternal triangle, and many of the same resolutions that are common for triangular relationships can be expected in the transvestite's marriage.

DISCUSSION

We have seen how the habit of masturbation with articles of feminine clothing is sometimes reestablished (or it may never have stopped) when there is a perceived difficulty in establishing successful masculine and heterosexual identity, combined with a blockage of the possibility of achieving a homosexual identity. When this pattern is taken up and the individual elaborates it into an entire feminine identity, he comes to find it gratifying in both sexual and social ways. When it becomes fixed in his identity he begins to relate toward himself, in some particulars, as if he were his own wife, and he receives many of the social and sexual rewards of the marital relationship by doing this. He thus mimics his goal of a heterosexual relationship without the threatening presence of a person of the opposite sex. His internal relationship may then be so strong that he will keep it up even after having established a real heterosexual relationship, and it will continue as his pattern of gratification, and his pattern of social relationship, for the rest of his life.

Culture provides certain patterns to which most people are easily socialized. Culture provides goals that individuals accept, but culture does not always provide for every individual the means to reach these goals. Certain common blockages produce certain conventional forms of deviant behavior. The transvestite is blocked from achieving either the cultural goal, which he shares, of a normal heterosexual masculine functioning, or the common variant, homosexuality. His response to this double blockage is to create a miniature society within himself in which he can achieve a cultural goal but without following the cultural pattern of achieving it through interpersonal relationships. [*He substitutes subjective reality for unattainable social reality goals.*]

Instead of the libidinal diffusion into object relationships which is socially expected and encouraged, which forms the bonds of society, the transvestite has discovered a gap in the culture's coercive patterns of involvement—a gap that has no particular social controls to prevent its use. He thus diffuses his libido within himself, but in a culturally prescribed direction, thus affirming his belief in the importance of the cultural object and affirming his inability to obtain it.

Some cultures, notably American Indian, provide a role for the transvestite (who may also have been a homosexual or a transsexual —the evidence is not clear) that puts his personal adaptation to societal use. They bring his cathexes back into the service of the social group, by giving him the opportunity for service in spite of his personal peculiarity. We have no such position in our culture. It is possible that this adaptation is characteristic of societies that have extremely strong cultural masculinity demands, such as being a warrior, which creates for many men the conditions conducive to transvestism. With many transvestites in a society a pattern of societal adaptation may arise wherein transvestites are given a job within the culture because they occur too frequently to be shrugged off. In our modern Western society relatively weak masculinity demands are made, and they are getting weaker all the time. There are more and more occupations that, objectively at least, can be performed by people of either sex. This means that there is a relatively small number of people who subjectively perceive the society as demanding so much masculinity from them that they can't make it, and, thus, there are probably relatively few transvestites. Since there are relatively few transvestites, and since most people do not routinely encounter them, the occasional transvestite arouses interest, mostly as an oddity, but not as a threat to the social fabric. In the last five years I have kept a careful but unsystematic watch on news items and publications dealing with transvestites and I have not seen a single horror story, and I have not talked with anyone who was particularly upset with transvestism except transvestites and, of course, their wives. Thus the problem of transvestism has not reached the level of public discussion which would be necessary to establish the position of "transvestite" as a respectable role-in-itself, so the transvestite must remain somewhat out of the institutional order of society. It is not, however, a major social problem, though it may be a problem for the transvestite.

When a transvestite seeks "therapy" it is pointless to tell him that transvestism comes from latent homosexuality, or that it is a sexual deviation. A possible therapeutic approach for the transvestite, based upon this theory, would be to explore with him the social functions of his transvestism. If he can come to objectivate the social gratifications it supplies, which he may not have thought of, and the sexual gratifications, which he is well aware of, he may be able to find other means for providing similar gratifications, and his internal wife may become less necessary. Given a supportive sociosexual milieu he may find transvestism less compelling, though it is probably a mistake to think that a simple, habitual, direct means of sociosexual gratification will be completely replaced without a considerable alteration in life style.

☐ ☐ ☐

With transvestism as with schizophrenia there are elements of the habit that make institutionalization unlikely. First, the transvestite adopts his behavior in retreat from others. Second, there is no necessity for having a partner or other person with whom reciprocal typifications could be made. Third, the transvestite can not really talk about his behavior openly without some negative response. As a consequence, the organizations of transvestites that do exist are not institutionalizations of transvestism, but places where mutual emotional support and defense may be found. Transvestism itself remains a "bad habit."

The third way in which a person may pick up a bad habit is through a simple failure to learn what the "good" habit is. This failure to learn may come from many causes: inability to learn the right way to do something, lack of knowledge on the part of the transmitter, or a discrepancy between the values of the symbolic universe and the behavior required in an institution. Again, in matters involving institutions of sexuality, the existence of values which make talk about sex unthinkable to some, and the reliance on informal transmission of "how to do it" knowledge about sex, means that many people will have large gaps in their knowledge that they will have to fill in on their own. Suppose that reading was only taught at home by parents, some of whom were ashamed of it, but that everyone was expected to read successfully. Some parents don't know how to read, others don't know how to teach. Many children, then, would be expected to read but would not have the knowledge. This is the situation with knowledge about sex. Very few people have a broad knowledge of sexual behavior, and a great number have important gaps in their sexual knowledge. If sexual experience were wide and free, people could be expected to learn from each other, but since the values in North America ideally require that a person have only one partner for life, and many people follow the corresponding institution of behavior, it is entirely possible that two people ignorant about the same details will become married to each other. They may, by experimenting, create the sexual habits necessary for reproduction, if not for enjoyment. On the other hand, they may not. Two people brought up in homes where sexual instruction was taboo may feel so ashamed that they never even experiment, or they try for a while and give up. At a somewhat less severe level of ignorance there are many couples who have figured out "how to do it" but do it badly. In the following adaptation, John Blazer studied the reasons why a thousand women had never had sexual intercourse with their husbands. Their lack of knowledge has kept them habitually virginal, in an institution defined in social reality as being sexual.

□ □ □

7
MARRIED VIRGINS
A Study of Unconsummated Marriages
JOHN A. BLAZER

One thousand American females of the Caucasian race were used as the sample. The sample was chosen from replies received from newspaper advertisements, personal appeals to men's and women's clubs, notices on college bulletin boards, clients appealing to a state psychological agency for assistance, leads from marriage counselors, and leads from gynecologists.

Ages in the sample ranged from 17 to 47 with a mean of 29 years:

1. Length of marriage (and period of nonconsummation) ranged from one to 21 years with a mean of eight years.
2. Length of marriage for 98 per cent had been more than three years.
3. Marriage took place between the ages of 20–29 for 76 per cent of the current sample.

Each subject in the present study was subjected to an examination by a gynecologist. In some cases (432), little or no physical evidence (hymen) substantiated the subject's claim to virginity. In such instances, the gynecologist was asked to render a medical opinion as to the virginity of the subject. In cases of doubt or suspicion, the subject was removed from the sample.

The gynecologist also rendered a medical opinion regarding the physical capability of the subject to experience intercourse. Vaginismus was diagnosed in 476 cases, but the entire sample was considered physically capable of experiencing intercourse.

Each subject remaining in the sample was interviewed by the author and asked a standard question: "Why are you still a virgin?" The subjects were prompted to speak until all details were revealed. All interviews were recorded on tape, and three licensed psychologists reviewed the tapes and agreed on the reasons as categorized. When the psychologists disagreed on categorization of a subject, the subject was removed from the sample.

To verify the gynecologist's opinion and to verify the wives' reasons for virginity, the husbands were interviewed separately. In almost all cases, the husbands supported the wives' statements. ["*Reasons*" *are the verbal legitimations for the bad habit of virginity in marriage.*]

Adapted from John A. Blazer, *Journal of Marriage and the Family,* Vol. 26, No. 2, May 1964, pp. 213–214. Reprinted with permission of the author and the National Council on Family Relations.

RESULTS

All the "reasons" for abstinence were subsumed under 15 general categories, which are listed below in descending order of prevalence in the sample.

1.   *Fear of pain in the initial intercourse* was expressed by 203 (20.3%) of the sample. Mutual masturbation to orgasm was practiced by 108 of these couples. The remaining 95 couples admitted to total abstinence.
2.   The sex act was considered to be *nasty or wicked* and a disgust for sexuality was expressed by 178 (17.8%) of the sample. All of these couples denied mutual masturbation, but 63 husbands practiced self-stimulation.
3.   *Impotent husbands* were blamed by 117 (11.7%) of the wives. Mutual masturbation was engaged in by 38 couples, and self-stimulation was practiced by 49 wives.
4.   *Fear of pregnancy or childbirth* was expressed by 102 (10.2%) of the wives. The husbands agreed, and in 12 cases, the husbands admitted to being more afraid than their wives. Mutual masturbation was practiced by 42 of these couples.
5.   *Small size of the vagina* was reported to prohibit intercourse by 82 (8.2%) of the subjects. On examination, neither partner was considered to be beyond the range of normality in size. Mutual masturbation was practiced by 38 of these couples.
6.   *Ignorance regarding the exact location of their organs* and, to avoid embarrassment and mistakes, avoidance of intercourse was reported by 52 (5.2%) of the wives. All of these couples denied mutual masturbation, but 18 husbands admitted self-stimulation.
7.   *Preference for a female partner* was stated by 52 (5.2%) as the excuse for denying their husbands. These couples denied mutual masturbation, but 12 husbands admitted self-stimulation.
8.   *Extreme dislike for the penis* was expressed by 46 (4.6%). The couples denied mutual masturbation, but 29 husbands admitted self-stimulation.
9.   *Intense dislike for intercourse without pregnancy* was expressed by 39 (3.9%). The couples agreed that pregnancy was completely undesirable up to the time of the study and expressed no intense dislike for intercourse *per se*. Twelve couples admitted mutual masturbation.
10. *Dislike of contraceptives* was indicated by 33 (3.3%). The couples agreed that intercourse could not be accomplished without contra-

ceptives in their case because of fear of pregnancy. Twelve of these couples admitted mutual masturbation.

11. *Belief that submission implies inferiority* was expressed by 31 (3.1%). These couples denied mutual masturbation, but 12 husbands and three wives admitted self-stimulation.

12. *General dislike of men* was expressed by 30 (3%). The subjects stated other reasons for their marriage ("the thing to do," "fear of being an 'old maid,'" "security," "dislike living alone," etc.). These couples denied mutual masturbation, but 11 husbands and two wives admitted self-stimulation.

13. *Desire to "mother" their husbands only* was indicated by 14 (1.4%), and such behavior did not include sexual intercourse. The couples denied mutual masturbation. Six husbands and two wives admitted self-stimulation.

14. *Fear of damaging the husband's penis* was expressed by 12 (1.2%). The couples denied mutual masturbation. Three husbands and two wives admitted self-stimulation.

15. *Fear of semen* was mentioned by nine (.9%) subjects. Three couples admitted mutual masturbation without discharge for the husband. Three husbands and two wives admitted self-stimulation.

DISCUSSION

Due to the manner of selecting the sample, no estimates of the prevalence of virginity in marriage within the general population can be made. However, the relative importance (as perceived by the wife) of 15 factors in the etiology of married virginity has been revealed. Moreover, the results of this study suggest that married women are ignorant of sexual matters. None of the factors reported in this study (with the possible exception of number 7 and, perhaps, 3) would destroy or distort the sexual relationship of the woman and her husband *if the woman had scientific knowledge of sex at her disposal.* Hence, each category is a facet of the underlying, disruptive cause—ignorance.

It is obvious that more general knowledge of sex imparted at an earlier age, especially to females, might prevent later behavior of the type categorized here. Similarly, where such a sexual relationship has already appeared, the wife can be given scientific instruction about sex.

□ □ □

Besides schizophrenia, transvestism, and married virginity, there are legions of bad habits that break one rule or another. Many times when we find a person unpleasant to be with, it is because of some habits he has that annoy us. The annoyance may be that our habits conflict at an individual level, or it may be that his habits do not fit in with those common to our group. Very often we are at a loss to understand exactly why some person is annoying; he just makes us feel creepy or uncomfortable. In most instances we get rid of the problem by relational social control; we avoid people who make us feel strange. By doing this we never confront the actual conflict of habits and remain self-satisfied in our own patterns. When a person's habits don't mesh with our group, conventional habits or not, he may find himself faced with an emergent group definition of himself as undesirable. For example, in a communal family that I have had a chance to observe, when people visit they are fairly quickly typed as fitting in or not. People who fit in have habits such as helping clean up after dinner and are sensitive to minor interaction cues. If they don't fit in they are gradually and subtly isolated until they go away. If the visitor's habits make the family positively upset the reaction will be even quicker and more direct—they will be told to leave. In one such instance a sexually available girl attempted to seduce all of the men in the family in rapid succession without much regard for the existing coordinations. Her sexual habits conflicted with the typifications within the family, causing great upset that was only resolved when she left the scene. Similar conflicts occur in all social settings; the number of rules of behavior that we all follow is immense. They arise from the coordinations and institutions of behavior in which we are involved. Every rule can be broken in countless ways, many of which are only discovered when they happen. Thus we all have, in some situations and at some times, habits that may be defined as bad by others. Whether anything worse than being avoided happens to us depends largely on the circumstances of the situation, and the nature of our habit. Thus a schizophrenic or a transvestite may well find himself encountering formal social control in the person of a psychiatrist, while a person who doesn't help with the dishes will normally encounter only relational social control.

BAD HABITS—REALITY CONFLICTS

While the residual rule breaker follows the values of the symbolic universe but violates the rules of institutions, the person with a reality conflict either believes in two realities at once, and violates the rules of institutions, or he believes in an unconventional reality, and violates the rules of institutions. Such behavior is probably always considered a sign of mental illness because the person neither believes nor does what he "should" do. Such a person may escape the mental hospital if he can work out a round of daily adaptations that do not bring him to the attention of the authorities. He may be considered "strange" but harmless, and a great many people—policemen, waitresses, hotel clerks, and newsboys—may take care of him as he wanders around his customary haunts. The origins of these adaptations are quite various —they are probably casualties of many different kinds of reality flaws.

BAD HABITS—RETREATISM

The final kind of bad habit that a person might have is total withdrawal from social life. This is a person who has given up on the outside world entirely; he has withdrawn from social reality and has not adopted an alternate reality, withdrawn from legitimate institutions and has not fol- lowed counter-institutions. Retreatism is the most desperate response to reality flaws—total withdrawal. It takes many forms. Sometimes the catatonic patient is a retreatist. The total heroin addict who lives from shot to shot is a retreatist. The total recluse is a retreatist. The anomic suicide is a retreatist. A person who stops wanting to live and just dies is a retreatist. The retreatist adaptation is halfway between life and death. A person totally withdrawn from others has small chance of a long life; he has no reason to live except that which he himself creates. His individual action is without reference to society or to others. Some- times a person retreats from society over a period of time as he finds himself successively less able to cope with it. Heroin addicts and alco- holics often follow this pattern. Other times the withdrawal is sudden, his reality structure and self-esteem are confronted by events and col- lapse, and he kills himself or dies.

The social habit upon which all other social structures depend is participation. A refusal to participate is the ultimate negation of society, and, from the point of view of social reality, the ultimate bad habit.

In the following adaptation Stewart Wolf writes about the final retreat. In certain circumstances the heart may be permanently "turned off" by the brain, resulting in voluntary death. Medical research into such deaths, which apparently have no organic cause, has increasingly come to be focused on the social factors that affected the individual. Appar- ently complete withdrawal from society, or complete expulsion from society as is the case in voodoo deaths, creates a situation of such overwhelming mental anomie or rootlessness that the brain "gives up" and signals the heart, through the vagus nerve, that it is time to die. No

more striking demonstration of man's dependence on socially constructed reality is possible. Dr. Wolf first explored the medical dimensions of such voluntary death, and then turned to an examination of the
psychosocial factors involved.

□ □ □

8
THE END OF THE ROPE
The Role of the Brain in Cardiac Death
STEWART WOLF

PSYCHOSOCIAL FACTORS

Since it appears that both cardiac arrest and ventricular fibrillation, potentially fatal as they are, can be induced via neural mechanisms that may be actuated through the highest integrative levels of the brain, it becomes interesting to explore those symbolic stimuli that may be relevant to these processes.

Dassberg, Assael and Dreyfuss have reported that myocardial infarction is disproportionately high among patients hospitalized for mental depression. [*Myocardial infarction is a sudden breakdown of part of the heart muscle tissue. Sometimes it is not fatal, other times it continues until the heart stops.*]

Our own group has observed that those who have suffered or died from myocardial infarction have been alienated to some degree from their culture or social setting. Bruhn and Adsett reported preliminary analyses of psychosocial data obtained at intervals over a five-year period on 24 patients with coronary disease who have since died. Two of them died as a result of suicide and the others as a result of recurrent myocardial infarction. In each instance the patients achieved higher depression scores on the Minnesota Multiphasic Personality Inventory over this time period than did their healthy matched controls. More of the patients than of the controls had experienced long-term frustration in their jobs and at home. They were unable to find meaningful satisfaction in leisure and social activities, and made either no attempts, or only slight attempts, to modify their way of life following myocardial infarction. [*The individual was not receiving the benefits of the institutions of behavior in which he was involved in the areas of labor, leisure, and family or territory as represented by the home, and he had apparently given up on attempts to change the situation.*] These characteristics appeared to exert an additive effect with the passage of time. The observations are in keeping with those of Paffenbarger *et al.*, who found that social and psychological exhaustion correlated significantly with subsequent death from coronary heart disease. [*The effects of the frustration with social reality build up over time.*]

In exploring psychosocial factors as they relate to sudden cardiac death, it is appropriate to consider the findings in Roseto, Pennsylvania,

Adapted from Stewart Wolf, "The End of the Rope: The Role of the Brain in Cardiac Death," *The Canadian Medical Association Journal,* Vol. 97, October 21, 1967, 1022–1025 by permission of the author and the publisher.

an Italian-American community where not only is the incidence of myocardial infarction in the first five decades of life remarkably low, but so also is the death rate following myocardial infarction in the older age groups. Roseto is a place where the populace is generally obese, where the diet is at least as rich in saturated fats as the average American diet, and yet where the death rate from myocardial infarction is less than one-half that of neighbouring communities, or of the United States at large. The most striking peculiarity of Roseto is its social structure. Unlike most American communities, it is cohesive and mutually supportive, with strong family and community ties. Because of the concern of the inhabitants for their neighbours there is no poverty and little crime in Roseto. Data gathered before death among the small number of Rosetans who have succumbed to myocardial infarction indicate that they were, to a large extent, alienated or excluded from the mainstream of their culture. [*In a tightly knit and mutually supportive social reality, exclusion from the reality or alienation from it is likely to be much more important than in a less structured reality where other alternatives are also present.*] Thus it would appear that some of the elements of voodoo death may be operative in our society today. The extent to which such factors may be responsible for our relatively high mortality from myocardial infarction is yet to be determined, but the available evidence certainly warrants more careful study of the possible relevance of psychosocial factors to myocardial infarction and sudden death.

DEATH AS ADAPTATION

Irrespective of the potential importance of emotionally significant stimuli, it does appear from the data that sudden cardiac death can be the result of an adaptive maneuver, representing the operation of a regulatory process rather than the breakdown of a mechanism. J. B. S. Haldane once wrote, "The growth of scientific medicine has been based on the study of the manner in which the human body expresses itself in response to change in the environment." In recent years evidence has accumulated that some diseases constitute simply exaggerated or inappropriate adaptations. Thus, disability and death may result from fundamentally protective reaction patterns gone awry. The adaptive significance of a mechanism that results in cardiac death must indicate that death at times is the ultimate solution to a pressing problem or difficulty. [*Possibly it is the only form of retreat left to an individual who has been withdrawing from social relations for some time.*] Thus, when intolerable suffering is imminent from an incurable disease or circumstances, death may serve as a blessed release.

☐ ☐ ☐

The experience–social reality conflict completely overwhelms the re-treatist. The definitions of situations that he accepts keep him from making any adaptation other than withdrawal, asocialization, and, possibly, death.

SOCIETAL REACTIONS TO BAD HABITS

Bad habits are individual behavior that require no social cooperation, and often inhibit social cooperation; the individual is isolated, working against society. Generally he has no very convincing reason or legitima-tion for his behavior so he is weaponless in his conflict with social reality. Whenever his bad habit causes social upset, he is potentially at the mercy of the people he has disgruntled. But most bad habits do not cause much social reaction, either because they are irrelevant to what is happening at the time or because the people affected do noth-ing about it. For example, a few weeks ago a young man came into my house. Since he had followed a friend of mine in I assumed that he had been invited, which turned out later not to be the case. After being silent for awhile he began saying "I love my lord Jesus," over and over again. He stared at the ceiling fixedly and with rising fervor and volume repeated again and again that he loved Jesus. After this had been going on for about a half an hour I asked my friend what was up. Upon finding that our visitor had just wandered in I gave a little thought to what to do about him. I didn't know whether he was on a drug-induced trip or was just more wrapped up in religion than is customary. Since I was not sure whether he had used drugs, or which drugs, I decided against offering him a tranquilizer. He didn't seem particularly dangerous, though of course the potential is always there; it was just annoying that he was sitting there making conversation impossible. I didn't even consider calling the police because, whatever his problem, a stay in jail or a psychiatric observation ward probably would be of little help and possibly could cause him great harm. Finally, I suggested that I loved Jesus too, but he was really sort of upsetting things, and I thought it better if he would leave. After some further dialogue in which he questioned my love for Jesus, he did so. Suggesting that he leave was a societal reaction on the part of myself and my friends to a person who had a bad habit. We exercised the social control of relations to exclude him from our group, but we did not bring the formal social control of the police or the psychiatric ward into the situation. His behavior, as far as we were concerned, was quite inconsequential. From his point of view, if he were on a drug trip, his behavior was a momentary aberrance resulting from the drug. He could easily deny to himself that this was a real part of his personality. If it were a psychotic break it could still be momentary and dismissable within terms of his subjective reality. Even if such behavior were a routine for him our reaction would not complicate his life much.

Most people react to strangers with bad habits in similar ways, leaving the person with the bad habit to work it out on his own. When our friend or relative has a bad habit, one that disturbs the coordinations or institutions of behavior in which we are mutually involved, we may try to change his habit, we may dismiss it as his eccentricity, or, if it disturbs us enough, we may call in the police or the psychiatrists. Sometimes the police discover people with bad habits on their own, and if the habit appears to break a law (as being a transvestite sometimes does), or if it does break a law (as being a heroin addict often does), or if it appears to be sufficiently threatening or disturbing to qualify as an emergency psychiatric detention case, they may take action on their own. They may not, however. Many, many people who are very strange are ignored by the police when they contact them, just as we might ignore them.

If a formal social control agent attempts to control the behavior of a person with a bad habit, various outcomes are possible. The person may get rid of his bad habit, it may be unaffected, or it may be reinforced. One thing that will certainly happen, however, is that it will be much harder for the individual to deny to himself that he did something. By taking official notice of a bad habit it becomes a social object, a thing, a piece of behavior with a written record. Since the individual is alone against this enforcement of social reality, and since he probably does not have much of a legitimation for his habit, at least not enough to have avoided formal social control at the outset, he may be compelled to think of this behavior as typical of himself, to make it a part of his self-image. The police or the psychiatrist will probably ask him how often he did this thing, thereby causing him to think of the previous times he had done the act, or something he now thinks of as similar, and he thus retrospectively constructs an image of himself as a person with this "bad habit." Once he has done this it becomes much more difficult for the bad habit to simply disappear in the normal course of changing situations; it has become a social object with a record, and a part of him. This may ultimately cause the habit to become an important part of his life.

If the habit is a response to a continuing reality flaw and it has been well embedded in the person's personality, formal control is unlikely to change it. Remember that there have been no cures for transvestism. If the bad habit is sporadic, formal control is probably more likely to reinforce it than to cure it; very few people are "cured" in mental hospitals or prisons. Suppose that I had called the police when the young man enamoured of Jesus dropped in. At the least the police would have come, talked with him, taken him away and let him go. We would have been thought of as anti-Christ and he would have been disturbed by having been detained. Suppose it were drugs and he was carrying others. He might face an incredibly long prison sentence, but would certainly go through arrest and processing, resulting in a life-long criminal record. If it were drugs, or a psychotic break, and he was taken in for psychiatric observation, he would probably be classified either as having latent schizophrenia with delusions triggered by drugs, or as having schizophrenia and delusions. In either event, when he was released, he would carry around in his mind the idea that he was mentally ill, an idea given to him with all the authority of a medical doctor, and possibly a hearing before a judge. These thoroughly legiti-mated experts in social reality have a great amount of prestige and he could not easily dismiss their judgment that he was ill. This mental image, coupled with the fact that his parents would probably be told about his bizarre behavior, would mean that both he and some of the people around him would be constantly looking for further signs of his "insanity." Any minor recurrence of his bad habit would then be inter-preted as further evidence of illness, and he might be encouraged to "face up to his problem" so that he can get rid of it. As this happens he would find himself in a position of being rewarded for saying he is sick, and punished for saying it was just a momentary freakout. This process might even lead to his acting out his bad habit more frequently, since everyone around him now agrees that this is the way he "really" is. The net result of bringing formal social control agents in might well be that a pattern of behavior that had a good chance of working itself out naturally will have been treated with such seriousness that it becomes a permanent bad habit.

Each step in the formal social control process thus has this possi-bility of "feeding back" and reinforcing the behavior it is supposed to control, a process known technically as "deviation amplifying feed-back." It often works in social response to bad habits, and, similar deviation amplifying feedback processes sometimes make counter-institutions of behavior stronger and more deviant.

Thomas Scheff's theory of mental illness has been formalized by Walter Buckley in the following adaptation. "Mental illness" is a cate-gory that exists in social reality to be applied to bad habits that are not understandable within the reality. It is a label given to many kinds of behavior produced in response to many different experience–social reality conflicts. It is also a convenient way of disposing of people whose behavior disturbs us by giving them a "not to be taken seriously" in reality status. We protect ourselves from discovering the reality flaws around us by not taking people who have experienced them seriously, which allows us to continue thinking that our socially constructed reality is total, logical, and explains everything, and that our institutions are perfect. A person comes to be defined as mentally ill in a process through which reality is protected from the chaos that would occur if its flaws were widely recognized. If this disturbs you, if you believe that mental illness is really a thing that "science" is going to get rid of if only they have enough money for research, let's examine the situation that existed in a theological symbolic universe. Then, bad habits were attributed to demonic possession and exorcised with bell, book, and candle. If this failed the sinner was perhaps given the water test, tied up and thrown into the water—if he sank and drowned he was innocent of demonic possession, if he floated and lived he was guilty and was then burned. Not only was this practiced on heretics who had other religions, but also on people who had bad habits, such as too much worldly success (which is not a bad habit in our reality, but was then). When a person was under arrest for suspicion of heresy, during the Inquisition, his property was taken, he and his family were turned out of doors, and anyone who was charitable to them was also suspect. Thus anyone whose habits varied from social reality was isolated from the community and given the "not to be taken seriously" status. By this method the church kept a tight control on the social definition of reality and eliminated countless people whose bad habits might have exposed its flaws. While the burning of "witches" seems outrageous to us, might not a future generation look back on the way in which we isolate people by socially defining them as "mentally ill" as similarly outrageous?

It is easy to see that this process might be relevant for a transvestite, for a person with sporadic patterns of schizophrenic communications, or even for a person who had started the process of withdrawing from society in a retreatist adaptation.

This is not to suggest that the formal social control of bad habits does no good at all; it does protect reality, and help some people over their experience–reality conflicts, and others can have the intensity of their conflicts reduced by sufficient and sustained doses of tranquilizers. However, comparative studies seem to indicate that for the bad habits called "mental illness," trying psychiatry or witchcraft, or nothing, effect about the same number of "cures."

9

SOCIOLOGY AND MODERN SYSTEMS THEORY

WALTER BUCKLEY

Thomas J. Scheff's recent sociological theory of mental illness represents a suggestive systematic and more detailed statement of this transactional generation of a different kind of deviance.* The accompanying flow-chart suggests the complex systemic nature of the process, including some of the deviation-amplifying feedbacks characteristic of the complex adaptive system we are studying. (See Figure 1.) In outline, the theory is as follows. For diverse causes—biological, psychological, and/or social—most individuals at some time or other engage in *residual rule-breaking* or unusual behavior that is potentially definable by some members of society as abnormal or wrong. (These "diverse causes," of course, call for the plugging in of sociological and psychological theories of strain generation.) [*Such as have been outlined in the Expanded Typology of Individual Adaptation and the various experience–social reality conflicts explored in this chapter.*] Most such residual rule-breaking is *denied,* not defined or reacted to as of consequence, and is thus not amplified; it is transitory and without issue. On the other hand, depending on the status of the individual, the visibility of his residual rule-breaking, community tolerance level, and so on, his behavior and its effects on family or friends may lead to a "public crisis" wherein it comes to be defined and "labeled" as "mental illness." These social responses of others significant to him, in conjunction with his own suggestibility at such a time of stress, and along with the stereotyped behaviors of the mentally disturbed he has learned during the normal socialization process, all contribute to his definition of himself as deviant. (This is very much the same process whereby *any* aspect of one's role and self-conception are socially elaborated, though without the stress and crisis.) Inasmuch as this is unsettling to an already disturbed person, his self-control is further impaired, making further episodes of "unusual" behavior likely. A deviation-amplifying feedback loop is thus set up as suggested in Figure 1, reverberating from "ego" and his behavior to significant others, to the public such as psychiatrist, court judge, family physician, or solicitous neighbor, and back to ego's self-conception. Ego's advance into overt deviant role-

Adapted from Walter Buckley, *Sociology and Modern Systems Theory* (Englewood Cliffs, N.J.: Prentice-Hall, 1967). Copyright © 1967. Reprinted by permission of Prentice-Hall, Inc., Englewood Cliffs, N.J. Pp. 169–171.

* Thomas J. Scheff, "The Role of the Mentally Ill and the Dynamics of Mental Disorder: A Research Framework," *Sociometry,* 26 (1963), 436–53; *Being Mentally Ill* (Chicago: Aldine Publishing Company, 1966).

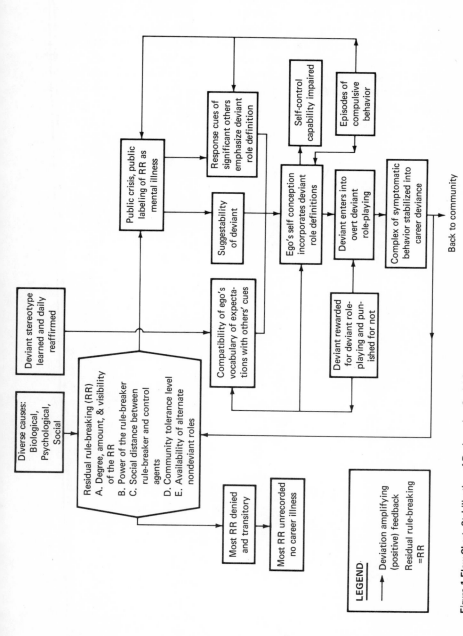

Figure 1 Flow Chart: Stabilization of Deviance in a Social System

playing is furthered when the psychiatrist, for example, attempts to fit ego's presumed symptomatic behaviors into traditional clinical categories, and inadvertently rewards ego for the "correct" behavior symptoms and verbal responses and punishes him for attempting to deny his deviant role. This also constitutes a potential deviation-amplifying source, contributing to the final stabilization of ego into the career deviant role—the neurotic or psychotic. Finally, the aggregation of such deviant roles has its feedback effects on the community, its structure, its tolerance level, and the consequent nature of the "social reaction" to further deviance.

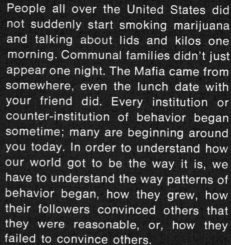

People all over the United States did not suddenly start smoking marijuana and talking about lids and kilos one morning. Communal families didn't just appear one night. The Mafia came from somewhere, even the lunch date with your friend did. Every institution or counter-institution of behavior began sometime; many are beginning around you today. In order to understand how our world got to be the way it is, we have to understand the way patterns of behavior began, how they grew, how their followers convinced others that they were reasonable, or, how they failed to convince others.

It is easy to lose sight of the fact that the things we do, and that others do, have not always been done. Things that started before our birth always appear to be such facts of life that it is hard for us to conceive of them as not existing. Most of the institutions of behavior that we follow we did not create; most of the counter-institutions of behavior were not created by the people within them either. These patterns in the world seem real, seem always to have

four

MEETING OTHERS

been there, and we may choose to follow or not. But this perspective makes our own behavior easy to understand, and the behavior of others incomprehensible. Even though the most common route into social deviance is following a counter-institution that already existed, we must see where these counter-institutions came from to understand why people choose to do disapproved things, and, more basically, how they have this choice.

Our basic premise is that socially constructed reality has flaws. The fact that social reality is never a cohesive whole that provides answers to everything, though most people believe it is, leaves many individuals with a sense of discomfort or despair. This discomfort may be caused by the values of the symbolic universe, the institutions of behavior legitimated within the universe, or maladjustments between these values and institutions—producing conflicts with individual experience. The individual sees possibilities that the reality held by others denies. For example, a man may become bored by his marriage but feel himself locked into it. His comings and goings, his purchases, his self-concept, his pattern of friendships, his mortgage, his entire style of life have been affected by the marriage institution. There are many parts of it with which he has no quarrel, but he is bored. The values of marriage, and probably his wife as a coparticipant in the actual institution, require him to be faithful. Perhaps in his job he meets many attractive women who are sexually free and available; he may even have a specific girl in mind. Within the terms of the marriage institution he may not stray; his daily participation in all the patterns of marriage continually reaffirms this definition of the situation; his time is so organized and routinized in patterns of coordination with his wife that finding time to stray would require a bit of thinking and lying. In other words, his social reality is so constructed as to keep him within the institution, abiding by its values. At the same time it may become painfully obvious to him that he could have an enjoyable sexual encounter with his girl from the office. What does he do? Does he try to forget his knowledge of the situation and the outside possibilities, or does he do a little discreet exploration, looking around for a way to segment his life so that he may enjoy the best of both worlds? Part of his existential knowledge is that other men cheat on their wives; he is also aware of the horrors of divorce and alimony. Ideally, the marriage institution should not allow him to see these choices if he is to remain faithful, but in this area experience has often conflicted with values, and has frequently led people to stray and become "deviants."

Another example might be the dilemma faced by a young man who is ordered to war by his country. Ideally, within the definition of reality fostered and spread by the territorial institutions of the institutional order, transmitted to him by the schools, it is his patriotic duty to fight.

But other institutions, also within the institutional order, such as his church, may have given him the idea that killing is wrong and immoral. What does he do with this conflict?

In both of these cases there is an incongruity between what the individual feels constrained to do and what he wants to do. This incongruity comes from unrationalized reality production processes, which leave gaps and contradictions in explaining what the individual should do with his life. If marriage and work were so organized that a married man would not meet available females, and if countries were bound to follow the morality of churches, there would not be these particular conflicts—but there would be others.

Any definition of reality is *imposed* on ongoing life. Reality includes ongoing life, but it also includes much from life that has gone on before. The values we have in our symbolic universe, the things people believe in, are somewhat tied together by a scientific outlook, somewhat tied together by a religious outlook, and have some organization from an Enlightenment philosophical standpoint. They came from many different sources and represent many different points of view: abstractions from the experience of societies living nomadic lives in the desert; points of view developed in Greek conversation clubs; rule enforcement concepts from little towns in England that lived under barons; morals from religious deviants who couldn't live in their homeland; from the work of a doctor in Vienna who had a middle-class clientele. And some of our values are being implanted in our heads between deodorant commercials. That is an awful lot of miscellaneous, historically accidental, abstractions to pile up on what we do every day. But that is what happens. We take this entire accidental collage into our heads and it is all supposed to "make sense." Since it doesn't have any inherent order, it has to be organized to make sense and a lot of people have different ways of trying to make sense of it for us. Small wonder that all these ideas don't fit together logically; they were produced in many different places under incredibly diverse conditions. Small wonder that all the people who try to make them fit together can't agree on how to do it. Among the people in our country are people who grew up elsewhere, people who have religions from outside of our symbolic universe, people who live every day in a tight, dangerous, boiling turmoil of collisions and meetings, help and horror, in the squalor and smog of our cities. *That* collection of abstractions is not going to always fit the everyday reality of *those* people. But since the construction of reality that *is* the symbolic universe is defended as being total, complete, and logical, the realities of some of the people living within it are denied. This is *necessarily true* for any abstraction from reality. To abstract is to overlook. It is in these flaws in reality, where abstractions don't fit experience but pretend to, that the people we call deviants reside. If you live in a reality flaw you will always have to choose, consciously, unconsciously, or as you drift, to do one of two things: acquiesce unwillingly to what "reality" requires, while dimming your vision of alternatives, or strike out on your own to create a reality that makes more subjective sense. Reality is something like a mother; you will be restrained, cajoled, and encouraged not to do things that are "bad for you." But as children begin to live in the world, some of them get into things and believe in things that their parents never did or thought about. And their parents don't "understand" that they are only living in accordance with their own reality.

The processes of reality definition go on in groups, laboratories, nations, solemn assemblies; they go on for all levels of abstraction from experience. Consequently large collections of people hold to a similar interpretation of some aspect of reality; were this not so any large-scale coordination of activity would be impossible. But—just as many share a similar interpretation of some realities, many are affected by similar reality flaws. Large-scale reality definition means large-scale exceptions, sometimes densely populated exceptions. There is not just one man or woman who is bored with marriage; there is not just one conscientious objector.

For every activity in which a person might engage there is at least potential for a reality flaw, and since the activities of many people are conditioned by similar social locations and similar biographies, when there *is* a conflict between experience and social reality it will generally have widespread effect. Not all of these people will be known to one another. Children usually have to work out their fates alone because they don't know enough other children with the same problem parents. But Blacks are beginning to really get to know one another.

Imagine what happens when a reality flaw begins to be recognized as important by a number of persons all at about the same time. This *category* of persons may well be widely distributed through society, though they may have one or many characteristics in common with one another. Some may know others who have the same conflict, others may not. Some may recognize that they have a conflict, others just accept being depressed, unhappy, and discriminated against because they still believe that the reality they live in has no flaws. The only thing they have in common is that they all share what may come to be defined as this particular reality conflict. The conflict may be crucial to their ongoing lives, threatening to their sense of self-esteem, or a fairly minor and unrecognized annoyance that is only relevant to one or two of the things they do. In any event a certain portion of the affected people will want to talk their problem over with others, to seek a solution, or to seek company in their misery. For these people there is a motivation, which contends with other motivations, to seek out others who have the same problem.

The socially defined reality, as articulated by its spokesmen, politicians, ministers, businessmen, labor leaders, and social scientists, is supposed not to have flaws. For these spokesmen and their subjective realities, it doesn't. As a result, solutions to the problems of reality flaws have usually been defined as immoral, illegal, or unreal. These negative definitions have usually been passed on to those who suffer from the flaw, in socialization before they encounter it as self-conscious adults, or in the institutions of behavior they follow. Consequently a person's self-control and his relational controls both discourage his open advertising of his problem. He would be publically admitting a "sin." Even if he overcame his self-control he might not want to shout his "immorality," "illegality," or "insanity" from the fire escape to people in the street. Many people can't overcome their self-control without going to a priest or a psychiatrist, a healer of problems for the social reality, only to be told that their problem is quite common and that behind the masks many others share it.

The person seeking to relieve the discomfort of a reality flaw is thus motivated to find others who share it, but at the same time is constrained to do so in a manner that will not expose him to the public reaction or condemnation that he expects might follow an open admission. The necessary preconditions for finding others who share the flaw are two: they must be identifiable, and there must be the possibility of effective communications.

It may be very hard to identify another person who had an authoritarian mother; the behavioral results are quite various. A great many bad habits remain only bad habits because the individuals involved can't identify others who have them. For example, even though they constitute a majority of the population, people who masturbate have never gotten together to force a redefinition of their habit from bad to good. They can't really identify one another easily, and it is not a serious enough problem for most that they would be compelled to try. Similarly, according to Kinsey, a majority of married people have engaged in oral-genital sexual relations but no one has yet started a Cunnilingus Society to overturn the laws that make this act a felony. Others are not identifiable because they believe what they do is bad and prefer outwardly peaceful, if inwardly anguished, anonymity.

People may be able to identify one another, but not be able to effectively communicate. This is true for schizophrenics and for people who stutter. In the following adaptation Edwin Lemert points out that stutterers do not form institutions even though they can identify one another and even though they suffer similar experience–social reality conflicts.

10
SPEECH DEFECT AND THE SPEECH DEFECTIVE
EDWIN M. LEMERT

Systematic deviation does not occur with stuttering, according to all available records. [*"Systematic deviation" means institutionalization and recruitment or transmission.*] Although several persons in the same family and members of different generations of the same family often show stuttering symptoms, there is no proof that this behavior is ever learned. There may be some communication of learning of techniques for covering up or handling blocks between stutterers in clinical situations, but beyond this it would be in error to claim any special culture for stutterers. Nor is there any indication of social organization among stutterers. As far as is known, stutterers outside of clinics do not seek out one another's company, nor do they form groups among themselves. In fact, the effort of one speech correctionist, known to the author, to organize a community group of stutterers failed conspicuously. It is not surprising that stutterers have no special group life when it is remembered that communication is the medium of culture and the requisite for social organization. The social situation is the nemesis of the stutterer, hence he tends to avoid it whenever he can, unless he can enter into it as a nonverbal participant. A further important reason for the absence of a behavior system of stuttering inheres in the nature of the societal reaction to this deviation.

.   .   .

THE SOCIETAL REACTION

While there is not such a definite and venerable folklore about stuttering as that which clusters around blindness, nevertheless a number of fallacious beliefs about this handicap have gained currency with the public. These largely concern the causes of the defect. Some of the commonly encountered folk explanations of stuttering are phrased in terms of injury, illness, bad heredity, shock, nervousness, imitating other stutterers, thinking too fast, and, perhaps most significantly, lack of will power. Some parents express the belief that stuttering is a phase through which all children must pass. The diffusion of scientific knowledge about stuttering seems to be at a minimum among members of the general public.

Stuttering more often provokes laughter and amusement among those who hear it than it does hostility or deep sympathy. Added to these is a degree of embarrassment and irritation, prevalent among those who empathize the reactions of the stutterer. This is perceived overtly in the impulsive tendency of a stutterer's auditors to supply words and finish sentences for him, or in other cases in the looking away and breaking eye contact with the person as he speaks. Some persons, often complete strangers, feel a responsibility to instruct the stuttering individual as to how he should overcome his handicap. From such persons come all the timeworn remedies which he has heard so many times before and which he knows will do him no whit of good. [*This is one experience–social reality conflict that stutterers share. The "timeworn remedies" are part of socially constructed reality; his knowledge of their uselessness comes from his experience.*] He is told to watch his breathing or to talk slowly, all with an unconscious arrogance that is humiliating and infuriating to the stutterer, who often is his unsought mentor's intellectual superior. Occasionally the stutterer becomes the butt of crude practical jokes.

□ □ □

ESTABLISHMENT OF RECIPROCAL TYPIFICATIONS

If a person is sufficiently motivated to overcome his reluctance, if he can identify others with the same problem, and if he can communicate with them, he still has one remaining problem—how to go about it. The answer is, discreetly. Without admitting the entire problem or conflict, without even mentioning it, he drops subtle cues to the people he identifies as possibly sharing his conflict with social reality. A word, a gesture, a silence in the context of an ongoing situation leaves a conversational avenue open for the other's development. The man bored with his marriage might by words or gestures discreetly indicate his availability to potential partners; the unwilling draftee might cautiously seek out others who might be opposed, but without antagonizing his draft board, fellow employees, or parents.

The person caught in a reality flaw might seek others for many reasons: Just to see if they have the same problem. To see if they are sympathetic or can help him to a new pattern of living. To see if another life style would avoid the problem through its definition of reality. To see if others have complementary needs (as, for example, a woman who would enjoy a sexual liaison but who is not interested in marriage might complement a man bored with his marriage). To see if with another they can begin to change social reality.

In the following adaptation Albert Cohen discusses the process of "feeling out" others in subculture formation. In the terms developed here he is describing the emergence of reciprocal typifications among people who inhabit similar reality flaws.

11
A GENERAL THEORY OF SUBCULTURES
ALBERT K. COHEN

HOW SUBCULTURAL SOLUTIONS ARISE

Now we confront a dilemma and a paradox. We have seen how difficult it is for the individual to cut loose from the culture models in his milieu, how his dependence upon his fellows compels him to seek conformity and to avoid innovation. But these models and precedents which we call the surrounding culture are ways in which other people think and other people act, and these other people are likewise constrained by models in *their* milieux. [*"Models" are ongoing institutions of behavior. "Precedents" are the abstractions of past realities.*] *These models themselves, however, continually change.* How is it possible for cultural innovations to emerge while each of the participants in the culture is so powerfully motivated to conform to what is already established? This is the central theoretical problem of this book.

The crucial condition for the emergence of new cultural forms is the existence, *in effective interaction with one another, of a number of actors with similar problems of adjustment.* [*A "new cultural form" is a new institution of behavior. "Problem of adjustment" is another way of saying reality flaw.*] These may be the entire membership of a group or only certain members, similarly circumstanced, within the group. Among the conceivable solutions to their problems may be one which is not yet embodied in action and which does not therefore exist as a cultural model. This solution, except for the fact that it does not already carry the social criteria of validity and promise the social rewards of consensus [*that is to say, it is not legitimated or enacted yet within the symbolic universe and the institutional order*], might well answer more neatly to the problems of this group and appeal to its members more effectively than any of the solutions already institutionalized. [*This, it seems, explains the emergence of new forms of group behavior outside of legitimated institutions, and also outside of existing counter-institutions.*] For each participant, this solution would be adjustive and adequately motivated provided that he could anticipate a simultaneous and corresponding transformation in the frames of reference of his fellows. Each would welcome a sign from the others that a new departure in this direction would receive approval and support. But how does one know whether a gesture toward innovation will strike a responsive and

Adapted with permission of The Macmillan Company from "A General Theory of Subcultures," *Delinquent Boys* by Albert Cohen. Copyright 1955 by The Free Press, a Corporation.

sympathetic chord in others or whether it will elicit hostility, ridicule and punishment? *Potential* concurrence is always problematical and innovation or the impulse to innovate a stimulus for anxiety.

The paradox is resolved when the innovation is broached in such a manner as to elicit from others reactions suggesting their receptivity; and when, at the same time, the innovation occurs by increments so small, tentative and ambiguous as to permit the actor to retreat, if the signs be unfavorable, without having become identified with an unpopular position. Perhaps all social actions have, in addition to their instrumental, communicative and expressive functions, this quality of being *exploratory gestures.* For the actor with problems of adjustment which cannot be resolved within the frame of reference of the established culture [*that is, social reality*] each response of the other to what the actor says and does is a clue to the directions in which change may proceed further in a way congenial to the other and to the direction in which change will lack social support. And if the probing gesture is motivated by tensions common to other participants it is likely to initiate a process of *mutual* exploration and *joint* elaboration of a new solution. My exploratory gesture functions as a cue to you; your exploratory gesture as a cue to me. By a casual, semi-serious, noncommittal or tangential remark I may stick my neck out just a little way, but I will quickly withdraw it unless you, by some sign of affirmation, stick *yours* out. I will permit myself to become progressively committed but only as others, by some visible sign, become likewise committed. [*This is the process of making reciprocal typifications of another in an area forbidden by guilt, taboo, and other sanctions of social reality.*] The final product, to which we are jointly committed, is likely to be a compromise formation of all the participants to what we may call a cultural process, a formation perhaps unanticipated by any of them. Each actor may contribute something directly to the growing product, but he may also contribute indirectly by encouraging others to advance, inducing them to retreat, and suggesting new avenues to be explored. The product cannot be ascribed to any one of the participants; it is a real "emergent" on a group level. [*That is, it is a new reciprocal typification of behavior, a pattern that did not exist before.*]

We may think of this process as one of mutual conversion. The important thing to remember is that we do not first convert ourselves and then others. The acceptability of an idea to oneself depends upon its acceptability to others. Converting the other is part of the process of converting oneself.

.   .   .

The emergence of these "group standards" of this shared frame of reference, is the emergence of a new subculture. [*The understanding of the two or more people who have formed this reciprocal typification about how they should behave is potentially the beginning of a counterinstitution of behavior.*] It is cultural because each actor's participation in this system of norms is influenced by his perception of the same norms in other actors. It is *sub*cultural because the norms are shared only among those actors who stand somehow to profit from them and who find in one another a sympathetic moral climate within which these norms may come to fruition and persist. In this fashion culture is continually being created, re-created and modified wherever individuals sense in one another like needs, generated by like circumstances, not shared generally in the larger social system. Once established, such a subcultural system may persist, but not by sheer inertia. It may achieve a life which outlasts that of the individuals who participated in its creation, but only so long as it continues to serve the needs of those who succeed its creators. [*An additional step in outlasting its creators is the recruitment of new persons to follow it, that is to say, its completion as an institution of behavior that can sustain itself. This is the next higher level of institutionalization from reciprocal typification, which will usually require a higher level of legitimation.*]

□ □ □

An individual begins to typify another as having a certain habitual pattern of activity that seems "interesting" in their experience–social reality conflict. The other responds and the reciprocal typification grows. This first step, however, is small. Possibly it is not consciously considered. It is probably very tentative. The person involved is often not subjectively conscious of any particular movement away from conformity, he simply finds some people with whom he feels more comfortable. At any stage in the emergence of this reciprocal typification the individual might be astonished to realize that he is doing something "wrong." People have many experiences in their everyday lives and a new reciprocal typification may be a very small part of what they are doing. People generally change their lives in small steps and fit the new in with the old, always retaining a fairly strong sense of biographical continuity and thus a sense that the situation is "normal." People can undergo amazing transformations of habits in a relatively short time without ever feeling that things are abnormal until one day they think back, recast their actions in new mental categories, and discover that they are doing something quite different. This is true for both legitimate and illegitimate changes in many instances. For example, over a period of a year and a half a girl that I knew who was "just doing a thing with her friends" was objectively transformed from a straight middle-class college student into a methedrine-shooting, acid-dropping, marijuana-smoking resident of a Haight-Ashbury commune. But she took up each new thing separately; in a group of her friends from high school who were also taking them up one at a time, over one-and-a-half full years, over four hundred daily rounds of activity, and it all seemed very normal and manageable until one day she realized that *she* was the hippie the newspapers were writing about. Hippies had always been strange people to her, strange and a bit unknown. It is in this context of gradual transformation that her comment, "I didn't even know what a hippie was, until I was one," makes sense. Most people who create new reciprocal typifications probably experience something of a surprise when they suddenly reorder their sense of biography and identity to take account of what they have been doing for a while.

ELEMENTARY LEGITIMATIONS FOR RECIPROCAL TYPIFICATIONS

In order for two people to coordinate their behavior they must at least understand what they, mutually, are doing. This means that they understand "how to do it," the very first recognition of the behavior as a distinct social object, and the first step in legitimating it. If their behavior is not totally innocuous, as meeting a friend for lunch usually is, they will eventually run into someone who will demand an explanation of the behavior, usually because it has upset him. At this point, the participants, who still have not progressed beyond the stage of reciprocal typification, may begin having to answer the question, "why did you do it?" When they come up with an answer they have taken the second step in legitimating their behavior. Legitimations at this level are not usually very convincing unless the behavior pattern is rapidly becoming a recruiting institution.

For an example of legitimation at this level let us look at what juvenile delinquents say when they are caught. We tend to think of juvenile delinquents as members of gangs that recruit new members, but this recruiting institution actually accounts for a small portion of all juveniles who commit delinquencies. Most juvenile delinquents probably form reciprocal typifications with a few friends that certain forms of activity such as smashing school windows, stealing hubcaps together, and getting laid are fun. They have probably mutually created as much of this behavior as they have learned from established delinquents. The juvenile gang has been called a "near-group" by Lewis Yablonsky, that is, something between the stages of reciprocal typification and a recruiting institution. Most juveniles have to make up legitimations for their actions on the basis of their general knowledge of social excuses—statements that are not really positive assertions of the value of a thing but indications that it is not totally without precedent nor totally evil. These explanations—legitimations—in response to the question "why," were called "neutralizations" by Gresham Sykes and David Matza in the following adaptation. These explanations "neutralize," at least for the delinquent, some of the criticism directed toward him, allowing him to fit his behavior into his biographical self-concept. Like most such elementary forms of legitimation they are not terribly convincing to others, but they allow the reciprocal typifications to be continued, and the behavior to be carried out.

□ □ □

12
TECHNIQUES OF NEUTRALIZATION
A Theory of Delinquency
GRESHAM M. SYKES AND DAVID MATZA

The difficulties in viewing delinquent behavior as springing from a set of deviant values and norms—as arising, that is to say, from a situation in which the delinquent defines his delinquency as "right"—are both empirical and theoretical. In the first place, if there existed in fact a delinquent subculture such that the delinquent viewed his illegal behavior as morally correct, we could reasonably suppose that he would exhibit no feelings of guilt or shame at detection or confinement. Instead, the major reaction would tend in the direction of indignation or a sense of martyrdom.* It is true that some delinquents do react in the latter fashion, although the sense of martyrdom often seems to be based on the fact that others "get away with it" and indignation appears to be directed against the chance events or lack of skill that led to apprehension. More important, however, is the fact that there is a good deal of evidence suggesting that many delinquents *do* experience a sense of guilt or shame, and its outward expression is not to be dismissed as a purely manipulative gesture to appease those in authority. [*Primary socialization inculcates values that conflict with the behavior reciprocally typified. "Guilt" or "shame" are the sanctions of "self-control."*]

. . .

In the second place, observers have noted that the juvenile delinquent frequently accords admiration and respect to law-abiding persons. The "really honest" person is often revered, and if the delinquent is sometimes overly keen to detect hypocrisy in those who conform, unquestioned probity is likely to win his approval. A fierce attachment to a humble, pious mother or a forgiving, upright priest (the former,

Adapted from Gresham M. Sykes and David Matza, "Techniques of Neutralization: A Theory of Delinquency," *American Sociological Review* Vol. 22, No. 6, December 1957, pp. 664–670. Reprinted with permission of the authors and The American Sociological Association.

* This form of reaction among the adherents of a deviant subculture who fully believe in the "rightfulness" of their behavior and who are captured and punished by the agencies of the dominant social order can be illustrated, perhaps, by groups such as Jehovah's Witnesses, early Christian sects, nationalist movements in colonial areas, and conscientious objectors during World Wars I and II. [*These, of course, are people operating within an alternate reality, who have very thorough and plausible legitimations for their actions.*]

according to many observers, is often encountered in both juvenile delinquents and adult criminals) might be dismissed as rank sentimentality, but at least it is clear that the delinquent does not necessarily regard those who abide by the legal rules as immoral. [*The delinquent is still connected to persons in legitimate institutions and his primary socialization to the values they uphold causes him to accept and value them for their honesty.*]

.　　.　　.

In the third place, there is much evidence that juvenile delinquents often draw a sharp line between those who can be victimized and those who cannot. Certain social groups are not to be viewed as "fair game" in the performance of supposedly approved delinquent acts while others warrant a variety of attacks. In general, the potentiality for victimization would seem to be a function of the social distance between the juvenile delinquent and others and thus we find implicit maxims in the world of the delinquent such as "don't steal from friends" or "don't commit vandalism against a church of your own faith." [*In other words, the typifications that constitute delinquency only operated in a few and selected parts of the delinquent's life. His involvement in other, legitimate, institutions protects them from his attack.*]

.　　.　　.

In the fourth place, it is doubtful if many juvenile delinquents are totally immune from the demands for conformity made by the dominant social order. There is a strong likelihood that the family of the delinquent will agree with respectable society that delinquency is wrong, even though the family may be engaged in a variety of illegal activities. That is, the parental posture conducive to delinquency is not apt to be a positive prodding. Whatever may be the influence of parental example, what might be called the "Fagin" pattern of socialization into delinquency is probably rare. [*That is, much of the behavior is created by the delinquents themselves, not passed on to them by counterinstitutional socialization.*]

.　　.　　.

The fact that a child is punished by parents, school officials, and agencies of the legal system for his delinquency may, as a number of observers have cynically noted, suggest to the child that he should be more careful not to get caught. There is an equal or greater probability, however, that the child will internalize the demands for conformity.

[*This child's reciprocal typification may be broken up; he may be moved back into conformity.*] This is not to say that demands for conformity cannot be counteracted. In fact, as we shall see shortly, an understanding of how internal and external demands for conformity are neutralized may be crucial for understanding delinquent behavior. But it is to say that a complete denial of the validity of demands for conformity and the substitution of a new normative system is improbable, in light of the child's or adolescent's dependency on adults and encirclement by adults inherent in his status in the social structure. No matter how deeply enmeshed in patterns of delinquency he may be and no matter how much this involvement may outweigh his associations with the law-abiding, he cannot escape the condemnation of his deviance. Somehow the demands for conformity must be met and answered; they cannot be ignored as part of an alien system of values and norms. [*The delinquent cannot isolate himself enough to build a complete and supported set of legitimations because of his dependency on people who are followers of legitimate institutions.*]

In short, the theoretical viewpoint that sees juvenile delinquency as a form of behavior based on the values and norms of a deviant subculture in precisely the same way as law-abiding behavior is based on the values and norms of the larger society is open to serious doubt. The fact that the world of the delinquent is embedded in the larger world of those who conform cannot be overlooked nor can the delinquent be equated with an adult thoroughly socialized into an alternative way of life. Instead, the juvenile delinquent would appear to be at least partially committed to the dominant social order in that he frequently exhibits guilt or shame when he violates its proscriptions, accords approval to certain conforming figures, and distinguishes between appropriate targets for his deviance. [*In other words, the delinquent's pattern of behavior is not supported by systematic legitimations, and is surrounded and penetrated by legitimate institutions, making the production of consistent legitimations quite difficult.*] It is to an explanation for the apparently paradoxical fact of his delinquency that we now turn.

As Morris Cohen once said, one of the most fascinating problems about human behavior is why men violate the laws in which they believe. This is the problem that confronts us when we attempt to explain why delinquency occurs despite a greater or lesser commitment to the usages of conformity. A basic clue is offered by the fact that social rules or norms calling for valued behavior seldom if ever take the form of categorical imperatives. Rather, values or norms appear as *qualified* guides for action, limited in their applicability in terms of time, place, persons, and social circumstances. The moral injunction against killing, for example, does not apply to the enemy during combat in time of war, although a captured enemy comes once again under the prohibition.

Similarly, the taking and distributing of scarce goods in a time of acute social need is felt by many to be right, although under other circumstances private property is held inviolable. The normative system of a society, then, is marked by what Williams has termed *flexibility;* it does not consist of a body of rules held to be binding under all conditions.

This flexibility is, in fact, an integral part of the criminal law in that measures for "defenses to crimes" are provided in pleas such as nonage, necessity, insanity, drunkenness, compulsion, self-defense, and so on. The individual can avoid moral culpability for his criminal action —and thus avoid the negative sanctions of society—if he can prove that criminal intent was lacking. *It is our argument that much delinquency is based on what is essentially an unrecognized extension of defenses to crimes, in the form of justifications for deviance that are seen as valid by the delinquent but not by the legal system or society at large. [These legitimations are learned in socialization as they are commonly used in the culture for excusing other behavior. The delinquent's use of them, however, is not convincing enough to be plausible to people in legitimate institutions, though they provide him with biographical legitimation.]*

These justifications are commonly described as rationalizations. They are viewed as following deviant behavior and as protecting the individual from self-blame and the blame of others after the act. But there is also reason to believe that they precede deviant behavior and make deviant behavior possible. *[In contemplating an act known to be illegitimate, the individual thinking about it, or the group talking it over, has to find some legitimacy to make the act psychologically possible.]* It is this possibility that Sutherland mentioned only in passing and that other writers have failed to exploit from the viewpoint of sociological theory. Disapproval flowing from internalized norms and conforming others in the social environment is neutralized, turned back, or deflected in advance. Social controls that serve to check or inhibit deviant motivational patterns are rendered inoperative, and the individual is freed to engage in delinquency without serious damage to his self image. In this sense, the delinquent both has his cake and eats it too, for he remains committed to the dominant normative system and yet so qualifies its imperatives that violations are "acceptable" if not "right." Thus the delinquent represents not a radical opposition to law-abiding society but something more like an apologetic failure, often more sinned against than sinning in his own eyes. We call these justifications of deviant behavior techniques of neutralization; and we believe these techniques make up a crucial component of Sutherland's "definitions favorable to the violation of law." It is by learning these techniques that the juvenile becomes delinquent, rather than by learning moral imperatives, values or attitudes standing in direct contradiction to those of the dominant society. In analyzing these techniques, we have found it convenient to divide them into five major types.

[*These are types of "social excuse" legitimations that protect self-esteem more than they really convince others.*]

The Denial of Responsibility ☐ In so far as the delinquent can define himself as lacking responsibility for his deviant actions, the disapproval of self or others is sharply reduced in effectiveness as a restraining influence. As Justice Holmes has said, even a dog distinguishes between being stumbled over and being kicked, and modern society is no less careful to draw a line between injuries that are unintentional, i.e., where responsibility is lacking, and those that are intentional. As a technique of neutralization, however, the denial of responsibility extends much further than the claim that deviant acts are an "accident" or some similar negation of personal accountability. It may also be asserted that delinquent acts are due to forces outside of the individual and beyond his control such as unloving parents, bad companions, or a slum neighborhood. In effect, the delinquent approaches a "billiard ball" conception of himself in which he sees himself as helplessly propelled into new situations. From a psychodynamic viewpoint, this orientation toward one's own actions may represent a profound alienation from self, but it is important to stress the fact that interpretations of responsibility are cultural constructs and not merely idiosyncratic beliefs. [*Delinquency, being a part-time affair, borrows legitimation formulas from the ongoing society.*]

The Denial of Injury ☐ A second major technique of neutralization centers on the injury or harm involved in the delinquent act. The criminal law has long made a distinction between crimes which are *mala in se* and *mala prohibita*—that is between acts that are wrong in themselves and acts that are illegal but not immoral—and the delinquent can make the same kind of distinction in evaluating the wrongfulness of his behavior. For the delinquent, however, wrongfulness may turn on the question of whether or not anyone has clearly been hurt by his deviance, and this matter is open to a variety of interpretations. Vandalism, for example, may be defined by the delinquent simply as "mischief" —after all, it may be claimed, the persons whose property has been destroyed can well afford it. [*This illustrates the ad hoc nature of these legitimations; they do not represent a consistent philosophy.*] Similarly, auto theft may be viewed as "borrowing," and gang fighting may be seen as a private quarrel, an agreed upon duel between two willing parties, and thus of no concern to the community at large. We are not suggesting that this technique of neutralization, labelled the denial of injury, involves an explicit dialectic. Rather, we are arguing that the delinquent frequently, and in a hazy fashion, feels that his behavior does not really cause any great harm despite the fact that it runs counter to law. Just as the link between the individual and his acts may be broken by the denial of responsibility, so may the link between acts and their consequences be broken by the denial of injury. Since society sometimes agrees with the delinquent, e.g., in matters such as truancy, "pranks," and so on, it merely reaffirms the idea that the delinquent's neutralization of social controls by means of qualifying the norms is an extension of common practice rather than a gesture of complete opposition.

The Denial of the Victim □   Even if the delinquent accepts the responsibility for his deviant actions and is willing to admit that his deviant actions involve an injury or hurt, the moral indignation of self and others may be neutralized by an insistence that the injury is not wrong in light of the circumstances. The injury, it may be claimed, is not really an injury; rather, it is a form of rightful retaliation or punishment. By a subtle alchemy the delinquent moves himself into the position of an avenger and the victim is transformed into a wrong-doer. Assaults on homosexuals or suspected homosexuals, attacks on members of minority groups who are said to have gotten "out of place," vandalism as revenge on an unfair teacher or school official, thefts from a "crooked" store owner—all may be hurts inflicted on a transgressor, in the eyes of the delinquent. [*Some people and legitimate institutions may well agree with him, and they may be secretly or openly pleased that the delinquent is carrying out dirty work that they favor by attacking homosexuals or minority groups. Many "Loyal Americans" were pleased when the Hell's Angels attacked anti-Vietnam marchers in Berkeley.*]

.   .   .

The Condemnation of the Condemners □   A fourth technique of neutralization would appear to involve a condemnation of the condemners or, as McCorkle and Korn have phrased it, a rejection of the rejectors. The delinquent shifts the focus of attention from his own deviant acts to the motives and behavior of those who disapprove of his violations. His condemners, he may claim, are hypocrites, deviants in disguise, or impelled by personal spite. [*He implicitly accepts and uses values from the symbolic universe in this process.*] This orientation toward the conforming world may be of particular importance when it hardens into a bitter cynicism directed against those assigned the task of enforcing or expressing the norms of the dominant society. Police, it may be said, are corrupt, stupid, and brutal. Teachers always show favoritism and parents always "take it out" on their children. By a slight extension, the rewards of conformity—such as material success—become a matter of pull or luck, thus decreasing still further the stature of those who stand on the side of the law-abiding. The validity of this jaundiced viewpoint is not so important as its function in turning back or deflecting the negative sanctions attached to violations of the norms. The delinquent, in effect, has changed the subject of the conversation in the dialogue between his own deviant impulses and the reactions of others; and by attacking others, the wrongfulness of his own behavior is more easily repressed or lost to view.

The Appeal to Higher Loyalties ☐ Fifth, and last, internal and external social controls may be neutralized by sacrificing the demands of the larger society for the demands of the smaller social groups to which the delinquent belongs such as the sibling pair, the gang, or the friendship clique. It is important to note that the delinquent does not necessarily repudiate the imperatives of the dominant normative system, despite his failure to follow them. Rather, the delinquent may see himself as caught up in a dilemma that must be resolved, unfortunately, at the cost of violating the law.

.　　.　　.

The most important point is that deviation from certain norms may occur not because the norms are rejected but because other norms, held to be more pressing or involving a higher loyalty, are accorded precedence. [*The people involved in the reciprocal typification and its patterns of behavior may be more important than the abstract rules of legitimate institutions.*]

.　　.　　.

"I didn't mean it." "I didn't really hurt anybody." "They had it coming to them." "Everybody's picking on me." "I didn't do it for myself." These slogans or their variants, we hypothesize, prepare the juvenile for delinquent acts. These "definitions of the situation" represent tangential or glancing blows at the dominant normative system rather than the creation of an opposing ideology; and they are extensions of patterns of thought prevalent in society rather than something created *de novo*. [*Because they are tangential and ad hoc, because they are dubious modifications of common values, they are inadequate for forming a consistent and transmittable set of legitimations.*]

□ □ □

I was able to see the formation of reciprocal typifications of behavior and the creation of legitimations for them in the communal family that I observed. Before the "family" came to be there was a couple living in a large house with a boarder. Another couple who needed a place to stay for a few weeks moved in and the five began to participate in common activities, listening and dancing to acid-rock records, watching old movies on television, getting high. There were always some other people around, friends of one or another of the five. When one of the new couple had to leave the city his girlfriend was asked by the original couple to stay on. The pattern of interaction and the dropping in of friends continued, which was much more pleasant for all four than the somewhat lonely lives each had lived previously. Reciprocal typifications began to arise within the group regarding work, who was to cook, who was to clean, how much money each would contribute, and typifications regarding a variety of sexual patterns, as each of the four had a variety of partners. Territory typifications, whose room was whose, how messy or clean different rooms should be, what different rooms would be used for what different activities, also emerged from the continuing interaction. Typifications of communication also arose as each of the four began to refer to items of common knowledge by shorthand references. These understandings and patterns of doing things developed naturally as problems arose. If the living room was not straight when company came, somebody would mention it and the others would then keep it clean. Strangers dropped in fairly frequently, so marijuana smoking was moved out of the living room. Certain rooms came to be defined as "work rooms" for one or another of the four, which the others would not disturb. Although there were some speculative legitimations around, such as the idea that the nuclear family did not work and that living together was more fun, there was no systematic legitimation of the collection of activities.

One day, after about a month of living together, the girl who had stayed on was involved in a telephone argument with her mother, who wanted her to live at home and do her "family duty" of being an obedient daughter. One of the original couple who overheard half of the conversation later suggested that the girl had a "family" in the house as well. The idea caught and the group began to refer to itself as "the family," giving the patterns of behavior of the four the legitimacy of a name which separated them from the outside world as a distinct unit. All of the patterns of behavior came to be seen as the way the family did things, and "the family" started entertaining occasionally as a cohesive group, rather than as a collection of individuals. Legitimations such as, "it's cheaper to live this way," and "we all have more freedom this way" became common understandings. With every contact with people living in conventional families came new ideas of the horrors that a voluntary collective family avoided. The problems of the conventional family, which all had experienced, was the "reality flaw" that caused the four to be receptive to the new pattern. At this stage in its development the family had coordinated a number of independent habits, created reciprocal typifications about them that allowed other new behavior to emerge, had given itself the legitimacy of a name, and was beginning to answer the question "why is it done this way?" about an increasing number of its activities. It had not yet had to systemize its legitimations because it had not yet recruited and convinced a new member, so the legitimations were understood and discussed by the four as isolated ideas. This pattern of development happens all the time for both legitimate and counter-institutions. If you think about any group that you have participated in forming you will see the same steps. These are the ways in which people respond to reality flaws and create new patterns of behavior, different from existing, legitimate institutions.

MOVING INTO ESTABLISHED COUNTER-INSTITUTIONS OF BEHAVIOR

Most people engaged in unusual behavior with others did not think the behavior up for themselves. First, not everyone is creative or experimental enough to create new forms of behavior even if they have the experience–social reality conflict that would make it desirable. Second, most of the problems caused by most reality constrictions are not new, and others who have faced them before have already created counter-institutions that can be followed. Third, through ideas thoroughly spread around, a person learns about many counter-institutions in his socialization. He generally learns negative things, but he at least knows that the patterns exist. We all know that mistresses exist, even if we don't have one or haven't been one. Robbers, prostitutes, dope fiends, and homosexuals abound in the daily newspaper and the six o'clock news. We even have some rough and generally inaccurate idea of the types of people who do deviant things, and the purported reasons for which they do them. It is sometimes possible to see ourselves in this position, and to understand the ways of following counter-institutions. For all of these reasons, people with an experience–social reality conflict usually choose to follow the existing patterns of counter-institutions rather than creating their own.

No one learns very much about how to do things from abstract descriptions. One generally learns things by watching and participating with others. As was suggested, one's social location and pattern of institutional involvements influences the type of institutions contacted, and thus the behavior which can be observed and learned. A child in a suburban school has far less chance of learning how to shoot heroin than a child in Harlem. A student living in an apartment is more likely to make friends who smoke marijuana and sleep around than a student living at home. An ex-prisoner is far more likely to know the techniques of safe cracking than the uncaught criminal. In the following adaptation Edwin Sutherland outlines his theory of differential association in the learning of criminal behavior. Although he was only writing about "criminal" behavior his points are equally applicable to all forms of counter-institutional behavior. "Criminal" is a subcategory of counter-institutional behavior that has had a certain kind of formal social control, legal control, applied to it by the institutional order. Something becomes "criminal" when it has a law passed against it, but the process of learning how to do it does not thereby become different. LSD use had similar institutions and legitimations before and after it became "criminal." Making it "criminal" affected the openness with which it could be practiced and may have made it more difficult for people in some social locations to contact, but they would still probably learn it in a small circle of friends. When Sutherland speaks of "legal codes" remember all the formal social control used by the institutional order— laws, official rules, psychiatric testing, and so forth.

□ □ □

13
PRINCIPLES OF CRIMINOLOGY
EDWIN H. SUTHERLAND

The scientific explanation of a phenomenon may be stated either in terms of the factors which are operating at the moment of the occurrence of a phenomenon or in terms of the processes operating in the earlier history of that phenomenon. In the first case the explanation is mechanistic, in the second historical or genetic; both are desirable. The physical and biological scientists favor the first of these methods and it would probably be superior as an explanation of criminal behavior. Efforts at explanations of the mechanistic type have been notably unsuccessful, perhaps largely because they have been concentrated on the attempt to isolate personal and social pathologies. Work from this point of view has, at least, resulted in the conclusion that the immediate factors in criminal behavior lie in the person-situation complex. Person and situation are not factors exclusive of each other, for the situation which is important is the situation as defined by the person who is involved. The tendencies and inhibitions at the moment of the criminal behavior are, to be sure, largely a product of the earlier history of the person, but the expression of these tendencies and inhibitions is a reaction to the immediate situation as defined by the person. The situation operates in many ways, of which perhaps the least important is the provision of an opportunity for a criminal act. A thief may steal from a fruit stand when the owner is not in sight but refrain when the owner is in sight; a bank burglar may attack a bank which is poorly protected but refrain from attacking a bank protected by watchmen and burglar alarms. A corporation which manufactures automobiles seldom or never violates the Pure Food and Drug Law but a meat-packing corporation violates this law with frequency.

The second type of explanation of criminal behavior is made in terms of the life experience of a person. This is an historical or genetic explanation of criminal behavior. This, to be sure, assumes a situation to be defined by the person in terms of the inclinations and abilities which the person has acquired up to that date. The following paragraphs state such a genetic theory of criminal behavior on the assumption that a criminal act occurs when a situation appropriate for it, as defined by a person, is present.

Adapted from Edwin H. Sutherland, *Principles of Criminology* (New York: J. B. Lippincott & Co., 1947), pp. 5–8, by permission of the publisher, J. B. Lippincott & Co. Copyright © 1969 by J. B. Lippincott & Co.

Genetic Explanations of Criminal Behavior

The following statement refers to the process by which a particular person comes to engage in criminal behavior.

1. *Criminal behavior is learned.* Negatively, this means that criminal behavior is not inherited, as such; also, the person who is not already trained in crime does not invent criminal behavior, just as a person does not make mechanical inventions unless he has had training in mechanics.
2. *Criminal behavior is learned in interaction with other persons in a process of communication.* This communication is verbal in many respects but includes also "the communication of gestures."
3. *The principal part of the learning of criminal behavior occurs within intimate personal groups.* Negatively, this means that the impersonal agencies of communication, such as picture shows and newspapers, play a relatively unimportant part in the genesis of criminal behavior.
4. *When criminal behavior is learned, the learning includes (a) techniques of committing the crime, which are sometimes very complicated, sometimes very simple; (b) the specific direction of motives, drives, rationalizations, and attitudes. [In our language "techniques of committing the crime" is the counter-institutional behavior, how to do it, and the "motives, drives, rationalizations, and attitudes" are the legitimations and their consequences for self-esteem.]*
5. *The specific direction of motives and drives is learned from definitions of the legal codes as favorable or unfavorable.* In some societies an individual is surrounded by persons who invariably define the legal codes as rules to be observed, while in others he is surrounded by persons whose definitions are favorable to the violation of the legal codes. In our American society these definitions are almost always mixed and consequently we have culture conflict in relation to the legal codes. *[And almost all other behavior required by the institutional order as well.]*
6. *A person becomes delinquent because of an excess of definitions favorable to violation of law over definitions unfavorable to violation of law. [Another way of putting this is that he sees more benefits in the counter-institution than in the legitimate institution.]*

This is the principle of differential association. It refers to both criminal and anti-criminal associations and has to do with counteracting forces. When persons become criminal, they do so because of contacts with criminal patterns and also because of isolation from anti-criminal patterns. Any person inevitably assimilates the surrounding culture unless other patterns are in conflict; a Southerner does not pronounce "r" because other Southerners do not pronounce "r." Negatively, this proposition of differential association means that associations which are neutral so far as crime is concerned have little or no effect on the genesis of criminal behavior. Much of the experience of a person is neutral in this sense, e.g., learning to brush one's teeth. This behavior has no negative or positive effect on criminal behavior except as it may be related to associations which are concerned with the legal codes. This neutral behavior is important especially as an occupier of the time of a child so that he is not in contact with criminal behavior during the time he is so engaged in neutral behavior.

7. *Differential associations may vary in frequency, duration, priority, and intensity.* This means that associations with criminal behavior and also associations with anti-criminal behavior vary in those respects. "Frequency" and "duration" as modalities of associations are obvious and need no explanation. "Priority" is assumed to be important in the sense that lawful behavior developed in early childhood may persist throughout life, and also that delinquent behavior developed in early childhood may persist throughout life. This tendency, however, has not been adequately demonstrated, and priority seems to be important principally through its selective influence. "Intensity" is not precisely defined but it has to do with such things as the prestige of the source of a criminal or anti-criminal pattern and with emotional reactions related to the associations. In a precise description of the criminal behavior of a person these modalities would be stated in quantitative form and a mathematical ratio be reached. A formula in this sense has not been developed and the development of such a formula would be extremely difficult.

8. *The process of learning criminal behavior by association with criminal and anti-criminal patterns involves all of the mechanisms that are involved in any other learning.* Negatively, this means that the learning of criminal behavior is not restricted to the process of imitation. A person who is seduced, for instance, learns criminal behavior by association but this process would not ordinarily be described as imitation.

9. *While criminal behavior is an expression of general needs and values, it is not explained by those general needs and values since non-criminal behavior is an expression of the same needs and values.* Thieves generally steal in order to secure money, but likewise honest laborers work in order to secure money. The attempts by many scholars to explain criminal behavior by general drives

and values, such as the happiness principle, striving for social status, the money motive, or frustration, have been and must continue to be futile since they explain lawful behavior as completely as they explain criminal behavior. They are similar to respiration, which is necessary for any behavior but which does not differentiate criminal from non-criminal behavior. [*Thus one must have a theory of experience–social reality conflict to explain the ways in which these general motivations incline people in particular life situations to counter-institutional affiliation.*]

It is not necessary, at this level of explanation, to explain why a person has the associations which he has; this certainly involves a complex of many things. In an area where the delinquency rate is high a boy who is sociable, gregarious, active, and athletic is very likely to come in contact with the other boys in the neighborhood, learn delinquent behavior from them, and become a gangster; in the same neighborhood the psychopathic boy who is isolated, introvert, and inert may remain at home, not become acquainted with the other boys in the neighborhood, and not become delinquent. In another situation, the sociable, athletic, aggressive boy may become a member of a scout troop and not become involved in delinquent behavior. The person's associations are determined in a general context of social organization. A child is ordinarily reared in a family; the place of residence of the family is determined largely by family income; and the delinquency rate is in many respects related to the rental value of the houses. Many other factors enter into this social organization, including many of the small personal group relationships.

□ □ □

Cohen's theoretical statement about the formation of counter-institutions of behavior illustrated the way in which new patterns arose. Sutherland's theory of differential association outlines the factors which incline a person to follow a counter-institution. In the following adaptation by Marie-Anne LeGrand we can follow the path of a person who has no particular values but who does both legitimate and counter-institutional things in the course of making out. The rounder is an illustration of Type 11 in the Expanded Typology of Individual Adaptations, a person whose behavior is conforming or deviant as the situation requires. The rounder is an extreme example of the searching behavior engaged in by a person with an experience–social reality conflict as he is looking for a stable pattern of adaptation. His associations teach him the techniques of many counter-institutions; he will eventually decide to follow one of them or to go straight. He is a "street person" who lives by his wits, but we can see elements of his behavior in the man who is bored with his marriage and possibly seeking an outside liaison, in the student who encounters both alcohol and drug using groups around campus, in the hippie or the ghetto dweller standing on the street corner, as well as the person following a liberal arts course in the university. They are undecided, tentatively sampling many things, not sure what form of behavior to finally follow.

☐ ☐ ☐

14
ROUNDERS

MARIE-ANNE LeGRAND

As one rounder put it: "The term has just always been; it's known to the police and to anyone who's been involved with rounders in one way or another."

Rounders are unspecialized deviants who earn their living by various illegal means—hustling, stealing, conning people, or prostituting themselves. The term "rounder" is used because these people make "rounds" every night seeking out situations where they can make "easy money" and are thus always "around," always available.

A rounder doesn't know specifically what he wants; only that he wishes to make money and will do it any way he can. [*No values, legitimate and counter-institutional behavior.*]

He usually begins by leaving home in his late teenage years or early twenties, and is either lazy or just can't get a job. For lack of things to do, he spends his time walking around the downtown area, sleeping in theatres, and comes into contact with vagabonds, prostitutes, hustlers, and other members of deviant society. Since he needs some money he will try conning someone, or, if desperate enough, will prostitute himself. At this point he has learned a fair amount about the rules and ways of the many deviant institutions and will start finding prostitutes for men, arrange a meeting for a couple of homosexuals—or whatever deal he can arrange that will give him a fair share.

Normally between 18 and 25 years old, a rounder can be anywhere from 13 years up. The maximum age is about thirty for by then he has usually found a specific area of deviance more interesting or profitable or he has rejoined the institutional order. The rounder is usually male but there have been cases of females. (One former rounder I observed was a chess champion and sat in the Honey Dew Restaurant from opening to closing playing chess with anyone who would risk losing a few dollars. *She* almost always won the game.)

The rounder is usually single and may be employed part-time (which constitutes a "good" rounder). In this way he always makes sure that he has enough money. A typical part-time job could be a parking-lot attendant, a salesman, or perhaps a small night-club manager.

Appearance varies. Some are untidy, but a good rounder will always be well dressed. If a well-dressed rounder is not working part-time, he has probably accumulated his wardrobe by: (a) a false credit account,

Adapted from Marie-Anne LeGrand, "Rounders" (unpublished manuscript, Sir George Williams University, Montreal, 1969). Reprinted with permission.

(b) conning people out of clothes in games or bets, (c) using counterfeit money, or (d) stealing clothes in suitcases or from cleaning trucks —wherever opportunity arises.

The usual length of time as a rounder is from about five to ten years —a fairly long prespecialization period, probably due to the ambivalence and lack of orientation most rounders exhibit. In many cases they prefer not to think about the future, subconsciously realizing that it is quite bleak. As one interview with a twenty-four year old rounder showed: "Oh, I don't know what I'll do. I'll get along O.K. I guess."

Some rounders prefer to work alone (a larger profit), but others will work in two's. They are straight-forward only with one or two people— usually their partners. If they work in two's, they will each have their own con-game. One may be a hustler and the other a booster (shoplifter). If they work together for a fairly long time, one will share his profits with his partner if the partner happens to be broke—but the partnerships they form usually are of a very short duration. Rounders know a lot of people, and are usually in and out of touch with them as the situation arises.

Usually during some period of the rounder's life he will have a "family." This is a group of people that he has working for or with him. It might consist of two girls whom he hires out, a couple of rounder-partners; or in some cases, a few rounders and their girl friends who all work together on different con-games and deals. Here, again, as in the case of the two rounders, the profits will be shared, or the rounders and their girls who are doing well will provide room and board for the other couple who is having bad luck. There are at least three or four of these families in every city.

A Rounder's Description: "Depending on how broke I am depends on what time of day I start. Also what particular con-game I am playing at the time.

"If I am playing a day-time game I will just be *around* (term rounder) at night to see and meet other rounders and friends, but if I have a chance to make a buck, I will.

"If I am playing a night-time game, I'll start anywhere from 2 P.M. to 6 P.M.

"Maybe I'll go to the main restaurant and see what friends are around and then go from one hang-out to another, pool-halls, restaurants, prostitute hang-outs, bus and train stations, "gay-joints," and later on in the evening to different bars, clip-joints, anywhere where I can find a mark, or run into the night people—to make a buck.

"After the clubs close it's good to go from restaurant to restaurant where people go to eat after clubbing— then I go back to the hang-outs 'til four or five in the morning.

"I will hustle a queer sometimes, but if not will find a hustler for the queer.

"I'll take any deal, from 25 cents to clothes, in plain English—anything possible."

An example of a deal: In following one rounder on his course, I noticed that he must have been hungry and stopped into the A. & W. He sat on one side of the counter and ordered a big meal—then sat on the other side of the counter and ordered a coffee. When he got up from the counter he went over and paid his coffee bill and left.

Rounders will usually try anything to get out of paying money.

They also seem to have a knack for spotting policemen and plain-clothes detectives. While I was accompanying one rounder on his round, he kept remarking every half-hour or so "There's one." Finally I realized he was referring to police detectives, and when I asked him how he was able to distinguish them, he just answered: "You can tell them a mile away."

The rounder legitimates his life by holding that his past work or his past acquaintances prevent him from getting a full-time "straight" job. He may blame his parents for driving him out of the house in the first place; or may justify himself by saying that if people want to be fooled, it is their own fault. Rounder: "I get a good laugh after, off the suckers I con."

To them every straight person is a "mark."

AFTER-EFFECTS

It is possible for the rounder to become a normal member of the institutional order, with a nine-to-five job—but he will usually find himself reverting back to some of his con-lines on occasions.

As one rounder put it: "You never completely stop once you've started—the effects are 'in your blood.'"

However, this was possibly a legitimation with some rounders for not making a full attempt to go straight.

Becoming part of the institutional order can be difficult for them; rounders often meet people they worked with or people they've conned. They are everywhere—so come into contact with a great number of people. They may have a police record, or they may be known to the police and be picked up for questioning from time to time.

CONCLUSION

In this paper, I hope to have presented the rounder as an essential and concrete interactive link between the various institutions of deviant society. The period of time as a rounder (approximately five to ten years) can be compared to the university training of members of the institutional order. Both are periods of prespecialization and of learning, relating and choosing; for the student, an accumulation of knowledge; for the rounder, a training in the ways and techniques of the deviant world.

☐ ☐ ☐

Institutions of behavior, legitimate or not, vary widely in their complexity and therefore in the instruction that a recruit requires. It requires more training to be a doctor than to be a truck driver. It requires more training to be a professional thief than to knock over a gas station. It requires more training to be a prostitute than to smoke marijuana. But even the most simple institution of behavior must have the "how to do it" knowledge transmitted if it is to be passed on, and this generally requires some legitimation.

In learning to smoke marijuana both techniques and legitimations are transmitted. The novice generally encounters a group where marijuana is already used. When he indicates that he would like to join in, the joint is passed to him. Anyone who has ever seen a person smoking marijuana for the first time knows what happens next: he takes too shallow a puff, doesn't hold it in long enough, and is so afraid that he has started on the road to heroin that he wouldn't notice any effect more subtle than a sledge-hammer blow to the back of his head. He must learn several things and redefine several things before he can really enjoy the mild intoxication that marijuana produces. First of all, he must learn how to do it: take a long drag followed by some air, and hold it until he *has* to exhale. Additionally he will have to learn the etiquette of smoking, passing the joint, not "hogging" the joint, and being cool about where he talks about it. In time he will have to learn how to roll joints, how to clean marijuana through a strainer, who to buy lids from, how to tell whether it has been sugared, what the going prices are for Acapulco Gold, Panama Red, California Brown, and the ordinary weed his dealer handles. Before he goes on to learn all this technical data, though, he must be "decontaminated" of all the incorrect knowledge of the drug he has received from his parents, newspapers, and the drug booklets put out by the Narcotics Bureau. He may have to learn that it is not addictive, that the effects are temporary, that it doesn't lead to shooting heroin, or to mass murders.

When the novice's head has been sufficiently decontaminated so that he can relax while smoking, the experienced users will point out to him the sensations caused by the drug, the ability to really get into music, typical "high" conversations, the fact that he is hungry, and that fruit juice tastes better than alcohol. After smoking a few times the novice has picked up the basic techniques, the basic legitimations, a knowledge of what it is like to be "high," and a more relaxed attitude toward the experience. At this point he will learn that it takes successively smaller quantities of marijuana to reach a pleasurable stage of intoxication, and while it took him five whole joints to go up the first time, he can now do it with three or four tokes. In the process of learning the counter-institution of behavior he also picks up the pattern of communication, the specialized words and ways of saying things which allow him to communicate within the group. I have used some of these words here; if you don't know what they mean, ask the first long-haired college student you meet for illumination and guidance. According to a May 1969 Gallup poll, over a fifth of the college students in the United States have smoked marijuana, and many would contend that this is now a serious underestimate. In any event, these are the three things that must be learned in beginning to follow a counter-institution: how to do it; why it is good; why it is not bad.

Behavior and Legitimations □ The behavior involved in learning to get high is not very complicated—not seriously more complicated than learning to get drunk without getting sick. Many counter-institutions are this simple. Others, such as prostitution, require a more extended training period because they are more complex, and because they are dominant life roles, occupations that require full-time attention. In the following adaptation James Bryan explores the apprenticeship period in learning to be a prostitute. The same *types* of things are learned— how to do it, why it is good, why it is not bad—but they are learned in much greater detail over a longer period of time.
□ □ □

15

APPRENTICESHIPS IN PROSTITUTION

JAMES H. BRYAN

This paper provides some detailed, albeit preliminary, information concerning induction and training in a particular type of deviant career: prostitution, at the call girl level. It describes the order of events, and their surrounding structure, which future call girls experience in entering their occupation.

The respondents in this study were 33 prostitutes, all currently or previously working in the Los Angeles area. They ranged in age from 18 to 32, most being in their mid-twenties. None of the interviewees were obtained through official law enforcement agencies, but seven were found within the context of a neuropsychiatric hospital. The remaining respondents were gathered primarily through individual referrals from previous participants in the study. There were no obvious differences between the "psychiatric sample" and the other interviewees on the data to be reported.

All subjects in the sample were call girls. That is, they typically obtained their clients by individual referrals, primarily by telephone, and enacted the sexual contract in their own or their clients' place of residence or employment. They did not initiate contact with their customers in bars, streets, or houses of prostitution, although they might meet their customers at any number of locations by pre-arrangement. The minimum fee charged per sexual encounter was $20.00. As an adjunct to the call girl interviews, three pimps and two "call boys" were interviewed as well.

Approximately two thirds of the sample were what are sometimes known as "outlaw broads"; that is, they were not under the supervision of a pimp when interviewed. There is evidence that the majority of pimps who were aware of the study prohibited the girls under their direction from participating in it. It should be noted that many members of the sample belonged to one or another clique; their individually expressed opinions may not be independent.

The interviews strongly suggest that there are marked idiosyncrasies from one geographical area to another in such practices as fee-splitting, involvement with peripheral occupations (e.g., cabbies), and so forth. For example, there appears to be little direct involvement of peripheral occupations with call girl activities in the Los Angeles area, while it

Adapted from James H. Bryan, "Apprenticeships in Prostitution," *Social Problems*, Vol. 12, No. 3, Winter, 1965, 287–297. Reprinted by permission of the author and The Society for the Study of Social Problems.

has been estimated that up to 10% of the population of Las Vegas is directly involved in activities of prostitutes. What may be typical for a call girl in the Los Angeles area is not necessarily typical for a girl in New York, Chicago, Las Vegas, or Miami.

.   .   .

All but two interviews were tape recorded. All respondents had prior knowledge that the interview would be tape recorded. The interviewing was, for the most part, done at the girls' place of work and/or residence. Occasional interviews were conducted in the investigator's office, and one in a public park. Interviews were semi-structured and employed open-ended questions. One part of the interview concerned the apprenticeship period or "turning out" process.

THE ENTRANCE

> I had been thinking about it [becoming a call girl] before a lot . . . Thinking about wanting to do it, but I had no connections. Had I not had a connection, I probably wouldn't have started working . . . I thought about starting out . . . Once I tried it [without a contact] . . . I met this guy at a bar and I tried to make him pay me, but the thing is, you can't do it that way because they are romantically interested in you, and they don't think that it is on that kind of basis. You can't all of a sudden come up and want money for it, you have to be known beforehand . . . I think that is what holds a lot of girls back who might work. I think I might have started a year sooner had I had a connection. You seem to make one contact or another . . . if it's another girl or a pimp or just someone who will set you up and get you a client . . . You can't just, say, get an apartment and get a phone in and everything and say, "Well, I'm gonna start business," because you gotta get clients from somewhere. There has to be a contact.

Immediately prior to entrance into the occupation, all but one girl had personal contact with someone professionally involved in call girl activities (pimps or other call girls) [*That is, they had an interactive contact that could be used to learn about the counter-institution.*] The one exception had contact with a customer of call girls. While various occupational groups (e.g., photographers) seem to be peripherally involved, often unwittingly, with the call girl, there was no report of individuals involved in such occupations being contacts for new recruits. The novice's initial contact is someone at the level at which she will eventually enter the occupation: not a street-walker, but a call girl; not a pimp who manages girls out of a house of prostitution, but a pimp who manages call girls.

Approximately half of the girls reported that their initial contact for entrance into the profession was another "working girl." The nature of these relationships is quite variable. In some cases, the girls have been long standing friends. Other initial contacts involved sexual relationships between a Lesbian and the novice. Most, however, had known each other less than a year, and did not appear to have a very close relationship, either in the sense of time spent together or of biographical information exchanged. The relationship may begin with the aspiring call girl soliciting the contact. That is, if a professional is known to others as a call girl, she will be sought out and approached by females who are strangers.

> I haven't ever gone out and looked for one. All of these have fell right into my hands . . . They turned themselfs out . . . They come to me for help.

Whatever their relationship, whenever the professional agrees to aid the beginner, she also, it appears, implicitly assumes responsibility for training her. This is evidenced by the fact that only one such female contact referred the aspirant to another girl for any type of help. Data are not available as to the reason for this unusual referral.

If the original contact was not another call girl but a pimp, a much different relationship is developed and the career follows a somewhat different course. The relationship between pimp and girl is typically one of lovers, not friends:

> . . . because I love him very much. Obviously, I'm doing this mostly for him . . . I'd do anything for him. I'm not just saying I will, I am . . . [After discussing his affair with another woman] I just decided that I knew what he was when I decided to do this for him and I decided I had two choices—either accept it or not, and I accepted it, and I have no excuse. [*The legitimation of love.*]

Occasionally, however, a strictly business relationship will be formed:

> Right now I am buying properties, and as soon as I can afford it, I am buying stocks . . . It is strictly a business deal. This man and I are friends, our relationship ends there. He handles all the money, he is making all the investments and I trust him. We have a legal document drawn up which states that half the investments are mine, half of them his, so I am protected. [*The legitimation of a business enterprise.*]

Whether the relationship is love or business, the pimp solicits the new girl.* It is usually agreed that the male will have an important

---

* Two of the pimps denied that this was very often so and maintained that the girls will solicit them. The degree to which they are solicited seems to depend upon the nature and extent of their reputations. It is difficult to judge the accuracy of these reports as there appears to be a strong taboo against admitting to such solicitation.

managerial role in the course of the girl's career, and that both will enjoy the gains from the girl's activities for an indefinite period:

> Actually a pimp has to have complete control or else its like trouble with him. Because if a pimp doesn't, if she is not madly in love with him or something in some way, a pimp won't keep a girl.

Once the girl agrees to function as a call girl, the male, like his female counterpart, undertakes the training of the girl, or refers the girl to another call girl for training. Either course seems equally probable. Referrals, when employed, are typically to friends and, in some cases, wives or ex-wives.

Although the data are limited, it appears that the pimp retains his dominance over the trainee even when the latter is being trained by a call girl. The girl trainer remains deferential to the pimp's wishes regarding the novice.

APPRENTICESHIP

Once a contact is acquired and the decision to become a call girl made, the recruit moves to the next stage in the career sequence: the apprenticeship period. The structure of the apprenticeship will be described, followed by a description of the content most frequently communicated during this period.

The apprenticeship is typically served under the direction of another call girl, but may occasionally be supervised by a pimp. Twenty-four girls in the sample initially worked under the supervision of other girls. The classroom is, like the future place of work, an apartment. The apprentice typically serves in the trainer's apartment, either temporarily residing with the trainer or commuting there almost daily. The novice rarely serves her apprenticeship in such places as a house of prostitution, motel, or on the street. It is also infrequent that the girl is transported out of her own city to serve an apprenticeship. Although the data are not extensive, the number of girls being trained simultaneously by a particular trainer has rarely been reported to be greater than three. Girls sometimes report spending up to eight months in training, but the average stay seems to be two or three months. The trainer controls all referrals and appointments, novices seemingly not having much control over the type of sexual contract made or the circumstances surrounding the enactment of the contract.

The structure of training under the direction of a pimp seems similar, though information is more limited. The girls are trained in an apartment in the city they intend to work and for a short period of time.

There is some evidence that the pimp and the novice often do not share the same apartment as might the novice and the girl trainer. There appear to be two reasons for the separation of pimp and girl. First, it is not uncommonly thought that cues which suggest the presence of other men displease the girl's customers:

> Well, I would never let them know that I had a lover, which is something that you never ever let a john know, because this makes them very reticent to give you money, because they think you are going to go and spend it with your lover, which is what usually happens. [*This is part of the technical knowledge of the counter-institution.*]

. . .

Secondly, the legal repercussions are much greater, of course, for the pimp who lives with his girl than for two girls rooming together. As one pimp of 19 years experience puts it:

> It is because of the law. There is a law that is called the illegal cohabitation that they rarely use unless the man becomes big in stature. If he is a big man in the hustling world, the law then employs any means at their command . . .

Because of the convenience in separation of housing, it is quite likely that the pimp is less directly involved with the day-to-day training of the girls than the call girl trainer.

The content of the training period seems to consist of two broad, interrelated dimensions, one philosophical, the other interpersonal. The former refers to the imparting of a value structure, the latter to "dos" and "don'ts" of relating to customers and secondarily, to other "working girls" and pimps. [*Legitimations and patterns of expected behavior.*] The latter teaching is perhaps best described by the concept of a short range perspective. That is, most of the "dos" and "don'ts" pertain to ideas and actions that the call girl uses in problematic situations. Not all girls absorb these teachings, and those who do incorporate them in varying degrees.

Insofar as a value structure is transmitted it is that of maximizing gains while minimizing effort, even if this requires transgressions of either a legal or moral nature. Frequently, it is postulated that people, particularly men, are corrupt or easily corruptible, that all social relationships are but a reflection of a "con," and that prostitution is simply a more honest or at least no more dishonest act than the everyday behavior of "squares." [*Legitimations that are useful for the self-esteem of the prostitute.*] Furthermore, not only are "johns" basically exploitative, but they are easily exploited; hence they are, in some respects, stupid. As explained by a pimp:

> . . . [in the hustling world] the trick or the john is known as a fool . . . this is not the truth . . . He [the younger pimp] would teach his woman that a trick was a fool.

Since the male is corrupt, or honest only because he lacks the opportunity to be corrupt, then it is only appropriate that he be exploited as he exploits.

> Girls first start making their "scores"—say one guy keeps them for a while or maybe she gets, you know, three or four grand out of him, say a car or a coat. These are your scores . . .

The general assumption that man is corrupt is empirically confirmed when the married male betrays his wife, when the moralist, secular or religious, betrays his publicly stated values, or when the "john" "stiffs" (cheats) the girl. [*This allows the condemnation of the condemners, mentioned by Sykes and Matza.*] An example of the latter is described by a girl as she reflects upon her disillusionment during her training period.

> It is pretty rough when you are starting out. You get stiffed a lot of times . . . Oh sure. They'll take advantage of you anytime they can. And I'm a trusting soul, I really am. I'll believe anybody till they prove different. I've made a lot of mistakes that way. You get to the point, well, Christ, what the heck can I believe in people, they tell me one thing and here's what they do to me.

Values such as fairness with other working girls, or fidelity to a pimp, may occasionally be taught. To quote a pimp:

> So when you ask me if I teach a kind of basic philosophy, I would say that you could say that. Because you try to teach them in an amoral way that there is a right and wrong way as pertains to this game . . . and then you teach them that when working with other girls to try to treat the other girl fairly because a woman's worst enemy in the street [used in both a literal and figurative sense] is the other woman and only by treating the other women decently can she expect to get along . . . Therefore the basic philosophy I guess would consist of a form of honesty, a form of sincerity and complete fidelity to her man [pimp].

It should be noted, however, that behavior based on enlightened self-interest with concomitant exploitation is not limited to customer relationships. Interviewees frequently mentioned a pervasive feeling of distrust between trainer and trainee, and such incidents as thefts or betrayal of confidences are occasionally reported and chronically guarded against.

Even though there may be considerable pressure upon the girl to accept this value structure, many of them (perhaps the majority of the sample) reject it.

> People have told me that I wasn't turned out, but turned loose instead . . . Someone who is turned out is turned out to believe in a certain code of behavior, and this involves having a pimp, for one thing. It also involves never experiencing anything but hatred or revulsion for "tricks" for another thing. It involves always getting the money in front [before the sexual act] and a million little things that are very strictly adhered to by those in the "in group," which I am not. . . . Never being nice or pleasant to a trick unless you are doing it for the money, getting more money. [How did you learn that?] It was explained to me over a period of about six months. I learned that you were doing it to make money for yourself so that you could have nice things and security . . . [Who would teach you this?] [The trainer] would teach me this. [*The "million little things" are all the minute techniques of "how to do it" that are transmitted to the novice.*]

It seems reasonable to assume that the value structure serves, in general, to create in-group solidarity and to alienate the girl from "square" society, and that this structure serves the political advantage of the trainer and the economic gains of the trainee more than it allays the personal anxieties of either. In fact, failure to adopt these values at the outset does not appear to be correlated with much personal distress. As one girl describes her education experiences:

> Some moral code. We're taught, as a culture . . . it's there and after awhile you live, breathe, and eat it. Now, what makes you go completely against everything that's inside you, everything that you have been taught, and the whole society, to do things like this? [*The legitimations have not been sufficient to overcome this girl's biographical discontinuity crisis that arose when she shifted into counter-institutional patterns.*]

Good empirical evidence, however, concerning the functions and effectiveness of this value structure with regard to subjective comfort is lacking.

A series of deductions derived from the premises indicated above serve to provide, in part, the "rules" of interpersonal contact with the customer. Each customer is to be seen as a "mark," and "pitches" are to be **made**.

[Did you have a standard pitch?] It's sort of amusing. I used to listen to my girl friend [trainer]. She was the greatest at this telephone type of situation. She would call up and cry and say that people had come to her door . . . She'd cry and she'd complain and she'd say "I have a bad check at the liquor store, and they sent the police over," and really . . . a girl has a story she tells the man . . . Anything, you know, so he'll help her out. Either it's the rent or she needs a car, or doctor's bills, or any number of things.

Any unnecessary interaction with the customer is typically frowned upon, and the trainee will receive exhortations to be quick about her business. One girl in her fourth week of work explains:

[What are some of the other don'ts that you have learned about?] Don't take so much time . . . The idea is to get rid of them as quickly as possible.

Other content taught concerns specific information about specific customers:

. . . she would go around the bar and say, now look at that man over there, he's this way and that way, and this is what he would like and these are what his problems are . . .
. . . she would teach me what the men wanted and how much to get, what to say when I got there . . . just a line to hand them.

Training may also include proprieties concerning consuming alcohol and drugs, when and how to obtain the fee, how to converse with the customers, and, occasionally, physical and sexual hygiene. As a girl trainer explains:

First of all, impress cleanliness. Because, on the whole, the majority of girls, I would say, I don't believe there are any cleaner women walking the streets, because they've got to be aware of any type of body odor . . . You teach them to French [fellatio] and how to talk to men.

Personal cleanliness is an attempt to counter the idea that prostitutes carry disease.

(Do they [pimps] teach you during the turning out period how to make a telephone call?) Oh, usually, yes. They don't teach you, they just tell you how to do it and you do it with your good common sense, but if you have trouble, they tell you more about it.

Interestingly, the specific act of telephoning a client is often distressing to the novice and is of importance in her training. Unfortunately for the girl, it is an act she must perform with regularity as she does considerable soliciting. One suspects that such behavior is embarrassing for her because it is an unaccustomed role for her to play—she has so recently come from a culture where young women do *not* telephone men for dates. Inappropriate sex-role behavior seems to produce greater personal distress than does appropriate sex-role behavior even when it is morally reprehensible.

> Well, it is rather difficult to get on the telephone, when you've never worked before, and talk to a man about a subject like that, and it is very new to you.

What is omitted from the training should be noted as well. There seems to be little instruction concerning sexual techniques as such, even though the previous sexual experience of the trainee may have been quite limited. What instruction there is typically revolves around the practice of fellatio. There seems to be some encouragement not to experience sexual orgasms with the client, though this may be quite variable with the trainer.

> . . . and sometimes, I don't know if it's a set rule or maybe it's an unspoken rule, you don't enjoy your dates.
>
> Yes, he did [teach attitudes]. He taught me to be cold . . .

It should be stressed that, if the girls originally accepted such instructions and values, many of them, at least at the time of interviewing, verbalized a rejection of these values and reported behavior which departed considerably from the interpersonal rules stipulated as "correct" by their trainers. Some experience orgasms with the customer, some show considerable affect toward "johns," others remain drunk or "high" throughout the contact. While there seems to be general agreement as to what the rules of interpersonal conduct are, there appears to be considerable variation in the adoption of such rules. [*The rules of counter-institutions may also produce experience–social reality conflicts, and may not be closely followed.*]

A variety of methods are employed to communicate the content described above. The trainer may arrange to eavesdrop on the interactions of girl and client and then discuss the interaction with her. One trainer, for example, listened through a closed door to the interaction of a new girl with a customer, then immediately after he left, discussed, in a rather heated way, methods by which his exit may have been facilitated. A pimp relates:

> The best way to do this [teaching conversation] is, in the beginning, when the phone rings, for instance . . . is to listen to what she says

and then check and see how big a trick he is and then correct her from there.

. . . with everyone of them [trainees] I would make it a point to see two guys to see how they [the girls] operate.

In one case a girl reported that her pimp left a written list of rules pertaining to relating to "johns." Direct teaching, however, seems to be uncommon. The bulk of whatever learning takes place seems to take place through observation. [*Important nuances of behavior are very difficult to explain formally; this is the value of guided experience in learning any complex job.*]

It's hard to tell you, because we learn through observations.

But I watched her and listened to what her bit was on the telephone.

To summarize, the structure of the apprenticeship period seems quite standard. The novice receives her training either from a pimp or from another more experienced call girl, more often the latter. She serves her initial two to eight months of work under the trainer's supervision and often serves this period in the trainer's apartment. The trainer assumes responsibility for arranging contacts and negotiating the type and place of the sexual encounter.

The content of the training pertains both to a general philosophical stance and to some specifics (usually not sexual) of interpersonal behavior with customers and colleagues. The philosophy is one of exploiting the exploiters (customers) by whatever means necessary and defining the colleagues of the call girl as being intelligent, self-interested and, in certain important respects, basically honest individuals. The interpersonal techniques addressed during the learning period consist primarily of "pitches," telephone conversations, personal and occasionally sexual hygiene, prohibitions against alcohol and dope while with a "john," how and when to obtain the fee, and specifics concerning the sexual habits of particular customers. Specific sexual techniques are very rarely taught. The current sample included a considerable number of girls who, although capable of articulating this value structure, were not particularly inclined to adopt it.

CONTACTS AND CONTRACTS

While the imparting of ideologies and proprieties to the prospective call girl is emphasized during the apprenticeship period, it appears that the primary function of the apprenticeship, at least for the trainee, is building a clientele. Since this latter function limits the degree of occupational socialization, the process of developing the clientele and the arrangements made between trainer and trainee will be discussed.

Lists ("books") with the names and telephone numbers of customers are available for purchase from other call girls or pimps, but such books are often considered unreliable. While it is also true that an occasional pimp will refer customers to girls, this does not appear to be a frequent practice. The most frequent method of obtaining such names seems to be through contacts developed during the apprenticeship. The trainer refers customers to the apprentice and oversees the latter in terms of her responsibility and adequacy in dealing with the customer. For referring the customer, the trainer receives forty to fifty per cent of the total price agreed upon in the contract negotiated by the trainer and customer.* The trainer and trainees further agree, most often explicitly, on the apprentice's "right" to obtain and to use, on further occasions, information necessary for arranging another sexual contract with the "john" without the obligation of further "kickback" to the trainer. That is, if she can obtain the name and telephone number of the customer, she can negotiate another contract without fee-splitting. During this period, then, the girl is not only introduced to other working colleagues (pimps and girls alike) but also develops a clientele.

There are two obvious advantages for a call girl in assuming the trainer role. First, since there seems to be an abundant demand for new girls, and since certain service requirements demand more than one girl, even the well established call girl chronically confronts the necessity for making referrals. It is then reasonable to assume that the extra profit derived from the fee-splitting activities, together with the added conveniences of having a girl "on call" allows the trainer to profit considerably from this arrangement. Secondly, contacts with customers are reputedly extremely difficult to maintain if services are not rendered on demand. Thus, the adoption of the trainer role enables the girl to maintain contacts with "fickle" customers under circumstances where she may wish a respite from the sexual encounter without terminating the contacts necessary for re-entry into the call girl role. It is also possible that the financial gains may conceivably be much greater for most trainers than for most call girls, but this is a moot point.

---

* The fee-splitting arrangement is quite common at all levels of career activity. For example, cooperative activity between two girls is often required for a particular type of sexual contract. In these cases, the girl who has contracted with the customer will contact a colleague, usually a friend, and will obtain 40%–50% of the latter's earnings. There is suggestive evidence that fee-splitting activities vary according to geographical areas and that Los Angeles is unique for both its fee-splitting patterns and the rigidity of its fee-splitting structure.

A final aspect of the apprenticeship period that should be noted is the novice's income. It is possible for the novice, under the supervision of a competent and efficient trainer, to earn a great deal of money, or at least to get a favorable glimpse of the great financial possibilities of the occupation and, in effect, be heavily rewarded for her decision to enter it. Even though the novice may be inexperienced in both the sexual and interpersonal techniques of prostitution, her novelty on the market gives her an immediate advantage over her more experienced competitors. It seems quite likely that the new girl, irrespective of her particular physical or mental qualities, has considerable drawing power because she provides new sexual experience to the customer. Early success and financial reward may well provide considerable incentive to continue in the occupation. [*Following the counter-institution provides benefits.*]

A final word is needed regarding the position of the pimp vis-à-vis the call girl during the apprenticeship period. While some pimps assume the responsibility for training the girl personally, as indicated above, as many send the novice to another girl. The most apparent reason for such referral is that it facilitates the development of the "book." Purposes of training appear to be secondary for two reasons: (1) The pimp often lacks direct contact with the customers, so he personally cannot aid directly in the development of the girl's clientele; (2) When the pimp withdraws his girl from the training context, it is rarely because she has obtained adequate knowledge of the profession. This is not to say that all pimps are totally unconcerned with the type of knowledge being imparted to the girl. Rather, the primary concern of the pimp is the girl's developing a clientele, not learning the techniques of sex or conversation.

The apprenticeship period usually ends abruptly, not smoothly. Its termination may be but a reflection of interpersonal difficulties between trainer and trainee, novice and pimp, or between two novices. Occasionally termination of training is brought about through the novice's discovery and subsequent theft of the trainer's "book." Quite frequently, the termination is due to the novice's developing a sufficient trade or other business opportunities. The point is, however, that no respondent has reported that the final disruption of the apprenticeship was the result of the completion of adequate training. While disruptions of this relationship may be due to personal or impersonal events, termination is not directly due to the development of sufficient skills. [*The career paths in counter-institutions are unlikely to be as formally rational as in legitimated institutions.*]

☐ ☐ ☐

We have now examined the two ways in which a person may come to be involved in counter-institutions of behavior, creating his own or joining an existing one. In each case the most important step was the beginning of face-to-face interaction with a person who shared the problem or a person already in a counter-institution. From this interaction, behavior and legitimations had to be created or learned. Most people join existing counter-institutions, a few create new ones. Institutions of behavior newly created in response to reality flaws are in many ways more interesting to study than existing counter-institutions. An emerging institution may go through many stages, it may grow or die, it may become finally defined as legitimate or illegitimate, and as it goes through these stages it illustrates many things about the workings of institutions and values in our socially constructed reality.

☐ ☐ ☐

□ □ □

People get together in new institutions because they feel that these patterns of behavior are better alternatives; they continue to follow these patterns of behavior because they find them rewarding. If enough people have similar conflicts with social reality and find the behavior forms of a counter-institution rewarding, the counter-institution will grow in numbers and influence. While these general assertions seem self-evident, the underlying processes are often quite complex. Let us examine some counter-institutions of behavior and see if we can find the factors that are involved in their growth, survival, or demise.

First, a counter-institution that maintains itself, but is probably not growing in numbers of influence—the bottle gang on Skid Row. The legitimate institutions of drinking include public drinking places, taverns and restaurants, and private drinking in homes. The inhabitant of Skid Row seldom has the money to patronize a tavern, and usually has no home in which to drink. His life experience conflicts with the

COUNTER-
INSTITUTIONS

institutions legitimated by social reality, and he establishes a counter-institution that serves his needs better—the bottle gang. In the following adaptation James Rooney describes the bottle gang as he observed it by living in the Skid Row sections of several California cities.

☐ ☐ ☐

16

GROUP PROCESSES AMONG SKID ROW WINOS
A Reevaluation of the Undersocialization Hypothesis
JAMES F. ROONEY

SOCIAL RELATIONS ON SKID ROW

Men on Skid Row clearly do not participate in social relations in a manner which characterizes the other classes in American society. Close examination reveals, however, that even the most enculturated groups of Skid Row drinkers manifest consistent efforts to structure situations so as to involve interpersonal contact and emotional reinforcement. The investigator in his field of work has found that winos do participate in cooperative activities and form social groups in which they experience the rewards of belonging, prestige, and a feeling of security. Yet they strive to accomplish these ends in ways distinctively different from those of other classes of society.

These unattached men attempt to satisfy their need for interpersonal contacts by structuring social relations around an activity which meets one of their major physical needs—purchasing and drinking wine. [*The counter-institution satisfies more than one requirement; it is not an independent act isolated from other living processes.*]

GROUP PROCESSES

The quality of the interactional pattern of winos perhaps may be best interpreted according to a dichotomy of group processes proposed by Hubert S. Coffey:* socio-group processes and psyche-group processes. The socio-group process is that by which the members consciously seek out external goals and direct their activities toward the selected goals. Psyche-group processes are those by which group members find satisfaction of their own emotional needs for interpersonal contact but are not concerned with the attainment of an external goal.

Coffey points out that few human groups fulfill either socio- or psyche-group functions exclusively. Most socio-groups have a latent function of partially meeting the members' psychic needs through the

Adapted from James F. Rooney, "Group Processes among Skid Row Winos: A Reevaluation of the Undersocialization Hypothesis," *Quarterly Journal of Studies on Alcohol,* Vol. 22, 1961, pp. 444–460. Reprinted with permission of the author and the Rutgers Center of Alcohol Studies, Rutgers University, New Brunswick, N.J.

*Coffey, H. S., "Socio and Psyche Group Processes: Integrative Concepts," *Journal of Social Issues,* 3, 65–74, 1952.

interaction which occurs in conducting the contractual relations. Conversely, most groups in which the members interact primarily for personal satisfaction accomplish this objective through participation in goal-focused activities. Hence, nearly every group combines both psyche-group and socio-group processes, and focuses on the business involved in achievement while simultaneously meeting the members' needs for interpersonal contact.

The Skid Row winos integrate these two aspects of group process in procuring their most imminent felt need: alcohol. Individuals band together, pool resources and purchase their wine communally. The purchasing of wine by a group of men fulfills two functions simultaneously: (1) it permits individuals with very limited financial resources to purchase the maximum amount of alcohol per monetary unit; (2) the interpersonal association resulting from this transaction permits satisfaction of emotional needs for personal contact. The former is a socio-group function; the latter is a psyche-group function. In the following section the economic aspect or socio-group functions of communal purchasing of wine will be examined.

FORMATION OF THE BOTTLE GROUP

Socio-Group Functions

Men who can afford to drink hard liquor in taverns, or who prefer beer, can meet social needs by associating with other tavern habitués. The men in the wino group cannot afford to purchase hard liquor nor can they satisfy their need for alcohol with beer. They are thus forced to drink fortified wine, the beverage which provides the most alcohol per penny. Purchasing wine by the bottle is much cheaper than wine over the bar. This places poverty-stricken winos in an economic dilemma, for they can purchase little wine with the small sums they beg or earn by odd jobs. Their poverty could prevent them from experiencing both the satisfactions derived from liquor and those of interpersonal contact. The winos, however, have capitalized on their deficits and have developed an alternate institution capable of satisfying both economic and social needs simultaneously. This institution is the wino bottle group.

The wino bottle group or "bottle gang" is similar to a corporate group in that a number of individuals pool their capital for a common goal. The management of the capital is handled by a leader who acts as general chairman. Each member is a stockholder and maintains rights to consumption of the communally purchased bottle of wine.

A bottle group is developed through the efforts of an initiator with some capital who recruits other members willing and able to contribute to the purchase of a bottle. [*Any institution of behavior must be enacted to exist. The knowledge necessary may exist in many minds but real people must actually follow the pattern of behavior for us to speak of an institution of behavior. Any joint effort must be started by someone, someone who has the motivation to exert himself.*] The initiator must have a "substantial" sum to start with—at least 10 cents. However, two or three regular associates may pool nickels and pennies to the amount of one-third or one-half the price of a bottle and then go out to look for other investors.

The initiator and the other members proceed along the sidewalk asking passers-by whether they are interested in "going in on a bottle." The solicitor has the obligation to inform the prospective partner of the amount of money collected and the number of men with whom he will have to share the wine, for example: "Three of us have 28 cents in on a bottle. Do you want to get in on it?" As the statement is made the leader holds the announced cash out in his hand so that the prospect may know the offer is genuine and that he is not being exploited to purchase wine for a group of destitute "promoters." Thus the prospective stockholder can appraise the value of the corporation before investing. [*Before a third party can be recruited he must be shown clearly how he will benefit from his participation in the counter-institution.*]

If the solicited person has sufficient money and is willing to participate, he gives his contribution to the leader. The handing over of money toward the purchase of a "jug" of wine establishes a contractual relation by which a contributor becomes a member of the group. The contract forms a corporation in which the members hold certain rights to the consumption of the proposed bottle of wine, and the leader has the obligation to purchase and share the wine with the members. The size of the group is governed by the price of a bottle and is usually between three and five men. The corporation continues in existence until the emptying of the bottle dissolves the contract. [*Enacting an institution of behavior places some obligation on the cooperating participants to interact with one another until the institution has run its course. This obligation may be self-interest, for the members, and reputation, for the leader.*]

Although the actual drinking group as such does not have temporal continuity, there are both temporary and quite regular associates in these bottle groups. Men living permanently in one Skid Row area may become regular associates by the fact of engaging in the common activity of group drinking. Because each individual frequently seeks drinking companions, these men often join forces and may thereby develop specialized patterns of interpersonal responses. Frequent participation may promote recognition of a special relationship between a group of men who then can come to regard themselves as a clique distinct from others. [*More or less extensive interpersonal relationships may grow up among people participating in a counter-institution.*]

Two factors prevent the development of a strong feeling of group solidarity: First, the boundaries of the clique are seldom defined. Almost any individual is substitutable for another. The only reason the clique has continuity is that the same men are there day after day in the same habitat. [*Mutual involvement in the institution of territory, Skid Row, facilitates the recurrent enacting of the counter-institution by the same individuals.*] Second, the members appear not to make close personal ties but, instead, tend to interact in an instrumental pattern, not making great adjustments to individual personality differences. [*The counter-institution may be enacted by almost any collection of individuals who have the same experience–social reality conflict.*]

Temporary associates are men who have never met previously or who meet only infrequently and hence have not developed any sense of group identity. The membership of the bottle group at any one time, however, is determined strictly by those available men who are willing and able to "go in on a bottle." [*The "how to do it" of this counter-institution is not difficult to learn; it can be transmitted in seconds.*] This most frequently will include those who associate regularly by reason of their spatial proximity, but actually includes also any available men who have funds to contribute. The so-called "permanent" bottle gangs, then, are composed of a core of regular associates with one or two strangers recruited expediently. The "temporary" groups are composed of men who most likely never met before but are brought together for an occasion of wine drinking and social interaction.

The bottle gang is not an on-going association with temporal continuity. As stated above, the emptying of the bottle dissolves the contract. At this time some members may leave. Those wishing to "go in on another bottle" then assess their finances and go out again to recruit the necessary additional individuals to finance another bottle. Although there may be carry-over of personnel, each group is started anew with each new bottle.

Psyche-Group Functions

The formation of a bottle gang and the consequent contractual relations, as described, are socio-group functions of wine-drinking activity. The psyche-group functions or structured interpersonal contacts which fulfill emotional needs will now be examined, beginning with the leader's role.

The Leader–Host ☐ The role of initiator or leader requires the performance of exactly prescribed duties. It calls for the exertion of more effort in soliciting additional members for the purchase of the bottle, as well as for serving as treasurer. In addition, the leader actually plays the psyche-function role of host to the men in the group. [*These rewards provide him with the motivation required for taking the initiative in enacting the counter-institution.*] When sufficient money has been acquired, the leader enters a liquor store or tavern and makes the purchase, selecting the variety of wine to be consumed. In California, tokay is by far the most popular variety on Skid Row, with muscatel, port and sherry following in order. Rarely does anyone make a suggestion as to which variety of wine should be selected. This is the prerogative of the leader. The purchase completed, the buyer places the bottle in an inner pocket of his coat and rejoins the group, which then moves to a place convenient for drinking.

It is best to consume the wine in a somewhat secluded spot in the Skid Row neighborhood rather than on the main street. A degree of seclusion is desirable for three major reasons: (1) The members can chat more easily and freely. (2) The possibility of annoyance by potential "moochers" is diminished. (3) It insures avoidance of the police who frequently arrest persons drinking on the street or in other public places. [*The legitimate institutions of drinking, in taverns and homes, are part of the institutional order. Drinking in public is outside of this order and is thus subjected to formal social control by the police, and is more open to exploitation by others outside of the institutional order, moochers.*]

The leader walks at the front of the group carrying the bottle. Upon arriving in a doorway or alley, the men form a circle. After looking around to see that no police are in sight, the leader takes the bottle from his inner pocket and nicks the celluloid protective band with his finger nail before removing it by grasping the raised edge of the band with his teeth. He then takes off the cap and offers the bottle to the first man on his left. Almost without exception the bottle is passed to the left because the leader generally uses his right hand to unscrew the cap. This necessitates holding the bottle in the left hand, which facilitates passing it to the left or in a clockwise direction. Each man takes two swallows in his turn as the bottle is passed to him. If an individual takes more than the allotted number of gulps, one of the members is certain to protest and to grab the bottle from his mouth. [*The counter-institution has rules of behavior to follow, and relational social control to enforce these rules.*] Not until the bottle has toured the entire group does the leader take his drink. Upon completing the circle, the cap is replaced on the bottle and it is returned to the leader's pocket for a few minutes until any member calls for another round. The leader, in his role of host, has the major obligation of leading the conversation, which consists of ego-building mechanisms and recapitulations of past experiences, with frequent disparagement of the local police force as grossly unjust, and condemnation of the gospel missions as "rackets." [*The counter-institution provides the "role" of leader–host, and this role includes patterns of behavior not directly connected with the mere purchase of a bottle. In the interaction that goes on while drinking, knowledge about items of mutual interest is transmitted, and attitudes about the police and missions are developed and reinforced. This means that the bottle gang is an important part of the cultural transmission process on Skid Row.*]

The leader–host feels he has prestige because the others are dependent upon him for providing the initial capital and especially the impetus to organize the group. By assuming such important socio-group functions the leader gains the right to play the psyche-group role of host, which consists of selecting the type of wine and regulating the consumption and conduct of his guests.

The Members □   For the other members of the group, too, participation in the contractual relations provides a structure for the operation of psyche-group functions, activities for the structuring of affective relations which meet the psychic needs of the members. [*These provide the motivations for following the counter-institution aside from wanting to drink.*]

The initial contractual relation forms a small primary group in which all members are aware of their statuses and of the exclusion of all others. While the wine is being consumed the men converse in a convivial mood and the group members tend to accept the stories and claims of each individual quite uncritically. During drinking the men exchange ego-boosting rationalizations, reaffirm their status as "good men," offer boastful stories of their accomplishments, and retell past experiences, especially experiences in common. [*These stories are often attempts to provide biographical legitimations that will ease the sense of failure pervasive on Skid Row.*]

A portion of the inveterate wine drinkers prefer to regard themselves still as members of the working class but temporarily out of the labor market. Although some may not have had stable employment for as long as 10 years, a few still cling tenaciously to their identification as working men. An individual can continue to maintain this rationalizing façade by talking only of his past work experience and not considering any future employment plans. [*This is an avoidance of the problem of biographical legitimation.*] By interacting with another individual who has performed the same kinds of work, or better yet, who has worked at the same places, a wino can engage in esoteric small talk about the specific details of the job. By this means a man is able to bolster his identification with his reference group and to keep alive for a while longer his illusion of being a participant in his former occupation. The fully encultured wino, however, has relinquished all identification with his former working class status and has come to accept Skid Row as "home."

The group drinking experience is the only situation in the Skid Row social system in which a man receives personal recognition and affectional response. The men may not know each other's names, perhaps never having met before. This does not dim or alter the nature of their feelings toward each other; for by contributing money toward the group goal a man automatically becomes an insider and is afforded full acceptance.

Equal Consumption Without Equal Contribution ☐ Another manifestation of the psyche-group functions of the bottle gang is the fact that although not all individuals contribute equally to the purchase of a bottle, all are full and equal members and consume the beverage in equal proportions. As the bottle is passed around the group, each man takes his two swallows in turn and passes the bottle on to the next man. The fact of contribution makes one a member; the amount of contribution is not a relevant factor. This may be due to mutual interdependence for obtaining the wine. [*Cooperation is necessary in this counter-institution.*]

The purchasing of the bottle is a group action which results in satisfaction of individual needs. No one individual has sufficient funds to purchase a bottle; hence, all members are mutually interdependent for the attainment of their individual goals. The wine becomes a group goal because its procurement is possible only through the group effort. Since no individual in the group had sufficient funds to buy a bottle for himself, the man with 25 cents had as much need for the man with 5 cents as the poorer man did for the more affluent one. All therefore share equally in the wine purchased through the combined efforts of the members. Furthermore, the desire for personal association is an independent additional motive in forming the group.

The banding together to purchase liquor is a contractual relationship, the structure of which permits the functioning of interpersonal contacts for the satisfaction of psychic needs. It is at this point that the desire for psyche-group relations alters the operation of the socio-group contractual relations. This is a nonpecuniary motive for forming the contractual relationship, and appears to influence the members to overlook all but the grossest monetary differences.

Economically the differential contributions may balance out through time, if the individuals are permanent residents in one Skid Row. The man who one day contributes a larger amount to a "jug" may have only a few pennies on the following day, but he will be fully welcome in a group because of his past associations. The men do not calculate the balance of monetary relationships over a period of time but rather accept a former drinking "buddy" because he is considered a "good guy."

.   .   .

Treating and "Chiseling" ☐ Another institution operating within this context is the "treat," in which one individual who has earned a substantial sum or who has just received a subsistence check purchases a bottle and shares it with one or two of his friends. "The treat is the Skid Row version of conspicuous consumption." The treater experiences a sense of prestige in being able to buy liquor for his less fortunate friends; it permits him temporarily to feel superior to his dependent associates. The treater has the right to tell the others his troubles and they in turn have the obligation to listen and to agree.

But the sharing of the wine incurs an obligation to reciprocate when one comes into money. At this point difficulties and animosities may arise. One who continually fails to return the treat, if suspected of being able to do so, soon finds himself excluded from wino society and is no longer invited to share drinks.

The obligation of eventual reciprocation can lead to trouble for an individual who wishes to maintain a large number of "treating" relationships but has insufficient income for treating. Financially the most advantageous manner of repayment is to invite former benefactors to share in a corporate bottle and thus to repay with wine for which the reciprocator has borne only part of the cost. That is, a man becomes a legitimate stockholder in a bottle gang by contributing his share toward the purchase of wine, and after the bottle has been purchased, if he meets former benefactors on the street, he invites them to have a drink out of "his" bottle.

By this method a man may repay debts to former hosts largely at the expense of other stockholders. This maneuver gains the shrewd operator future invitations to share drinks, since he has "returned the compliment" to his benefactors. But this frequently leads to arguments, resentments, and eventual banishment of the offender. Such a person is called a "chiseler." Chiselers attempt to persuade the other members to invite the outsiders because they are "old buddies" and "such nice guys" that it would be a severe breach of etiquette not to offer them a drink. This low-cost technique of providing for a future liquor supply is most frequently tolerated by the group members because many of them do not care to appear rude. There may be protest by some. The outcome is determined by the relative strengths of the appeal of the inviting man balanced against the strengths of the protests. Usually the most vociferous win. [*"Chiseling" is a violation of the pattern of behavior required by the counter-institution, and as such is subjected to relational social controls.*]

Although there is some resentment by the group members when outsiders are invited, this is compensated to some degree by a sense of superiority because of the dependency relationship of the outsider. The resentment is a natural result of a breach of the contractual or socio-group relations. The compensating feeling of superiority is a psyche-function which alters the operation of the initial contractual relations. Nevertheless, some resentment remains against both the outsider and, especially, the chiseler. An individual who continually treats his own friends at the expense of group members is likely to find himself excluded from wino society.

EXPEDIENCY VERSUS PERSONALITY

In wino society, personnel for interaction and emotional rapport must be recruited most of the time on the basis of expediency. The psyche-group functions are structured around the socio-group functions. And the socio-group functions consist of the contractual relations by which money is collected for the purchase of wine. Ability to participate in the bottle gang is influenced at any particular time by the individual's financial resources. Hence the social relationships of each individual are determined solely by his pecuniary condition.

Selection on the basis of expediency does not allow focus on the value of a particular personality and thus prohibits the formation of a close personal bond. Rather, the choice of an individual for interaction, of necessity, must be with one who can meet the necessary financial requirements by which the bottle—the focal point of the social relations—is purchased.

The overt form of interaction is the affirmation of one's status as a "good man" and the expression of ego-boosting rationalizations. To this end, one only needs others who will cooperate in these sets of behavior patterns. Because the majority of winos in the Skid Row population can participate in this social institution, a great number of individuals can be easily substituted for any man. Thus there is no need to make a strong investment of libido in any individual.

The selection of associates on the basis of expediency is shown quite clearly in the acceptance of Negroes into white drinking groups. Negroes comprise 10 to 15 per cent of the Skid Row population of the California cities studied. Negroes were excluded by the management from the majority of "flophouses" and low-priced hotels. This exclusion was sanctioned by the white residents of the area who professed that Negroes were "dirty" and "low," and that the majority were untrustworthy in that they would pilfer from other hotel residents and even "cut up" those who attempted to stop them.

In soliciting membership for a bottle group, however, Negroes as well as whites on the streets of the Skid Row area were asked to participate. No willing Negro was refused membership if he had the cash. Negro members appeared to be accorded the same degree of acceptance in the psyche-group relationships as were the white members. Interaction, thus, does not appear to involve mutual adjustment of personalities by which individuals invest part of themselves, through the mutual exchange of libidinal bonds, to form affective ties. Rather, there is selection of personalities according to ability and willingness to participate in a preestablished pattern of behavior. [*This counter-institution may be enacted by willing individuals with the money regardless of their other personal characteristics. This means that the counter-institution can be carried out by anyone who shares the experience–social reality flaw and the territorial location.*] Selection on such a basis does not call for investment of self. The prevalence of this phenomenon inhibits the formation of strong personal ties among Skid Row winos.

☐ ☐ ☐

The main reason that "bottle ganging" is not sweeping the country is that there are fewer and fewer men living in Skid Rows relative to the rest of the population. For people who are not simultaneously homeless and destitute there are few reasons for joining a bottle gang. We might abstract from this the general idea that a counter-institution is limited by the population that experiences the particular experience–social reality conflict that it resolves. If a great many people have a particular conflict there will be a large pool of potential converts. There are numerous variables which come between a counter-institution and this pool; social distance, lack of communications, the other involvements of potential recruits in legitimate institutions, lack of recognition of their conflict, aversion to counter-institutions—all of these affect the number of converts a counter-institution can make. An outside limit, however, is the absolute number of people who experience the conflict.

The bottle gang provides rewards for those who follow it, not all the same for the various members. The leader–host experiences a number of psychological gains from enacting his role; the members of the bottle gang gain both drinking and companionship. From this we can see that counter-institutions, like institutions, provide roles for their members, and different and differential rewards for enacting the various roles required to carry them out.

The bottle gang also provides rewards for its members for recruiting more members, up to a point. If there are not enough men in on the bottle there won't be one, if there are too many men in on the bottle there will not be enough for each to drink. We saw a similar pattern of rewards for transmitting the institution to new members among call girls—taking on apprentices made the work of the trainer easier and provided more money. Any institution or counter-institution that recruits new members must provide some rewards for doing the recruiting, or there will be little motivation to recruit. These rewards may be in many different realms: alcohol, money, spiritual advancement, fulfilling the requirements of the job, prestige, love . . . the list could be endless. What is important is that *some* reward, which is valued by the person who does the recruiting, is normally associated with transmitting the pattern of behavior to another. Additionally, these rewards may be self-limiting or essentially limitless. Too many people on a bottle is self-limiting, the salvation of souls is limitless.

In order to sell the institution to new recruits, there must be a sales pitch, an explanation of the benefits to be derived. "Three of us have 28 cents in on a bottle. Do you want to get in on it?" is all the sales pitch that a bottle gang needs. Convincing someone to join a communal family, to make a radical alteration in a large part of his life, requires a much more complete, extended, and sophisticated sales pitch. The rewards that the recruit could gain will have to be made clear to him. This is the reason that an institution that recruits new members will have to have an answer to the question, "why," with a legitimation more complete than a simple description of what is done.

Recruiting a new person for a pattern of behavior that is not conventionally legitimate will probably involve more complex arguments if the institution covers a large part of daily behavior. If a girl is to become a prostitute she will be spending many hours a day at it, and she will require a more thorough training than someone learning to share a bottle. Similarly, counter-institutions that provide alternate patterns to the predominant institutions of labor, sex, territory, and communications will require more thorough working out than counter-institutions that substitute for less important legitimate institutions. Counter-institutions that have a large impact on other behavior, such as being an open homosexual, will be more difficult to "sell" than institutions that can be segregated, such as cheating on one's wife at a convention. The social visibility of the behavior, and the importance of the rules it violates, may also be important in a person's decision to follow or not. This emphasis on recruiting should not obscure the fact that the recruit is often willing, and sometimes even searching for the counter-institution. He may have already prepared himself to follow the counter-institution even before meeting the first person involved in it. Bryan suggested that potential prostitutes often took the initiative in approaching current prostitutes.

People involved in counter-institutions of behavior may be particularly vulnerable to exploitation by others because the counter-institution cannot call upon the protection and formal sanctions of the institutional order as a legitimate institution can. A moocher can be evicted from a tavern, and arrested, but he can only be thrown out of a bottle gang, and not too violently at that. IBM can sue a competitor if employees carry trade secrets when they change jobs; a call girl trainer cannot call the police when her apprentice steals her book, which contains her trade secrets. A homosexual beaten by juvenile delinquents may be reluctant to report it to the police. The lack of formal sanctions means that there is more victimization of people involved in counter-institutions, and that protection against such victimization is also more direct and interpersonal. The Mafia seldom sues those who double-cross.

Most institutions and counter-institutions of behavior do not require the full and undivided attention of the people enacting them. This means that there will usually be a chance for the participants to talk with one another both about what they are doing and about other things. Since they share at least the behavior in which they are participating in common, and perhaps many other things, they may well get to know one another better, create new legitimations for what they are doing, pass on additional knowledge, learn about other counter-institutions, and make further connections between what they are doing and other aspects of their lives. In this regard they are little different from gatherings of couples with babies, who talk about babies, and gatherings of divorced men who talk about alimony—people tend to talk about the things they have in common. People smoking marijuana together may hear about new shipments, about psilocybin that's around, about some celebrity who smokes. They may develop attitudes about political figures, about working stoned, and about law enforcement in general. These attitudes are likely to differ from those developed in conversations at Rotary Club meetings. In other words, initial participation in a counter-institution facilitates more participation, and it opens access to more and different counter-institutions. Differential association has the potential of being progressive; a slight change in social location opens the possibility of further change.

The bottle gang, being a limited affair, provides for its own legitimation as an institution—this is how it is done—but does not provide its members with any particular biographical legitimations. A counter-institution that organizes extensive behavior will probably develop biographical legitimations for the people who follow it. These legitimations may be just a front for dealing with the straight world as are the prostitute's answers to her customer's routine question, "what's a nice girl like you doing in a place like this?" or they may be elaborate biographical reconstructions that explain to the individual himself how he came to be where he is. Lest we fall into the trap set by our socially constructed reality we must realize that these biographical legitimations are not "rationalizations" in the bad sense; they are the same explanations we all have for what we are doing. It's just that people who are involved in counter-institutions don't usually have the ready-made, pretested, culturally approved "explanations" that are available to a doctor, housewife, or student. Because deviants are doing things that are not "understandable" in socially constructed reality, any explanation they make will be viewed from within the reality as a "rationalization," a self-serving explanation of the unexplainable. The processes involved are the same, but a person in a counter-institution does not have the overarching legitimations of the symbolic universe to fall back upon as do people in legitimate institutions. When a counter-institution begins to be followed by a significant number of people within a society more persuasive biographical legitimations will be developed, along with more convincing institutional legitimations.

A LIMIT TO COUNTER-INSTITUTIONS—
PHYSICAL BODY DESTRUCTION

In some cases the counter-institution never develops a high level of legitimation because of inherent handicaps in the behavior it requires. Heroin addiction, for example, has never developed many convincing legitimations. This is due partially to its nature, and partially to the structure of "antagonistic cooperation" that makes other heroin addicts unreliable.

Heroin causes physical addiction, which is extremely hard to eliminate. This physical addiction plays an indirect part in explaining the behavior and health of the addict. If a person has reasonable access to a stable supply of heroin he might enjoy a relatively unaffected life, just as a diabetic who has a stable source of insulin can lead a relatively normal life. Such is the case with most physician addicts who manage to carry out full and useful lives so long as their addiction is not discovered by the law. Physical addiction, however, in conjunction with an unstable and illegal source of supply results in the "junkie" pattern, the counter-institution of addiction. The price of heroin is high because law enforcement is relatively effective, and dealing entails considerable risk. Because the price is high the addict must come up with large amounts of money to get the heroin which he physically needs. He may have to be out at any hour of the day or night, in almost any place, to score. Needing much money and living an unstable life, the addict finds that ordinary jobs don't pay enough and are too restricting. As a consequence he may turn to theft in order to have enough money to take care of his physical needs. Making opiates available under medical supervision might not cure the addict, but it would have a high probability of allowing him to lead a more stable life.

In the following adaptation a girl addict gives a first-hand account of the process of starting with heroin, getting into the counter-institution of addiction, discovering retrospectively that she was part of the counter-institution and finding out the consequences.

☐ ☐ ☐

17

THE FANTASTIC LODGE
The Autobiography of a Girl Drug Addict

HELEN MacGILL HUGHES, editor

I knew that Bob'd been using heroin and I thought at first that maybe the feelings he had for me could substitute, in part at least, for the heroin. But then I didn't know much about heroin in those days. I knew everybody was doing it and it was just a socially accepted thing. More than that, you just *had* to. It was like just the next most natural step for anyone to take, after joining that group. [*Many counter-institutions recruit people who have become affiliated with groups in which the behavior is common. Affiliation with the group may come from other, legitimate, institutions of behavior that insiders and outsiders share, such as love.*]

So Bob didn't stop and I found out that the one time I felt apart from him was when he made it, you know. Then he was mostly snorting up. When that happened, when he'd make it, then we were apart for the first time. And at first I couldn't understand it and that, I saw, was because he was in an entirely different world, and I just wasn't there. So I gave up; I don't think I'd ever tried, anyway. And one night I told him to turn me on. Well, we both lied to one another. I told him I'd made it before. And he said "Yes," knowing that I hadn't, "So, solid! I'm not really turning you on for the first time"—that sort of thing, both absolving one another.

We were at my mother's house, that particular night. It was the first time I ever saw anything as far as ritual is concerned with any of the opping, you know. He got out a mirror and a razor blade—I was fascinated—and the caps and started cutting it into lines. Then he rolled the straw, the dollar bill, to snort it up with. I made it that night and it's difficult for me to remember exactly what my feelings were. Why, I don't know, when I can remember other things so well. But the first thing I noticed about it after I made it was when I got up to change a phonograph record that was playing. As I reached out to get the arm of the phonograph, I had the same feeling, almost identically, to the feeling I had when I was in the hospital and I'd gotten a shot of morphine—this tremendous physical joy in the sensation of moving your arm. But outside of that, nothing much was shaking and I used to get very sick the first couple of times.

. . .

If it had stayed like that, maybe I would never even have stood around with it, any more. But after we got down to the Key that's when I really started digging it, what was happening. We walked into that place and everything was a hundred miles away. First kicks on horse are strange, just the strangest, just the biggest gas in life, you know. I guess that's why you keep on it. [*The counter-institution provides benefits.*]

. . .

But we were staying over at my mother's in between apartments. And that was when I started taking off.

I say that with a feeling of horror. We'd been making it every night, first of all. That was the first thing, you know, just snorting up. Going back to my mother's with Bob, even for a week or a week and a half was all I needed; that was it. There I was in the same old eternal situation. A situation that frightens me beyond all reality. We couldn't talk or do anything, there's no door between the two rooms, so we would just go out on the landing at night and snort up out in the stairway, get out of our minds, come back in and go to bed. [*Participation in a counter-institution may become more extensive because it seems preferable to the legitimate institutions in which a person is currently involved.*]

So one night we were walking down the street, just to be out of the pad and I said to Bob, "Is that a drugstore?" and he said, "Yes." And I said, "Well, go in and buy a twenty-six-and-a-half insulin needle." He looked at me and he said, "Do you know what you're doing?" I said, "I know." I smiled. I don't know what I thought was so funny. So he went in and got the stuff for the fix and we made it. I had made it once before at the hotel one time, but I didn't dig it. I thought snorting up was craziest because this made me too, you know, falling out. I had too much eyes to sleep or stay. I didn't dig nodding out then.

But this second time I made it, I got my first flash and I never felt anything like that before. I dug it, completely. And if I thought the world had been all right when I snorted, it was insane and solid and smooth and crazy when I made it in my arm.

And that was about the time that Ron Slater came in town. He made arrangements for Bob and some other cats to make a gig with him, and Bob and Ron just dug each other completely from the word go. So Bob started bringing Ron over all the time and he is a nice cat. It's impossible not to like him because he's such a cool cat in spite of the terrible, terrible habit he has. This was my first experience with a real out-and-out junkie. A cat that would do anything to get heroin.

One night we went out to see Ron and someone said he was staying under the basement where they were playing and we wondered what the hell. We went down there, in this cold, brick-lined, damp, sweating basement—this was in the middle of winter, incidentally—there was no heat, of course, nothing. It was about twenty below zero down there. There was an old mattress on some newspapers. Any resemblance between it and a real mattress by this time was coincidental. And there was Ron on this filthy mattress with his only clothes that he owned, a pair of huaraches on his feet, I remember, and his overcoat, if you can call it that, thrown over him. And the only other items in that room was a carton sitting upright and on top of it empty caps, thousands and thousands and thousands of empty caps, and about six points and two spoons and several setups, everything, you know. That was immaculate, that little corner of the room. Jesus, you know, it was too much.

. . .

[*Discovering that you are part of the counter-institution.*] This is when this started. I wouldn't get up to eat, to comb my hair, to answer the phone, nothing. I just stayed there and that was that. Usually I'd just knock myself out with seconal, heroin, or whatever I could get my hands on. Sometimes I'd just sleep for forty-two, forty-seven hours—something like that—couple of days in a row.

And I was getting all kinds of tremendous symptoms at this point. The waking-up business was bad enough, but then it started in the other way, too: I couldn't go to sleep at night. Terrible insomnia! I could do anything, I could take anything and it wouldn't knock me out and I just went crazy for lack of sleep. And all of it, all of the tensions, all of the fears and feelings and nightmares and everything made it that much easier to hurry up and score.

And so, really, all this time, I was getting hooked. The first couple of times that I was sick, I couldn't believe it. I always thought that was a bunch of stuff about withdrawal symptoms, you know, that everyone was handing me. Well, you certainly can't be very sick from stuff, I thought. Then one night I remember coming from Bob's parents, and we hadn't made a fix all day and I said, "You know, I think I'm coming down with a cold," to Bob as we were driving along. He said, "What's the matter, dear? Don't you feel good?" And I said, "I don't know, I'm so uncomfortable and restless. My back aches, my nose is running," I said, "I just feel rotten, you know." I said, "We'd better go home and get some pot or something. I don't like the way I feel." He looked at me and said, "You're sick," and I said, "What do you mean, I'm sick?" He said, "You need some stuff." He said, "Even I'm starting to feel a little sick." I said, "You're kidding? Is this what it is, the way I feel now?"

and he said, "Yeah." And I started asking him all about it. How sick could you get? And how many hours after your last fix are you liable to get sick? And, well, if you make it three days in a row, does that mean the fourth day, if you stay off, you get sick?—things like that. And he told me the whole story that night. [*Learning to recognize withdrawal symptoms, combined with the knowledge that more heroin will make them go away, has been recognized as a critical step in the addiction process.*]

That was the point when I got hooked. I didn't see it that way at the time, but—looking back—up to that time I was able to handle it and after that time I was unable to. When you're hooked, it's different. The cool feeling you had when you're not hooked gradually diminishes, the amount that you have to take always getting larger, and with it having less and less effect as you go along. In the beginning, the way you get hooked in a lot of ways is because of this tremendous relief that you feel because of all of these problems, anxieties, and so forth becoming resolved all of a sudden. Here you've been worrying about them your whole life and they just got resolved, wham, like that. And you think, well, why didn't I ever think of this before? Everything is going to be cool. And naturally subconsciously, unconsciously, you connect that feeling with the horse and you think about getting high. But it isn't getting high, it's getting straightened out, you know, in a sense.

Then, as you go along, that's when you begin to find out that horse is a cheat, a real cheap cheat. Before this, you can have a whole evening or a whole day of wonderful I'm-great-and-the-world-is-all-cool feeling. But after you get hooked, you have to take eight to ten caps to get that feeling and even after you take your ten caps it is just sort of a re-creation of that old relief. It isn't really there, because for one thing just after you've taken off, you're already back in the position within an hour, maybe, you're going to have to look at things in the cold gray light of dawn already. And so, desperately hoping to hang on to this much nicer, much finer world and in order to keep re-creating this capable-of-coping-with-things feeling, you must keep opping a cap every few hours. [*At this point heroin addiction becomes a "retreatist" form of adaptation, Type 16 in the Expanded Typology of Individual Adaptation.*]

· · ·

That's when we first started making half a package between us a day, regularly, taking off at regular times. Pretty soon it was a whole package between us. Then it was two packages, then it was everything we could get our hands on. And that was when we had to start crawling and doing all the rest of the things you have to do. We were screwing everybody, burning everybody now, getting money any way we could think of. I would make up fantastic lies to my mother and get some bread. Bob would go out and make up to his old man and get some bread. Anything to get money! Consequently we stopped eating, we stopped doing anything, you know. Every cent we had we hated to even spend. There were only two things, heroin and cigarettes. We were in contact with nothing but junkies twenty-four hours a day; we had to be. It's the group you know, the kind of people you know. [*At this point there is total involvement in the counter-institution of behavior only for the retreatist motivation of obtaining heroin.*]

It's funny, when I look back since the first time I was really hooked, there were different phases. For a while you see, maybe, one or two junkies, almost exclusively. And then, all of a sudden, for some reason or other, you either hype him too much or he hypes you too much, or it's mutual disgust. You know, how long can one junkie stand another junkie? That is the question. And you go on to the next, and so forth. It's like a bunch of cripples getting together at a convention and pooling their crutches, in order that one or two of them can sort of stagger around. It's really one of the best examples of cooperative animosity that I've ever seen. Because actually I think those people hate each other. I don't like any of them sincerely, I mean, if I wasn't hooked, would I know any of them? I wonder. I don't think so. I might know them, but I certainly wouldn't be as intimate with them as I am. [*The pattern of behavior within the counter-institution is antagonistic cooperation, a mutual sharing of individual adaptations. Even the people involved don't like it, so no great legitimations are developed, and the counter-institution does not become organizationally elaborated.*]

· · ·

[*Formal social control seen from the outside.*] On the lower level— the uniformed nab, the squad-car nab, the guy who's driving the paddy wagon, the small-time matron—the junkie is somebody you can kick the life out of and nobody can do anything to you because they're nowhere: they're junkies, you know. When you get up on the higher levels, at the Narcotics Unit itself, and when you get to the point where there is more information about junk, there's more tolerance and the attitude becomes one of "Oh, well, we have to do this. The public is down on everything. There's a lot of publicity and a lot going on. But, oh, what a drag." I don't think anyone really wants to be bothered there. And certainly they don't want to be bothered enough to do anything genuine that's going to help anything. They pick up junkies as regularly as possible and book as many as they can as much as they can and send them away for as much as they can. Then they can say in their weekly statistics, "Four out of five junkies sent up for a year," or something.

But the people at the very top, the judges and the rest who should know most and who should be attempting most, after seeing these thousands and thousands of cases and not having a real understanding of any of them and just expecting them to straighten up after they get out of court and seeing them come back again, time after time, they've developed a tremendously cynical attitude. I mean, their philosophy about junk and junkies is very definitely that the junkie is no good to anyone, has no feeling toward anyone, and that maybe something more should be done for them; but under the existing laws that all they can do is —"two years!"

.   .   .

[*General public, seen from the outside.*] But the general public, now, they *do* feel abhorrence; the junkie frightens them, I think. The junkie frightens them because they realize that this is something that no human is prepared to cope with at all; that even they, with a warm, normal home and lovely background and a setup in society and so forth, could somehow be hooked in the end. And it's true. That's another reason why I'm very suspicious of those people and of their feelings, because, actually, in all these loud protestations about "Throw them all in jail! Get rid of them, preying on society!" et cetera, et cetera, all I can see is the terror underneath it. And all that terror indicates to me is that they have eyes almost, in a weird sense, I could never trust anyone with an attitude like that, ever. Not simply because of what they can do to you, some pretty horrible things, but because they have just as irrational an attitude as the junkie has.

☐ ☐ ☐

Anthropological reports of other societies testify to the diversity of socially created realities, the diversity of institutionalizations of behavior. There are, however, outside limits to what is possible with social reality construction. If some form of behavior actually destroys the body, or alters it permanently, the concrete physical fact cannot be done away with by any definition of the situation. The counter-institution of heroin use creates a definition of the situation, creates legitimations ("where there's dope, there's hope"), that are at variance with the actual socially structured consequences of physical addiction. The recruiting of the counter-institution eventually results in a compulsive pattern of usage. This physical dependency, in combination with a fluctuating and expensive supply, eventually changes the individual from a counter-institution participant who is deriving benefits from it, into a retreatist who cooperates within the counter-institution only to assuage his physical dependency. Likewise, no amount of advertising can make disappear the fact that cigarette smoking causes lung cancer. Were cigarettes to be subject to the same legal control as heroin a similar counter-institution of behavior would arise, though it would not be as certain a route to retreatism because cigarettes are slightly less habituating.

Whether a form of behavior is or is not inherently destructive is often a matter of debate. If the behavior is legitimated within the socially constructed reality of a society there will be many who are ready to assert that it is not destructive. Smokers, cigarette manufacturers, tobacco growers, and all those who depend on them, have a stake in claiming that the physical destruction caused by tobacco is "not proven." If the behavior is not legitimated by social reality the nature of proof shifts, and "conclusive proof" that the pattern is harmless is required. The facts that marijuana has been used for 3,500 years—about 3,000 years longer than tobacco—and that there are no proofs of physical harm from its use, are "not enough" for concluding that it is harmless. Now it is claimed that *enough* tetrahydrocannabinol (THC) will produce temporary psychosis (a social reality word for ununderstandable behavior) in anyone, and since THC is similar to one of the many THCs in marijuana, therefore marijuana use is harmful. Social reality now defends itself with pseudoscience.

In any event, physical body destruction puts certain limits on the forms of institution which can be structured around it. Since this limit currently seems to apply only to the counter-institutions supporting heroin use, masochism, and Russian roulette, it is not important for most counter-institutions.

THE PERVASIVE NORMALCY OF EVERYDAY REALITY

Change proceeds by small increments in our everyday lives. Some new form of behavior, or some connection that will eventually lead to a new form, may occupy only a thousandth of our attention during the day it happens. Though we may later look back and see this beginning as a momentous event, it seldom appears this way at the time. One small connection may lead to another and a pattern of behavior may arise that may later be seen as quite different from what went on before. The girl who "didn't know what a hippie was, until she was one" is a good example. Because we seldom recognize all the consequences of our actions we often get deeply involved in a new pattern of behavior before realizing its full consequences for our old way of doing things.

As people feel one another out and find that they have mutually satisfying activities in common, they tend, through conversation and association, to get to know one another better. The man bored with his wife may become involved with a mistress, the reluctant draftee may find that he has become a war resister very much concerned with the movement. As involvement grows along these several dimensions, enactment of the counter-institution becomes a routine. As the participants interact and talk they extend their definition of the situation into less and less obvious areas, at the same time solidifying the basic activities of their counter-institutions. Since not all participants start at the same level of understanding, the basic definitions will have to be repeated over and over again to bring everyone to the usual level of coordination. This internal explanation process sharpens and clarifies the definition of the situation for the participants, reinforcing its reality for them.

Since the people involved in a counter-institution will also be involved with others in legitimate institutions, parents, co-employees, families and so on, there is a good chance that they will have to explain and defend their atypical behavior. The people around the bored husband will raise their eyebrows at his mistress, his boss may call him in for a chat, the corner baker may fall unaccustomedly silent when he enters the bakery with her. The reluctant draftee-turned-war-resister may have a soul-searching talk with his girl friend, his parents may send him to see a psychiatrist because he "must" be having problems, his college friends may begin feeling uncomfortable with him in the cafeteria. In the process of presenting and defending the counter-institution many legitimations will occur to its participants. People involved in counter-institutions *need* these legitimations to deflect the reactions of conventional people. These reactions constitute relational social control, and the legitimations are shields to turn away barbed words.

As these legitimations are developed by individuals they are passed along to others in the same position. They are "good things to say" when people ask. And as they are passed, they begin to have a life of their own, becoming agreed upon by participants in the counter-institution. These agreed upon legitimations will then be used by most members of the counter-institution when they are defending or transmitting their view of reality to those not involved. Bored husbands may communicate among themselves verbally, war resisters through underground newspapers.

A special case of the transmission of legitimations occurs when the counter-institution is passed along to potential recruits. The recruit, possibly dubious or guilt-ridden, may require a thoroughgoing processual legitimation that will allow him to see the counter-institution as necessary, and his following it as honorable. Such a legitimation might take the form, "My wife's psychiatrist thinks she has definite neurotic tendencies, at any rate we haven't gotten along for years, and the love that you and I share is such a beautiful thing." Or, "Yes, I used to think that the peaceniks were communist dupes, but then I began to understand war resistance when I met people in it. Now I see that the things I had been told were untrue, they had just been produced by the system." Having attempted to deflect attacks on the counter-institution they might then go on to transmit and legitimate their behavior, explaining why it was right and logical, and why anyone, at least anyone in the position of the recruit, should follow the counter-institution. Whether the recruitment is formal or informal, the process of explaining the institution to a naïve potential member requires an act of reflective consciousness on the part of the tutor, who must make his own reasons and justifications sharper and more logical. The recruiter himself thus becomes more confirmed in his belief in the counter-institution as he convinces others of its truth. The counter-institutional definition of reality becomes solidified and more firmly held by the participants as they recruit, or as they talk with those who recruit. Some counter-institution organizations have recognized this phenomenon and require *all* their members to do missionary work among the unenlightened, bringing in more recruits and creating more conscious participation.

The counter-institution can now exist as a functioning behavior pattern with its own rules, and its own relational and self-control for those who follow it. It transmits itself, or is apprehended by others, through the same processes that legitimate institutions use. Its one constant handicap in recruiting is that it is outside the institutional order. This is important—it provides the greatest barrier to recruitment, the most constant questioning of legitimations, and the most serious threat to the group-defined reality held within the counter-institution. A great many of the actions of people in counter-institutions can only be understood as responses to the surrounding socially constructed reality. Many kinds of counter-institutions are condemned in similar ways because of the characteristics of their response to social pressure. Were there no social pressures the reactions would be unnecessary and the counter-institution might be seen as considerably less threatening.

Constant contact with unbelievers, people in legitimate institutions, may cause the followers of a counter-institution to grow more firm, rigid, and fanatical in their beliefs. When a person feels an underlying ambiguity about his actions, possibly conflicting values in his self-control, he may have to defend his new position very strongly to others to convince himself. This too is a reaction to the ideas planted in his head in his primary socialization. Freud called this process "reaction formation." I suspect that a large part of the fanaticism of American Maoists comes from trying to maintain a definition of reality quite at variance with the residual self-concepts internalized from their early socialization. Some counter-institution organizations consciously require their members to engage in extreme actions to reap the benefits of the more total conviction which follows. Leon Festinger suggested, in *When Prophecy Fails,*[1] that a disconfirmed prophecy caused the members to believe even more strongly. This is the same process of reaction formation—too much self-esteem has been invested to admit failure.

The defense of a counter-institution against socially constructed reality takes place in many ways—from debates by theoreticians of both sides to actual conflict of enacted institutions of behavior. When the people involved in a counter-institution encounter straight people they may flee, or fight, in many ways. They may fall silent, they may legitimate. They may leave the scene, they may attempt to control the scene. In the following adaptation Sherri Cavan describes the way in which homosexuals defended their scene, a gay bar, against straight people who wandered in. The gay bar is a counter-institution of territory and an offshoot of the counter-institution of homosexuality. The gay bar is a place to meet, to retreat, to enjoy oneself without the restraints necessary in the outside world. As a result of these benefits the appearance of straight people is distinctly unwelcome, something like a skunk showing up at a picnic.

☐ ☐ ☐

---

[1] Leon Festinger, *When Prophecy Fails: A Social and Psychological Study of a Modern Group That Predicted the Destruction of the World* (New York: Torch Books, Harper and Row, 1956).

18
INTERACTION IN HOME TERRITORIES
SHERRI CAVAN

In the following sections I would like to focus on the patterns of inter-action which occur in a public bar which is also defined as a home territory by homosexuals and which, by virtue of both its location in the city and its reputation of being a unique night spot is frequently infiltrated with outsiders. At these times, when strangers invade the bar, the character of the interaction within the bar can be described best in terms of the indigenous population bending, abridging and breaking the interaction rules of polite society in such a way as to maintain their definition of the bar as a home territory.

The Hangout is a relatively small bar, located in the entertainment area of San Francisco. For about the past 15 years the Hangout has been operated as a gay bar, and though rarely listed in guide books, it is a "spot" for tourists in the know and sophisticated residents of the city in search of diversified entertainment. But even without prior knowledge about the bar, since it is on the fringe of the entertainment area of the city, many, walking along the street, are drawn into the noisy, active bar.

The area of the bar is no more than 100 feet by 50 feet, and the front door opens directly onto the street. The bar itself extends along the left side of the room, and the remaining area is a crowded complex of small tables, which are occasionally, along the far right side, pushed end to end. At the back of the room on the bar side is a tiny kitchen, and on the right there is a small stage with a piano which occupies almost half the area of the stage.

Between the kitchen and the stage is a small room which is used for storage of both bar supplies and employees jackets, shoes, etc.; next to this room is a short hallway leading to the bathrooms.

The decor of the bar is a planned decadence, with large papier-mâché figures decorating the walls and ceiling, as well as a number of murals along the lower part of the right wall. There are two large paint-ings (done by the same artist who did the papier-mâché work and the murals) which feature a number of people who at one time or another were regulars of the bar. The upper part of the right wall is usually hung with paintings by local artists who are also either frequenters of the bar or friends of the regular customers.

In contrast to the obviously planned aspect of the decor, there are always beer cases and mix cases piled high along the walls, and the

Adapted from Sherri Cavan, "Interaction in Home Territories," *Berkeley Journal of Sociology,* Vol. 8, 1963, pp. 17–32. Reprinted by permission.

floor is typically covered with sawdust and littered with ashes and cigarette butts, deposited there by the waiters who clean the ashtrays on the tables and the bar by emptying them on the floor.

The bar is usually open by 11:30 A.M., and while drinks are available at this time, the biggest attraction is the buffet lunch. Although the patrons of the Hangout at this time are drawn from the gay community as well as from those who work in the area (in the numerous offices and shops of the financial district and Jackson Square) during the early afternoon the Hangout is both officially and unofficially a public eating establishment.

The patrons eat their lunch both at the bar and the tables, and almost every afternoon the delivery truck drivers congregate at one end of the bar to eat, chat, drink, discuss racing with the afternoon bartender, and play poker dice.

By 2:00 P.M. the lunch period is over, and there may be only two or three customers present prior to the late afternoon, when the bar begins to fill up again with what is then called by the employees, the "cocktail crowd."

The majority of those present from cocktail time on, and particularly during the week, are homosexuals, though it is not unlikely that upon occasion the non-homosexuals who have lunched at the Hangout will return for a drink after work.

The use of the physical area within the bar is unequal. The majority of the customers use the bar, and the tables under most circumstances are used by the non-homosexuals. Members of the indigenous population coming in usually begin to seat themselves at the end of the bar farthest from the door, gradually filling the area towards the door. Unless it is particularly crowded, the door end of the bar is usually left vacant, but if all the stools are taken, the customers may stand two or three deep at the bar.

Whether or not there are others standing at the bar, the people at the bar typically sit facing away from the bar, toward the center of the room. This means that activity occurring at the tables and in the small open area between the tables and the bar is under constant surveillance from those at the bar, and at the same time, if there are others standing at the bar, the face-to-face distance between those standing and those sitting will be quite small.

From early evening on, anyone entering the bar is an object of attention at least at his moment of entrance, and his future treatment in the bar is dependent upon what he is classified as—an old friend, a possible new friend, or an outsider. Acquaintances entering the bar are almost invariably greeted vocally, and most likely will situate themselves in the proximity of the one proffering the greeting, at least initially. The category of "possible acquaintances" are typically proffered a silent greeting—a welcoming nod, an invitational glance to recognize their presence. But where they will locate is variable. The treatment of the entering outsider, is both decisive and obvious. And while he may be totally ignored by the majority of the patrons at the bar, more likely than not, some member of the indigenous population of the bar will, in some unequivocal manner, announce their presence.

Though from the standpoint of those who make the Hangout their home territory, no homosexual is an outsider, not all non-homosexuals are outsiders. Three categories of non-homosexuals are recognized within the bar: straight friends, possible trade, and tourists.

The category of straight friends encompasses non-homosexuals who are either known outside the bar or who have, during the course of time, established relationships with the members of the indigenous population during the lunch period operation of the bar. They are most likely to form part of the cocktail crowd, though they may be present on weekends or Sundays.

Within the gay community, the Hangout is not known as a "cruisey bar." That is to say, it does not have the reputation of being a place where impromptu homosexual assignations are likely to occur, although this is always a possibility in any gay bar. But since the bar is known for what it is throughout most of the city, it is a place where trade, or non-homosexuals who might be willing to enter into a sexual relationship for either money or a lark, may frequently be found. Almost all males who enter the bar unaccompanied are seen as possible trade, and most service men, even if they enter with others in uniform, fall into this category. Once inside the bar, those who are initially categorized as possible trade undergo a continuing process of evaluation, for their behavior within the bar is used as a sign of whether they are in fact homosexuals, trade, or tourists.

Women, mixed couples and groups, and four or more apparently straight males, unless categorized as old friends, are tourists who by definition are outsiders, and as such, they are singled out for special treatment.

Inasmuch as the Hangout is defined first as a public drinking place and only alternatively as a home territory for homosexuals, the degree to which the invasion of outsiders can be curtailed by the indigenous population is limited. The interest of the owner in maintaining the bar as a profitable business establishment tends to set the limits to which the bar can be converted into a private territory. In this sense then, no outsider can be forceably removed from the area unless he can be categorized as a public nuisance. But on the part of the indigenous population, the difference between legitimate customers and public nuisances is often vague and in general almost all outsiders are classified somewhere in between, as objects which can be officially treated in improper ways. [*The counter-institution does not control the territory completely; it merely occupies it. Thus they do not have the power of formal social control, the power to define people they disagree with as public nuisances to be removed by the police, and they must use relational social control to effect their ends.*]

While the definition of the bar as a business establishment serves as one type of limitation on the defense behavior which the indigenous population can engage in, there also appear to be certain rules limiting behavior which are formulated within the group itself. For example, public displays of affection which might be repugnant to outsiders are rare when outsiders are present and though the outsider may be publicly announced as an ingroup member, this category is rarely actualized in behavior toward him, which is to say that he is never in fact treated as if he actually were homosexual.

.   .   .

To the degree that the character of the behavior pattern of any behavior setting can be known in advance, people can enter established behavior settings with an expectation about whether or not they will be taking active or passive parts in the proceedings, whether or not their behavior will constitute a performance. The patrons of public places usually expect at most to be customers and, if the place is known to be frequented by certain groups, they may expect their position to be only that of onlooker or audience. Thus, one of the ways in which the indigenous population can make trouble for the invader is to breach his expectations about his (the patron's) degree of involvement and responsibility in the proceedings.

An outsider rarely enters the physical premises of the Hangout unnoticed. His approach to the door may be loudly proclaimed by the patrons at the end of the bar and the waiter may usher him from the door to the center area of the room in such a way that the entire proceedings are disrupted and the outsider immediately becomes the focus of attention. Once inside the territory, the outsider may remain as an object of attention for the duration of his stay, by being handled in a noisy and obtrusive manner, having chairs and tables rearranged for him and his orders for drinks yelled across the room, while waiters or patrons engage in loud performances at his table.

Making the outsider the focus of attention serves to define his position as that of an active rather than passive one in the proceedings. And as such, this definition breaches the expectations which the entering outsider has with regard to the bar as a public place. Rather than being an onlooker, audience or mere customer, the outsider becomes an active performer in the ongoing interaction: He becomes the key figure in a parody of deference which is played out around his mere presence in the bar.

And, while the rule for proper behavior towards others is that "when a person is caught out of face because he has not expected to be thrust into interaction ... others may protectively turn away from him ... to give him time to assemble himself,"* no such consideration is offered the outsider. His loss of face and subsequent embarrassment is also to be attended to. If a waiter caresses his hair while taking his order and the outsider blushes or requests that he stop, someone may announce that he has just "come out." ("Coming out" is the phrase which is used among homosexuals for both one's recognition of oneself as a homosexual or one's entrance into the ongoing stream of homosexual life, specifically into the bar system and the privately organized social affairs.) The waiter may publicly cry, "Sweetie, don't be shy. We were made for each other." [*This sort of attention attacks the outsider's sense of identity and self-esteem.*]

Frequently the definition of the outsider as an object of attention includes offering him a nefarious role, or a status below the one he puts forth as his rightful status. The shows usually begin with a brief welcome and then the statement, "Don't worry about your reputation. The moment you walked in here it was ruined."

Women are frequently ushered from the entrance with a brusque "This way, Busters" and their male companions are greeted with exclamations as to the effect that it has been so long since they were last seen there. On a Sunday morning, a group of young women were announced to all present as "The Lesbians paying their Sunday call."

Women in excessively feminine attire are open either to the direct accusation of "My, you're so butch" or to an aside addressed to their male companion, "Who's your butch friend?" The woman herself rarely responds to either remark. If her companion responds in her defense by restating what her actual status is, e.g. girlfriend, wife, etc., the counter response is made directly to his status and indirectly to hers. The male in this case is defined as both a regular customer of the Hangout and a particularly intimate acquaintance of the waiter, by remarks such as, "I didn't know I was merely another woman" or "Why haven't you ever told me you were married?"† Occasionally the waiter may even pronounce the escort's status to the rest of the bar with a loud, "My God—a bisexual!"

Older women who are present are frequently handled by somewhat less obvious, though equally devastating, methods. Rather than being

---

* E. Goffman, "On Face Work," *Psychiatry*, 18:213–231, 1955, 219.

† Statements alluding to surprise at finding a married man there with his wife are so frequently taken as a dig that, on one occasion, when such a statement was made in all sincerity, the reaction was as if in fact the intent was to discredit the other's moral role.

directly degraded, they often receive a fond gaze, and then a public proclamation is made that "Another mother has discovered her son is a faggot."

While the united action of territory defense on the part of the indigenous population can be viewed as one way in which the group can, so to speak, close ranks and more clearly define their own position for themselves, this is not to say that the mere presence of the outsider prevents the occurrence of behavior which the indigenous population itself considers improper. For example, while hustling drinks is frowned upon in general, outsiders are frequently used in this way. In the same light, when one member of the indigenous group was chastised for engaging in a prolonged session of low camp (behavior characterizing female mannerisms), he responded with, "The tourists expect it. I'm no longer a mere faggot; I'm show bizz!" [*Participants in many counter-institutions often put on and put down straight people by staging "minstrel shows" or "freak shows."*]

CHALLENGES TO TERRITORIAL DEFINITIONS

Thus far the description of behavior has focused on the ways in which the indigenous population can make the outsider feel uncomfortable at having invaded another's home territory. Counters to these defensive actions can be viewed as challenges by the outsiders to the indigenous population's definition of the territory.

In the face of the attacks of the indigenous population, the outsider can engage in three possible behavioral tacks. (1) He can leave, and by so doing, acknowledge the indigenous population's definition of the bar as a home territory, (2) He can attempt to counter the defense of the territory with his definition of the bar as a proper public place or (3) he can accept his role of invader with "good graces" until such time as he can terminate his stay.

Unsuccessful challenges of invaders in home territories tend to be more frequent than successful challenges; the futility of challenging the indigenous population in their home territory appears to be based on the fact that (1) the indigenous group has greater immediate support for their position and (2) the outsider has a limited supply of arms. [*This is the reverse of the usual situation, but it is one reason why people can feel comfortable outside of legitimated institutions. At certain times and at certain locations that they frequent, the participants in a counter-institution are an effective majority.*]

The first point refers to the fact that the outsider can muster numerically fewer allies from those present to support his position. But beyond this, the indigenous population has a tendency to present a united front, and this is not the case with the outsiders. Insofar as the indigenous population attacks each outsider individually, the attack of each outsider becomes the object of attention of the entire audience: for not only the indigenous population but also the object of attention for the other outsiders who are present. In this sense, the successful challenge must be against not only the definition which is explicitly offered by the indigenous population, but against the implicit acceptance of that definition on the part of the other outsiders present.

.   .   .

The second point refers to the fact that there are very few successful lines of attack open to the challenging outsider. Since the indigenous population has already defined the bar as a place where there is no moral respectability to be had for anyone, there is no base from which the outsider can start his attack. Furthermore, almost any challenge can be utilized by the indigenous population to further discredit the outsider. For example, the challenge two women once presented regarding the sex of the waiter's bed partners was countered with a statement to the effect that such interest was obviously indicative of a voyeuristic predisposition.

In general the situation is most frequently one in which the outsider acts with good graces. To act with good graces is essentially to respond in the mode of action which has been defined by the indigenous group, and in this sense, to acknowledge their control within the situation. [*Capitulation to relational social control from a counter-institution is relatively easy to accept if one defines it as temporary and situational.*]

This typically takes the form of attempting to disattend the proceedings as much as possible (by becoming overly involved with one's drink, one's cigarette, or the decorations around the room) and when such disattention is no longer possible, by behaving in such a way as to show that whatever is happening is actually all a very funny joke, of no real consequence. Thus the outsider who finds the waiter on his lap may pat him on the knee and then grin broadly to both his companions at the table and to everyone else who is observing the event.

Occasionally an outsider will respond with a challenge, but the specific encounter will terminate by the outsider not only accepting the position which the indigenous group has defined him in, but also further extending the interaction with the indigenous group on their own terms. Typically such behavior appears only when the outsider is with a larger group, that is, with more than one or two companions. For instance, a male in a group of four couples, dressed in blue jeans, straw hats and western cotton dresses was singled out one evening by the Hangout entertainer as a farm boy who (1) had tired of animals,

(2) was really not interested in the woman he was with and (3) who really would like to be in drag. The outsider attempted to refute each of these attributes, going as far as taking off his shirt to display his tattoos. In the end, he initiated an exchange of his straw hat for the entertainer's sequined cloche, which in essence signified his desire to eventually terminate the interchange without ill will.

.   .   .

Sometimes the outsider attempts a challenge only at the termination of his stay, when, because of his leaving the physical area, a counter to this challenge is impossible. He may call, "So long, sister" in a tone of voice which implies disgust, or he may engage in a mocking swish out the door. In any case, though he has had the last word, he is no longer present to enforce this victory, which in the last analysis can only be measured by the extent to which his actions have controlled the subsequent actions of the indigenous group.

☐ ☐ ☐

COUNTER-INSTITUTIONS WITHIN THE INSTITUTIONAL ORDER

Not all counter-institutions of behavior exist entirely outside the institutional order. It is possible that an institution will be legitimate within the symbolic universe but that counter-institutions which violate the values of the symbolic universe will be allowed to exist within these legitimated institutions. The performance of industrial espionage wherein one company attempts to steal the secrets of another is widely known, but it is also secretly sanctioned by many otherwise legitimate companies. These counter-institutions within legitimate institutions generally have legitimations that run from "efficiency" to "have to do it to survive." The housewife who becomes a part-time prostitute to help with the grocery bills, the newsstand dealer who carries a little pornography under his counter, the use of an expense account for personal bills, are all counter-institutions that exist within legitimate institutions.

In the Expanded Typology of Individual Adaptation this pattern of behavior and belief would be Type 3: believing the values of the symbolic universe but doing legitimate and illegitimate things. While we might think that this would produce an intolerable conflict for the person doing it, the ability of people to compartmentalize their lives and their legitimations often allows it to be carried out.

There are many questionable practices in business that go on inside of otherwise legitimate institutions. These may run from cutting a few corners on income tax matters to systematically cheating customers at every opportunity. In some legitimate institutions, such as automobile and electronics repair, the counter-institution of cheating the customer is so well established that it is the predominant form of behavior. Survey after survey conducted by organizations from the *Reader's Digest* to the Better Business Bureau have shown that the average customer is more likely to be cheated than to get an honest job when he takes his radio, television, or car to be repaired. The customer will be charged for work not done, for parts not installed. He will be lied to about the condition of his car or appliance, parts in perfect working order will be replaced, and underlying defects will not be corrected so they will eventually produce a return trip. I recently took my Volkswagen bus in for its 6,000 mile maintenance service. When I picked it up, I noticed that it was dripping oil from the transmission; the drain plug had been left loose. Deciding to find out what else was wrong, I went over the list of things for which I had been charged. Of the twenty-seven items on the list only twelve required operations that left physical traces of whether or not they had been done. Of these twelve, only three had been done. When I returned to the dealer to watch the mechanic do them right, I was informed that the other nine procedures were not really necessary. Perhaps so, but I had been charged full price for a one-quarter job. The service manager attempted to give me a run-around until I demonstrated that I knew what I was talking about and could prove the omissions. This is not to single out my Volkswagen dealer as uniquely guilty; this happens routinely with automobile repairs. Automobile shops often conceal their activities from customers by refusing to let customers enter the shop, citing as a legitimation that "our insurance won't allow it." This defense of territory could be compared with the hecklers in a gay bar—"insurance" just *seems* more legitimate while serving the same purpose. The basic reason for counter-institutions within business is profit, and the fact that the customer can rarely know he has been cheated.

In the following adaptation a former student of mine writes about the counter-institutions in his family business. Because it was a family business, and because many of his relatives are still running such businesses he has asked to remain anonymous. It is a good example of the counter-institutions that are to be found within seemingly legitimate organizations.

□ □ □

19

CRIMINAL DEVIANCY IN A SMALL BUSINESS: SUPERIOR TV

ANONYMOUS

From the summer of 1964 to the end of the summer of 1966, I worked for a now bankrupt and dissolved Television and Appliance company called Superior TV. I served in the capacity of stockboy, salesman, deliveryman and handler of credit accounts. As a participant-observer for two years with this company, I gained some knowledge of the complexities, motivations and attitudes found within the company.

DESCRIPTION OF ENVIRONMENT

Superior TV is located amidst a variety of retail stores. They include a drugstore, two small markets, a bar and liquor store, a bank, and most importantly, a large factory which employs some three to four thousand people on three shifts. The street is fairly active throughout the day, with many people shopping from store to store. This traffic is known as "street trade" and the store takes advantage of it by using brightly colored signs, window displays, TV sets showing different channels, and music pumping continuously from hi-fi sets. In this carnival atmosphere, the customer is at a disadvantage from the start. His reason is somewhat suspended by the diversions of sight and sound, and by his eagerness to own one or more of the bright new TV's, hi-fi's etc. The customer is further encouraged in his psychological set by the salespeople who appear extremely friendly, charming and eager to please. This gives the customer a feeling of importance and dignity, together with some elation. The perfect atmosphere to sell a person anything.

HOW THE STORE FUNCTIONS

The store is divided into seven departments: Service, Sales, Advertising, Buying, Delivery, Clerical and Financing. Each department has its own functions and responsibilities, however, each department works reciprocally with the others and overlapping of duties often occurs. For example, a customer may bring in a used TV into the service

Adapted from "Criminal Deviancy in a Small Business: Superior TV" (unpublished manuscript). Reprinted by permission of the author.

department for repairs, the service man may then offer to accept the used set as a trade-in on a new one. Thus the service department may on occasion sell new merchandise. This is also true for the delivery personnel who are encouraged to "load" a customer. Methods of loading a customer (selling additional merchandise) vary from store to store and from department to department. The basic method used by delivery personnel is usually as follows: The delivery boy delivers a piece of merchandise to a customer's home. While in the house he surveys the furnishings, especially the kitchen. He may notice that the customer has an old refrigerator. He can then explain that the refrigerator could have a high trade-in value on a new one, and since the finance company has accepted his account, why not add a new refrigerator to the original contract for a few dollars a month more.

PERSONNEL

At the time I was working for the company, the total personnel numbered five. Mr. A, co-owner, in charge of bookkeeping, service and some financing. Mr. B, in charge of sales and buying. Mrs. A, co-owner, in charge of financing, credit, and some clerical compiling and telephone sales. Mr. C in charge of delivery and maintenance (janitorial) and myself, man Friday, handling all areas except advertising, buying and bookkeeping.

I have listed the personnel and their functions in order to illustrate later in this paper the unique cooperation and team action that is necessary in the day-to-day operation of the store.

CLIENTELE

In looking into the operations of any small enterprise, it is necessary to find what type customer the company is approaching. Stores vary in their clientele, and certain goods and services may not be appropriate for certain areas. For example, fine men's specialty shops and high quality stereo components are not going to be sold in the slums. However, discount shoe stores and co-op supermarkets may find these particular areas ideal for their business.

Superior TV was designed to sell to the lower socio-economic classes. The store location was deliberately planned for the area and the store advertising (window displays) were designed to attract the attention of these lower classes. Displays offered little or no down payment, easy credit terms, two for one sales and so on. Superior TV also appealed to a transient class of people through advertising. These people were predominantly young single office workers living in the downtown areas. They were approached through the radio (a pop station). The radio "spot" offered a TV in the house that same night for ten cents a day on the "meter plan." I will discuss the Meter Plan later in this paper in conjunction with the "Switch."

Superior TV was a pioneer in this technique of selection of clientele in the appliance business. The store appealed to the people on the street in a particular fashion, while at the same time offering a different perspective for telephone callers. This gave the company a great area of influence, and a potential for volume business, without the overhead of a large, high rent store.

DEPARTMENTAL TECHNIQUES

The Service Department

The service department was a money making enterprise in itself. It advertised in the paper as a "Radio and TV service company," however its main purpose was to practice the "Switch." The switch was simply talking the customer into buying a new set rather than spending money in fixing his present set. The switch can sometimes be legitimated, in that the broken set may really be a bad investment with chronic problems that will cost the customer more, in the long run, than the purchase of a new set.

Mr. A was the master of the switch for the service department. He had the technical training and the jargon necessary to impress a customer. Often he conducted a flawless switch on a perfectly functioning set a customer had brought in to have cleaned. He would claim that the picture tube had been "boosted," which makes the picture brighter but shortens its life. Other claims used to make a switch involved bad tubes, wiring, shorts, and all kinds of electrical hangups. Mr. A had a vivid imagination in this area of phony diagnoses and often convinced me of their authenticity when I knew damn well the set only needed $6.00 worth of tubes.

When the "switch" could not be used, the serviceman could still use the phony diagnosis in order to make more money on the repairs. I know of a particular case where the repair bill added up to $56.00 and the only thing wrong with the set was a bad antenna connection, that I fixed myself in ten minutes. In this case Mr. A did an easy switch into a new color television combination for $650.00. He told the bereaved customer that he need not pay for the repairs on his old set, in fact Mr. A would let him have a $56.00 discount on the color set. The customer came out with a smile, leaving a signed contract for over $700, and his original used set we sold later for $90.00.

Buying

Buying is one area where dishonest practices are seldom used. Although a good buyer is essential for a business, and thus a great amount of stress is placed on the buyer, he has little opportunity to use dishonest practices because the people he deals with are also businessmen, and he must rely on them in a continuing face-to-face relationship. This does not mean that the whole buying transaction is legitimate, this simply means that the people involved (factory representatives, wholesalers and retailers) tend to remain honest with one another. There are two notable exceptions, price fixing and double transfers. Price fixing is a common occurrence and often agreements are made between the retailers and wholesalers of a particular brand name, usually imported, to sell the product for a high price or an exceptionally low price in order to beat the discount houses at their own game.

One technique Superior TV used, was called the "double transfer." To work this scheme you need an appliance outlet in a discount house. What the buyer does, say, is to buy $10 thousand worth of fair traded merchandise, on consignment, to be delivered to Superior TV; when the goods arrive, a delivery crew moves them to the stockroom at the discount house, where they are sold, from the stockroom, to discount buyers. This seems foolish at first glance. Why discount fair-traded merchandise, which is against the law, when you could sell the merchandise legitimately in the retail store? The answer to this question is fairly simple. Ten thousand dollars worth of merchandise is a lot of risk. A risk which would not necessarily pay off in a retail store because everybody advertises the same merchandise at the same price. However, if you discount the merchandise in the stockroom of a discount house, the $10 thousand risk would probably liquidate itself in a few weeks. This is great because it is on consignment anyway, so you make money before you even have to pay for the merchandise. The "double transfer" is a risky operation because, if the factory representative ever finds out he can call back all the merchandise of his brand, demand full payment, and also take you to court for discounting fair-traded merchandise.

In the case of Superior TV we had over $85 thousand worth of R.C.A.'s in the stockroom of a discount house when the factory representative came to take inventory of our retail store. Not finding the products at the store, and knowing we had a discount operation, he almost fainted. After several hours of heated argument a compromise was reached with the factory representative. We would guarantee the pullout of all R.C.A.'s from our discount operation in 48 hours, and we would also write the factory representative a personal check for $500. Cheap at double the price.

Financing

Financing is a complicated business that I have little license to go into in detail. I can, however, submit some examples from experience with semi-honest or downright dishonest activities that occurred in the two years I was with Superior TV. One technique used by the store was the "cut-in" or the "payoff in the dark." These terms refer to cash payments made to credit managers in order to finance risky accounts. The credit manager is in the hot seat, because if enough of the accounts accepted by his finance company because of his approval, bounce, in other words have to be repossessed, the credit manager is handed his walking papers—he's fired.

The "big bust" is a term used when many accounts go bad. In 1965, a major finance company suffered a big bust. Over 3 million dollars worth of financed contracts defaulted (customers refused to pay on the contracts). In the controversy and investigation that went on over the next three months, it was found that seven credit managers had accepted bribes, over a three year period, from retail appliance stores throughout the area. The finance company almost went bankrupt.

"Loading" in financing, leads to the big bust. Loading means piling up thousands of dollars worth of bad accounts on a particular finance company. Prior to the declaration of bankruptcy, Superior TV loaded three different finance companies with over $400 thousand worth of bad accounts, and then officially declared bankruptcy, leaving the finance companies with no alternative but to collect on the accounts as best as possible. Since we were dissolved legally through bankruptcy, the finance companies could not make us buy back the accounts. We came out clean.

Delivery

The delivery department's main responsibility is to deliver merchandise to the customer as quickly and as efficiently as possible. The reason for this rapid and dependable service was to keep the customer from reconsidering the transaction and cancelling out before the merchandise reached his home. Another function of the delivery man was to soothe the customer of any apprehensions regarding the transaction. This is similar to the confidence man's technique of "cooling the mark out" described by Goffman.* Thus an alert delivery man must keep the

* E. Goffman, "On Cooling the Mark Out: Some Aspects of Adaptation to Failure," *Psychiatry*, 15:451–463 (1952).

customer sold, and must be sharp enough to try for an additional "load" as described in the beginning of this paper.

Clerical

This department, under the genius of Mr. and Mrs. A, maintained a strictly honest system of records and filing. In fact Mr. A said, "Any store that maintains written records of any kind must continually be wary of any dishonest or sloppy organization—for this is the evidence most likely to be brought into a court of law for close scrutiny." [*Counter-institutions protect themselves from the response of the institutional order.*]

Advertising

"Advertising practices as a general rule, are by definition, a misrepresentation," said Mr. B who was in charge of advertising at Superior TV. [*This is a form of legitimation.*]

Many media were used at Superior TV for promotion of merchandise. We advertised through the newspapers, radio, phone book, direct mail, and hand circulars. Every advertising gimmick was employed through these media at one time or another. Here are some examples:

1. "Rent to Own Plan" Advertised only on radio. Basically it offered a 19-inch portable television for ten cents a day on a rental plan with the idea of eventually owning the set. In reality, however, you could not rent the set, nor could you pay ten cents a day. The set was financed at $10 a month for 24 months, and you had to purchase the set.
2. "The Meter Plan" Advertised on radio and in the daily paper. Offered any new appliance on a month-to-month rental with an option to buy. A coin meter would be attached to the set in which you made your payments. After the customer called in, in response to the ad, he was told differently. A typical conversation went something like this—"Yes the meter plan applies to 19-inch Philco TV's." "Actually we don't attach a meter to the set because we find it unattractive for the customer to have a meter attached to the TV, therefore we simply ask you to make monthly payments of $10 a month." "No this does not apply to strict rental plans, as you probably heard, this is a rent with option to buy, this means your payments apply to the TV so actually you are owning the set—wouldn't you rather own the set for the same price?"

3. Merchandise Certificates   Usually these are given through direct mail, although we did have them appended to circulars that we passed out in given areas. Merchandise certificates have been used in promotional schemes for years. Actually they are worthless, but they are the bait to bring in customers. Superior TV printed thousands of merchandise certificates that gave a $50 discount on products over $300. When a customer comes into the store with a certificate and presents it to the salesman, he simply tells the customer to pick out a piece of merchandise worth over $300. He finds one that he likes and asks the price. (No prices were marked on our appliances.) The salesman says "$450, however you have a certificate, so for you $400." The customer saves nothing, because the salesman simply raised the original cost by $50.

4. Drawings and Raffles   Drawings and Raffles are widely used in all business. They offer something for nothing in order to get the customer into the store. Superior TV had a drawing in 1964 offering $10 thousand in prizes. In reality there was only one prize: a $500 color TV. The additional $9,500 in prizes were the phony merchandise certificates. The color TV, to be given away on a raffle, was not given away to just a randomly selected person, though it seemed that way to the customers; it was given to one of our customers who had previously bought merchandise from us. In "winning" the color set, this customer could be depended on to remain a satisfied customer and to continue buying from us and to contribute to our "image" of good will.

5. "Leaders"   "Leaders" are discounted merchandise heavily advertised to get people into the store. When a person comes in looking for the leader, a salesman uses the "switch" and sells him something for more money.

6. "Mystery Tune" Identification   Done over the radio. A listener calls the station and identifies the tune (usually an easily identifiable song). He wins the phony $50 merchandise certificate.

7. "Double Billing"   Double billing is a method by which the store can rob a company like Philco out of hundreds of dollars a month. When you advertise a brand name over the radio, that brand name will cooperate in paying your advertisement. This is called "co-op" advertising. To ascertain how much you pay out for advertising, Philco requires that you furnish receipts for the amount of air time on a particular radio station. Superior TV had co-op advertising with Philco on a fifty-fifty basis; in other words they would pay half the advertising fee if we advertised Philco. Mr. B, in charge of advertising, simply bribed the advertising salesman for the radio station into giving him blank invoices. Mr. B then added any price for the ads which he pleased, and submitted them to Philco for the

50 percent reimbursement. For a period of six months Superior TV did not pay a cent in advertising, yet advertised to the tune of $1,000 a month.

SALES

The areas in which dishonesty enters sales is truly extensive. A whole paper could be written on the subject without scratching the surface. Again, I must only cite examples from what I observed and, alas, what I learned to do myself. Assuming that we have a customer in the store, due to some misleading advertisement, there are many techniques which can be employed depending on the customer, the salesman's inclinations, and the nature of the ad the customer bit on. If the customer comes in to see a discounted TV (leader) the salesman uses the switch. He can say the leaders have all been sold, or he can be less dishonest and say they have freight damage. Either explanation will suffice for a good salesman to make a switch. Another technique is called the "burn." The burn is used when a woman comes in without her husband. She is shown the store, and she may ask the price of a particular piece of merchandise. The salesman quotes a very low figure, not so low she buys it on the spot, but high enough so she must go home to bring back her husband. When she returns with her husband, the salesman tells her that the set she looked at was sold an hour ago, "however we have another sale on this set here—originally $450, now $350."

Price quotes are easily made without the customer knowing where they came from. Since no prices are put on the merchandise, the customer can only guess as to their legitimacy. Superior TV used special codes for all merchandise on the floor. Codes are used in almost all types of enterprises, and some are almost impossible to decode, unless you know the system. Our price codes were fairly simple. A $500 item, retail, was coded 99005. The two nines were used only to mask the important numbers, 005, which is 500 backwards. These codes were pasted on all merchandise, and thus gave the salesman opportunity to bargain with the customers about prices only the salesman knew for sure.

Often a customer would come in wanting to buy a TV set, but wanting to trade in a used set. The salesman looks at the code on a TV (99005) and says, "this set normally sells for $550, but I'll allow you $50 on your old set." Another technique often used is the "special closer." This special closer is the salesman who finally concludes the sale after one or more salesmen have filled the buyer with misconceptions. Mr. B was the special closer at Superior TV and I have not seen another closer work as well as he does. Once, just as a joke, I approached a customer on the floor who was looking at a hi-fi stereo priced around $350. I told him I'd give him the set for $300 plus a 19-inch Philco portable for no additional charge. I then stepped out, leaving Mr. B to finish the sale. Mr. B switched this customer into a hi-fi stereo color combination for over $1,000.

Often fishy sales techniques become downright funny as in the case of what I call "bogus roles." Bogus roles are used in handling customers who are mad and demanding, usually over balloon prices or bad services. The customer walks in mad, demanding to see the manager. Mr. A introduces himself as the janitor, refers him to Mr. B who identifies himself as "just a salesman" and passes him off to Mrs. A who finally gives him to Mr. C or me. By this time the customer is so confused and infuriated that he doesn't know what to do—then we all start laughing and Mr. A introduces himself as the manager, slaps the customer on the back, and asks him his problem—it is another way of "cooling the mark out." In more serious cases, we employed bogus roles for process servers, members of the Better Business Bureau, and for collectors.

THE PHILOSOPHICAL MOTIVE
[LEGITIMATIONS OF THE COUNTER-INSTITUTION]

In outlining aspects of fraud, corruption, and criminality in this paper, I realize that the reader must wonder how we justified our practices— were there no feelings of remorse, guilt, qualms of conscience? Often after store hours, the five of us would gather around the display counter drinking and discussing aspects of the business day. These were the times when we got reflective—Mr. A wanted to get out of this filthy business into a more legitimate venture. Mr. B wanted to retire and fish. Mrs. A wanted just to be a housewife. Mr. C wanted to travel, and I wanted to go back to school. [*Notice the weakness of the biographical legitimations of the counter-institution—not strong enough to overcome a feeling of guilt.*]

I think that we all agreed that it was a "filthy business," but that our actions were justified and due to the vicious competition and the natural stupidity of our clientele. People discuss Social Darwinism as a relic of the turn of the century—as an outdated philosophical approach [*i.e. no longer a relevant symbolic legitimation for action*]. I submit that the Social Darwinistic philosophy still exists to a large extent, perhaps throughout the business world and politics. [*Or at least, the counter-institutions in these worlds find the philosophy of the "survival of the fittest" a useful legitimation.*]

Our justification for deviance in this area follows the Darwinian line. We were up against tough, vicious competition, our competitors used the same techniques of fraud and robbery that we did, often times more ruthlessly and calculatingly than our own techniques. The people were naturally stupid, how else could you account for the day-to-day success of our operations?

When a value system of this magnitude is continually being reinforced, it is rather simple to accept it not only in the business world, but in all areas of interaction. [*The legitimation of Darwinistic philosophy fits the counter-institution into the institutional order fairly well, though it fails for biographical legitimation.*] Therefore I find it fairly easy to detect people with this set of values simply by talking with them for a short time. There are phrases that often come up, like, "What's in it for me?" and "It's a dog eat dog world."

☐ ☐ ☐

It is a truism that individuals and institutions directly affected by counter-institutions are most likely to produce some social response, some form of social control. Whether this control is relational or formal depends on a great many things: whether or not there is a law against the behavior, whether or not a response is possible, whether or not a response is practical, the effect of continuing dependence on the counter-institution, and other factors. The counter-institution that victimizes others from within a legitimate institution is perhaps safest from both relational and formal control, because its illegitimacy is not immediately obvious. It is very difficult to get satisfaction after being cheated as a consumer; it can cost far more to go to court than could be recovered. Just as legitimate institutions of behavior can defend themselves, counter-institutions can often win out when only relational social control is used. The counter-institution, while not legitimate, may be more powerful in its territory than the ordinary person who would want to attack it. It may also be far more ready for a conflict, as attack is part of its expectations.

☐ ☐ ☐

□ □ □

Almost all human behavior is guided by informal social control. The ideas regarding what is right and wrong, what is good and bad, what one should and should not do that the individual has taken into himself are called to consciousness many times every day, and continue to be guides even when not called to conscious thought. The encouragements and warnings of the people around him, particularly those with whom he shares some relationship, keep him attuned to the forms of behavior that will be rewarded and the forms which will be punished.

If you will think of the multiple relationships in which you are involved, many cross-cutting, situational, and dependent ideas you have about proper courses of action, you can begin to see the complexity of the network in which informal social control takes place. Our multiple involvements, our relative attachments to each, and our complex biographies always influence the nature of the social control that we give off and that which is directed toward us; they also affect whether or not the

INFORMAL
SOCIAL CONTROL

control will work. Just to take a simple example of a student deciding whether or not to smoke marijuana can give us an idea of the multiple involvements, situations, and cross-pressures that exist in any informal social control situation. Perhaps the student has heard that marijuana is not harmful from some of his friends who use it. He has heard that it is harmful from his parents and the newspapers. He wants to do well in school and is afraid of the consequences of smoking marijuana. He also knows it is illegal, but doesn't think the chance of being caught is very great. His recently acquired girl friend, with whom he has gone to bed a few times, but doesn't know really well, smokes marijuana occasionally when she is with some of her friends, but not when she is with others. He lives in a dormitory and has some beer drinking friends, some people he knows from classes, and some people he nods to. He sees his parents about once a month, and over vacations. He knows some other adults, teachers, relatives, and friends of his parents, but he doesn't know them very well. He doesn't know any "heads" really well, though he sees them around campus. He digs rock music and occasionally goes to a concert or dance. He studies enough to keep up a "B" average but it doesn't take up all of his time. These are the people, thoughts, and commitments that might incline him to try marijuana, or to avoid it. But it is not just the weights of various positive and negative controls that determine his actions, because the weights are constantly shifting, and one day one thing is more important, while another day it is something else. He is also involved in situations that are more or less conducive to smoking, surrounded by favorable and unfavorable others and favorable and unfavorable circumstances. He is extremely unlikely to start smoking at the dinner table at home, or in class, or alone in his dormitory room, or with beer drinking friends. Both these situations and the others present would informally control him not to. Even when he is alone his self-control and the anticipations of the reactions of these others would keep him from it. He is much more likely to smoke when he is passed a joint by his girl friend at a small party in an off-campus apartment where everyone else is smoking and none of his straight friends, acquaintances, or relatives will know of it.

Taking any action has potential consequences for many other people and things. While most people might consider some form of unconventional behavior or the other, by itself, it is never by itself. There are always fears, hopes, and others who approve or disapprove.

Any attempt at informal control over another person's behavior will be considered in this matrix, so the success of every attempt at control is problematic. Controls can be accepted, seemingly accepted, rejected, and avoided. Fronts can be established that make attempts at control unlikely; fronts can be breached.

Particular moods, preceding events, affections or distastes, momentary desires, and dispositions toward conformity or rebellion may all play a part in determining which controls will work when for whom, which controls will backfire, and which controls will be ineffectual.

Bearing in mind the complexity of actual situations, let us examine some of the controls that keep conventional people conventional, those that bring them back to conventionality when they have done something unconventional; the controls that urge a conventional person into "deviance," and the controls that keep a deviant person deviant. Many of the following examples were suggested by Jane Wright, Margaret Fleming, Alina Garrett, Maureen Komlos, Donna McCombs, Sheila Aronoff, Bill Horan, and Bobby Lomon in the course of a class assignment to study informal social controls.

CONTROLS THAT KEEP CONVENTIONAL PEOPLE CONVENTIONAL

People usually feel or anticipate feelings of pride at doing something right, and guilt at doing something wrong. One young lady became a nurse because her upbringing favored humanitarian forms of endeavor, because her mother was a nurse, and because her father thought it was a great idea. Thus she could feel pride in her occupation.

On a hot evening a couple across the alley moved their television set out on the balcony, and set it up with their backs to their neighbors' apartment window, so as not to invade the privacy of the apartment. Noticing this the apartment dwellers closed their blinds so as not to invade the privacy of the newly extended living room. These reciprocal actions kept either from improperly invading the space of the other.

Proprieties of conversation are often maintained, even at the expense of communication. A waitress, dealing with a customer who didn't speak English, needed to know if the customer wanted a chicken leg or breast. She said "leg" and pointed to her leg. Then she said "breast" and pointed to her arm.

Bodily contact is regulated by many norms. One woman pointed out that she was always upset when any man kissed one of her young daughters on the mouth; she felt this type of kiss should be reserved for lovers.

A young lady working for a Labor College would never drink her favorite beer, which was made by nonunion labor, when she was out with other union people, though she would at home.

On a first visit to a couple's home, a student observed a single leather chair and a long sofa in the living room. Though she would rather have sat in the chair, she felt it might have been the "favorite" chair of the man in the house, and to avoid even minor dislocation she sat on the sofa.

Inappropriate laughing in public is felt to be a breach of the impersonal face we are supposed to maintain in such situations. One young lady who was overcome with a need to laugh at something that had happened earlier was so constrained by being on a bus full of strangers that she got off the bus to laugh.

Our conceptions of what others might think, or what conclusions they might draw about our behavior, often cause caution even when there is no need. Even the appearance of straying is avoided, for example, by the man whose wife is out of town and is afraid to come home late because the neighbors will see his car, and might talk. A young boy on a bus looks around to see if anyone is watching before he sneaks a glance at the girls in the lingerie ads. A woman on a bus conceals her lurid paperback behind the cover of a best seller.

Most people have a very conventional set of self-controls that keep them from being tempted by the rewards of counter-institutions. They are concerned with what others would think, often flattering themselves that others care enough to think about them. These self-controls are created and supported by the institutions and others around them. In most cases they keep the individual conventional.

At a relational level, the others around us are constantly exercising control over our behavior. For the most part this control is vested in the coordinations required by the institutions we share with them, and never needs be mentioned. They control our behavior positively by accepting us, and negatively by avoiding or correcting us.

Work situations, for example, can command our loyalty. Students who have been hired for a fair wage by a friendly employer may go out of their way to give him a hand when he needs it, even when it conflicts with their work as students. The owner of a small grocery store gets to know his customers, and will cash checks for those he trusts. Bus drivers automatically hand transfers to those who indicate by their gestures that they want them. Each of these activities rewards us for behaving conventionally.

Families often guide their children into conventionality by providing them with rewards for being dutiful. One family, for example, went out of its way to decorate their daughter's room, to give her things she wanted, to praise her for her achievements, in the hope that she would continue to live at home while attending university, and in the hope that she would meet a nice boy of the same religion to marry.

Sometimes deviants can help a person to remain conventional by excluding him from their activities. A clean-cut college student who sits down at a cafeteria table occupied by freaks may be pointedly ignored on the assumption that he is not one of them, and may be an informer. Since he doesn't make contact he is forced back to conventionality. Likewise the individual who wanders into a gay bar and is verbally assaulted is speedily returned to his conventional ways.

Expressions of displeasure at lapses in social conduct can take many forms.

There is an impersonal order that others often assume is shared by all. They act on this assumption, and penalize anyone who is outside of the order. For example the assumption is that people sleep at night and work during the day, so a day sleeper is discomfited and awakened by pneumatic hammers starting at 7 A.M., and by telephone calls starting at 8 A.M. Callers are apologetic for waking one from eight to ten, slightly apologetic from ten until noon, and self-righteous from noon until 2 P.M., when no decent person should be sleeping.

Credit buying has become so universal that a person who habitually pays in cash is penalized by having no credit rating when he needs to buy a car.

People often express their displeasure by a pointed glance. One office worker reported that in her office the coffee break was taken at the desk, and the majority of the employees bought something to eat during their break. Since she was trying to save money she didn't buy anything, and she suddenly noticed that her boss was giving her "sharp glances" when she talked with the other workers. It turned out that "coffee break" was composed of both talking and eating, and if one didn't eat, one was expected to keep on working. Similarly, waitresses who have been standing in a group chatting, waiting for customers to come to their tables, can be scattered to their stations by a glance from the manager.

Deprecatory comments are often made, even by strangers, about things they consider out of order. One mother, whose nine-month-old son had adopted an old pipe as a teething object, was almost reduced to tears when passers-by glanced at the baby in the carriage with the pipe in his mouth, then at her, and muttered words like "disgusting" and "terrible."

Anxieties over the appearance of deviance are often handled by making it a joke. One young man reached across the back of another, and momentarily his arm rested across his shoulders. The second young man jumped up, laughing, dropped his wrist, and said, "Be careful— you know I'm not that kind."

Adherence to certain routines is often demanded, with various woes reserved for those who break them. One young man felt constrained to call his wife exactly at 9 P.M. every evening he worked late. If he failed she would worry until he got home and scold him for worrying her. A bridge club may institutionalize certain conversational conventions, such as an unwritten rule that only trivia is to be discussed. Anyone who ventures a new line of conversation will find the topic of conversation immediately changed to something trivial.

Others will sometimes give us a slight nudge if we don't appear to them as if we are about to do what we are supposed to. This may be in a check-out line in a grocery store, not starting quickly enough on a green light, or standing paralyzed at the thought of taking the first step down the aisle to get married. It is for no small reason that the father escorts the bride, and the best man the groom, safely to the altar.

Another effective technique of control is silence. When everyone falls silent upon our entrance to a room, when a father pointedly refuses to speak to his daughter's boy friend, when attempts at brilliant conversational ploys are rewarded by embarrassed silence, when people who *ought* to say something don't say anything, we see the control of silence.

On another level we are controlled by our overlapping plans and obligations in many of our institutionalized endeavors. Before all our obligations are cleared up in one institution we have contracted more in others. At the moment I am writing this it is the middle of the winter, in Montreal, the temperature outside is twelve below zero, and I would really like to be lying on the beach in Mexico. But I've got an important dinner engagement this weekend, I have to finish this book, I have to meet my classes, I have to grade some students' papers so they will know what to do for the rest of the year, and I have to finish a paper of my own by the end of the month so that I can go to a conference next summer. If I left for Mexico I would leave many people stranded, so I don't go. I might say to hell with any one of these obligations, but to throw over the entire pattern would signal a dramatic shift in my life. It is similar patterns of overlapping obligations and plans that keeps more men and women from committing adultery, getting divorced, and/or quitting their jobs. It is simply impossible to look upon social control as a simple yes-no dichotomy. It is always yes here, no there, yes somewhere else, and maybe in another place. If we took all of our obligations seriously, as we are trained to do in middle-class homes, we would never have the time to do anything deviant.

I have tried to give both positive and negative examples of the self-control and the relational control that keep people conforming to conventional and legitimate institutions. Given their vast number and their apparent power over our behavior, the most interesting thing about them is that they don't always work. When they don't work, and someone becomes deviant, there are other controls to bring him back to conventionality.

CONTROLS THAT RETURN DEVIANTS TO CONVENTIONALITY

The person who is trained to deviance at his mother's breast and through his entire socialization is a special case that need not much concern us here. Most people have been at least somewhat socialized to conventionality, and have only later moved into various forms of unconventionality. Their early training to conventionality remains with them always (unless they undergo a complete conversion and totally reinterpret their past) and is always a lever that may be used to return them to conventionality. The lever is variably effective, however, because there may be no one around to work it, and the individual may have created a sheltering structure of legitimations for his activities that keeps him from wanting to work it.

But the individual's self-control does often bring him back to conventionality.

The prototypical self-reaction that returns a person to conventionality is "Oh God, what am I doing among these perverts, I'll never stray from morality again." Anyone whose self-control seriously conflicts with his unconventional behavior is ripe for a return to conformity. The triggering incident may be almost anything, a sudden vision of himself being punished, losing his conventional life, seeing an unusually outrageous scene, or simply being overcome by fright. A number of students are treated to an episode of irrational behavior at a party where they are smoking marijuana, mostly for the first time. Several go home that night vowing never to touch the evil weed again. A young man has a stripper sit beside him in a cabaret and puts his hand on her breast, as she orders an expensive drink, on him. He leaves. A young man accosted by a prostitute goes to her room, sees her in the light, is overwhelmed by what he is doing and asks for his money back. A teenager realizes that if he keeps on stripping cars he will get caught, and suddenly becomes more involved with a conventional friend.

Many people returning to their parents or in-laws for a visit will take care to remember special traits that should or should not be exhibited while there. Their self-controls lead them to behave, at least temporarily, as conventional people are expected to.

A girl who is working as a prostitute, or as a cocktail waitress, may decide to pick up a conventional skill, such as teaching, to provide her with a return path to conventionality when her present occupation becomes too taxing or unrewarding.

A bisexual is very much attracted to another boy at a party, but doesn't ask him to dance because he fears the reaction of the heterosexuals around him.

In many situations an individual will drift into an unconventional scene without giving much thought to it. He goes along for other reasons, because he likes someone, because he doesn't know what the scene is, because he had felt confident that he could carry it off. He is not really convinced by the legitimations that others have for the behavior, and suddenly normalcy calls him back with a flash of guilt. Put another way, a lot of people try some deviance and return to conventionality because it scares them and makes them feel bad.

Probably the strongest force making a person become conventional again is provided by those others with whom he has relationships in legitimate or illegitimate institutions.

It is widely recognized in motorcycle clubs, for example, that the first baby kills the motorcycle. Similarly it is recognized among street-corner boys that after a fellow gets married and gets a job he is not going to be available very much. The fact that about 80 percent of juvenile delinquents do not become adult criminals testifies to the rewards of conventionality.

Sometimes conventional others can mobilize the deviant's self-control, by making him frightened of the consequences of his behavior. Police officers often act as informal control agents when they lecture or give a reprimand instead of arresting an individual.

Even more effective than police officers are significant others who sometimes argue against the behavior in quite subtle ways. A girl friend who becomes cold and distant when one smokes marijuana, and is thoughtful and loving at other times. The wife who allows her husband to have a mistress only on the condition that he bring her home so she can destroy her. The company that will promote the homosexual only if he is married and has children.

The problem that significant others face in luring or shaming the deviant back to conventionality is to frustrate a particular desire while rewarding him in other ways. Blanket prohibitions have a way of making people choose; if they are bludgeoned into becoming conventional they may hate the person who did it, and if the bludgeon fails they may become more confirmed in their deviance.

Nonsignificant others may just provide warnings and harassment, intentionally or unintentionally. Rude jokes about homosexuals may strike the covert homosexual painfully. Cries of "why don't you go back to Russia," "why don't you cut your hair," "hippie," and "we don't serve your kind here" may eventually become taxing to such a point that the deviant becomes conventional or inconspicuous.

There is always a strong control from overlapping conventional institutions. Deviance in one area perils progress in others, which many people are ready to point out whether it happens to be true or not in the particular case.

A number of people make it their business to give deviants a hard time. Doormen, unless they get a cut, will threaten to turn prostitutes in. Hotel clerks may be suspicious of couples without luggage. Restaurant managers often refuse to admit persons improperly attired. Busybodies and neighborhood gossips can spread the word of scandal. These forms of control tend to be less effective in large cities, where people can live somewhat anonymously and move around more freely.

The other participants in a counter-institution may even exercise informal control to return a person to conventionality. Most commonly this probably comes from their not opening up to him, not letting him in. The gang that has control over prostitution or drugs in an area may use extortion or violence to keep a newcomer out. After a few death threats and beatings conventionality may not look so bad. Positive control, where the veteran takes the neophyte aside and whispers, "You better get outa 'dis kid, we always lose. I'm too old to go straight, but you've got a wife and family and your whole life ahead of you," probably happens mostly in the movies. Few counter-institutions reject a willing recruit, and if they do so it is generally because he is incompetent or uncool, not because they are interested in his welfare.

On occasion, attempts at informal control take the form of attempting to destroy the legitimations of the counter-institution. This is a double-edged sword, however, because in the very process of verbalizing the legitimations the individual may become more committed to them. Few people are won over in debates, anyway. A more plausible approach is to remain silent on the counter-institutional legitimations and give legitimations, not directly contradictory, for the various other institutions of conventionality.

A person may be "blacklisted" by his union for breaking union rules, which effectively shuts off his employment.

Organizations often suggest that a young man shave his beard or cut his hair if he wishes to remain employed.

Druggists address girls with prescriptions for birth control pills as "Mrs." and sometimes become rude when the girl indicates that she is "Miss."

The entrance of a lady into most pool halls renders the habitués inarticulate; her mere presence shuts off about 90 percent of their language.

Sometimes an attempt is made to mobilize common values to return people to conventionality. In a church arts project one lady was so disturbed at the continuing mess that she hand-painted a sign for the wall that said "Clean Up With Christ."

Minor deviancies may be met with the silent treatment, significant others simply refuse to talk to the violator for several days. One lady reported that she attended a Halloween costume party in the suburbs, attired as a stripper, and was as ostracized as if she had actually been a lady of ill-repute.

Among high school students the interpersonal controls may be such that almost no one will dare to wear yellow or green on Thursday, or red on Friday, for fear of being baited as homosexual or pregnant.

Relational control starts in childhood, when the child says "Stupid Daddy," and is told, "no, bad, no." It continues through our lives, bringing us back to conventionality, and our relatives have to deal with it as they arrange our proper funeral.

With this barrage of self and relational controls keeping us conventional and bringing us back from deviance it is hard to see how anyone can be involved in a counter-institution without its being an intolerable hassle. The answer is, of course, that counter-institutions use informal controls as well.

CONTROLS THAT LEAD TO DEVIANCE

Internalized self-control is neither all-encompassing nor always relevant to an individual. If it were, the only sort of deviants we would find would be those who created their own emergent counter-institutions before everyone's self-controls were socialized to reject it.

Self-control is not all-encompassing, and it is complex. An individual may never have been taught that some particular behavior was bad, or if he was taught he might not have been taught well. He might feel that some other value, such as friendship, acceptance, or money is more important than his reluctance to be unconventional. Even given normally strong self-control an individual can be involved in a situation where that control is not very relevant. Suppose you were in a position to steal $20,000 you needed for your family from a large corporation that was insured against theft, and that you *knew* that it was 100 to 1 that no one would find out, and if you *were* found out you would be allowed to return the money without any charges being pressed—would you not be tempted? Our potential marijuana smoker is in a situation somewhat like this when he is offered a joint in an apartment. Many forms of counter-institutional activity may be attempted with a relatively high chance of being rewarded and a relatively low chance of being caught. A person may act first in such a situation, find it rewarding, and further weaken the self-controls he might have against it.

It is possible that a person's self-controls will lead him toward a counter-institution without his ever having contacted it. This is somewhat similar to the idea that deviance is rebellion, against parents, against authorities. Clearly not everyone likes his parents. Many parents are not likeable. A parental value system that condemns deviant behavior may become a negative map of the social world, for a person who hates or wants to hurt his parents. An old saying goes, "The enemy of my enemy is my friend." The value structure of disliked parents, or other authorities for that matter, may become a guide to one's potential friends. I don't know the proportions, but I have the impression that a lot of the teen-age runaways in hip communities came from families appalled by the hip phenomenon.

Sometimes one self-control directly contradicts another. One student reported that she had been outraged when another woman handed in a paper that had been plagiarized and got a higher grade than she did for her own work. Her first reaction was to report the plagiarism, or at least to tell the woman of her displeasure, but the woman was the wife of her employer and they mixed socially. In lieu of risking losing her job or alienating someone she had to be with, she swallowed her outrage and silently fumed. Her self-controls led her to value her employment more highly than her outrage.

Especially in a time of massive change many counter-institutions arise which individuals were not socialized against. Even their current legitimate involvements may not preclude trying these emergent counter-institutions. Nobody ever told me that marijuana was bad when I was a child; few people even knew about it. I was a beginning graduate student when I first read about it, and the article I read indicated it was harmless.

As I indicated in the last two sections, self-control is one of the major barriers to attempting or continuing deviance, but it is an incomplete barrier in a society cross-cut with many unintegrated moral traditions, many different communities, and many different kinds of parental values. A person may be frightened out of participating in a counter-institution because of his self-control, but he may also find participation rewarding and his former fears groundless. It is logical to assume that counter-institutions that are growing and spreading rapidly are not having a hard time overcoming the self-controls people have against them.

People in counter-institutions, of course, often reward others for following the counter-institution, and following it usually provides benefits in itself. The apprentice prostitute gets a quick increase in income, the bottle gang member gets his drink, the gay bar patron gets to cruise, the marijuana user gets high, the transvestite solves his problem, and the delinquent gets friends, protection from other gangs, and money.

Counter-institutions may also have elaborate negative controls that are used to keep participants from going straight. When someone from the outside visits a moonshine still in one of the hollows of eastern Kentucky he may well be asked to throw a piece of wood on the fire under the still. It is then pointed out to him that he is now an accomplice and would go to jail with the rest of them should he tell anyone the whereabouts of the still. Some counter-institutions don't object to an individual getting out of the game so long as he doesn't blow the whistle on the people he leaves behind. Inevitably, as the neophyte picks up the counter-institution the others will paint a black picture of the conventional world and often indicate their disapproval of his continuing involvement in it. A mistress may press a man to divorce his wife, using all her wiles to get the message across. It may be suggested that the apprentice prostitute not go home to visit her family until she has her cover story straight. The homosexual may be teased for going out with a girl. The delinquent may be called chicken if he doesn't want to go along on a robbery, or if he backs out of a fight.

One paradox that has fascinated sociologists is the way in which conventional people encourage others to become deviant or more deviant by either rewarding them or rejecting them. This will be discussed at the group level in the chapter on deviation amplifying feedback, but we can see how it works for individuals here. There is no contradiction in suggesting that both rewards and rejection can encourage deviance, because they occur in different situations. Say, for example, that a boy steals a car and a pretty girl is willing to go out with him in spite of the fact that she knows the car is stolen; he is rewarded for stealing the car. If the pretty girl exercises negative controls and won't go out with him because he stole the car, he is rejected for stealing the car. Perhaps this relational control works and he becomes contrite and returns the car. On the other hand he may say, "stupid girl," and go out to pick up another girl who is a member of the gang and enjoys riding in stolen cars, thus getting himself deeper into the gang. We often give prestige to money without questioning its source. Anyone who has the cash can live in a luxury apartment and enjoy most of the other things that a conventional person with money can. Women often prefer to have their hair styled and their homes decorated by homosexuals, because they are not potentially threatening males. The conventional world rewards deviants in many ways.

Attempts at rejection that fail to reject the behavior without rejecting the person, result in expelling the deviant from conventional society and increasing the likelihood that he will find his home in the counter-institution. The impersonal rejection of passers-by is particularly likely to result in increasing the individual's isolation from these annoyances. The man with long hair may move to a hip ghetto where he is normal, the radical may form stronger bonds with other radicals, and the alcoholic may move to skid row to be with his "buddies" who don't look down on him.

Thus, in certain situations, the rewards and punishments of informal social control can move an individual from conventionality to deviance.

CONTROLS THAT KEEP DEVIANTS DEVIANT

After a person has been participating in a counter-institution for a time many of his self-controls will no longer belong to the conventional world. Most of his activities and most of his self-controls will still be conventional (unless, of course, he has shifted to a new reality), but in the areas of his counter-institutional activity he will have started to internalize a new set of self-controls based upon the counter-institution and its legitimations.

He may feel proud of his skills in picking pockets or opening safes. The prostitute may feel that she is performing a useful social service, taking care of the handicapped, the lonesome, and the strange ones who might otherwise be on the streets undoing innocent girls. The bottle gang member might feel good about being a "regular guy" who is asked to share the bottle. The delinquent may feel pride in the power and loyalty of his gang. The marijuana smoker may have an almost missionary zeal for spreading this beautiful way of seeing the world. The crooked businessman may feel a pride in his sharpness, while the heroin addict may feel pride in his coolness. The homosexual may be truly involved in a love relationship. The mafioso may feel that he is really doing well for himself and his family. In short, anyone thoroughly involved in a counter-institution feels some pride, on some basis, in what he is doing.

Negatively there might be a fear of the straight world, a fear of rejection if it is ventured into carelessly, a feeling that people who work for a living are saps, any of which might restrain him from becoming conventional. There may also be immense guilt at the thought of selling out or not supporting friends and comrades-in-arms. The delinquent may feel that he has to go to a fight. The marijuana smoker might feel shame and embarrassment if company drops over and he has no grass to offer. In short, by both positive and negative self-controls the individual supports his continued activity in the counter-institution. These, of course, are unlikely to be any more effective than the self-controls of conventional people, but both usually keep most of the people in their behavior patterns most of the time. The deviant is far more likely to have cross-cutting and contradictory self-controls than is the conventional person simply because he is in many ways still conventional. On the other hand, he may have built better defenses against these conflicts because his new self-controls probably displaced old ones and he probably had to go through a certain amount of self-examination to achieve his present state.

In many ways the relational controls that helped a person to become deviant are the same ones that help him to remain so. The same pattern of rejection and reward from the straight world continues, and many of the positive and negative controls of the counter-institution members are the same. The rejection by the straight world may be more thorough, the acceptance within the counter-institution may be more complete.

Here again, as in the conventional world, there may come to be overlapping patterns of involvements that constitute together an extremely powerful network of controls. The heroin addict may have to keep up his thefts to keep up his addiction, the prostitute may have girls she is training and a pimp that she loves, and debts that she owes on her fines or charge accounts that keep her in prostitution. The marijuana smoker may be the only source of supply for a circle of friends, and dealing may provide his only income; he may have to schedule trips to score, and his social contacts may always be in smoking circles. The homosexual may buy his daily necessities from homosexuals, sell his merchandise to homosexuals, own part of a gay bar, live in an apartment house reserved for homosexuals, and be "married" to a homosexual. Since the pattern of overlapping obligations of the conventional world includes all the institutions of labor, sex, and territory, it may well be that the deviant's pattern of overlapping obligations within the deviant world is not as extensive, and part of his obligations may be in the conventional world. The fact that he has obligations in two worlds may well provide him with a constant battle of segregation and integration. Even so, his overlapping involvements in counter-institutions constitute a powerful force stabilizing him in his deviant world.

A further adaptation to being in a counter-institution is the development of various "fronts" that are useful for projecting an image of conventionality or deflecting attempts at informal social control. These differ from legitimations in that they are mostly what Goffman calls techniques of "impression management."

A student, knowing that the telephone company doesn't trust students and requires a large deposit before installing a phone for them, told them that he was a visiting professor from India and that his name was Hare Krishna. He got the phone with no mention of a deposit.

A married woman whose mother lived upstairs in the apartment building cleaned whenever she felt like it, but carefully left the vacuum cleaner in the middle of the living room, so that when her mother dropped in, as she often did, it would look as if she were in the middle of cleaning.

A couple who made their own wine, but who had a group of friends who were teetotalers, would always bake homemade bread and buns when the wine was fermenting in the basement so that their friends would think that the strong yeast odor came from the baking.

A businessman who has an extramarital relationship with his secretary always leaves the office fifteen minutes before she does and meets her at a prearranged spot.

A divorcee whose boyfriend sleeps with her every weekend carefully messes up the sofa bed so that her older daughter will think he slept in the living room.

Marijuana smokers burn incense to disguise the smell of marijuana in the air.

A homosexual and a lesbian may get married to project the image of a normal family.

A smart delinquent will act very polite and middle-class to a police officer.

A prostitute may become a fashion model. A crooked business may spend a lot of money on its office decorations to impress clients with its stability and honesty.

A communal family may spend a fair amount of time painting the outside of its house so that the neighbors will not complain about it.

We all use impression management in our daily lives to avoid informal and sometimes formal social controls. For the counter-institution and the people who follow it, it becomes a total first line of defense against informal social control. It usually deflects the attempts at control, and makes living far less problematic.

Informal social control is a kaleidoscope of shifting patterns of influences and attempted influences, directed to many different ends in never constant situations. To select out as I have the one dimension of conformity and deviance is to vastly oversimplify this pattern.

Should you care to become attuned to the nuances of control in your mind and your surroundings you will find complex patterns beginning to appear, and you will understand the many other things that are influenced besides conformity and deviance.

□ □ □

Now we turn to the more formal kinds of social reaction—the sort effected by major institutions in the institutional order, or by agents hired by the institutions and directed to enforce the "legitimate" ways of behaving on the people in their jurisdiction. We have seen that the institutional order is a collection of somewhat independent institutions of behavior that contend with one another as well as cooperate. We have seen that the symbolic universe is made up of a number of independent and mutually disputed traditions loosely organized under the rubrics of science, philosophy, theology, and mythology. We have seen that agencies of government are institutions like others in the institutional order, pushing and pulling for influence, legitimacy in their enterprises, and hegemony over the relations of other institutions. It is from this mixed bag that formal social control over counterinstitutions is developed.

The social reality developed from these sources is not total or logical; the formal social control is not either.

FORMAL
SOCIAL CONTROL

It was developed through social processes in response to behavior that upset some people at some point in history. As Thurman Arnold noted in *The Symbols of Government*,[1] law is not scientific, nor even rational, since it comes from so many sources over such a long historical period. In the Province of Quebec, to take an extreme example, there is a combination of English criminal law, French civil law, and some American corporation law, all overlaid with Canadian law and precedents. The kind and sort of laws we have reflects the beliefs and practices of diverse groups in positions of political power in our history. If you are of the belief that all laws should be enforced "without fear or favor" read copies of all the various criminal and civil codes that apply to your jurisdiction. It should be enlightening.

Law is the most codified basis for formal social control. The control over morality exercised by social workers is less codified but springs from similarly diverse sources. Popular morality, left-over "lady bountiful" concepts of welfare, and academic prescriptions of the ways in which the poor should behave are subtly enforced as the social worker works with her "clients."

The control over subjective realities exercised by mental hospital psychiatrists is similarly based on middle-class conventions, tests of reality orientation based on assumptions of years ago, and psychoanalytic theorizing. While there is a great deal in both social work and mental hospital psychiatry that is logical and rational within the terms of socially constructed reality, they both had historical developments that have produced inconsistent forms of social control. They are both, also, intended to enforce part of the social definition of reality, and to provide "therapy" for those who stray.

Formal social control is a response to the behavior of people with an experience–social reality conflict. In a rough way the amount of formal control that a society employs may be taken as an indicator of the amount of reality constriction it has. When a society puts an ever-increasing portion of its population in jails and mental hospitals, it is an indication that an increasing number of people are experiencing a conflict with the social definition of reality being enforced. A totalitarian state with its constricted definition of reality must have more police, more jails, more mental hospitals than a pluralistic state that grants legitimacy to a broader range of behavior.

Mental hospital psychiatrists and social workers generally effect social control against individuals with bad habits; law is generally used against counter-institutions of behavior. Since most counter-institutions of behavior have been around for a long time the laws that respond to

---

[1] Thurman W. Arnold, *The Symbols of Government* (New Haven: Yale University Press, 1935).

them have been long in force. In order to see the process of law construction, the process of formal social reaction to counter-institutions, we will have to examine the enactment of a law to prohibit a relatively new counter-institution, for example the smoking of marijuana.

When a counter-institution comes to public attention many people will be indifferent to it, especially if it has no impact on their lives. Other people will adopt it, and still others will want to ban it. Those who wish to prohibit a new counter-institution generally do so because it violates a value that they hold as their own, or because it disturbs an institution of behavior that they follow. Either an individual or a legitimate institution may take the lead, and in either case the goal is the same: to pass a law that will authorize the agents of formal social control to eliminate and destroy the counter-institution. The process of getting a law passed may be quite difficult if its passage affects other legitimate institutions; it may be quite easy if the behavior is isolated and enacted by powerless people.

People rarely do things involving much effort from which they derive no rewards. The benefits to be derived from passing a law against something are thus frequently most important to the people most involved; they may be considerably less important to other people and institutions. An individual may start a moral crusade because he has been thoroughly socialized to one of the values of the symbolic universe and the world will not seem right to him unless the counter-institution is outlawed. An institution may start a moral crusade because it can gain power and influence by outlawing a competing institution, or because it can insure its survival in the push and pull of the institutional order by giving itself more work to do. Antiunion legislation was prompted by business interests, antimarijuana legislation helped the Narcotics Bureau to survive. Whether started by an individual or an organization, the crusade to pass a law must gain the support of enough people and institutions to actually get the law through. This may be facilitated by common adherence to the value of the symbolic universe as well as by trading and deals among interacting institutions. In the following adaptation Howard Becker examines the process of law creation by looking at the activities of individuals.

☐ ☐ ☐

20

OUTSIDERS
Studies in the Sociology of Deviance

HOWARD S. BECKER

RULE CREATORS

The prototype of the rule creator, but not the only variety as we shall
see, is the crusading reformer. He is interested in the content of rules.
The existing rules do not satisfy him because there is some evil which
profoundly disturbs him. He feels that nothing can be right in the world
until rules are made to correct it. He operates with an absolute ethic;
what he sees is truly and totally evil with no qualification. Any means is
justified to do away with it. The crusader is fervent and righteous, often
self-righteous. [*The symbolic universe, with its claim to total reality
organization, often inculcates such adherence to values through socialization. The crusader is different from others in that he is willing to
devote more energy to his views.*]

It is appropriate to think of reformers as crusaders because they
typically believe that their mission is a holy one. The prohibitionist
serves as an excellent example, as does the person who wants to suppress vice and sexual delinquency or the person who wants to do
away with gambling.

These examples suggest that the moral crusader is a meddling busy-
body, interested in forcing his own morals on others. But this is a one-
sided view. Many moral crusades have strong humanitarian overtones.
The crusader is not only interested in seeing to it that other people do
what he thinks right. He believes that if they do what is right it will be
good for them. [*The legitimate values are held to be inherently good.*]
Or he may feel that his reform will prevent certain kinds of exploitation
of one person by another. Prohibitionists felt that they were not simply
forcing their morals on others, but attempting to provide the conditions
for a better way of life for people prevented by drink from realizing a
truly good life. Abolitionists were not simply trying to prevent slave
owners from doing the wrong thing; they were trying to help slaves to
achieve a better life. Because of the importance of the humanitarian
motive, moral crusaders (despite their relatively single-minded devo-
tion to their particular cause) often lend their support to other
humanitarian crusades.

.　　.　　.

Moral crusaders typically want to help those beneath them to achieve a better status. That those beneath them do not always like the means proposed for their salvation is another matter. But this fact— that moral crusades are typically dominated by those in the upper levels of the social structure—means that they add to the power they derive from the legitimacy of their moral position, the power they derive from their superior position in society. [*Not only do they have the power of symbolic legitimacy, but they also can sway legitimate institutions in which they are leaders.*]

Naturally, many moral crusades draw support from people whose motives are less pure than those of the crusader. Thus, some industrialists supported Prohibition because they felt it would provide them with a more manageable labor force. Similarly, it is sometimes rumored that Nevada gambling interests support the opposition to attempts to legalize gambling in California because it would cut so heavily into their business, which depends in substantial measure on the population of Southern California.

The moral crusader, however, is more concerned with ends than with means. When it comes to drawing up specific rules (typically in the form of legislation to be proposed to a state legislature or the Federal Congress), he frequently relies on the advice of experts. Lawyers, expert in the drawing of acceptable legislation, often play this role. Government bureaus in whose jurisdiction the problem falls may also have the necessary expertise, as did the Federal Bureau of Narcotics in the case of the marijuana problem. [*Various legitimate institutions must be coordinated to draft acceptable laws.*]

As psychiatric ideology, however, becomes increasingly acceptable, a new expert has appeared—the psychiatrist. [*The rise of psychiatry indicates that bad habits have been taken out of theology and are now being "explained" by "science" in social reality.*] Sutherland, in his discussion of the natural history of sexual psychopath laws, pointed to the psychiatrist's influence.* He suggests the following as the conditions under which the sexual psychopath law, which provides that a person "who is diagnosed as a sexual psychopath may be confined for an indefinite period in a state hospital for the insane," will be passed.

First, these laws are customarily enacted after a state of fear has been aroused in a community by a few serious sex crimes committed in quick succession. This is illustrated in Indiana, where a law was passed following three or four sexual attacks in Indianapolis, with

---

* Edwin H. Sutherland, "The Diffusion of Sexual Psychopath Laws," *American Journal of Sociology*, LVI (September, 1950), 142–148.

murder in two. Heads of families bought guns and watch dogs, and the supply of locks and chains in the hardware stores of the city was completely exhausted. . . .

A second element in the process of developing sexual psychopath laws is the agitated activity of the community in connection with the fear. The attention of the community is focused on sex crimes, and people in the most varied situations envisage dangers and see the need of and possibility for their control. . . .

The third phase in the development of these sexual psychopath laws has been the appointment of a committee. The committee gathers the many conflicting recommendations of persons and groups of persons, attempts to determine "facts," studies procedures in other states, and makes recommendations, which generally include bills for the legislature. Although the general fear usually subsides within a few days, a committee has the formal duty of following through until positive action is taken. Terror which does not result in a committee is much less likely to result in a law.*

In the case of sexual psychopath laws, there usually is no government agency charged with dealing in a specialized way with sexual deviations. [*It was a categorization of many bad habits into a single category—sexual psychopath—that had not existed before. The specialists in dealing with bad habits are psychiatrists.*] Therefore, when the need for expert advice in drawing up legislation arises, people frequently turn to the professional group most closely associated with such problems:

In some states, at the committee stage of the development of a sexual psychopath law, psychiatrists have played an important part. The psychiatrists, more than any others, have been the interest group back of the laws. A committee of psychiatrists and neurologists in Chicago wrote the bill which became the sexual psychopath law of Illinois; the bill was sponsored by the Chicago Bar Association and by the state's attorney of Cook County and was enacted with little opposition in the next session of the State Legislature. In Minnesota all the members of the governor's committee except one were psychiatrists. In Wisconsin the Milwaukee Neuropsychiatric Society shared in pressing the Milwaukee Crime Commission for the enactment of a law. In Indiana the attorney-general's committee received from the American Psychiatric Association copies of all of the sexual psychopath laws which had been enacted in other states.† The influence of psychiatrists in other realms of the criminal law has increased in recent years.

* *Ibid.,* pp. 143–145.
† *Ibid.,* pp. 145–146.

In any case, what is important about this example is not that psychiatrists are becoming increasingly influential, but that the moral crusader, at some point in the development of his crusade, often requires the services of a professional who can draw up the appropriate rules in an appropriate form. The crusader himself is often not concerned with such details. Enough for him that the main point has been won; he leaves its implementation to others.

By leaving the drafting of the specific rule in the hands of others, the crusader opens the door for many unforeseen influences. For those who draft legislation for crusaders have their own interests, which may affect the legislation they prepare. It is likely that the sexual psychopath laws drawn by psychiatrists contain many features never intended by the citizens who spearheaded the drives to "do something about sex crimes," features which do however reflect the professional interests of organized psychiatry. [*In the competition within the institutional order every institution does its best to benefit from any coordination of activities, often at the expense of another legitimate institution.*]

□ □ □

An individual must always begin something. The actions of organizations are the coordinated actions of many individuals operating toward a common goal. Becker focused on the role of the individual in creating a moral crusade, a crusade that affirmed a value of the symbolic universe, in response to counter-institutions of behavior. Of course individuals cannot accomplish great changes without convincing other individuals, and without bringing together many institutions and organizations in a common definition of a situation. In the final "societal response" the interests of these other individuals and various institutions will play some part. Whether the part is major or minor is an outcome of interinstitutional bargaining. His mention of prohibition is interesting because in this case the moral crusade was one to expel an existing, legitimate, institution from the legitimations of the institutional order. The failure of prohibition testifies to the resiliency of institutions of behavior, and to the limits of societal reactions.

In the following adaptation Donald Dickson shows the way in which an institution may benefit itself by playing the role of moral entrepreneur. He points out the various struggles and conflicts in the institutional order that affected the Federal Narcotics Bureau, and the benefits that the institution hoped to derive by outlawing marijuana.
□ □ □

21

BUREAUCRACY AND MORALITY
An Organizational Perspective on a Moral Crusade
DONALD T. DICKSON

A CASE STUDY: THE U.S. BUREAU OF NARCOTICS

The Bureau as a Public Bureaucracy

This case study will be limited to an analysis of the policies of the
Narcotics Bureau and the effects of these policies on salient elements
of its environment. This approach is preferable to a more general
organizational analysis of the Bureau—examining its structure, recruitment, boundary defenses, and myriad environmental transactions—
because in these respects the Bureau is not unlike most other governmental bureaucracies. Further, in its efforts to mold public opinion in
support of its policies, it is not unlike many organizations, especially
those with a moral commitment. The W.C.T.U. carried on the same sort
of campaign—including propaganda, attacks on its critics, and legislative lobbying. What makes the Bureau unique from many other organizations which have tried to influence their environments is that the
campaign was and is carried out by a governmental organ.

Several ramifications of this difference are immediately apparent.
There is the element of legitimation. [*Government is usually one of the
most thoroughly legitimated set of institutions within the institutional
order. This ceases to be true only when a revolution comes close to
overthrowing the government.*] The public is far more likely to accept
the pronouncements of a federal department than a voluntary private
organization. There is the element of propaganda development. Due to
its public nature, a federal department is more skilled in dealing with
the public and in preparing propaganda for public consumption. There
is the element of communication. A federal organization has far more
means available for the dissemination of the information than a private
one—by press releases, publications, or lectures and speeches—and
it is likely to have representatives based in major population centers
to disseminate the information. There is the element of coercion. A
federal department can bring a wide range of pressures to bear on its
critics. [*Any legitimate institution can use some of these tactics, but the
government, claiming to represent the entire institutional order, can use
them more freely and to better effect.*]

Adapted from Donald T. Dickson, "Bureaucracy and Morality: An Organizational Perspective on a Moral Crusade," *Social Problems*, Vol. 16, No. 2, Fall 1968, pp. 143–156.
Reprinted with permission.

Finally, at a different level, a federal bureau differs in the area of survival. Private organizations have considerable control over their future. They may decide to expand, continue as before, disband, merge, alter their aims, or reduce their activities. The attitude of their environments will have great bearing on this decision, to be sure, but the final decision rests with the organization. A federal department may go through any of the above stages, but frequently the final decision does not rest within the department but with the congressional, executive, or judicial body that created it. A bureau created by congressional enactment will continue to be unaltered except by internal decision only as long as Congress can be convinced that there is no need to alter it. Although there may be some question of degree, there is no question that public opinion will be a major factor in the congressional decision. [*These are the interinstitutional transactions that this particular bureau must deal with.*]

Therefore the federal department must convince the public and Congress: 1) that it serves a useful, or if possible, a necessary function; and 2) that it is uniquely qualified to do so. The less the department is sure of its future status, the more it will try to convince Congress and the public of these.

Background to Environmental Change: The Emergence and Development of the Bureau

In the late nineteenth and early twentieth centuries, narcotics were widely available: through doctors who indiscriminately prescribed morphine and later heroin as pain killers, through druggists who sold them openly, or through a wide variety of patent medicines.

> The public . . . (in the early twentieth century) had an altogether different conception of drug addiction from that which prevails today. The habit was not approved, but neither was it regarded as criminal or monstrous. It was usually looked upon as a vice or personal misfortune, or much as alcoholism is viewed today. Narcotics users were pities rather than loathed as criminals or degenerates . . .*

In 1914 Congress through the passage of the Harrison Act attempted to exert some control over the narcotics traffic. This act remains today the cornerstone of narcotics legislation. Rather than eliminate the use of narcotic drugs, the act was passed in order to honor a previous international obligation stemming from the Hague Convention of 1912, and to control the criminal encroachments into the drug trade. Nowhere in the act is there direct reference to addicts or addition.

* Alfred R. Lindesmith, *Opiate Addiction,* Bloomington, Ind.: Principia, 1947, p. 183.

Its ostensible purpose appeared to be simply to make the entire process of drug distribution within the country a matter of record. The nominal excise tax (one cent per ounce), the requirement that persons and firms handling drugs register and pay fees, all seemed designed to accomplish this purpose. There is no indication of a legislative intention to deny addicts access to legal drugs or to interfere in any way with medical practices in this area.*

Medical practices were specifically exempted:

Nothing contained in this section . . . shall . . . apply . . . [t]o the dispensing or distribution of any drugs mentioned . . . to a patient by a physician, dentist, or veterinary surgeon registered under section 4722 in the course of his professional practice only.†

Thus, the act did not make addiction illegal. All it required was that addicts should obtain drugs from registered physicians who made a record of the transaction.

A narcotics division was created in the Internal Revenue Bureau of the Treasury Department to collect revenue and enforce the Harrison Act. In 1920 it merged into the Prohibition Unit of that department and upon its creation in 1927 into the Prohibition Bureau. In 1930 the Bureau of Narcotics was formed as a separate Bureau in the Treasury Department.

Legitimation: The Process of Changing an Environment

After 1914 the powers of the Narcotics Division were clear and limited: to enforce registration and record-keeping, violation of which could result in imprisonment for up to ten years, and to supervise revenue collection. The large number of addicts who secured their drugs from physicians were excluded from the Division's jurisdiction. The public's attitude toward drug use had not changed much with the passage of the Act—there was some opposition to drug use, some support of it, and a great many who did not care one way or the other. In fact, the Harrison Act was passed with very little publicity or news coverage.

Thus at this time the Narcotics Division was faced with a severely restricted scope of operations. Acceptance of the legislation as envisioned by Congress would mean that the Division would at best con-

---

* Alfred R. Lindesmith, *The Addict and the Law,* Bloomington, Ind.: Indiana U., 1965, p. 4. See also Rufus King, "The Narcotics Bureau and the Harrison Act: Jailing the Healers and the Sick," *Yale Law Journal,* 62 (1953), p. 736; and William B. Eldridge, *Narcotics and the Law,* New York: American Bar Foundation, 1961. The Act is placed in a statutory perspective in "Note: Narcotics Regulation," *Yale Law Journal,* 62 (1953), pp. 751-787.

† *U.S.C.* 4705(c) (1954 Code).

tinue as a marginal operation with limited enforcement duties. Given the normal, well-documented bureaucratic tendency toward growth and expansion, and given the fact that the Division was a public bureaucracy and needed to justify its operations and usefulness before Congress, it would seem that increased power and jurisdiction in the area of drug control would be a desirable and, in fact, necessary goal. Adaptation to the Harrison Act limitations would preclude attainment of this goal. Operating under a legislative mandate, the logical alternative to adaptation would be to persuade the Congress and public that expansion was necessary and to extend the provisions of the Harrison Act.

Also at this point, the public's attitude toward narcotics use could be characterized as only slightly opposed. Faced with a situation where adaptation to the existing legislation was bureaucratically unfeasible, where expansion was desirable, and where environmental support—from both Congress and the public—was necessary for continued existence, the Division launched a two-pronged campaign: 1) a barrage of reports and newspaper articles which generated a substantial public outcry against narcotics use, and 2) a series of Division-sponsored test cases in the courts which resulted in a reinterpretation of the Harrison Act and substantially broadened powers for the Narcotics Division. Thus the Division attained its goals by altering a weakly-held public value regarding narcotics use from neutrality or slight opposition to strong opposition, and by persuading the courts that it should have increased powers. [It thus brought into play the public opinion that it mobilized and focused, along with the other law-making institution besides Congress—the courts. A reinterpretation of law requires far less effort than the creation of a new law.]

Though the resources of the Division were limited, it was able to accomplish its goals because it was a public bureaucracy and as such had the aforementioned advantages which arise from that status. Since the ability to develop propaganda and the means to communicate it were inherent in this status, as was the propensity by the public to accept this propaganda, environmental support could be generated with less resource expenditure. Further, the Division as a public bureaucracy would be assumed to have a familiarity with governmental processes not only in its own executive branch, but also in the congressional and judicial branches as well. This built-in expertise necessary for the Division's expansion might be quite costly in time and resources for the private bureaucracy but again was inherent in the Division's status.

One typical example of the public campaign was a report cited and relied upon by the Narcotics Division for some years. It is an interesting combination of truth, speculation, and fiction, a mix which the Division and the Bureau which succeeded it found to be an effective public persuader for many years. In a report dated June, 1919, a committee appointed by the Treasury Department to study narcotics reported *inter alia* that there were 237,665 addicts in the United States treated by physicians (based upon a 30 percent response by physicians queried), that there were over one million addicts in the country in 1919 (a figure based upon a compromise between projections based on the percentage of addicts in Jacksonville, Florida in 1913 and New York City in 1918), that there was extensive addiction among children, that narcotics were harmful to health and morals, and that they were directly connected with crime and abject poverty. Among the physical effects noted were insanity; diseased lungs, hearts, and kidneys; rotting of the skin; and sterility.

This "scholarly report" is an interesting example of the propaganda effort, for it appears to the casual reader to be credible (especially given its source), and contains charges which seem to be designed to generate widespread public disgust toward narcotics users and support for the Division and its efforts. Many of the same charges were applied to marihuana when the Bureau campaigned against its use.

While the Division was carrying out its public campaign, it was also busy in the courts. Between 1918 and 1921 the Narcotics Division won three important cases in the Supreme Court and persuaded the Court, essentially, to delete the medical exception from the Harrison Act thereby broadening its position as an enforcement agency. In the first case, *Webb v. United States,** the court held that a physician could not supply narcotics to an addict unless he was attempting to cure him and in so doing made illegal the work of a large number of physicians who were supplying addicts with drugs under the registration procedures of the Harrison Act. This decision was supported in the two following cases: *Jin Fuey Moy v. United States*† and *United States v. Behrman.*‡ In *Behrman,* it was held that physicians could not even supply drugs to addicts in an attempt to cure them. The medical exception was nullified. The cases were skillfully chosen and presented to the court. Each was a flagrant abuse of the statute—in *Webb,* the physician's professional practice seemed to be limited to supplying narcotics to whoever wanted them. In the other two cases, the physicians supplied huge amounts of drugs over short periods of time to a small number of patients—patently for resale at a later time. Yet the Division did not argue for and the court did not rule on the cases as violations of the statute as it was intended, but instead regarded all of these as normal professional practices by physicians and held that, as such, they were illegal.

* 249 *U.S.* 96 (1918).
† 254 *U.S.* 189 (1920).
‡ 258 *U.S.* 280 (1921).

Three years after *Behrman,* the court somewhat reversed itself in *Linder v. United States.** Here the doctor supplied a small dosage to a patient who was a government informer. The court rejected the government's case in a unanimous opinion, holding:

> The enactment under consideration . . . says nothing of "addicts" and does not undertake to prescribe methods for their medical treatment, and we cannot possibly conclude that a physician acted improperly or unwisely or for other than medical purposes solely because he has dispensed to one of them, in the ordinary course and in good faith, four small tablets of morphine or cocaine for relief of condition incident to addiction.†

The court went on to warn the Division:

> Federal power is delegated, and its prescribed limits must not be transcended even though the ends seem desirable. The unfortunate condition of the recipient certainly created no reasonable probability that she would sell or otherwise dispose of the few tablets entrusted to her and we cannot say that by so dispensing them the doctor necessarily transcended the limits of that professional conduct with which Congress never intended to interfere.‡

Though *Linder* might have reintroduced doctors into the area, the Narcotics Division successfully prevented this by refusing to recognize *Linder* in its regulations, thus creating a situation where few would accept the risks involved in testing the doctrine, and by launching an all-out campaign against doctors—closing the remaining narcotics clinics, imprisoning rebellious doctors, and publicizing records and convictions of physician addicts. [*This is the development of a counter-institution within a legitimate institution, developing a pattern of behavior prohibited by law.*]

Rufus King comments on this period of growth:

> In sum, the Narcotics Division succeeded in creating a very large criminal class for itself to police . . . instead of the very small one Congress has intended.§

The success of this campaign was reflected not only in the increased number of potential criminals, but in financial growth as well. Between 1918 and 1925, the Bureau's budgetary appropriations increased from $325,000 to $1,329,440, a rise of over 400 percent.

* 268 *U.S.* 5 (1924).
† 268 *U.S.* 5 at 15 (1924).
‡ 268 *U.S.* 5 at 20 (1924).
§ King, *op. cit.,* p. 738.

The Marihuana Tax Act of 1937: A Bureaucratic Response

There are many other examples of efforts by the Bureau to create and maintain a friendly and supportive environment—through other publicity campaigns, through lobbying in Congress, and through continued and diligent attacks upon and harassments of its critics—which have been amply chronicled by others, although not as part of an organizational process.

The Bureau's efforts to induce passage of the Marihuana Tax Act deserve special mention, however, in light of Becker's finding that the legislation was the result of what he terms a "moral enterprise." Becker concludes that Narcotics Commissioner Anslinger and his Bureau were the motive forces behind the original 1937 legislation and the increasingly severe penalties which have since been imposed. This is readily conceded. But he argues that the motivation behind this desire for the marihuana legislation was a moral one. He presents a picture of a society totally indifferent to the use of marihuana until Anslinger, in the role of a moral entrepreneur, "blows the whistle" on marihuana smoking. Again, it is conceded that Commissioner Anslinger throughout his long career with the Narcotics Bureau has opposed drug and narcotics use on moral grounds. This theme runs consistently through his writings. What Becker ignores is that Anslinger was also a bureaucrat and thus responsive to bureaucratic pressures and demands as well. The distinction between these roles is difficult to make but it is fundamental in analyzing the legislation. [*In other words, Becker argued that the value of the symbolic universe motivated an individual who led an institution, while Dickson argues that the institution's own problems of survival motivate both the individual and the institution.*]

To understand whether the marihuana legislation was to a large degree the result of bureaucratic processes similar to the Bureau's expansion after the Harrison Act or whether it was instead the result of an individual's moral crusade, it is necessary to focus not only on the individual, as Becker has done, but upon the Bureau and its environment during this period. Through this method, certain parallels with the post-Harrison Act period become evident.

The Marihuana Tax Act which imposed a prohibitively costly tax on the sale of marihuana was passed by both houses of Congress with practically no debate and signed into law on August 2, 1937. While Becker seems to argue that the Bureau generated a great public outcry against marihuana use prior to the passage of the Act, his data supporting this argument are misleading if not erroneously interpreted. While marihuana use seems to have increased since the early 1930's, there appears to have been little public concern expressed in the news media, even in 1937. Few magazine articles were written about the subject, and if the *New York Times* is any indication, newspaper coverage was also slight. The final presidential signing of the act received minimal coverage from the *Times*. In short, rather than the Bureau-generated public turmoil that Becker indicates, it seems that public awareness of the problem, as well as public opposition to it, was slight.

While it cannot be shown conclusively that the Marihuana Tax Act was the result of a bureaucratic response to environmental conditions, similarities between this period and the post-Harrison Act period are evident. Marihuana opposition, like narcotics opposition before, appears to have resulted from a weakly held value. In both situations, publicity campaigns were launched. In both cases, one through the courts and one through Congress, efforts were exerted to expand the power of the Bureau. In both cases, there were substantial numbers of potential criminals who could be incorporated into the Bureau's jurisdiction.

Perhaps more convincing than similarities are the budgetary appropriations for the Bureau from 1915 to 1944 presented in Table 1. In 1932, when the Bureau's appropriations were approaching an all time high, the Bureau stated:

> The present constitutional limitations would seem to require control measures directed against the intrastate traffic of Indian hemp (marihuana) to be adopted by the several State governments rather than by the Federal Government, and the policy has been to urge the

TABLE 1 BUDGETARY APPROPRIATIONS FOR THE U.S. NARCOTICS BUREAU (1915–1944)*

Year†	Total Appropriation	Year	Total Appropriation
1915	$ 292,000	1930	$1,411,260
1916	300,000	1931	1,611,260
1917	325,000	1932	1,708,528
1918	750,000	1933	1,525,000
1919	750,000	1934	1,400,000
1920	750,000	1935	1,244,899
1921	750,000	1936	1,249,470
1922	750,000	1937	1,275,000
1923	750,000	1938	1,267,000
1924	1,250,000	1939	1,267,600
1925	1,329,440	1940	1,306,700
1926	1,329,440	1941	1,303,280
1927	1,329,440	1942	1,283,975
1928	1,329,440	1943	1,289,060
1929	1,350,440	1944	1,150,000

* Source: Appropriations Committee, U.S. Senate, *Appropriations, New Offices, etc., Statements Showing Appropriations Made, New Offices Created, etc.,* 1915–1923; U.S. Bureau of the Budget, *The Budget of the United States Government,* Washington: Government Printing Office, 1923–1945.

† Fiscal year the appropriation was made. Each sum was appropriated for the following fiscal year.

State authorities generally to provide the necessary legislation, with supporting enforcement activity, to prohibit the traffic except for bona fide medical purposes. The proposed uniform State narcotic law . . . with optional text applying to restriction of traffic in Indian hemp, has been recommended as an adequate law to accomplish the desired purpose.*

At this time, according to the Bureau, sixteen states had enacted legislation in which "the sale or possession (of marihuana) is prohibited except for medical purposes."† One year later, 18 more states had enacted the desired legislation, and by 1936, it appears that the Bureau's policy had succeeded completely for all 48 states had enacted legislation which governed the sale or possession of marihuana.‡

Despite this apparent success and despite former questions concerning the constitutionality of the measure, the Bureau in 1937 pressed for the enactment of the federal marihuana act. For Anslinger, the moral entrepreneur, 1936 should have been a year of victory. In every state the marihuana menace was subjected to statutory control.§ But for Anslinger, the bureaucrat, 1936 seems to have been another year of defeat. His budgetary appropriation remained near a low point that had not been seen in over a decade, which to some extent reflected the general economic conditions of the time. His request for fiscal 1933 had been cut $100,000 below the general Treasury Department reduction for all bureaus.‖ In succeeding years, reductions in actual operating expenses were greater than those reflected in Table 1, for varying sums were deducted from the appropriations and held in a general trust fund as part of the government's anti-depression program. The Bureau's actual operating funds remained at about one million dollars from fiscal 1934 to fiscal 1936. In his appearances before the House Subcommittee of the Committee on Appropriations that considered the Treasury Department budget, Anslinger repeatedly warned that the limited budget was curtailing his enforcement activities. By 1936, his budget had decreased over $450,000 from its high four years before, a fall of almost 26 percent.

---

* U.S. Bureau of Narcotics, *Traffic in Opium and Other Dangerous Drugs for the Year Ending December 31, 1932,* Washington: Government Printing Office, p. 43.

† *Ibid.,* p. 43.

‡ U.S. Bureau of Narcotics, *Traffic in Opium and Other Dangerous Drugs* . . . , Washington: Government Printing Office, 1932–1936.

§ It can be argued that a federal measure was still necessary because: 1) state legislation was poorly drawn, or 2) state enforcement was inadequate. The former is doubtful since by 1937, 39 states (as compared to four in 1933) had enacted the Uniform Narcotic Drug Act, the very legislation the Bureau felt would best control marihuana use. The latter situation, even if true, could have been rectified by means other than federal legislation.

‖ *Hearings Before the Subcommittee of the House Committee on Appropriations,* 72nd Congress, 1st Session, in charge of the Treasury Department Appropriations Bill for 1933, January 14, 1932, pp. 375–393.

Again in 1937 Anslinger, the moralist, would be expected first to convince the general public that marihuana use was evil and immoral, while Anslinger, the bureaucrat, would be more concerned with attaining passage of legislation which would increase the Bureau's powers and then proceed to generate environmental support for these powers. In fact, the latter occurred. The great bulk of Bureau-inspired publicity came after the passage of the act, not before.

Faced with a steadily decreasing budget, the Bureau responded as any organization so threatened might react: it tried to appear more necessary, and it tried to increase its scope of operations. As a result of this response, the Marihuana Tax Act of 1937 was passed.* Whether the Bureau's efforts were entirely successful is questionable. One beneficial result for the Bureau was that violations and seizures under the Marihuana Tax Act contributed substantially to the Bureau's totals, which had been declining for some time. (When arrests, convictions, and seizures were on the increase, these were faithfully reported to the House Subcommittee as evidence of the Bureau's effective use of funds.) In 1938, the first full year under the Marihuana Tax Act, one out of every four federal drug and narcotic convictions was for a marihuana violation.†

Financially, the enterprise was less successful. Though the budgetary decline was halted, expected increases for enforcing the new legislation did not immediately materialize. Anslinger pointed out this problem in a 1937 subcommittee hearing in connection with the fiscal 1939 appropriation:

Comm. Anslinger: We took on the administration of the marihuana law and did not get any increase for that purpose. The way we are running we may have to request a deficiency of $100,000 at the end of the year; but I sincerely hope you will not see me here for a deficit. Beginning the first of the year, Mr. Chairman, I shall control all travel out of Washington. That is a hard job. I have to do that to make up some of this money. We went ahead at high speed and broke up ten big distributing rings, and now we find ourselves in the hole financially.

Mr. Ludlow: You have to find some way to recoup?

Comm. Anslinger: Yes; and keep the enforcement of the Marihuana

* U.S. Bureau of Narcotics, *Traffic in Opium and Other Dangerous Drugs for the Year Ending December 31, 1938,* Washington: Government Printing Office, pp. 77–79.

† *Hearings Before the Subcommittee of the House Committee on Appropriations,* 75th Congress, 3rd Session, in charge of the Treasury Department Appropriations Bill for 1939, December 14, 1937, p. 380.

Act going. Not a dollar has been appropriated in connection with the enforcement of the Marihuana law. We have taken on the work in connection with the Marihuana Act in addition to our other duties.

While the Bureau's budgetary appropriations since that time have in general increased, the period of the late 1930's and early 1940's, where increases might be expected to be the largest, was a period of small advances and then a gradual decline. Of course the major factor in that period was the massive redirection of funds from non-military areas, and thus these figures do not accurately reflect the Bureau's enterprise.

In conclusion, it should be reiterated that this paper does not presume to refute the moral entrepreneur approach—for in many instances it is a valid and useful means of analysis—but rather it attempts to demonstrate an alternative explanation that may frequently be appropriate. It would be either naive or presumptuous to deny that some combination of both moral and bureaucratic factors exist in any given crusade. The problem for analysis is to determine the relative importance of each, and the consequences stemming from a particular combination. The utility of the organizational approach lies in that it can be extended to other similar moral crusades or to entire social movements, where the emphasis so far has been on the work of individual crusaders rather than on the organizations and their environments. Further, to the extent these movements follow the general societal pattern and become increasingly complex, organized, and bureaucratic, the organizational approach will become even more important in analysis and prediction.

☐ ☐ ☐

Some combination of individual and institutional moral entrepreneurship accounts for the passage of new laws to counteract counter-institutions, whatever they may be. The specific individuals and institutions that take this leadership role in the creation of new laws will usually be those for whom the counter-institution is the most threatening or those for whom its suppression can be the most profitable.

The development of a reaction to some pattern of behavior follows the institutionalization of the pattern, its social definition as a pattern (the definition of sexual psychopath, for example), and some public, individual, or institutional assertion that it does not fit into the legitimate institutional order. There are many patterns of behavior that might possibly be defined as counter-institutional, or, technically, illegal, that have not come to be so defined because of the high status of the participants, lack of public outcry about the behavior, or lack of a legitimate institution that would benefit from defining it as a counter-institution. Many intoxicants that might be declared as illegal have not been. Many forms of sexual practice have not come to public attention and so have not been made illegal. Many corporations cheat consumers through still legal practices. The world is full of things to make deviant should anyone care to do so.

INSTITUTIONS OF FORMAL CONTROL

"There's a law." So what? Law is not a magic wand that makes counter-institutions disappear. Law is an abstract statement setting up minimal requirements for behavior. It is abstracted from experience with particular counter-institutions at particular times. It is passed by one legitimate institution, the legislature, and written down in books. So long as it remains only in books it has little influence on behavior; there are many laws which are not enforced, just records of a decision made sometime by some law-making body. In order for a law to be a formal social control it must be enforced by someone, an agent. Agents of formal social control are people, and in the process of enforcing laws they work in organizations and form institutions of behavior. These formal social control agencies, of which the police and the various federal bureaus are the most obvious, are charged with enforcing the laws that have been created. But they are also organizations that exist in the environment of the institutional order, and as organizations they have other goals besides simply enforcing laws. This often creates a paradox wherein enforcement of a law would be detrimental to the organization's other goals. This paradox is resolved by many small decisions; *when* to enforce the law, *against whom* to enforce the law, *which* laws to enforce, and *how much* to enforce the law. The abstract and formal law comes once again to be cloaked with institutional and individual needs when it is enforced against a counter-institution of behavior, because it is interpreted through the various institutional and organizational relationships that are relevant to the enforcers. This interpretation cannot be allowed to go unchecked, because the enforcement agencies might then act more in their own interests than in the interests of the institutional order. As a consequence other laws have been enacted that provide for court review of the actions of the agents of formal social control.

THE POLICE AS FORMAL SOCIAL CONTROL AGENTS

When a policeman encounters a person engaged in illegal behavior, he may make a complicated assessment of the situation before he acts to invoke formal control through arrest. One of the most frequent judgments made is whether the individual usually has legitimate self and relational controls operating upon him. If the offender is polite to the police officer and gives evidence of having a home, a family, and a job, the police officer often assumes that these other institutions will control the behavior, that arrest is unnecessary, and that a reprimand will suffice. If the offender is impolite or by his dress or location gives evidence of being outside of these legitimate institutions, the officer assumes that only arrest will control the behavior.

The police officer himself uses a great amount of relational social control in enforcing the standards of the community as he sees them. His powers under law are limited, he sees many community demands outside of law, his own behavior is controlled by the police organization and by the coordinations that have grown among police officers. He is a complex actor in a complex environment. Policemen frequently rely on friendships, on reason, on warnings, on force, threats, and lying, to accomplish what they think must be done, rather than using the law.

For the working police officer the community that he is supposed to serve is an abstraction, as it is for everyone else. The community may be behind him, but it is like having a fog behind him, apparently solid from a distance but offering no concrete support or backing. His true guides to behavior, the information he can trust, the pathways for guiding him through the legal jungle, have been learned through repeated contact with other institutions in his environment; the restaurants where he eats free, the businessmen who give him discounts and expect not to get parking tickets, the police reporter who can make or break his career, the community influentials who get special service, the informers who trade information for immunity, other police agencies, the District Attorney's Office, the parole officers who will let him arrest someone he wants to investigate on a parole violation charge, and his special clique of friends within the department. It is these institutions that the officer must take into account in his calculus of action if he is to function in the institutionalized role of policeman.

The policeman also prefers to work within popular morality because it makes his job easier. When counter-institutions of behavior are followed by many people, possibly a majority on the policeman's beat, he is faced with an impossible situation. He cannot fully enforce the law, and yet he cannot refuse to enforce the law. His usual solution is to arrest only the most flagrant violators. In San Francisco, for example, the police daily walk by people smoking marijuana in the Haight-Ashbury section and in Golden Gate Park. They "don't notice" anymore. Formal social control begins to break down when a counter-institution grows large enough.

The individual agent of formal social control enforces laws while paying attention to a great many other situations. His enforcement is a complex social product rather than an automatic reaction.

Formal social control agencies themselves have many problems of getting along and surviving in the institutional order. While select agencies, such as the Narcotics Bureau, may be able to manipulate their environments, most agencies, such as local police departments and psychiatric wards, cannot, and thus must seek other modes of adaptation to their environments. In our separate researches into the workings of social control agencies Professor Karl Kreplin (Sir George Williams University) and I have found similar organizational modes of adaptation to environmental uncertainty and we have collaborated on the next section of this chapter to show the way in which part of the stability of the institutional order and the stability of the day-to-day operations of social control agencies are served by paying differential attention to the people they are charged with controlling.

DEVIANTS AS CLIENTS AND AS FILLERS FOR SOCIAL CONTROL AGENCIES

Formal social control organizations confront a dilemma. There are a certain number of serious "cases" that they *must* take care of to fulfill their role of providing control for the institutional order. The police, for example, would be criticized if they did not arrest armed robbers, murderers, rapists, thieves, and rioters. Psychiatric wards would be criticized if they turned away psychotics, suicide attempts, and the patently disturbed. The dilemma is that the number of such cases that come to their attention fluctuates up and down, daily, weekly, and monthly. If they hired just enough people to take care of the average case load they would be unable to cope with periods of overload, because they would not have enough staff, or even enough space. If they hired enough people to take care of the peak load most of them would be idle a large part of the time. Since formal social control agencies are part of governmental bureaucracies such continual idleness would be questioned. The organization's budget might be cut, the level of staffing reduced, and it would become unable to deal with peak loads again.

Formal social control agencies do not have any way to manipulate the number of serious cases that come in. When there have not been any murders for a while the police can't really go out and create them.

When there have not been any suicide attempts for a while a psychiatrist can't go out and encourage someone to attempt to kill himself, just to fill his ward.

These organizations find their bureaucratic salvation in the less serious cases with which they also deal. They give priority to their serious cases and fill the remaining time and the remaining space in their jails or wards with less serious cases. Thus they always look busy. They have a steady flow of cases. They have a reserve capacity to take care of peak loads. And, most important from the point of view of a bureaucrat, this policy guards against budget cuts.

The people within the various agencies make the distinction between "clients," those cases they must take care of, and "fillers," those cases they may take care of, in various ways. The police make a distinction between "real police work" and "humbug." The psychiatric ward staff makes a distinction between the "sick" and the "freeloaders."

While each agency has its specialized types of clients, and its own special requirements for fillers, many agencies draw upon a common pool of fillers—down-and-out alcoholics.

The cause of alcoholism is usually untreatable, but the symptoms can be alleviated; alcoholics rarely get well, but they rarely die. No one expects the agencies to be able to do much for them. They have an extraordinarily long career before total organic damage sets in (twenty to forty years of being fillers for various agencies). The supply of down-and-out alcoholics is copious, available, obvious, degraded, in need of help, and constant. In every city they exist in sufficient numbers to fill the police officers' time, the jails, the courts, the psychiatric wards, the hospitals, the welfare agencies, and the gospel missions.

Alcoholics steal enough and are enough of a danger to themselves to constitute a police problem, they are confused enough to constitute a psychiatric problem, sick enough to constitute a health problem, destitute enough to constitute a welfare problem, and lost enough to constitute a religious problem. Alcoholics are God's gift to social control agencies. If all the down-and-out alcoholics were to be given specialized treatment as alcoholics, all these agencies would have to fill themselves from some other source. Perhaps recreational drug-users will supplant alcoholics as universal fillers.

In the course of gathering data for my doctoral dissertation on the police I worked as a uniformed police reserve officer for thirteen months. I observed the way in which the police managed to create a steady work load for themselves by giving selective attention to crimes of various kinds.

Police officers working in bar districts may arrest two to three thousand drunks in a year. Most other officers arrest drunks when there is no "real" police work to do, on quiet nights, or on weekends when they have a free moment. When an officer sees a drunk on the street he may or may not arrest him, partially at his own discretion, but more frequently in relation to his current work assignment. If he has been assigned to a call by radio, or if he is otherwise involved in "real" police work he will probably ignore the drunk, or plan to come back later. The radio room will "hold" reports of drunks until the officer on the street is free to deal with them. There is an inverse relationship between the amount of "real" police work to be done and the number of drunks arrested.

The work load that the jailers have also regulates the flow of drunks into jail. If the jailers are busy they will tell the officer not to bring in any more drunks. One evening a number of drunks asked to be arrested because it was raining and cold, and they had no place to sleep. As we took the seventh drunk of the evening in, one jailer said, "What are you working on, a point system?" Another jailer suggested, "Why don't you leave them out there so they'll freeze to death and we won't have to worry about them any more." After those comments we only took in two more, leaving many others on the street.

Traffic tickets serve a similar function. The patrol officer in the department I observed is expected to write one moving-violation ticket a day. "A ticket a day keeps the sergeant away," is the way they put it. Patrol officers write few tickets on the weekends when they are busy with "real" police work, but they may fill their week's quota on a quiet Wednesday night, keeping themselves busy. Officers assigned to traffic are expected to average two tickets an hour, which keeps them busy. The traffic division of a police department is a riot squad keeping busy until a riot breaks out.

A riot is a peak load situation for a police department, one which they are expected to take care of. When a riot occurs the police stop writing traffic tickets and arresting drunks, and turn their attention to the rioters. A large number of officers become available to arrest rioters, and the drunks may be chased out of jail to make room for arrested rioters. The organization has concealed this reserve capacity from bureaucratic review by using "fillers," and can take care of a peak load of "clients" when the need arises.

Drunks represent the largest category of offenders dealt with by most metropolitan police departments, which largely reflects their value as fillers rather than their danger to the community.

The down-and-out alcoholic may even search around to find an agency that needs filling. One pattern that came to my attention was for the alcoholic to try the gospel mission first. After being fed some soup and being prayed over for an hour, he discovers that there are no beds available that night. With the fifty cents he has saved for this emergency he buys a bottle of cheap wine, enjoys himself drinking it, and then lies down across the sidewalk to sleep. The first police officer who happens along then has to arrest him for obstructing the free use of the sidewalk, which the drunk was planning on. He joins his buddies in the jail, takes up his usual job as a trustee, and has solved his bedroom problem for another few days.

Karl Kreplin spent nine months working in a psychiatric ward making observations for his master's thesis on commitment procedures. He observed another way in which a social control agency meets its needs by using fillers, again mostly down-and-out alcoholics. The county hospital, in which the psychiatric ward is located, receives payments from the county and the state according to the number of beds filled. A full census assures the maximum monetary support from both the state and the county.

The supply of involutional psychotics, acute schizophrenics, and chronic schizophrenics coming to the hospital fluctuates up and down, but these are the "clients" that the ward staff feels they have been trained to deal with.

The admitting psychiatrist would wait until ten or eleven in the evening to see what the day would produce in the way of clients, and then he would admit alcoholics until the beds were filled for the census. Frequently the alcoholics who present themselves at the admissions ward know which symptoms to exhibit to get themselves admitted.

The ward staff views the alcoholic as basically nonpsychotic, and a freeloader. He is seen as a burden on ward routine who cannot benefit from the services of the ward. Consequently they spend less time in the diagnosis and treatment of the alcoholic than they do for their true clients. Since 20 to 25 percent of the patients on the ward at a given time are alcoholics the ward staff is able to give proportionately more time to their clients. They could give even more time to clients if alcoholics were not admitted, but they would not receive the large and steady supply of funds that the admission of alcoholics provides.

In the psychiatric ward as well as the police department, the use of fillers allows the agency to take care of fluctuating client loads, to keep busy, to get maximum support from the government, and to keep its place in the competition of the institutional order.

While I have concentrated on the police and the psychiatric ward to illustrate the way in which organizational requirements affect the social control function, a somewhat similar argument would hold for other social control agencies as well. Agencies are bureaucratic organizations. As such they compete for funds with other governmental agencies. They have many goals in addition to those of providing social control, and these other goals are frequently more important in the bureaucratic calculus than their particular legitimating ideologies would indicate.

In the courts, for example, most cases do not come to trial. Rather, the prosecuting attorney and the defense attorney work out a compromise. The prosecution will offer to substitute a lesser charge in return for a guilty plea. If this is accepted by the defense it remains only for the court to pass sentence on the guilty plea. The court does not have time to try all the cases.

Karl Kreplin observed that in the psychiatric committal court the hearings are often so well organized that the patient will barely have a chance to sit down before his case is decided.

Prisons, with few exceptions, place primary emphasis on custody—making sure that prisoners do not escape. Very little in the way of rehabilitation is provided. After spending a number of years adjusting to prison life and being socialized to convict society, the prisoner is released. About half of them come back to prison again. Delinquents in the San Francisco area refer to San Quentin as "postgraduate school." They use their time in prison to learn how to commit more professional crimes.

Mental hospitals are also primarily custodial institutions, where the offender's "sentence" is at the discretion of the psychiatrist. Except for the well to do who can afford a private mental hospital, the experience of most inmates is with tranquilizers, electroshock therapy, occasional contact with the psychiatrist, and eventual discharge when they have been acting normal for a while.

FORMAL SOCIAL CONTROL AND COUNTER-INSTITUTIONS

The effectiveness of formal social control in suppressing counter-institutions is about what could be expected from blindfold target-shooting in a moving room using a gun that frequently jams. Counter-institutional behavior is "not understandable" within social reality so the laws that are created rarely attack the reality flaws that produced it. The laws themselves are the compromise product of institutional interactions that may serve various legitimate institutions better than they attack the counter-institution. Laws are enforced by people and organizations more interested in keeping their own organizations steady than in attacking any *particular* counter-institution. The decision they make to divide their work into clients and fillers has little to do with the origins or effective control of the behavior. The police only solve about a quarter of the crimes they know about, and they don't officially "know about" many other crimes that are quite obvious. The courts frequently overturn convictions because some legal procedure has been violated. Even if a person winds up in a prison or mental hospital his chance of being "rehabilitated" or "cured" before he is released is slight and not really known. Perhaps formal social control serves well as a symbol of the rules of the institutional order; it doesn't work very effectively in practice. It may keep a lot of people in prisons and mental hospitals, but it eliminates few counter-institutions and bad habits.

For the people involved in counter-institutions, formal social control is little more than a risk in their environment. It may be a large risk or small risk. The amount of risk probably depends more on the nature of the counter-institution than on the nature of the formal control applied against it. Self-controls and relational controls derived from legitimate institutions prevent the bad habits and counter-institutionalization that can be prevented. Formal control harasses what has not been prevented.
☐ ☐ ☐

□ □ □
When you do something one way you
are necessarily not doing it in the other
ways it could have been done. When a
number of people follow one pattern of
behavior they are not following the
other patterns that might accomplish
the same ends. There are many different ways in which we could do most of
the things we do every day. Our time is
limited. Our choices are votes. When
we follow one pattern of behavior we
enact it, we keep it alive in the minds of
others. The patterns we don't follow
disappear gradually from the minds of
all. Some patterns of behavior complement others; they take care of different
aspects of our lives. Other patterns of
behavior contend with each other to
take care of one aspect of our lives.
Those who follow a certain pattern of
behavior find it rewarding and wish to
continue it; the same is true for people
following other patterns. In their explanations of the superiority of their
form of behavior people compare it
with the alternatives. This comparison
is something like a debate where each
makes points for his side. It is a debate

**UNORGANIZED
RESPONSES**

that goes on among large and ill-defined teams, some well-coordinated, others not. Some teams have many members who find the debate important, others have few. Some have troops to capture the members of other teams, resolving the debate by force. These teams belong to the mutual defense pact of the legitimate institutional order that is sometimes fully honored, other times not so fully. They debate among one another, but their use of troops is infrequent, and when occurring, limited. Every form of behavior contends in debate and the ones which field enthusiastic and well-coordinated teams have an advantage over others which don't. When the troops are called out the enthusiastic and well-coordinated team has a better chance of avoiding them, rescuing captured members, and arranging a cease-fire, than the unorganized team. This chapter is about some of the ways a team gets organized and enthusiastic, and what happens to it if it doesn't. It is about what happens to counter-institutions when they have unorganized responses, in the debate, and in dealing with the formal social controls used against them.

As we saw in the last chapter, formal social control fields a rag-tag army with the troops often operating on contradictory commands, but an army nonetheless, and with some organization, which can often win a battle against individuals hiding in the alleys, small groups rallied to fight, or large groups in a panic. Behind formal social control is the debating team of the institutional order: maintaining theoreticians who plan strategy and think up new arguments for the debate; important men who often make up in conviction and single-mindedness their lack of debating skill; and many, many people who don't know much about the debates going on around them but who find what they do rewarding, and who know some of the party line.

Counter-institutions seldom have troops, because the outcome of battle is almost certain defeat. When they try to defend themselves against the formal control troops their best strategy is to try to win the debate and have the troops called back. To win, their theoreticians must be good, their important men must have conviction and single-mindedness, and their people must know about the debate, and know the party line.

The institutional order debates on many fronts, with many different teams. Counter-institutions should have a single goal, however complex their strategy, and they should come up with good, consistent, and appealing legitimations if they are to stand any chance of winning the debate. The most important point they have to make is that they are not the kind of people against whom formal control should be used. Since being targets of formal control depends upon being defined as people against whom formal control *should* be used they must attempt to alter this definition, to change the law of psychiatric orthodoxy that defined them. There are many other debates to be won as well, with important people and with little people, and these will affect the central debate, but winning the central debate makes the counter-institution a de facto part of the institutional order. It makes it an institution against which debate will still be carried on, but against which formal control cannot be legitimately used.

In order to have a debate at all some things must be agreed upon, some basic values must be accepted by both sides. When there is no agreement on the basic organization of reality there cannot be a debate, only segregation or war. Thus the counter-institution must work within the symbolic universe that legitimates the institutional order if it wishes to become a de facto part of the order.

If a counter-institution produces only sporadic, disorganized responses, if it produces only unappealing, unconvincing legitimations that are not clearly within the value structure of the symbolic universe, the forces of the institutional order will stabilize it, force it to go underground, or defeat it.

When a counter-institution is stabilized in its conflict with the institutional order the behavior continues to be enacted, continues to exist, but the sporadic conflict keeps its growth in check. When a police official speaks of "managing" crime he is speaking of stabilizing it. He does not have enough officers to eliminate crime, so he assigns his forces to apply differential pressure to keep various counter-institutions in check. If there is a public outcry about prostitution he uses more officers to arrest prostitutes, if the armed robberies go up in a district he assigns more officers to patrol that district, if street demonstrations take place he creates a riot squad. He tries to keep the lid on many counter-institutions by selective assignment of his officers.

A stabilized counter-institution is one that has reached some sort of equilibrium with the forces of the institutional order. The reality flaws that produce it will not let its enactment fall below a certain level; social control will not let it rise above another level. The levels, of course, may change, but within them there is a homeostatic process that limits the counter-institution. The stabilization may come from debate as well as from the use of troops. Mothers may persuade their sons not to stick up gas stations, and intense police patrol may catch some of the unpersuaded. Most unorganized criminal activity is stabilized by these forces if only temporarily.

When a counter-institution is forced to go underground it continues to exist and may even grow, but it reduces its visibility. This reduction may affect the counter-institution's potential for reaching recruits, and for this reason the withdrawal is often thought to be a kind of victory by social control forces. When intense police pressure forces prostitutes off the street and they become call girls they are out of sight but still in practice. The overt conflict is reduced, which may be a satisfactory outcome for both sides.

Counter-institutions, once established, are rarely extinguished by formal social control, though they might disappear if the reality flaw that produced them disappears. For example if skid row residents all had enough money to drink in taverns the bottle gang might not continue. Horse stealing has become much less frequent, as has claim jumping.

There are many factors that keep a counter-institution from creating an organized response to its social definition. One of the most important of these is a lack of communications among people who follow the counter-institution.

LACK OF INTERNAL COMMUNICATIONS

Before actions can be coordinated, before legitimations can be developed, before the institutional order's negative definition can be challenged, there must be institutionalized patterns of communication among those who enact the counter-institution.

In a literate society, a counter-institution composed of functional illiterates is at a distinct disadvantage in formulating legitimations and plans. With almost universal literacy in North America this handicap is relatively unimportant, though some segments of the population still suffer. Keeping a population that might form counter-institutions illiterate has been an historical method of social control. Black slaves in the United States were forbidden to learn to read and write in many places. The Burmese attempted to keep the Karen minority illiterate during most of the nineteenth century. As literacy has spread many counter-institutions that were very much ad hoc have developed organization and legitimations; the rise of "welfare rights" groups among the recipients of public welfare, for example.

The increasing importance of electronic communications means, however, that the ability to read and write may be becoming less crucial. This is certainly true in many parts of the Middle East and Africa where the radio has replaced the town newspaper reader as a source of information and orientation. Electronic communications provide a second channel in a literate society; the words in rock songs carry as much meaning as underground newspapers, and to a wider audience.

If the followers of a counter-institution are dispersed geographically, communication becomes more difficult because face-to-face interactions are more rare and other methods of communication take more conscious effort. The bottle gang depended for its continuity on the common residence of its members on skid row. Even if others enacting the same counter-institution are known, distant communications are not likely to encourage the elaboration of the counter-institution as personal contact does.

If the followers of a counter-institution are dispersed throughout the social structure, and are not highly visible, communications cannot be directed at *known* fellow members and must be foregone or watered down sufficiently to be innocuous. Mate swapping arrangements, for example, had to depend on *very* discreet newspaper advertisements until specialized publications appeared.

If the people who share a reality flaw keep it secret because of guilt, and they don't have an elaborated and understood way of communicating with one another that is subliminal for people not sharing the flaw, they will not be able to communicate enough to form reciprocal typifications, much less counter-institutions. Transvestites, for example, had almost no way of meeting one another until *Transvestia* magazine was published.

If the followers of a counter-institution believe that informers are present they will restrict their communications drastically. The use of informers in Chinese Communist prisoner of war camps prevented the formation of escape committees among the American prisoners. The use of informers keeps many criminals from joining together.

The followers of counter-institutions may lack communications media. Access to the legitimate institutions of communications, television, radio, and newspapers, may be denied in the name of propriety or morality or as an explicit control measure. Additionally these legitimate institutions may misrepresent, ignore and editorialize against counter-institution legitimations and communications. Imagine trying to present the case for cunnilingus on your local television station. Michael McClure's play, "The Beard,"[1] was raided by the police in San Francisco, Berkeley, and Los Angeles, and the cast was arrested fifteen straight nights in Los Angeles for *acting* as if they were performing cunnilingus on stage.

If a counter-institution establishes its own media of communications it may be suppressed by the postal authorities, or the police. Vendors of underground newspapers are often arrested for not having licenses, licenses never required for vendors of the local daily that presents the institutional order's views. Radio stations that allow counter-institutional views to be presented sometimes have their license renewals held up, often on a pretext. All of this is part of the mutual defense pact of the institutional order.

Legitimations may never be developed and communicated if the behavior does not provide a basis for group cooperation. Most bad habits

[1] Michael McClure, *The Beard* (New York: Evergreen, 1969).

remain unlegitimated for this reason. If the counter-institution functions on the basis of antagonistic cooperation, as is the case with heroin addicts, the presentation of a united front is very difficult.

Various counter-institutions may be mutually antagonistic and may never achieve a common legitimation. Professional thieves will not associate with the less professional ones.

The counter-institution may lack the ability and resources to come to an evaluation of the theories that might form the basis for its legitimations, and there may be enough internal division and local variation so that no definable spokesman can be said to speak for the behavior. Timothy Leary does not speak for all drug users, LeRoi Jones does not speak for all black power advocates. This is true for both internal and external communications.

Handicaps of people who follow the counter-institution may make coordination and communication difficult. The mentally retarded do not communicate well with one another, though they may have common interests and reality flaws in their everyday lives. Children may lack expertise and access to communications, though there surely are as many reality flaws in grade schools as there are in universities. Poor people may not take the communications of other poor people as seriously as those from someone better off. The plight of stutterers has already been mentioned.

All of these problems in establishing internal communications limit the development of legitimations, often keep those following the counter-institutions ignorant of the debate and the party line, and keep the coordination of efforts to a minimum. Without internal communications and debate cannot be entered; without effective internal communications it cannot be won.

LACK OF EXTERNAL COMMUNICATIONS

In order to have any hope of becoming legitimate, effective communications must be established with the opposition. These need not be verbal; a sufficient number of people following a counter-institution makes a point by itself. Assuming that legitimations have been developed within the counter-institution the problem is effective presentation. The followers of a counter-institution may lack the knowledge or ability to make their presentation to the appropriate audience in the appropriate way. The audience may refuse to listen. There may not *be* an appropriate audience.

Certain key institutions and individuals must be convinced that the counter-institution is not bad, or that using formal social control against it is unfair or produces bad results. In addition, enough of the concerned members of the general public must be convinced so that the law can be dropped without public outcry, or so that the bad habit can be redefined. Winning the debate will not immediately change the relational and self controls used against the counter-institution—even if homosexuality is legalized many will still be opposed to it, and many institutions will still discriminate against homosexuals.

Often, the legitimate channels of communications will be closed to counter-institutions, keeping them from making their case to the public, or communications will be rejected with comments like, "just a bunch of perverts trying to rationalize their behavior."

The counter-institution may squander its resources because its participants have not developed a thought-out strategy for presenting their case in the most effective manner. The communications may be aimed at the public, when an official would be more appropriate, at an official when a newspaper would be better, at a newspaper when a civil-liberties association would be better. Counter-institutions rarely have the resources and organization to hire a public relations firm, that is, a legitimation specialist, even if one would take the account. Legitimate institutions often use public relations firms to make their case against other legitimate institutions, or to justify their place in the institutional order, but prostitutes might have difficulty in finding such a firm. Often public relations are used after some behavior has become partially legitimate, as when John D. Rockefeller hired an agent to erase his public image as a "robber baron." The same principles apply to hiring legislative lobbyists, frequently used by legitimate institutions to protect and improve their positions in the institutional order. Most large universities maintain them, but they are not often available to counter-institutions.

Because participation in a counter-institution is usually segmental and does not provide total organization for the daily round of a participant's activities, he will often find himself involved with others in legitimate institutions. He may find that he has to direct his explanations at these others. For various reasons they may take him more or less seriously. More seriously if he is important in the legitimate institution, less if he is unimportant or subordinate. Additionally, he may share values with these others because of a common pattern of socialization, and a shared value may cross-cut the implicit values of his legitimation. If this is the case he will not be able to communicate the totality of the legitimation developed within the counter-institution. A teenager may have difficulty in explaining to his parents why long hair is important.

Even given good internal and external communications and the development of persuasive legitimations, the outcome of the debate is in doubt.

THE IMPORTANCE OF CONVICTION

Some counter-institutions are faced with relatively widely shared and firmly held opposition, others are not: mores and folkways, for example. Armed robbers, who violate values of person and property, are faced with fairly unified opposition. Most criminal counter-institutions that victimize others would have a hard time becoming legitimate no matter what they said. Alcoholics, on the other hand, do not violate such centrally held values, and the United States Supreme Court has ruled that they may not be arrested just for showing the symptoms of their "disease" in public. The "disease" legitimation has taken the alcoholic out of police hands and put him in medical hands, at least in theory. The formal control used against alcoholics has become less punitive, a bit less certain, though he still encounters control, even if from a different source and with a different rhetoric.

Some counter-institutions develop the conviction among their followers that gives them the motivation to debate, others do not. In general, patterns of behavior that comprise a large part of a person's life and involve other parts tangentially are likely to develop more conviction than those that are only part-time. Thus homosexuals are developing the conviction to debate while bottle gang members are not.

The more widely shared and firmly held is opposition to a counter-institution the more likely that this opposition will have been transmitted even to the people following it, through socialization when they were children, and through their other interactions as adults. This means that some of their self-control and some of their relational controls will be in opposition to their behavior, making the development of conviction difficult. It is in these cases especially that a counter-institution strategy of encouraging extreme action may develop strong conviction through a "reaction formation" process.

It should be possible to predict with some accuracy whether or not a counter-institution will become legitimate by considering the factors mentioned in this chapter. Counter-institutions that develop good legitimations, communicate them effectively and with conviction, that face scattered opposition, have a good chance of becoming legitimate. Those that lack any of these factors have less of a chance, and those that lack all have no chance.

In the following adaptation Clive Copeland and Norris McDonald discuss the life of the prostitute and point out the difficulties that prostitutes face in becoming legitimate.

☐ ☐ ☐

22

PROSTITUTES ARE HUMAN BEINGS
An Unorganized Counter-Institution

CLIVE L. COPELAND AND NORRIS A. McDONALD

There are many prostitutes living and working within any big city. Why don't prostitutes fight collectively to make their profession legal? What keeps them from organizing to press for legitimacy? Homosexuals have fought for legalization of homosexuality—what is there about prostitution that prevents prostitutes from doing the same?

We have interviewed a number of prostitutes, who work as call girls and also as hustlers, and we will attempt to present here the "call-girl hustler's" view of the world. In other words we will try to let the prostitute speak for herself, to give her definition of the situation, and then to bring this information into sociological perspective. We found in the course of taking their world seriously that in some ways the girls made us see "our world" in an entirely new way—in fact, more sociologically.

Neither of us had had any prior connection with prostitution when we undertook this project so we were somewhat vague about our objectives when we started. However, we planned our questions before attempting to make contacts. We reasoned that the girls would be used to hearing customers ask "how did a nice girl like you get started in a business like this?" so we opened our interview by asking her about the police. We attempted in this way to gain the girls' confidence and to show that we were sympathetic. This approach worked well.

When we started we had a list of about twenty questions designed to tap the prostitute's career, her work situation, her legitimations, and her relationship to the "external world." By the end of the study our list had grown to about 200 questions, and we had asked another 150 in the course of interviewing.

In September 1968, we made our first contacts through the evening manager of a cocktail lounge. The manager offered to introduce us as prospective customers to "one of the girls." He believed that if we started out stating that we were researchers the girls would think we were either police, or crazy. (This manager we later found out was a "rounder.") [See article 14, "Rounders," by Marie-Anne LeGrand for definition.] The lounge was a relatively affluent midtown establishment catering to middle and upper-middle-class clients. It also attracted some student trade. The girls who hustled in the lounge were generally reasonably intelligent, clean, inclined to be honest, and open—as a result they were easy to understand and talk to. (Our sample thus has

Adapted from "The Meter Maids of Montreal," an unpublished manuscript, Sir George Williams University, Montreal, 1969. Reprinted by permission.

a bias toward middle-status prostitutes; pure call girls and street-walkers are not represented.)

We interviewed seven girls, usually in their apartments. The interviews lasted from two to five hours at a sitting—when the girls could give us the time. Three of the girls were interviewed numerous times, and in depth. Their answers were recorded on tape, or with a note pad. The interviews with the other girls were not as extensive. We followed the girls' work life through repeated interviews for three weeks, at the shortest, to eight months for the most extended case history.

Some of the girls' general comments about their work and their feelings provide a good introduction to their perspective.

> I think you're going to have very hard time to make the people believe that the hooker is human being like everybody else. You gonna have hard time to convince people, if you do, that she has feelings, that she is normal.

. . .

> The girl is in a profession. . . . It's a profession which requires experience . . . which requires skill like any profession. . . .

. . .

> She must be mature, and she must be prepared that she gonna be rejected by the society. She must be strong enough to understand, and to take it.

We found that a number of factors in the work situation of the prostitute inhibited the growth of an organization of prostitutes, and thus kept their counter-institution relatively fragmented and easily "managed" by the police.

COMMUNICATIONS

Prostitutes have not developed any very distinctive occupational argot with the exception of a few terms used for customers and for various sexual acts. Most of their conversation is with their relatively straight clients, rather than with other prostitutes. In fact, in our sample, other prostitutes avoided talking with the newcomer until she had become part of the gang. [*Prostitutes lack the reality defining power of their own distinctive language.*]

The prostitute finds out a great many things that she cannot talk about with anyone. From the other night people she meets, both as clients and as acquaintances, she finds out about goings-on in the underworld . . . who just pulled off a bank robbery, who is selling what drugs, what the Cosa Nostra is doing. To speak of these things is to invite a beating or death.

She is also aware of the "top businessmen" who use her services, of judges, lawyers, and policemen who take bribes. But to speak of these things is to invite repeated arrests and heavy jail terms.

Thus the prostitute talks mostly with her clients and does not develop a strong or coherent communications system with other prostitutes. [*This inhibits the formation of an organization and the development of legitimations.*]

INTERACTIONS WITH OTHER PROSTITUTES

Prostitutes tend to find themselves in antagonistic cooperation with one another. Girls who are "loners" (who work without a pimp, and don't work in a night club or a house) feel the most insecure. These girls see one another as rivals; they help each other only if it does not "put them out" too much.

Even the girls who work in the same club together have a very tenuous sense of community. They will not really help one another, especially when it costs a lot of money:

> If it's a question of ten, twenty dollars, and I know the girl, and she is a good working girl, I will help her. But if it's a question of "put up the bail, or question of big money," no. . . . Tomorrow, if it gonna happen to me, who gonna give it to me, right.

The prostitutes are aware of their "stigma," and tend to accept the fact that they are part, therefore, of a community of sorts. But this community feeling tends to be limited to contacts with other girls during 'business hours' in bars, lounges, etc. Also her usual acquaintances are connected with illegal institutions, or the subculture of counterinstitutions. She mingles with members of Cosa Nostra (Mafia), other call girls, pimps, waitress-cum-prostitutes, rounders, bookmakers, shylocks, etc., all of whom have something in common—they are the "night people."

> I mean I know one thing, that I don't belong to the society of decent people. I know this for sure; I have nothing in common, I mean I feel bad, I don't feel security, I don't feel I belong there. I belong to the people who steal, I mean uh, drugs, pushers. This is where I belong. This is where I can talk. I have something in common.

But she tends to be a *fringe* member of the "night people" institutions, as well as of the "straight" people institutions.

The prostitutes' occupational role requires youthfulness—their career is usually short-lived. They know that they will eventually have to become madams of their own houses or turn cheaper and cheaper tricks if they stay in prostitution. Thus they tend to look out for their own interests rather than for the interests of prostitutes as a whole. They tend not to think much about the future although they all seem to have some dreamlike goal in mind.

> I'd like to be a photographer's model—glamor pictures but not total nude shots. I would like to move to California where my modelling pictures might help me to get started in a movie career.

> . . .

> I try to make some money to put away, maybe open some business. But, so far . . . (What kind of business?) A little store with bras, panties, imported things like that. Not dresses, because there's so many stores like that. I don't see where all my money's going though. I more or less live day to day.

INSECURE CONDITIONS OF WORK

Most of the girls we talked to were not strictly speaking 'call girls' but also hustled (therefore, call-girl hustlers). 'Steady customers' usually don't last for more than three months, and thus the necessity to go out and hustle some more.

> First thing, if she want to be a call girl, she must, she cannot start being call girl because she decides to. She must start hustling and get her calls, she must find her tricks. . . . It's never enough, that you can make a living only on the phone. Best thing she must get off her ass and go and get clientele. Then, of course, she must have her apartment and get the phone, automatically.

By going out 'hustling' the girl naturally places herself at a disadvantage. The 'morality squad' knows the hangouts and also the girls who make use of them; as a result the girls tend to worry about being picked up and charged.

The girls also tend to work in one area.

> I used to have special area, but today I change. I almost get pinched today. You get used to one place, one spot. You get used to the people, you know the owner, you know the place, you know suckers over there. So you go over there. . . . Not many call girls gonno go to night club, not at all . . . I will say mostly they work, more or less, in hotel lounges, little cocktail lounges, where they have good steady clientele.

Their job engenders a great deal of insecurity, and known locations give the girls a relative sense of security. But, as a result, the morality squad can control them more effectively because their habits are known. Not only do the girls remain in a specific locale for security, but also because in other areas (e.g., night clubs) their entrance would be looked upon dimly by prostitutes (or management) who already work there.

> She might wake up in General Hospital. The girls are very sensitive when you go to new place, and they don't want you. They resent you, they give you trouble.

[*Working in one location makes prostitutes more predictable for the police, and limits their contacts with other prostitutes.*]
Even though their work environment is relatively constant, the girls would never say that they had "roots." They prefer to state that they are transients. They are always ready to move to another city when police pressure becomes too strong. [*Lack of roots means that the prostitute has little reason to stay where she is and fight for legalization—it is easier to move.*]

A prostitute also has few or no friends in the straight world; usually she has lost contact with old school friends who are not in the same profession. Even if she wished to leave her profession for a job in the straight world, she would have a difficult time obtaining employment. Few employers hire girls who have been imprisoned for prostitution (except those firms with house prostitutes on the payroll). [*The prostitute has few reliable friends and few allies. Thus she is forced to rely upon herself rather than trying to organize prostitutes to gain more general ends.*]

LEGITIMATIONS

Berger and Luckmann note three levels of legitimation that are developed in institutions. [*Prostitutes have not developed a high level of legitimation, probably as a consequence of the lack of organization of the counter-institution.*]

So far, in our sample, the legitimations we have heard have been at the first two levels. The first legitimation they have is "prostitution exists everywhere, all over the world, and has existed for thousands of years —it's the oldest profession."

Throughout history, prostitutes have been the only source or outlet for sex maniacs, criminals, or whatever—or so societies (and some theologians, such as St. Augustine of the fourth and St. Thomas Aquinas of the thirteenth century) have claimed. It has also been claimed that nonmarital sex is a necessary outlet for the male of the species and therefore prostitutes cater to this 'need.'

But many sectors of society believe that prostitutes pose a threat to the institution of the family: their availability (for cash) turns a "good" man's head. The prostitute reverses this statement.

> . . . When [the customer] goes home, his wife she lies like a piece of wood, right? Most of them. . . . When he's at home, his wife's bored, or she's tired. You know—all that bullshit!

> •   •   •

> Perhaps in 2000 years from now, it gonna be different. But, so far as I am concerned, for another 50 years ahead, prostitution is going to exist. Perhaps it's going to be a different kind of prostitution, different way of asking; society and people and everything changes. But prostitution is going to always exist. A man, he perhaps like his wife, but you are not going to find many men, I would say 45–50, who don't try to cheat his wife. . . . No, he always going to try, and always going to try one or two times.

The first- and second-level legitimations are mingled in the above quote. The first is, "that's the way things are." The second would be, "More marriages would break up if it wasn't for us." But there the prostitutes stop. There does not appear to be a third-level legitimation. "Counter-institutions infrequently rise to this level of legitimation unless they are well on the way to becoming integrated into the institutional order of society (e.g., marijuana smoking, homosexuality)."

The second-level legitimations that they have are, "If prostitutes did not exist, there would be many more sex crimes, rapes, etc." Why? "Because in marriage the wife lies like a piece of wood, and the man is not satisfied. More marriages would break up if it wasn't for us." Also on this level she sees it as an occupation that in some ways is not so bad: "It's not every day the same routine. You go always with different people, you talk to the people, you have chance to have a few drinks, you have free hours; you work when you want; you sit where you want, you make more money, you are more free. I feel revolted at beginning, rotten. Now I am used to it."

However, because they have not reached the third level of legitimation at this point, they present no actual threat to "society" and are therefore "controlled" rather than completely accepted or completely rejected. That is, they have no "organization," their contacts with every institution in society are peripheral, and among themselves there is rivalry.

FORMAL SOCIAL CONTROL—THE POLICE

How does the call-girl hustler cope with her occupational role? Probably not very successfully, since she feels harassed by the morality squad who pick her up mainly on charges of "vagrancy," who have "increase-the-arrest-rate drives" every so often.

The call-girl hustler's contact with the police is threatening and frustrating. We had a notion that the girls would see the police as perpetrators of stupidity and morality, that they would be bitter toward them. To date, most of the girls have stated that the cops, after all, are only doing a job—although they maintain that the cops, too, are crooks.

Some of the girls state that members of the morality squad receive additional "incentive" pay for each arrest involving prostitution. Also, the girls said the morality squad tended to "pick on" prostitutes as this was easier than cracking a gambling or dope ring, for example. This was one way the arrest rate was either raised or at least maintained at a steady level. In fact, the prostitutes indicated a considerable knowledge of the policeman's vocation. It could be said that the prostitutes and the police tend to have a close relationship and, therefore, that the institutions are intertwined.

> The only police I know is morality squad. So they are a bunch of crooks, because, for example, for a long time [this night club] was paying off and I saw many policemen coming over there, and they knew what was going on. I mean I slept with one free, you know, so they are not angels.

The prostitute faces the legal system alone and helpless. Unable to borrow bail money she awaits trial and almost certain conviction—even on a bum rap.

> If you have a record, and they (the police) are not telling the truth, who is going to believe you? There are two or three of them (the police) telling the same story and I am alone, no witnesses, but I am telling the truth. I lose the case anyway.

THE PROSTITUTE'S REACTION TO SOCIAL CONTROL

How do the girls respond to all these social pressures? As previous quotes have shown, she tends to condemn the people she interacts with (including her colleagues) and especially her customers.

> All my customers are sickening bastards. They look on hookers as cheap fucking sluts—but they can't get fuck-all else, and that's why they're here. And they think they're such fucking great lovers. I can't stand them.
>
> · · ·
>
> Some of them I don't mind to have some conversation with and spend some time with them, but sexually I don't feel anything. . . .

I don't ilke too the way some behave, the way they talk, and they try to . . . they feel superior, they are in a rush, they give you the money and want to get it over with. At the same time they need you and I mean they don't have time to treat you like a human being, just like a machine they use which they need, and that's all. Many of them, they say "if you see me anyplace outside, you don't know me." I say, you don't have to tell me that. If you see *me* anyplace outside you don't know me either, okay!

As can be discerned this kind of reaction to social pressures does not actually alleviate their situation. [*It is a condemnation of the condemners, as Sykes & Matza noted.*]

Although the girls were tolerant toward the police, they were nervous about police action; formal, routine police action. They were apprehensive if the telephone rang and they didn't know the person who was on the line. They were afraid to go to their hustling area as the police might be waiting to pick them up. Miss M. was busted five times in six weeks. She was beginning to show the strain: she drank more, talked more about money, and was not as available (for interviews) as usual. Obviously, she feared being arrested again, that this time the "key might be thrown away." Also, it was costing her a great deal of money, and kept her from "hustling."

CONCLUSIONS

Call-girl hustlers do belong to a subculture of sorts. It is not a strong subculture; ties between the members are only as strong as their stigmatized occupation. And since they tend to be tolerated as a "necessary evil" by most segments of society, their stigma is not like that of, say, murderers. However, the fact that they have few or no friends in the straight world also indicates a community of sorts. The weakness of the subculture is also indicated by their definite locality, their rivalry, and their ignorance of many other areas that might, or might not, be good for business.

Their role is bounded by their deviant label. They are negatively sanctioned in some way by most segments of society that they come into contact with, thereby increasing the likelihood of communal necessity. But since they are harassed individually their communal feeling is fragmented. [*Thus they have not organized to fight back.*]

☐ ☐ ☐

There are many counter-institutions that face some of the difficulties Copeland and McDonald noted for prostitution. These are the counter-institutions that continue but do not become legitimate. Prostitution, however, well illustrates that a lack of communications, antagonistic cooperation, a hostile environment including routine interaction with the police, and a consequent lack of legitimation and organization mean a fragmented and individualized response to social control.

COMMUNICATION THROUGH ACTION

On occasion even an unorganized counter-institution can communicate a message through its actions. For example, a riot communicates the discontent of the rioters. Since the message is physical rather than verbal, its "meaning" must be interpreted, and the interpretation may vary with the social position of the interpreter. Thus some might interpret riots as being the work of "outside agitators" or "Communists," while other might see a meaningful reaction to a flaw in social reality. In the following adaptation Russell Dynes and E. L. Quarantelli explore the "meaning" of the looting that goes on during ghetto uprisings. This meaning was not articulated by the participants as an explanation for their behavior but was interpreted from their actions.
☐ ☐ ☐

23
WHAT LOOTING IN CIVIL DISTURBANCES REALLY MEANS

RUSSELL DYNES AND E. L. QUARANTELLI

The occurrence of looting in civil disturbances needs no further documentation. And selectivity can be seen in the fact that, in racial outbreaks, looters have concentrated overwhelmingly on certain kinds of stores. In Watts, Newark, and Detroit, the main businesses affected were groceries, supermarkets, and furniture and liquor stores. In contrast, banks, utility stations, industrial plants, and private residences have been generally ignored. Apartments and homes have been damaged, but only because they were in or near burned business establishments. Public installations such as schools and Office of Economic Opportunity centers have also been spared. There has not been indiscriminate looting. Certain kinds of consumer goods have been almost the only targets.

Looters in civil disturbances are also likely to receive support from many people in their community. Spiraling support coincides with shifts in property redefinitions, and these shifts occur in three stages. Initial looting is often a symbolic act of defiance. The second phase, in which more conscious and deliberate plundering develops, is possibly spurred on by the presence of delinquent gangs that loot more from need or for profit than for ideological reasons. Finally, in the third stage, there is widespread seizure of goods. At this point, looting becomes the socially expected thing to do. For example, a sociological survey at U.C.L.A. found that nearly one-fourth of the population participated in the Watts outbreak (although all of these participants probably did not engage in the looting).

If looting means strictly the taking of goods, little of it occurs in the first phase of civil disturbances. Instead, destructive attacks are most frequently directed against symbols of authority in the community. Police cars and fire trucks are pillaged and burned. [*These are symbols of the institutional order. The police are also the troops that have been used against Black counter-institutions.*]

.   .   .

The full redefinition of certain property rights occurs next. The "carnival spirit" observed in the Newark and Detroit disturbances did not represent anarchy. It represented widespread social support for the new definition of property. In this phase, there is little competition for goods. In fact, in contrast to the stealthy looting that occasionally occurs in disaster situations, looting in civil disturbances is quite open and frequently collective. The looters often work together in pairs, as family units, or in small groups. Bystanders are frequently told about potential loot. And in some instances, as in the Watts outbreak, looters coming out of stores hand strangers goods as "gifts."

Looting in civil disturbances is by insiders—by local community members. These looters apparently come not only from the low socio-economic levels and from delinquent gangs, but from all segments of the population. During disturbances in Toledo, 91 percent of the 126 adults arrested for taking goods had jobs. A random sample in Detroit found that participants in the outbreak came more or less equally from all income brackets.

In both disasters and civil disturbances, there is a redefinition of property rights within the community. The community authorities, however, respond very differently to the two situations. In disasters, responsible officials tolerate, accept, and encourage the transition from private to community property. In civil disturbances, community authorities see looting as essentially criminal behavior—as a legal problem to be handled forcefully ʼʏy the police. [*The institutional order uses force to maintain its institutions, in this case private property.*] And many segments of the larger community, especially middle-class people, with their almost sacred conception of private property, tend to hold the same view. [*It is they who benefit from the institution of private property, not those without property.*] This view of looting in civil disturbances fits in neatly with the ideas they already have about the criminal propensities of certain ethnic groups, notably Negroes.

LOOTING AS A MASS PROTEST

At one level, there is no question that looting in civil disturbances is criminal behavior. But the laws that make it so are themselves based on dominant conceptions of property rights [*the symbolic legitimations of private property*]. Widespread looting, then, may perhaps be interpreted as a kind of mass protest against our dominant conceptions of property.

Mass protest is not new in history. According to George Rudé's analysis, in his book *The Crowd in History,* demonstrating mobs from 1730 to 1848 in England and France were typically composed of local, respectable, employed people rather than the pauperized, the unemployed, or the "rabble" of the slums. The privileged classes naturally regarded these popular agitations as criminal—as fundamentally and unconditionally illegitimate. Rudé notes, however, that such protest effectively communicated the desires of a segment of the urban population to the elite. E. J. Hobsbawm, in his analysis of the preindustrial "city mob," takes the same position: "The classical mob did not merely riot as a protest, but because it expected to achieve something by its riot. It assumed that the authorities would be sensitive to its movements, and probably also that they would make some immediate concession . . . This mechanism was perfectly understood by both sides."

In current civil disturbances, a similar mechanism and a similar message may be evolving. An attack against property rights is not necessarily "irrational," "criminal," or "pointless" if it leads to a clearer system of demands and responses, in which the needs and obligations of the contending parties are reasonably clear to themselves and to one another. The scope and intensity of current attacks indicate the presence of large numbers of outsiders living within most American cities [*people outside the institutional order*]. If property is seen as a shared understanding about the allocation of resources, and if a greater consensus can be reached on the proper allocation of these resources, many of these outsiders will become insiders, with an established stake in the communities in which they live. [*In other words, the institutional order must respond to the counter-institutional pressure to eliminate a reality flaw or be in a position of constantly having to defend itself with troops and guns.*]

□ □ □

When a reality flaw results in communications through action rather than debate the first response is usually also action. In the case of ghetto uprisings there is rarely anyone with whom to debate. Actions may produce concessions that debate would not. A riot establishes one-way communications with the institutional order; they get the message but except for an escalation of violence they cannot reply. The institutional order may have to figure out on its own what concessions to make, and make them to see if they reduce the reality flaw. Thus unorganized action is imperfect but often effective.

□ □ □

□ □ □
If a counter-institution has the handicaps mentioned in the last chapter it
will be held down—either it will never
develop as an institution, or it will
never develop a good explanation for
being an institution. If it doesn't have
these handicaps, it *may* fight back.
The attempt at control may make the
participants more confirmed in their
behavior, not less. This can happen
when a person stabilizes a "bad"
habit, as shown by Scheff and Buckley. It can also happen in a counter-
institution. What happens, in essence,
is that social reaction conveys the
message, "You are doing a bad thing,
and we are going to punish you for it."
And the "deviant" who enacts the
counter-institution doesn't say, "I am
guilty, punish me, I deserved it. I will
be better." He says, "I am proud of
what I am doing, and society is wrong
to condemn me for it."

In other words, at least some legitimate institutions have attempted to
define a counter-institution as being
"bad," illegal, and outside the institutional order. The institutional order

DEVIATION
AMPLIFYING
FEEDBACK

attempts to communicate this definition of social reality to the people in the counter-institution, to make its negative definition *the* definition of social reality. The definition is rejected. The people who follow the counter-institution have developed their own reality, at least about what they are doing. It is their own creation, based on their own experiences and conversations. You take a lot of physics on faith, but when your broiler catches fire you *know* that grease has a low ignition point. You will clean out the broiler in the future without even asking a physicist whether grease burns. If someone starts to broadcast the idea that it is paranoid to think that grease might catch fire, you are still going to clean the broiler. So it is with a person involved in some kinds of counter-institutions. Their experience and their friends create one reality and somebody "important" off in the distance tries to enforce another reality. If they check around and find that nobody who has done it finds anything wrong with it except that other people who have not done it told them it was wrong, they'll usually go along with their friends, and reject or evade the attempt at control.

We are constantly changing our views of reality to correspond with the views of others around us. We change our self-concept, we become something different from what we were. This happens no matter what the "direction" of the change—whether the new thing that we have become was good or bad according to our old way of looking at it. John Kinch offered an example in his article "A Formalized Theory of the Self Concept."[1] A group of graduate students, playing with the idea that a person would change to fit the reactions they got from others, all began to date a rather plain girl, telling themselves she was beautiful. Although it was difficult for the first of the men it gradually became easier because the girl began to fix herself up, to look as pretty as these men seemed to think she was. By the time the last man's turn came she had become so pretty and popular that she didn't have time for him. If you wander into a communal family and everybody treats you like a member of the family, you soon come to think of yourself as a member of the family. If you get married you soon come to think of yourself as a married person, because everybody around you reacts to you as if you were. If you smoke marijuana with your friends you will soon come to think that it is not as bad as the Narcotics Bureau says it is. Since what the Narcotics Bureau says—it makes you psychotic, it leads to heroin, delusions, and intellectual impairment—does not describe the experience that you or your friends have, you may begin to wonder why the Bureau is trying to put everybody on. If you get arrested for using marijuana you may suddenly find your world split in two—your smoking

[1] John Kinch, "A Formalized Theory of the Self Concept," *The American Journal of Sociology*, January 1963, Vol. 68, No. 4.

friends who are outraged and bail you out or at least sympathize, and a lot of people who won't talk to you because they think you're a dope fiend who might rape their daughters. Now you've really got a choice. Do you say, "I'll be a good boy, you were right," and *believe* it, to try to make it with all those people who won't talk to you? This is what social control would make you do if it worked as it is supposed to. Or do you say, "I'll be good" to the judge and trip out smoking with your friends? Might you not say, "the system is unjust, it must be changed/destroyed," and work to prod your friends to change or destroy the system? Depending on their situations, and their subjective realities, people do all three. If they go straight, control worked. If they go back to their friends and continue quietly, the counter-institution will at least be maintained. If they decide to fight the system, they may make an alteration in the structure of social reality. It's hard—the institutional order fights back—but it is possible.

Let's look at what are called "juvenile delinquents" for a moment. Most boys are only arrested once, and the subjective realities make them fear ever being arrested again. In their cases social control worked. For some boys, however, the first arrest is the start of a criminal career. Taking another hypothetical example, suppose a boy is out with his friends and one of them decides to steal a car that has the keys in it. They all go for a joyride, and are caught by the police. He goes to juvenile court and is placed on probation. When he goes back to school he finds that his teachers think of him as a potential troublemaker, and sometimes show it. (Teachers' assumptions often affect their students' performance. In a recent study teachers were led to expect that randomly selected students would "show great promise." The students' IQ's increased significantly.[2]) Some of his classmates' parents may have told them not to run around with him. His girl friend may refuse to see him, possibly on her parents' orders. His probation officer spends a fair amount of time asking about his illegal behavior. His parents show him that they are afraid he will be arrested again in the way they ask him about what he is doing. To a greater or lesser extent he begins to find that his one act, which might have been a lark if he had not been caught, has influenced others' definitions of him in many of his interactions. If his friends are still around he may find that it is most comfortable to spend his time with them. At least they don't look on him as being bad—they may even be proud of him. He may find that he can get along much better with his friends than with those who think badly of him. So he stays in the gang and gets arrested again and again, and possibly even becomes

---

[2] R. Rosenthal and L. Jacobson, *Pygmalion in the Classroom* (New York: Holt, Rinehart & Winston, 1968).

an adult criminal. Because the delinquent's legitimations for car stealing are not very good, as Sykes and Matza pointed out, the boy is unlikely to say "the system is unjust, it must be changed," but instead he just goes on stealing cars. This process of becoming more confirmed in deviant behavior as a response to social pressure has been called "secondary deviation" by Edwin Lemert. The process of social identification of a person as a "deviant" has been called "labeling theory" and has been explored by John Kitsuse, Kai Erikson, and Howard Becker.

When a counter-institution like a juvenile gang or a group of marijuana smokers finds itself under attack by various legitimate institutions, it has some advantages over an individual who is being attacked. The individual faces his environment, most of it disagreeing with him, alone. He deals with his parents as a participant in legitimate family institutions. He deals with his employer as one employee among many. He deals with the police or psychiatrists as a cowed individual. His secondary deviation may be involuntary, a consequence of his primary deviation and the social response, but a consequence over which he has little control. The alcoholic who drinks to forget the problems caused by his drinking is involved in secondary deviation with his bad habit. He may not have consciously chosen this path; he may have drifted into it. When somebody who enacts a counter-institution faces a negative definition from the straight world, he can seek support from others in the counter-institution. When he deals with negative definitions he can speak with the backing of or as a spokesman for a group, not as an individual.

Within the counter-institution various kinds of social controls are discussed, and ways of avoiding them or dealing with them become common knowledge. The individual becomes prepared for situations that have not happened to him yet, indeed may never happen to him. Much of the so-called "paranoia" of recreational drug users is simply the watchfulness that has diffused through the counter-institution, perhaps stimulated by a sense of fear, lack of knowledge of police procedures, and a lively imagination. Insofar as being watchful keeps one from being arrested it is a realistic and useful habit, within the reality generated by the counter-institution. Explanations for the counter-institution are developed for use in encounters with social control, particularly when exercised by parents rather than police. Speaking these legitimations not only defends the counter-institution but also helps the individual to make the explanations "real" for himself, helping to make them part of his self-concept, and his self-control. He begins to define his behavior as "right" and as what one "should do" when he is in these particular circumstances.

The counter-institution creates its own self-controls, its own sense of morality, which is bolstered by its relational controls. When a drug user who turns informer on his friends and has them arrested suddenly dies under mysterious circumstances, for example, by falling forty-two stories to the ground, many other users will feel that justice and morality have been served.

For less extreme violations of the counter-institution's expected forms of behavior, such as talking too openly about it, other relational controls will be applied, such as exclusion from the group. The important thing about these relational controls is that they are supported by self-controls—the members subjectively feel that the violators were more or less properly dealt with. Not every drug user would agree to killing informers, but many would not be terribly disturbed. Most drug users would probably agree to keeping uncool people away from critical information, information that if revealed could lead to disaster.

The social control within the counter-institution may be increased when strong formal social control is applied against it. The more danger formal control provides, the greater the legitimation for fighting against it. A prostitute who gets arrested looks at it almost as a business expense; she knows whether she will get a fine or thirty days or three months. If she is caught and not morally degraded by the officers, she usually will go along quietly. Her friends would be upset if she killed the officer because it might bring a crackdown on them. But when a third conviction for selling marijuana might result in a longer prison term than a conviction for murder some people will choose murder and others in similar positions will understand. The group enacting the counter-institution has come to define and control behavior in much the same way that those following legitimate institutions define and control behavior. The ultimate sanction may be called "murder" rather than "execution" but its social origins are similar.

The fact that formal social control is used "legitimately" against a counter-institution may be the *only* distinction it has from some legitimate institution. It is an important distinction with many consequences for the followers of the counter-institution. The use of alcohol, which is now legitimate, was once a counter-institution. While it was a counter-institution it created gangs, murder, fortunes, and many negative attitudes toward formal social control, some of which still persist. It no longer produces these results because it has become legitimate. When recreational drug use becomes legitimate we might expect it to have a similar career.

Many legitimate institutions, if not most, were counter-institutions at one time; some individuals and other legitimate institutions may still so define them. Thus even widely accepted and widely legitimated institutions may occasionally have to defend themselves from attack—antiliquor local option elections, antitrust suits, and the mother who doesn't want her adult daughter to move into an apartment. Even if an institution is not currently under attack many of its legitimations were developed when it was and may be useful if it is attacked again. They keep, sometimes. The counter-institution is *currently* developing and using its legitimations. It is doing this because it is under attack by formal social control.

It is easy to see how formal social control helps to make a counter-institution fight back. But this is not what formal social control is supposed to do, according to sociological equilibrium theories. Formal social control is supposed to counteract deviance and return the "social system" to a steady state. What is it doing making the system less stable? The answer is that "equilibrium" theories only apply to counter-institutions like prostitution, which are disorganized. The system can "manage" disorganized deviant behavior, but equilibrium theory fails when one system attacks another. The study of processes of stability and change at an abstract level is called cybernetics, and it provides a useful way of describing why social control sometimes results in social change. In the following adaptation Dr. Paul Wender illustrates several instances of "Deviation Amplifying Feedback" (DAF) in different systems. When a counter-institution is already producing and maintaining its own reality, formal social control usually creates a deviation amplifying feedback system with the counter-institution. The followers of the counter-institution band together to say, "social control is unjust, it must be changed." The attempt at control creates or augments communications, legitimations, self- and relational controls, motivations and enthusiasm all directed at changing the social reality that made the attempt at control possible. This reaction is quite parallel to what takes place in a nation, or a tribe, in wartime. Internal divisions are forgotten, patriotism rises, and the group "closes ranks" to face the enemy.

☐ ☐ ☐

24
VICIOUS AND VIRTUOUS CIRCLES
The Role of Deviation Amplifying Feedback in the Origin and Perpetuation of Behavior
PAUL H. WENDER

It is the purpose of this paper to call attention to a mechanism which has been used by behavioral scientists in a variety of fields—as well as by the man in the street—to explain the origin and continuance of much human behavior. This explanatory mechanism is usually introduced ad hoc so that its generality and applicability are not recognized. It is most commonly identified in its pathological form, the *vicious circle,* although the similar mechanism, with beneficent effects, has been noted and called the *virtuous circle.* Both vicious and virtuous circles are examples of what is called, in cybernetic terms, positive feedback, or what Maruyama has called "deviation amplifying feedback" (DAF).*

In the past, many of those concerned with the relevance of cybernetics to behavior have focused on the mechanism of negative feedback, in which feedback serves as a stabilizing principle. Common examples of negative feedback are the linking of a furnace and a thermostat to maintain constant temperature, or the various homeostatic mechanisms in the mammalian body—for example, those maintaining the constancy of glucose level in the blood.

The mechanism of deviation amplifying feedback (DAF) has been less clearly explicated despite the fact that this mechanism is operative in many biological and social systems. An understanding of it permits a better understanding of the genesis and perpetuation of behavior and suggests methods for the alteration of such behavior. Simply stated, DAF is a mechanism which explains how small variations in a system can (or must) become associated with large effects—how small perturbations can generate chains of events that can result in gross alterations. It is a process in which the output of the system is fed back (either directly or indirectly) into that system in a manner such that output continues to increase or decrease. This last statement may seem

Adapted from Paul H. Wender, M.D., "Vicious and Virtuous Circles: The Role of Deviation Amplifying Feedback in the Origin and Perpetuation of Behavior," *Psychiatry,* Vol. 31, No. 4, November 1968, pp. 309–324. Copyrght © 1968 by The William Alanson White Psychiatric Foundation, Inc. Reprinted by special permission of the author and The William Alanson White Psychiatric Foundation.

* Magoroh Maruyama, "The Second Cybernetics: Deviation-amplifying Mutual Causative Processes," *Amer. Scient.* (1963) 51:164–179. Common parlance recognizes DAF as "snowballing," the military as "escalation."

quite abstract and general, but a few concrete examples should show that this is not the case.

Consider (as Maruyama does) the fate of a boulder in a temperate climate. The process of DAF acts to increase the probability that such a boulder will eventually be replaced by gravel. This is so because if a random perturbation—a crack—appears, the process of DAF will act to increase the probability that further cracks will develop. Let a minor nick be introduced. With the succession of seasons rain will fall, freeze, and expand and further enlarge the crack into a fissure. With successive cycles the fissure grows and new ones are formed. It becomes increasingly probable then that organic material or plant seeds will find their way into the interstices, grow, further enlarge the cracks, cause new ones to form, and so forth. The first small nick does not shatter the rock, but given the specific properties of the environment (rain, freezing temperatures, the fact that water expands when it freezes, the presence of plant life), the occurrence of a minor deviation results in a major effect. Given a different environment, say a dry cave, the initial crack would not produce this sequence of events. It is important to note that without a knowledge of the specific properties of the system one would not know that his mechanism would operate in it.

Another simple physical example of the operation of DAF would be an amplification system in which a fraction of the output is fed back and added to the initial stimulus. This effect often occurs in public address systems or in hearing aids when they are not being worn. Random electronic noise is generated, amplified, and fed back to the microphone and re-amplified. As a result, a small hum rapidly increases to a howl or a roar. Other natural examples of the operation of DAF are shown in the formation of meanders in rivers and ripples in dunes, and in the development of "moguls" on ski slopes. A striking and important biological example is the evolution of new species of life. Random mutations which are better suited to a given ecological niche than the existing species have an increased probability of survival. Continued selection of such mutations is favored until optimal adaptability is achieved.

. . .

Note that in the examples given above the DAF process proceeds to a certain magnitude and then levels off. This effect is that of "dampening." In the case of the amplification system, dampening occurs because the physical properties of the components are such that they cannot amplify signals above a certain strength; when the input is increased to that level no further amplification occurs. In biological evolution, dampening occurs for a variety of reasons: For example, further amplification may lessen survival value—the Brontosaurus apparently exceeded a size capable of dealing with a fluctuating environment. It should be noted that the causes of dampening are as specific as those of the DAF process itself—that they, too, cannot be predicted without a detailed knowledge of the individual components of the system.

At this point it would be useful to define and list some properties of DAF systems:

(1) An event (A) may be positively linked with a succeeding event (B) so that a change in A is followed by a change in B in the same direction. (If A increases B increases; if A decreases B decreases.) This linkage will be indicated by a "+". Or,

(2) An event (A) may be negatively linked with a succeeding event (B) so that a change in A is followed by a change in B in the opposite direction. (If A increases B decreases; if A decreases B increases.) This linkage, seen in homeostatic systems of negative feedback, will be indicated by a "—".

(3) Consequently, if a system contains no negative links or an even number of negative links the system will manifest DAF. If there are an odd number of negative links the system will show negative feedback and tend to be stable.

(4) A given event may participate in more than one cycle so that several cycles can be linked together.

(5) The overall effects of such linked cycles will depend on their relative strengths. This last assertion is a statement of ignorance. Whereas in the case of a single loop (e.g., the amplifier example) the direction of change could be predicted by Proposition 3, in more complex systems prediction can be made only with a detailed knowledge of the component events.

(6) The DAF process may lead into one in which negative feedback exists so that the deviation which has occurred will then be stabilized. (Consider, for example, the case of the Brontosaurus. Presumably mutant Brontosauri who were larger were selected against and their size, which presumably had increased through DAF, was stabilized.)

To illustrate the use of this notation let us examine an ecological system (quasi-Australian) involving predators (wolves), their prey (rabbits), the rabbits' food source, and a virus disease that attacks rabbits. As Figure 1 indicates, given a system consisting only of wolves, rabbits, and rabbit food, a stable equilibrium can be predicted although the numbers of animals and amounts of forage at equilibrium cannot be predicted a priori. However, when the virus is introduced into the system the outcome can only be predicted probabilistically. This is so because a new equilibrium would be achieved only if mutant rabbits immune to the virus appeared, and this change can only be assessed probabilistically.

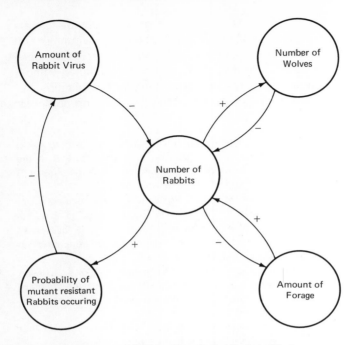

Figure 1 The Operation of DAF in a Hypothetical Ecological System

I shall now turn to the role of DAF in human behavior. It will be seen that as a consequence of DAF:

(1) It is often the case that an arrangement of events that are unstable exists between individuals or within an individual.
(2) When such unstable conditions exist, change will occur. This change will often be large and result in the establishment of a new and stable equilibrium.
(3) Unstable equilibria can often be generated by small shifts from the stable condition.

.   .   .

DAF IN INTERPERSONAL RELATIONS

The mechanism of DAF plays a large role in the formation of an individual's own personality and in his behavior with others. As will be seen, minor fluctuations in an individual's expectations and/or behavior often result in major alterations in his interpersonal environment, and these alterations then produce more substantial shifts in the individual himself.

. . .

Development of the Self-Image

George Herbert Mead employs the mechanism of DAF to explain the origin of a person's self-perception.* He suggests that much of a person's (A's) view of himself results from an incorporation of the generalized other's (B's) view of person A. In many—but not all—instances, B's perception is a product of A's behavior. Since A's behavior in part results from the self-image, the DAF mechanism can operate here (see Figure 2). If B's views of A are not a product of A's behavior, but rather are stereotyped and unchanged by variations in A's behavior, the mechanism does not operate. For example, if A is a child reared by a consistently depreciating mother, A's self-esteem will be low no matter how he behaves, since his behavior cannot alter his mother's view of him. In general, however, the DAF mechanism does operate, so that A's behavior helps to construct his self-image. Furthermore, since A is apt[†] to behave in a manner consonant with his self-image, both the self-

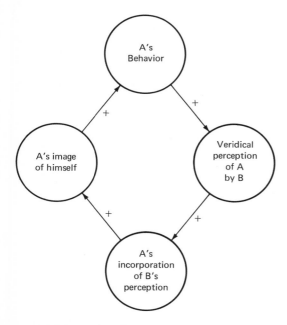

Figure 2 DAF and the Perception of Self

* George Herbert Mead, *Mind, Self and Society;* Univ. of Chicago Press, 1934.

† A is *apt*—but not certain—to behave in a manner consonant with his self-image. In many instances he will act quite differently, as in counterphobic or compensatory behavior.

image and the behavior are likely to polarize. For example, aggressive behavior in A will produce a self-perception by A that he is an aggressive person; this in turn is apt to increase the probability of aggressive behavior by A. [*This is the problem faced by a person with a "bad" habit. It is usually difficult to break out of the cycle of DAF, as Buckley showed.*]

This model has obvious implications for behavior change: if B's perception is both inaccurate and fixed, no change in A's behavior can alter B's perception of A, and the only way (logically) by which A can alter his self-perception is by replacing B with a new "significant other." How difficult this is to accomplish is exemplified by people who, despite great accomplishments, maintain the low self-esteem that once reflected a significant other's perception. If B's perception of A is accurate, the most expeditious way of changing A's view of himself is by changing A's behavior. That is, A's behavior is most expeditiously changed by changing A's behavior! If A can be induced, persuaded, cajoled, or forced to role-play, that role should eventually become real.

The Self-Fulfilling Prophecy

Merton describes the mechanism of the "self-fufilling prophecy," a mechanism by which someone's expectations are apt to bring about their own fulfillment even if they originally may have been based on a faulty judgment of reality. Merton adds a quotation from Thomas, ". . . if men define situations as real, they (i.e., the situations) are real in their consequences."* DAF is frequently the operative mechanism. Merton's example is that of a bank-run in the pre-FDIC era. The anxious belief that a bank could not reimburse its depositors would lead to a rush on the bank, which was *only then* unable to meet its obligations; fear of bank failure thus could lead to its occurrence. The theory of the self-fulfilling prophecy, Merton states, ". . . though it lacks the sweep and precision of a Newtonian theorem . . . possesses the same gift of relevance, being instructively applicable to many, if not most, social processes."

The self-fulfilling prophecy and its DAF chain play a frequent role in interpersonal relations. Let A, for whatever reason, approach B with the expectation that B is a "son of a bitch." [*This is an example of the way in which labeling works, the label in this case being "son of a bitch."*] A will then select from B's behavior those aspects that are consistent with this hypothesis and discount those that are inconsistent with it.

* Robert K. Merton, "The Self-Fulfilling Prophecy," in *Social Theory and Social Structure;* Glencoe, Ill., Free Press, 1957; p. 421.

If B is friendly, he is being deceptive; if B is angry, he is showing his true colors. A will treat B as an S.O.B. and B in general will react in kind. It is necessary to note that A need not be conscious of his expectations or set. In fact he often is not. A's conscious report then that people are "no damn good" need not be a distortion. His report may be an accurate report of people's behavior toward him. What A does not notice is that he is the generator of this behavior. Parenthetically, B's behavior can of course be either matching or complementary to A's behavior. That is, B may respond to A's hostility with either counter-aggression or passivity; B may respond to A's warmth by either approach or avoidance. The operation of DAF is then dependent upon A's character structure. If avoidance increases A's approach, DAF will operate. If A responds to avoidance (rejection) by withdrawal, DAF will not operate. Not all B's will "play into" A's DAF circles, as most of us A's and B's should know. [*This is an example of the reduction of visibility response of prostitutes becoming call girls.*]

□ □ □

Dr. Wender illustrated the operation of deviation amplifying feedback, generally with reference to individual behavior. He noted, however, that it could also take place at a group level, and illustrated this by the self-fulfilling prophecy. Deviation amplifying feedback can often be found in groups. Military escalation, confrontation politics, and ghetto uprisings are good examples. Taking the black ghetto as an example it is easy to see the progression of events that leads to a riot and the communication of a "message" through this "unorganized" action. Many ghetto residents have an experience–white social reality conflict. There is a fair amount of escape through drink, there is a fair amount of violence and crime, usually inflicted on other ghetto residents. The "high crime rate" brings intense police patrol, which often does little to protect the residents. The police often stop innocent people out on the street late at night for informal questioning. This breeds resentment. The police sometimes use violence in their arrests. In some cases the violence is a response to violence, in others it is police initiated. This violence is often witnessed by a crowd of already resentful people. The police come to be defined as an occupying army. Some such incident touches off a riot, and looting takes place. An occupying army of police come to put down the uprising and to seal off the other parts of the city. It has happened in many cities; some people have been impressed with the importance of the reality flaw that lays the groundwork for the DAF escalation of violence. As a whole, however, the institutional order seems to be responding with more troops and more gas and more guns, which has started something of an arms race between ghetto residents and the police. Perhaps a dampening effect will operate sooner or later, but a great many people may be killed first.

It is in organized responses that deviation amplifying feedback produces new patterns of legitimation. Frequently the legitimations that a counter-institution develops are specifically designed to counter the negative definition created by socially constructed reality. Since the symbolic universe is complex, open to interpretation, and the source of legitimacy for the institutional order, a value adapted from those available in the symbolic universe is often selected to legitimate the counter-institution. Such legitimations, which may purport to show why the pattern of behavior is "functional" or "necessary," may not convince many people in the institutional order, but they will probably provide biographical and institutional reasons for the behavior that are adequate for the participants.

A more strategic approach than merely countering the negative definition on its own terms is finding a new legitimation to outflank the negative definition of reality that called for the use of formal social control. The selection of certain legitimations makes continued pressure from the institutional order very difficult. For example, if some value from the symbolic universe can be found that no conventional person would want to deny (say, freedom of speech), and if it can ·be attached to the counter-institution (say, pornography, which has been defined as sinful), the institutional order is placed in the difficult position of having to attack its own values when it attacks the counter-institution. This may create division within the institutional order. The attack may begin to falter. If the counter-institution has some other requisites—a fairly wide following, some power within legitimate institutions, and a face-saving "out" (such as upholding the Constitution) for those who might remove the legal controls—such confounding legitimations may begin to open the possibility of accommodations with the institutional order.

In the following adaptation, which was first published in 1951, a theoretical legitimation for the position of the homosexual in society is developed. This legitimation has been taken up by many homosexuals, and by homosexual groups, and has provided a basis for organizing many actions on the part of homosexuals.

□ □ □

25

THE UNRECOGNIZED MINORITY

DONALD WEBSTER CORY

In recent years the world has become extremely conscious of minority problems. Upon industry, government, and indeed upon society as a whole, there is a constant pressure to recognize the rights of minorities. Usually by biological accident, sometimes by intellectual choice, many people find themselves outside the pale of the mainstream of life, unable to enjoy the benefits of civilization side by side with their fellowmen. Their plight is recognized; one constantly hears that human rights must be granted, regardless of race, religion, color, or political creed. The attitude toward minorities has, in the opinion of many, become a touchstone by which the progressive character of an individual or a nation may be judged. [*In other words, it is a value of the symbolic universe.*] Minority rights, many contend, have become the challenge of this century; they are regarded as the cornerstone upon which democracy must build and flourish, or perish in the decades to come. The lack of recognition of the rights of dissident and non-conforming minorities is the most distinguishing characteristic of totalitarianism. [*In other words, people who suppress minorities are antidemocratic and totalitarian, something no legitimate institution in the United States would want to be.*]

The struggle for advancement by groups that are denied their place in society at large takes place simultaneously on two levels. It is a struggle that is fought by those who, voluntarily or involuntarily, are in the ranks of the few. Almost without exception, they believe that they are deserving of full freedoms, and they strive to achieve them. They have an awareness of their problems that follows them without cease; their escape is only occasional, momentary, and fleeting. They see life as divided into two seemingly hostile and irreconcilable camps; and seldom do they stop to inquire of themselves whether they display toward other minority groups the attitudes they demand be shown toward themselves. On occasion one discovers the rare individual of such stature that his attitude of deep sympathy for all human beings transcends his own identification with a group of people.

At the same time, the minority is not infrequently strengthened by the activities of some individuals from the dominant world who, whatever their motives might be, identify themselves with the aspirations of a group without being a member of the group. Their entire philosophy

Adapted from Donald Webster Cory, *The Homosexual in America* (New York: Chilton Books, 1951). Copyright 1951 by Greenberg: Publisher. Reprinted by permission of the Chilton Book Company, Philadelphia.

may be libertarian, their endorsement of the outcast may be prompted by personal, psychological, humanitarian, intellectual, or other experiences. But what matter the motive; history judges the deed. And history has taught them that the many cannot prosper while the few wither; that the majority cannot achieve a true happiness in a world in which a minority is deeply condemned.

Out of these majority-minority relationships grow literature, protest, search for change. The more articulate describe what it means to live as a member of the minority—the blind alleys and the dead-ends ... the discrimination ... the sneer, the joke, the abusive language ... the humiliation and self-doubt ... the struggle to maintain self-respect and group pride. As these people describe and protest, their voices are complemented by those of the allies found in another world, people who can never fully know the psychological impact of a hostile culture on those whom they are aiding, but who are peculiarly well situated to further a cause without fully understanding it. [*From the point of view of the institutional order people who further causes without fully understanding them might be called "dupes."*]

The minority question has been studied exhaustively in recent years. Attention has been focused on the Jewish people in Germany and elsewhere in the world, the Hindus and Moslems in India and Pakistan, the Catholics in Ulster and the Protestants in Italy, the Negroes in America. Nor are religion, race, and color the sole aspect of minority problems; the rights of Communists in the Western democracies are debated, and rights for non-Communists in the Eastern European states are demanded. The privileges of atheists on the one hand, or Jehovah's Witnesses, on the other, fall within the scope of the study of minority problems.

It is my belief that another phase of the minority problem is demanding the attention of America. We who are homosexual constitute a minority that cannot accept the outlook, customs, and laws of the dominant group. We constitute a minority, and a unique one. [*This defines homosexuality as a minority problem, like others, demanding similar respect and attention within the symbolic values of democracy.*] Some will protest against the classification of the homosexuals as a minority, on the grounds that the term usually encompasses ethnic groups, and that the latter constitute a number of people grouped together by act or accident of birth. Even the religious minorities are not exempt from the fact of being grouped in this manner, inasmuch as religious creeds are generally passed on from parents to children. However, such a concept of the minority, aside from the narrowness of the considerations, is significant only insofar as it emphasizes the involuntary and inescapable nature of group belonging. As I shall show in a section of this book devoted to the genesis of homosexuality, and as is conceded by psychiatrists, the fact of being homosexual, and therefore of belonging to a group, is as involuntary as if it were inborn, despite the fact that it is not inborn; and as I shall demonstrate in my discussion of therapy, the fact of retaining homosexual desires, whether one indulges or suppresses, and whether or not a bisexual adjustment is made, is virtually as ineradicable as if it involved the color of one's skin or the shape of one's eyes. [*Since homosexuality is involuntary for the individual it is unfair to discriminate against him.*]

It goes without saying that there are some fundamental differences between homosexuals and the conventionally recognized minority groups. A minority, according to a rather narrow definition, would be any outnumbered people. But, in its broader connotations, a minority group must consist in the first place of people who have some important trait in common that not only unites them to each other, but differentiates them from the rest of society. Group psychology, writes Sigmund Freud, is "concerned with the individual man as a member of a race, of a nation, of a caste, of a profession, of an institution, or as a component part of a crowd of people who have been organised into a group at some particular time for some definite purpose."* From this definition, it can be seen that not only Christians and Jews, Negroes and whites, constitute groups, but Communists are a group, deaf-mutes are a group, as are physicians and psychoanalysts. But a minority group, from a sociological viewpoint, must have another characteristic, and that is its lower or unequal status in society. The physicians would therefore not be a minority, in such a sense, and it is even possible for the minority group, as has been pointed out, to be a numerical majority, the classic example being the South African Negroes.

By such a definition, the homosexuals are a minority group, consisting of large numbers of people who belong, participate, and are constantly aware of something that binds them to others and separates them from the larger stream of life; yet a group without a spokesman, without a leader, without a publication, without an organization, without a philosophy of life, without an accepted justification for its own existence. [*All of this was true in 1951. Homosexuals now have the communications and legitimations mentioned.*] In fact, there is surely no group of such size, and yet with so few who acknowledge that they belong. And, were it not for social pressure to acknowledge, or for biological ease of identification, would not other minorities likewise lose a large portion of their groups?

·   ·   ·

* Sigmund Freud, *Group Psychology and the Analysis of the Ego* (London: International Psycho-analytical Press, 1922), p. 3.

The prejudice of the dominant group, seen everywhere and displayed in countless forms, is most demoralizing when we homosexuals realize to what extent we have accepted hostile attitudes as representing an approximation of the truth. Here and there, in a book, a sociological document, or a psychological treatise, there will be a justification, but it does not negate the overwhelming weight of antipathy. [*These are social scientific legitimations.*] A person cannot live in an atmosphere of universal rejection, of widespread pretense, of a society that outlaws and banishes his activities and desires, of a social world that jokes and sneers at every turn, without a fundamental influence on his personality.

That influence I find to be complex. First, there is what can be characterized as self-doubt, but this in turn evokes its own response, which comes out of the need for self-acceptance. The reaction against the world which insists that we are inferior beings is the search for a fallacy in that thinking. Some of us may take refuge in the involuntary nature of our predilections. Inferior or equal, whatever the verdict of the world may be, we are homosexuals in spite of ourselves. How, we ask ourselves in amazement, can a world condemn an individual for being what he was made to be? Despite the widespread view to the contrary, we homosexuals are utterly incapable of being other than what we are.

More than that, if we are to believe in ourselves, we must reject the entire theory of the inferiority status which the heterosexual world has imposed upon us. And therein we find a reaction common among people who live in a special minority category: we create a new set of beliefs to demonstrate that our gay world is actually a superior one. [*The counter-institution is not just as good as the legitimate institution —it is better, for such and such a reason.*] For some reason or other that few of us stop to investigate, we come to believe that homosexuals are usually of superior artistic and intellectual abilities. Everywhere we look, we seize upon outstanding examples of brilliant people, either in our own circles or in the public domain, who are gay, or are supposed to be gay. How is it, we ask ourselves, that our friends are always outstanding among their business associates; that members of our group frequently graduate from universities with the highest honors; that at least four of the giants of modern French literature were sexual inverts. The list could be continued, although it includes only those recognized; what of the many who have achieved success and have hidden their secret even from those who share their burden?

Whether or not there is a factual basis for this belief in our own superiority is of secondary importance. Whether illusion or reality, the belief exists, and it stems from a desperation, deeply imbedded in people who find themselves despised by the world, and who require a belief in themselves in order to bolster an ebbing confidence and enable themselves to function in society.

Thus the homosexuals constitute what can be termed the unrecognized minority. We are a group by reason of the fact that we have impulses in common that separate us from the larger mass of people. We are a minority, not only numerically, but also as a result of a caste-like status in society. As I shall demonstrate in these pages, our minority status is similar, in a variety of respects, to that of national, religious, and other ethnic groups: in the denial of civil liberties; in the legal, extra-legal, and quasi-legal discrimination; in the assignment of an inferior social position; in the exclusion from the mainstreams of life and culture; in the development of the protection and security of intra-group association; in the development of a special language and literature and a set of moral tenets within our group. [*These are some of the major dimensions for any counter-institution.*]

On the other hand, one great gap separates the homosexual minority from all others, and that is its lack of recognition, its lack of respectability in the eyes of the public, and even in the most advanced circles. It has become a sign of worthiness to take up the cudgels for almost any minority group, except the homosexuals. One is a "hero" if he espouses the cause of minorities, but is only a suspect if that minority is the homosexual group.

As a minority, we homosexuals are therefore caught in a particularly vicious circle. On the one hand, the shame of belonging and the social punishment of acknowledgment are so great that pretense is almost universal; on the other hand, only a leadership that would acknowledge would be able to break down the barriers of shame and resultant discrimination. Until the world is able to accept us on an equal basis as human beings entitled to the full rights of life, we are unlikely to have any great numbers willing to become martyrs by carrying the burden of the cross. But until we are willing to speak out openly and frankly in defense of our activities, and to identify ourselves with the millions pursuing these activities, we are unlikely to find the attitudes of the world undergoing any significant change.

☐ ☐ ☐

The legitimation of being a "minority group," and one with many worthwhile characteristics, is a far cry from the individual homosexual who feels that he is sick, and takes the medical–psychiatric cop-out. Legitimations at this level of generality begin to answer wide sets of questions—not just how-to-do it and why we do it, but also why the counter-institution is a valuable addition to the institutional order.

Indeed, it is possible to discuss legitimations at this level of abstraction as constituting an ideology.

In Philip Selznick's book *The Organizational Weapon*,[2] several functions were listed for ideology: much of it is designed to bolster the group's own ranks; it strengthens cohesion and discipline and gives members a unique sense of mission. (A theoretical legitimation makes the members feel that they are saving the world.) Further, "Although ideology, to be translated into power, requires organization, effective organization also requires ideology." Thus a dialectical relationship exists between explicit *theoretical* legitimations and the creation and articulation of structured groups or organizations among the followers of a counter-institution. This means that at the point in its reaction to social control that a counter-institution begins to create a spokes-group, an organization that works for the legitimacy of the counter-institution, it will also have a great need for explicit and strategic theoretical legitimations. Likewise, pure theory is not a useful debating weapon without a means for its strategic deployment. Spokes-groups create theoreticians; theoreticians create spokes-groups; together they challenge social reality.

Here again, as in the process of becoming a counter-institution, the physical body may provide a dampening effect both on the creation of ideology and on the spread of the institution, although to less extent than might be supposed. The reason that physical body effects are not more important than they are, at this point, is because our symbolic universe gives us our ideas of what good and bad body effects are; it is possible, though not easy, to reject these ideas. Within the symbolic universe, however, what people presume to be connected with the physical body may limit the actions they take and the ideas they form, not because of its actual effect, but because of their ideas about its effect. Homosexuality limits its legitimations to being a harmless minority because of the common presumption that being homosexual is something distinctive that people either have in their minds and bodies or don't have. Homosexuality is a *role* that many people may enter involuntarily, but that anyone *can* enter with a little effort. Homosexuals *could* create ideas that it is fun to try—"Be gay for a day,"—if they did not accept the idea that it was an innate characteristic. The presumed body destruction of heroin keeps it from producing a legitimating ideology, but alcohol seems almost as destructive and is legitimate. Dr. Joel Fort prepared the following drug chart, which provides a great deal of information about various drugs. Notice the lack of coordination between the potential for abuse (column 10) and the form of legal

---

[2] Philip Selznick, *The Organizational Weapon, A Study of Bolshevik Strategy and Tactics* (New York: Macmillan, 1960.

regulation and control (column 14), or between the usual long-term effects (column 13) and the form of legal regulation and control. We create our realities. Realities are real to us. We are limited by our realities. But we can create new realities.

It is important to note that the "characteristics" of an institution have little relationship to its integration within the institutional order. Drugs can be dangerous, so can alcohol. Homosexuality is nonreproductive, so is heterosexuality using contraceptives. Armed robbery victimizes others, so does price-fixing. Murder is the taking of the life of another, so is execution. But, you protest, murder and execution are "different," as are each of the others, and you can undoubtedly come up with many explanations that you don't even have to think about that tell you why they are "objectively" different. This "objectivity" is what social reality creates. Which institutions are legitimate and inside of the institutional order, and which institutions are illegitimate and outside, are products of historical events and decisions—"objectivity" legitimates history.

Look at the experience of the American Indians when alcohol was introduced into their lives. They had no cultural way of dealing with it, so it was "objectively" bad and dangerous for them. The Indians didn't have the training we get in the use of alcohol: not to drink before five in the afternoon, not to drink more than two before dinner, count your drinks when you are driving, shut your friends' supply off if they get too loaded, help them home if they are too drunk to make it, drinking to your friends' health, drinking as part of communion with God, drinking as part of seduction scripts, how to handle drunks, how to avoid hangovers, what to do about hangovers, and all the various forms of alcohol and things that might be mixed with it. That is a lot of culture, a lot of knowledge.

The Indian picked up a bottle of whiskey and drained it. Their behavior became aggressive, uncontrolled, and unpredictable—because their culture didn't make allowances for and provide knowledge about drunks. An Indian "psychiatrist" who observed this behavior might say that overdoses of alcohol caused "psychosis." Similar problems with "psychotic" drunks arise in cultures where marijuana and hashish are commonplace but drinking is prohibited. Westerners visiting the East are sometimes made to register as "alcohol addicts" before being allowed to buy liquor. We create reality, reality creates us.

The following adaptation is an explicit theoretical legitimation for a counter-institution, the use of marijuana. In a coordinated, factually accurate, and theoretically sophisticated manner, Allen Ginsberg attacks the ontology of the negative definition of marijuana, where it came from, who it benefited, and the purposes it serves for the institutional order. He also offers and illustrates legitimations for alterations

	1 Official name of drug or chemical	2 Slang name(s)	3 Usual single adult dose	4 Duration of action (hours)	5 Method of taking	6 Legitimate medical uses (present and projected)	7 Potential for psychological dependence*	8 Potential tolerance (leading increased dosage)
A	Alcohol Whisky, gin, beer, wine	Booze Hooch	1½ oz. gin or whisky, 12 oz. beer	2–4	Swallowing liquid	Rare, Sometimes used as a sedative (for tension).	High	Yes
B	Caffeine Coffee, tea, Coca-Cola No-Doz, APC	Java	1–2 cups 1 bottle 5 mg.	2–4	Swallowing liquid	Mild stimulant. Treatment of some forms of coma.	Moderate	Yes
C	Nicotine (and coal tar) Cigarettes, cigars	Fag	1–2 cigarettes	1–2	Smoking (inhalation)	None (used as an insecticide).	High	Yes

D	Sedatives
	Alcohol—see above
	Barbiturates
	  Nembutal
	  Seconal
	  Phenobarbital
	Doriden (Glutethimide)
	Chloral hydrate
	Miltown, Equanil
	  (Meprobamate)
		Yellow jackets
		Red devils
		Phennies
		Goofers
			50–100 mg.
			
			500 mg.
			500 mg.
			400 mg.
				4	Swallowing pills or capsules	Treatment of insomnia and tension. Induction of anesthesia.	High	Yes

E	Stimulants
	Caffeine—see above
	Nicotine—see above
	Amphetamines
	  Benzedrine
	  Methedrine
	  Dexedrine
	
	Cocaine
		Bennies
		Crystal
		Dexies or Xmas trees (span-sules)
		Coke, snow
			2.5–5.0 mg.
			
			Variable
				4	Swallowing pills, capsules or injecting in vein
					
					Sniffing or Injecting
						Treatment of obesity, narcolepsy, fatigue, depression.
						
						Anesthesia of the eye and throat.
							High	Yes

F	Tranquilizers
	Librium (Chlordiazep-oxide)
	Phenothiazines
	  Thorazine
	  Compazine
	  Stelazine
	Reserpine (Rauwolfia)
			5–10 mg.
			
			10–20 mg.
			10 mg.
			2 mg.
			1 mg.
				4–6	Swallowing pills or capsules	Treatment of anxiety, tension, alcoholism, neurosis, psychosis, psychosomatic disorders and vomiting.	Minimal	No

G	Cannabis (marihuana)	Pot, grass, tea, weed, stuff	Variable—1 cigarette or 1 drink or cake (India)	4	Smoking (inhalation) Swallowing	Treatment of depression, tension, loss of appetite, sexual maladjustment, and narcotic addiction	Moderate	No
H	Narcotics (opiates, analgesics) Opium Heroin Morphine Codeine Percodan Demerol Cough syrups (Chera-col, Hycodan, etc.)	Op Horse, H	10–12 "pipes" (Asia) Variable—bag or paper w. 5–10 percent heroin 15 mg. 30 mg. 1 tablet 50–100 mg. 2-4 oz. (for euphoria)	4	Smoking (inhalation) Injecting in muscle or vein Swallowing	Treatment of severe pain, diarrhea, and cough.	High	Yes
I	LSD Psilocybin Mescaline (Peyote)	Acid, sugar Cactus	150 micrograms 25 mg. 350 mg.	12 6 12	Swallowing liquid, capsule, pill (or sugar cube) Chewing plant	Experimental study of mind and brain function. Enhancement of creativity and problem solving. Treatment of alcoholism, mental illness, and the dying person. (Chemical warfare).	Minimal	Yes (rare)
J	Antidepressants Ritalin Dibenzapines (Tofranil, Elavil) MAO inhibitors (Nardil, Parnate)		10 mg. 25 mg., 10 mg. 15 mg., 10 mg.	4–6	Swallowing pills or capsules	Treatment of moderate to severe depression.	Minimal	No
K	Miscellaneous Glue Gasoline Amyl nitrite Antihistaminics Nutmeg Nonprescription "sedatives"		Variable 1–2 ampules 25–50 mg. Variable	2	Inhalation Swallowing	None except for antihistamines used for allergy and amyl nitrite for some episodes of fainting.	Minimal to Moderate	Not known

Copyright by Joel Fort, M.D., San Francisco, 1969.

* The term "habituation" has sometimes been used to refer to psychological dependence; and the term "addiction" to refer to the combination of to ance and an abstinence (withdrawal) syndrome.

† Drug Abuse (Dependency) properly means: (excessive, often compulsive use of a drug to an extent that it damages an individual's health or socia

9	10	11	12	13	14
Yes	High	To relax. To escape from tensions, problems and inhibitions. To get "high" (euphoria), seeking manhood or rebelling (particularly those under 21). Social custom and conformity. Massive advertising and promotion. Ready availability.	CNS depressant. Relaxation (sedation). Sometimes euphoria. Drowsiness. Impaired judgment, reaction time, coordination and emotional control. Frequent aggressive behavior and driving accidents.	Diversion of energy and money from more creative and productive pursuits. Habituation. Possible obesity with chronic excessive use. Irreversible damage to brain and liver, addiction with severe withdrawal illness (D.T.s).	Available and advertised without limitation in many forms with only minimal regulation by age (21, or 18), hours of sale, location, taxation, ban on bootlegging and driving laws. Some "black market" for those under age and those evading taxes. Minimal penalties.
No	None	For a "pick-up" or stimulation. "Taking a Break." Social custom and low cost. Advertising. Ready availability.	CNS stimulant. Increased alertness. Reduction of fatigue.	Sometimes insomnia or restlessness. Habituation.	Available and advertised without limit with no regulation for children or adults.
No	Moderate	For a "pick-up" or stimulation. "Taking a Break." Social custom. Advertising. Ready availability.	CNS stimulant. Relaxation (or distraction) from the process of smoking.	Lung (and other) cancer, heart and blood vessel disease, cough, etc. Habituation. Diversion of energy and money. Air pollution. Fire.	Available and advertised without limit with only minimal regulation by age, taxation, and labeling of packages.
Yes	High	To relax or sleep. To get "high" (euphoria). Widely prescribed by physicians, both for specific and nonspecific complaints. General climate encouraging taking pills for everything.	CNS depressants. Sleep induction. Relaxation (sedation). Sometimes euphoria. Drowsiness. Impaired judgment, reaction time, coordination and emotional control. Relief of anxiety-tension. Muscle relaxation.	Irritability, weight loss, addiction with severe withdrawal illness (like D.T.s). Diversion of energy and money. Habituation, addiction.	Available in large amounts by ordinary medical prescription which can be repeatedly refilled or can be obtained from more than one physician. Widely advertised and "detailed" to M.D.s and pharmacists. Other manufacture, sale or possession prohibited under federal drug abuse and similar state (dangerous) drug laws. Moderate penalties. Widespread illicit traffic.
No	High	For stimulation and relief of fatigue. To get "high" (euphoria). General climate encouraging taking pills for everything.	CNS stimulants. Increased alertness, reduction of fatigue, loss of appetite, insomnia, often euphoria.	Restlessness, irritability, weight loss, toxic psychosis (mainly paranoid). Diversion of energy and money. Habituation. Extreme irritability, toxic psychosis.	Amphetamines, same as Sedatives above. Cocaine, same as Narcotics below.
No	Minimal	Medical (including psychiatric) treatment of anxiety or tension states, alcoholism, psychoses, and other disorders.	Selective CNS depressants. Relaxation, relief of anxiety-tension. Suppression of hallucinations or delusions, improved functioning.	Sometimes drowsiness, dryness of mouth, blurring of vision, skin rash, tremor. Occasionally jaundice, agranulocytosis.	Same as Sedatives above, except not usually included under the special federal or state drug laws. Negligible illicit traffic.
No	Moderate	To get "high" (euphoria). As an escape. To relax. To socialize. To conform to various sub-cultures which sanction its use. For rebellion. Attraction of behavior labeled as deviant. Availability.	Relaxation, euphoria, increased appetite, some alteration of time perception, possible impairment of judgment and coordination. (Probable CNS depressant.)	Usually none. Possible diversion of energy and money.	Unavailable (although permissible) for ordinary medical prescription. Possession, sale, and cultivation prohibited by state and federal narcotic or marihuana laws. Severe penalties. Widespread illicit traffic.
Yes	High	To get "high" (euphoria). As an escape. To avoid withdrawal symptoms. As a substitute for aggressive and sexual drives which cause anxiety. To conform to various sub-cultures which sanction use. For rebellion.	CNS depressants. Sedation, euphoria, relief of pain, impaired intellectual functioning and coordination.	Constipation, loss of appetite and weight, temporary impotency or sterility. Habituation, addiction with unpleasant and painful withdrawal illness.	Available (except heroin) by special (narcotics) medical prescriptions. Some available by ordinary prescription or over-the-counter. Other manufacture, sale, or possession prohibited under state and federal narcotics laws. Severe penalties. Extensive illicit traffic.
No	Moderate	Curiosity created by recent widespread publicity. Seeking for meaning and consciousness-expansion. Rebellion. Attraction of behavior recently labeled as deviant. Availability.	Production of visual imagery, increased sensory awareness, anxiety, nausea, impaired coordination; sometimes consciousness-expansion.	Usually none. Sometimes precipitates or intensifies an already existing psychosis; more commonly can produce a panic reaction when person is improperly prepared.	Available only to a few medical researchers (or to members of the Native American Church). Other manufacture, sale or possession prohibited by state dangerous drug or federal drug abuse laws. Moderate penalties. Extensive illicit traffic.
No	Minimal	Medical (including psychiatric) treatment of depression.	Relief of depression (elevation of mood), stimulation.	Basically the same as Tranquilizers above.	Same as Tranquilizers above.
No	Moderate	Curiosity. To get "high" (euphoria). Thrill seeking. Ready availability.	When used for mind-alteration generally produces a "high" (euphoria) with impaired coordination and judgment.	Variable—some of the substances can seriously damage the liver or kidney.	Generally easily available. Some require prescriptions. In several states glue banned for those under 21.

onal adjustment; or is otherwise specifically harmful to society.

ays to be considered in evaluating the effects of these drugs is the amount consumed, purity, frequency, time interval since ingestion, food in the
ch, combinations with other drugs, and most importantly, the personality or character of the individual taking it and the setting or context in which
aken. The determinations made in this chart are based upon the evidence with the human use of these drugs rather than upon isolated artificial experi-
l situations or animal research.

* scattered, inadequate health, educational or rehabilitation programs (usually prison hospitals) exist for narcotic addicts and alcoholics (usually out-
t clinics) with nothing for the others except sometimes prison.

in perceptual reality, and he suggests positive values of these altered perceptions. Strip-searched at U.S. Customs for traces of marijuana, nearly "set up" for a "bust" by narcotics agents, formal social control has inspired another counter-institutional theoretician through deviation amplifying feedback.

□ □ □

26
THE GREAT MARIJUANA HOAX
First Manifesto to End the Bringdown
ALLEN GINSBERG

How much there is to be revealed about marijuana in this decade in America for the general public! The actual experience of the smoked herb has been clouded by a fog of dirty language perpetrated by a crowd of fakers who have not had the experience and yet insist on downgrading it. [*Truth is to be discovered through experience, not through statements and conjecture.*] The paradoxical key to this bizarre impasse of awareness is precisely that the marijuana consciousness is one that, ever so gently, shifts the center of attention *from* habitual shallow, purely verbal guidelines and repetitive secondhand ideological interpretations of experience to *more direct, slower, absorbing, occasionally microscopically minute engagement with sensing phenomena.* [*In other words, the routinization of habits and thoughts disappears. Thinking things through results in a clearer understanding of what one is doing, and often leads to realizations closed off by imitative habits.*]

A few people don't *like* the experience and report back to the language world that it's a drag. [*Experience must be separated from its description in language. Linguistic descriptions impose meaning on experience.*] But the vast majority all over the world who have smoked the several breaths necessary to feel the effect, adjust to the strangely familiar sensation of Time slowdown, and explore this new space thru natural curiosity, report that it's a useful area of mind-consciousness to be familiar with. Marijuana is a metaphysical herb less habituating than tobacco, whose smoke is no more disruptive than Insight.

This essay, conceived by a mature middle-aged gentleman, the holder at present of a Guggenheim Fellowship for creative writing, a traveler on many continents with experience of customs and modes of different cultures, is dedicated to those who have *not* smoked marijuana, who don't know exactly what it is but have been influenced by sloppy, or secondhand, or unscientific, or (as in the case of drug-control bureaucracies) definitely self-interested language used to describe the marijuana high pejoratively. I offer the pleasant suggestion that a negative approach to the whole issue (as presently obtains in what are aptly called square circles in the USA) is not necessarily the

Adapted from Allen Ginsberg, "The Great Marijuana Hoax: First Manifesto to End the Bringdown," *Atlantic Monthly,* November 1966, pp. 104–112. An original (more extended) version of the essay, dated appropriately, was written for and published in *The Marijuana Papers,* Bobbs-Merrill, 1966. Reprinted with permission of the author and publishers. Footnote numbers refer to Ginsberg's "A Little Anthology of Marijuana Footnotes," which begins on page 309.

best, and that it is time to shift to a more positive attitude toward this specific experience.[1] If one is not inclined to have the experience oneself, this is a free country and no one is obliged to have an experience merely because friends, family, or business acquaintances have had it and report themselves pleased. On the other hand, an equal respect and courtesy are required for the sensibilities of one's familiars for whom the experience has not been closed off by the door of Choice.

The black cloud of negative propaganda on marijuana emanates from one particular source: the US Treas. Dept. Narcotics Bureau.[2] [*The legitimate institution most involved in suppression is self-interested.*] If the tendency (a return to common sense) to leave the opiate problem with qualified M.D.'s prevails, the main function of this large Bureau will shift to the persecution of marijuana. Otherwise, the Bureau will have no function except as a minor tax office, for which it was originally purposed, under aegis of Secty. of Treasury. Following Parkinson's Law that a bureaucracy will attempt to find work for itself, or following a simpler line of thought, that the agents of this Bureau have a business interest in perpetuating the idea of a marijuana "menace" lest they lose their employment, it is not unreasonable to suppose that a great deal of the violence, hysteria & energy of the anti-marijuana language propaganda emanating from this source has as its motive a rather obnoxious self-interest, all the more objectionable for its tone of moralistic evangelism. This hypocrisy is recognizable to anybody who has firsthand experience of the so-called narcotic; which, as the reader may have noticed, I have termed an herb, which it is—a leaf or blossom —in order to switch from negative terminology and inaccurate language. [*A change of reality requires a change of language, from "narcotic" to "herb," which does not have the negative connotations.*]

A marvelous project for a sociologist, and one which I am sure will be in preparation before my generation grows old, will be a close examination of the actual history and tactics of the Narcotics Bureau and its former chief Power, Harry J. Anslinger, in planting the seed of the marijuana "menace" in the public mind and carefully nurturing its growth over the last few decades until the unsuspecting public was forced to accept an outright lie.[3] [*See Dickson's Article in Chapter VII.*]

I must begin by explaining something that I have already said in public for many years: that I occasionally use marijuana in preference to alcohol, and have for several decades. I say occasionally and mean it quite literally; I have spent about as many hours high as I have spent in movie theaters—sometimes three hours a week, sometimes twelve or twenty or more, as at a film festival—with about the same degree of alteration of my normal awareness.

I therefore do know the subjective possibilities of marijuana and therein take evidence of my own senses between my own awareness of the mysterious ghastly universe of joy, pain, discovery, birth & death, the emptiness & awesomeness of its forms and consciousness described in the Prajnaparamita Sutra central to a Buddhist or even Christian or Hindu view of Kosmos which I sometimes experience while high, as for the last two paragraphs, and the cheap abstract inexperienced version of exactly the same thing one may have read in the newspapers, written by reporters (who smoke pot themselves occasionally nowadays) taking the main part of their poorly written squibs of misinformation from the texts & mouths of Chiefs of Narcotics Bureaus, Municipal or Federal—or an occasional doctor notorious in the profession for his ungracious stupidity & insulting manners. [*The experience conflicts with the description of it legitimated by socially constructed reality. This is one part of the reality flaw.*]

What was this criminal vision of marijuana presented by the Narcotics Department for years in cheap sex magazines and government reports? Who invented the myths of base paranoia close to murder, frothing at the mouth of Egyptian dogs, sex orgies in cheap dives, debilitation and terror and physiological or mysterious psychic addiction? An essentially grotesque Image, a thought-hallucination magnified myriad thru mass media, a by-product of Fear—something quite fiendish—"Dope Fiend," the old language, a language abandoned in the early sixties when enough of the general public had sufficient personal experience to reject such palpable poppycock[4] & the bureaucratic line shifted to defense of its own existence with the following reason: necessary to control marijuana because smoking leads to search for thrill kicks; this leads to next step, the monster Heroin. And a terrible fate.

In historical context this recent excuse for repression of marijuana seems to the author so irrational that it is impossible to disprove. Yet public confusion may warrant some precise analysis: A) There are no legitimate sociological/medical study documents warranting the Narcotics Department's assertion of causal relation between use of marijuana and graduation to opiates. B) There never had been any hint of such association before the two classes of drugs were forcibly juxtaposed in black market by said department; Anslinger testified to that in 1937. C) A greater percent of opiate users started with bananas, cigarettes & alcohol than started with marijuana—no causal relationship is indicated in any case. D) The number of millions of respectable Americans who smoke marijuana have obviously not proceeded on to opiates. E) In test sociological cases, i.e., societies such as Morocco and India where marijuana use is universal, there is very small use of opiates, and no social association or juxtaposition between the two classes of drugs. What juxtaposition there is in America has been created and encouraged by the propaganda and police repression tactics of the Narcotics Bureau. (*Pharmacological Basis of Therapeutics* 1965, and

1965 California Atty. General's Report both characterize the claimed causal relationship as "unproved.") [*In other words, examining the Bureau's statements, using the methodology legitimated by the scientific symbolic universe, leads to the conclusion that, scientifically speaking, the Bureau is wrong.*]

In sound good health I smoked legal ganja (as marijuana is termed in India, where it is traditionally used in preference to alcohol), bought from government tax shops in Calcutta, in a circle of devotees, yogis, and hymn-singing pious Shaivite worshipers in the burning ground at Nimtallah Ghat in Calcutta, where it was the custom of these respected gentlemen to meet on Tues. and Saturday nights, smoke before an improvised altar of blossoms, sacramental milk-candy & perhaps a fire taken from the burning wooden bed on which lay a newly dead body, of some friend perhaps, likely a stranger if a corpse is a stranger, pass out the candy as God's gift to friend and stranger, and sing holy songs all night, with great strength and emotion, addressed to different images of the Divine Spirit. Ganja was there considered a beginning of sadhana (Yogic path or discipline) by some; others consider the Ascetic Yogi Shiva Himself to have smoked marijuana; on His birthday marijuana is mixed as a paste with almond milk by the grandmothers of pious families and imbibed as a sacrament by this polytheistic nation, considered by some a holy society. The professors of English at Benares University brought me a bottle for the traditional night of Shivaratri, birthday of the Creator & Destroyer who is the patron god of this oldest continuously inhabited city on Earth. "BOM BOM MA-HADEV!" (Boom Boom Great God!) is the Mantra Yogis' cry as they raise the ganja pipe to their brows before inhaling.

All India is familiar with ganja, and so is all Africa, and so is all the Arab world; and so were Paris and London in smaller measure in high-minded but respectable nineteenth-century circles; and so on a larger scale is America even now. Young and old, millions perhaps, smoke marijuana and see no harm. And we have not measured the Latin-American world, Mexico particularly, which gave the local herb its familiar name. In some respects we may then see its prohibition as an arbitrary cultural taboo. [*In other cultures it is a normal part of life; why is reality different here?*]

There has been a tendency toward its suppression in the Arab world with the too hasty adoption of Western rationality & the enlarged activity of the American fanatic Mr. Anslinger, retired from the Narcotics Bureau but now US representative to the UN World Health Organization Narcotic Drugs Commission, a position from which he circulates hysterical notices and warnings manufactured in Washington's Treas. Dept. to the police forces of the cities of the world—so I was told by a police official in Tel Aviv, an old school chum who laughed about the latest release, a grim warning against the dangers of Khat, a traditional energizing leaf chewed by Bedouins of Arabia & businessmen & princes in Ethiopia, as well as a few traditional Yemenite Jews.

Professor Alfred R. Lindesmith in *The Addict and the Law* (Indiana University Press) has already objected in public print to the Department's manipulation and attempted quashing of various medical-juridic reports; the impartial LaGuardia Report of 1944 was rudely attacked by Anslinger; a President's Judicial Advisory Council Policy Statement (1964) has characterized the activities of the Bureau as exceeding legal rightfulness in "criminalizing" by executive fiat & administrative dictum those addicted to addicting drugs who for decades have been prevented from going to a doctor for treatment unless it was under the aegis of Lexington Jail, and thru police channels. Memory of the British East India Hemp Commission report, the largest in history, done in the 1890s, which concluded that marijuana was *not* a problem, has been ignored,[5] memories of our own Panama Canal military reports giving marijuana a clean bill of health have been unavailing in considerations of the Bureau,[6] thousands of intelligent citizens have been put in prison for uncounted years for possession or sale of marijuana, even if they grew it themselves and only smoked in private; youths have been entrapped into selling small or large quantities of the grass to police agents and consequently found themselves faced with all the venomous bullshit that an arbitrary law can create, from the terrors of arrest to the horror of years in jail; the author receives letters of complaint and appeals for help, from many US cities, from acquaintances, fellow litterateurs, even scholarly investigators of the subject writing books about it, as well as from one energetic poet founding a fine project for an Artist's Workshop (John Sinclair in Detroit, sentenced to six months for letting an agent buy marijuana for the second time.) [*Sinclair is in prison again, this time for ten years, for possessing two joints.*] Ken Kesey, the novelist, is now in exile; 21,931 arrests for marijuana from 1963 to 1965 reported from California alone, according to Prof. Alfred R. Lindesmith. The whole scene is so shrouded in bureaucratic mystery that there are no national figures available anywhere.

One becomes awed by the enormity of the imposition. It is not a healthy activity for the State to be annoying so many of its citizens thusly; it creates a climate of topsy-turvy law and begets disrespect for the law and the society that tolerates execution of such barbarous law,[7] and a climate of fear and hatred for the administrators of the law. [*Large-scale reality flaws require an immense social expenditure and produce many strains.*] Such a law is a threat to the existence of the State itself, for it sickens and debilitates its most adventurous and sensitive citizens. Such a law, in fact, can drive people mad.

It is no wonder then that most people who have smoked marijuana in America often experience a state of anxiety, of threat, of paranoia, in fact, which may lead to trembling or hysteria, at the microscopic awareness that they are breaking a Law, that thousands of Investigators are trained and paid to smoke them out and jail them, that thousands of their community are in jail, that inevitably a few friends are "busted" with all the hypocrisy and expense and anxiety of that trial & perhaps punishment—jail and victimage by the bureaucracy that made, propagandized, administers, and profits from such a monstrous law.

From my own experience and the experience of others I have concluded that most of the horrific effects and disorders described as characteristic of marijuana "intoxication" by the US Federal Treasury Department's Bureau of Narcotics are, quite the reverse, precisely traceable back to the effects on consciousness not of the narcotic but of the law and the threatening activities of the US Federal Treasury Department Bureau of Narcotics itself. [*That is, the bad effects claimed for the practice do not inhere in the practice but are a consequence of the social construction of reality.*] Thus, as the Buddha said to a lady who offered him a curse, the gift is returned to the giver when it is not accepted.

I myself experience this form of paranoia when I smoke marijuana, and for that reason smoke it in America more rarely than I did in countries where it is legal. I noticed a profound difference of effect. The anxiety was directly traceable to fear of being apprehended and treated as a deviant criminal & put thru the hassle of social disapproval, ignominious Kafkian tremblings in vast court buildings coming to be judged, the helplessness of being overwhelmed by force or threat of deadly force and put in brick & iron cell.

This apprehension deepened when on returning this year from Europe, I was stopped, stripped, and searched at customs. The dust of my pockets was examined with magnifying glass for traces of weed. I had publicly spoken in defense of marijuana and attacked the conduct of the Bureau, and now my name was down on a letter/dossier at which I secretly peeked, on the Customs search-room desk. I quote the first sentence, referring to myself and Orlovsky: "These persons are reported to be smuggling (or importing) narcotics. . . ."

On a later occasion, when I was advised by several friends and near acquaintances that Federal Narcotics personnel in NYC had asked them to "set me up" for an arrest, I became incensed enough to write a letter of complaint to my congressman. He replied that he thought I was being humorless about the reason for my being on a list for Customs investigation, since it was natural (I had talked about the dread subject so much in public); anyway, not Kafkian as I characterized it. As for my complaint about being set up—that, with my letter, was forwarded to the Treasury Dept. in Washington for consideration and reply. Thus, the reply received December 22, 1965: "I would advise you that I have been in touch with the Bureau of Narcotics and am of the opinion that nothing has been done in your case that is illegal or inconsistent with law enforcement practices designed to enforce the narcotics laws." In this case it was police request to arrested friends that they carry marijuana to *my* apartment and to that of the novelist William S. Burroughs. [*The mutual defense pact of the institutional order allows illegal actions in the name of "social control" on occasion.*]

Rather than radically alter the preceding composition written in 1965 —let it remain for the reader who has not smoked marijuana a manifestation of marijuana-high thought structure in a mode which intersects our mutual consciousness, namely language—I wish to add here a few thoughts.

I have spent half a year in Morocco, smoking kif often: old gentlemen & peaceable youths sit amiably, in cafés or under shade trees in outdoor gardens, drinking mint tea, passing the tiny kif pipe, and looking quietly at the sea. This is the true picture of the use of kif in North Africa, exactly the opposite of the lurid stereotype of mad-dog human beings deliberately spread by our Treasury Department police branch. And I set this model of tranquil sensibility beside the tableau of aggravated New York executives sipping whiskey before a 1965 TV set's imagery of drunken American violence covering the world from the highways to Berkeley all the way to the dirt roads of Vietnam.

No one has yet remarked that the suppression of Negro rights, culture, and sensibility in America has been complicated by the marijuana laws. African sects have used pot for divine worship (much as I have described its sacred use in India). And to the extent that jazz has been an adaptation of an African religious form to American context, marijuana has been closely associated with the development of this indigenous American form of chant & prayer. Use of marijuana has always been widespread among the Negro population in this country, and suppression of its use, with constant friction and bludgeoning of the Law, has been a major unconscious, or unmentionable, method of assault on negro Person.

Although most scientific authors who present their reputable evidence for the harmlessness of marijuana make no claim for its surprising *usefulness,* I do make that claim: [*These are legitimations that describe the benefits of the institution.*]

Marijuana is a useful catalyst for specific optical and aural aesthetic perceptions. I apprehended the structure of certain pieces of jazz & classical music in a new manner under the influence of marijuana, and these apprehensions have remained valid in years of normal consciousness. I first discovered how to see Klee's Magic Squares as the painter intended them (as optically three-dimensional space structures) while high on marijuana. I perceived ("dug") for the first time Cézanne's "petit sensation" of space achieved on a two-dimensional canvas (by means of advancing & receding colors, organization of triangles, cubes, etc. as the painter describes in his letters) while looking at *The Bathers* high on marijuana. And I saw anew many of nature's panoramas & landscapes that I'd stared at blindly without even noticing before; thru the use of marijuana, awe & detail were made conscious. These perceptions are permanent—any deep aesthetic experience leaves a trace, & an idea of what to look for that can be checked back later. I developed a taste for Crivelli's symmetry; and saw Rembrandt's *Polish Rider* as a sublime Youth on a Deathly horse for the first time—saw myself in the rider's face, one might say—while walking around the Frick Museum high on pot. These are not "hallucinations"; these are deepened perceptions that one might have catalyzed not by pot but by some *other* natural event (as natural as pot) that changes the mind, such as an intense Love, a death in the family, a sudden clear dusk after rain, or the sight of the neon spectral reality of Times Square one sometimes has after leaving a strange movie. So it's all *natural.*

At this point it should be revealed for those unaware that most of the major (best and most famous, too) poets, painters, musicians, cineasts, sculptors, actors, singers & publishers in America and England have been smoking marijuana for years and years. I have gotten high with the majority of the dozens of contributors to the Don Allen *Anthology of New American Poetry 1945–1960;* and in years subsequent to its publication have sat down to coffee and a marijuana cigarette with not a few of the more academic poets of the rival Hall-Pack-Simpson anthology. No art opening in Paris, London, New York, or Wichita at which one may not sniff the incense fumes of marijuana issuing from the ladies' room. Up and down Madison Avenue it is charming old inside knowledge; and in the clacketing vast city rooms of newspapers on both coasts, copyboys and reporters smoke somewhat less marijuana than they take tranquilizers or Benzedrine, but pot begins to rival liquor as a non-medicinal delight in conversation. Already eight years ago I smoked marijuana with a couple of Narcotics Department plainclothesmen who were trustworthy enough to invite to a literary reception. [*Many important people in legitimate institutions follow the counter-institution, including some agents who are paid to suppress it.*] A full-page paid advertisement in the New York *Times,* quoting authoritative medical evidence of the harmlessness of marijuana, and signed by a thousand of its most famous smokers, would once and for all break the cultural ice and end once and for all the tyranny of the Treasury Department Narcotics Bureau. For it would only manifest in public what everybody sane in the centers of communication in America knows anyway, an enormous open secret—that it is time to end Prohibition again. And with it put an end to the gangsterism, police mania, hypocrisy, anxiety, and national stupidity generated by administrative abuse of the Marijuana Tax Act of 1937.

It should be understood, I believe, that *in this area* we have been undergoing police-state conditions in America, with characteristic mass brainwashing of the public, persecution & jail, elaborate systems of plainclothes police and police spies and stool pigeons, abuse of constitutional guarantees of privacy of home and person from improper search and seizure. The police prohibition of marijuana (accompanied with the even more obnoxious persecution of sick heroin addicts who all along should have been seeing the doctor) has directly created vast black markets, crime syndicates, crime waves in the cities, and a breakdown of law and order in the State itself. For the courts of large cities are clogged with so-called narcotic crimes and behind schedule, and new laws (such as the recent NY Rockefeller Stop & Frisk & No-Knock) spring up against the citizen to cope with the massive unpopularity of prohibition.

Not only do I propose end of prohibition of marijuana but I propose a total dismantling of the whole cancerous bureaucracy that has perpetrated this historic screw-up on the United States. And not only is it necessary that the Bureau of Narcotics be dismantled & consigned to the wax museum of history, where it belongs, but it is also about time that a full-scale congressional investigation with all the resources of the embattled medical, legal & sociological authorities, who for years have been complaining in vain, should be undertaken to fix the precise responsibility for this vast swindle on the administrative & mass-media shoulders where it belongs. What was the motive & method in perpetrating this insane hoax on public consciousness? Have any laws of malfeasance in public office been violated? [*Not only call off the troops but dismantle the agency that created the reality flaw in the first place. These are logical consequences of alterations in social reality.*]

Not only an investigation of how it all happened but some positive remuneration is required for those poor citizens who have been defenseless against beatings, arrest, and anxiety for years—a minority directly & physically persecuted by the police of cities and states and by agents of the nation; a minority often railroaded to jail by uncomprehending judges for months, for years, for decades; a minority battling idiotic laws, and even then without adequate legal representation for the slim trickery available to the rich to evade such laws. For the inoffensive charming smokers of marijuana who have undergone disgraceful jailings, money is due as compensation. This goes back decades for thousands of people, who, I claim, are among the most sensitive citizens of the nation; and their social place and special honor of character should be rewarded by a society which urgently needs this kind of sensibility where it can be seen in public.

I have long felt that there were political implications to the suppression of marijuana, beyond the obvious revelation (which Burroughs pointed out in *Naked Lunch*) of the cancerous nature of the marijuana-suppression bureaucracy. When the citizens of this country see that such an old-time, taken-for-granted, flag-waving, reactionary truism of police, press, and law as the "reefer menace" is in fact a creepy hoax, a scarecrow, what will they begin to think of the whole of taken-for-granted public REALITY?

What of other issues filled with the same threatening hysteria? The specter of Communism? Respect for the police and courts? Respect for the Treasury Department? If marijuana is a hoax, what is Money? What is the War in Vietnam? What are the Mass Media? [*The entire structure of social reality is called into question by a deliberately created reality flaw that now affects a large portion of the population.*]

As I declared at the beginning of this essay, marijuana consciousness shifts attention from stereotyped verbal symbols to "more direct, slower, absorbing, occasionally microscopically minute engagement with sensing phenomena" during the high. Already millions of people have gotten high and looked at the images of their Presidents and governors and representatives on television and seen that all were betraying signs of false character. Or heard the impersonal robot tones of radio newscasters announcing mass deaths in Asia.

It is no wonder that for years the great centers of puritanism of consciousness, blackout & persecution of the subtle vibrations of personal consciousness catalyzed by marijuana have been precisely Moscow and Washington, the centers of the human power war. Fanatical rigid mentality pursuing abstract ideological obsessions make decisions in the right-wing mind of America, pursuing a hateful war against a mirror-image of the same "sectarian, dogmatic" ideological mentality in the Communist camp. It is part of the same pattern that both centers of power have the most rigid laws against marijuana. And that marijuana and versions of the African ritual music (folk-rock) are slowly catalyzing anti-ideological consciousness of the new generations on both sides of the Iron Time curtain.

I believe that future generations will have to rely on new faculties of awareness, rather than on new versions of old idea-systems, to cope with the increasing godlike complexity of our planetary civilization, with its overpopulation, its threat of atomic annihilation, its centralized network of abstract word-image communication, its power to leave the earth. A new consciousness, or new awareness, will evolve to meet a changed ecological environment. [*After demonstrating that the use of marijuana could be legitimated within the scientific symbolic universe, he also suggests its legitimacy for the new generation and its environment.*] It has already begun evolving in younger generations from Prague to Calcutta; part of the process is a re-examination of certain heretofore discarded "primitive" devices of communication with Self and Selves. Negro worship rituals have invaded the West via New Orleans and Liverpool, in altered but still recognizably functional form. The odd perceptions of Zen, Tibetan Yoga, Mantra Yoga, & indigenous American peyotism and shamanism affect the consciousness of a universal generation, children who can recognize each other by hairstyle, tone of voice, attitude to nature, and attitude to Civilization. The airwaves are filled with songs of hitherto unheard-of frankness and beauty.

These then are some of the political or social implications of the public legitimization of marijuana as a catalyst to self-awareness.

A LITTLE ANTHOLOGY OF MARIJUANA FOOTNOTES

FOOTNOTE 1:

The English Journal of Medicine, *The Lancet,* Editorial, November 9, 1963. "At most of the recent conferences the question was raised whether the marijuana problem might be abolished by removing the substance from the list of dangerous drugs where it was placed in 1951, and giving it the same social status as alcohol by legalizing its import and consumption.

"This suggestion is worth considering. Besides the undoubted attraction of reducing, for once, the number of crimes that a member of our society can commit, and of allowing the wider spread of something that can give pleasure, a greater revenue would certainly come to the State from taxation than from fines. Additional gains might be the reduction of interracial tension, as well as that between generations; for 'pot' spread from South America to Britain via the United States and the West Indies. Here it has been taken up by the younger members of a society in which alcohol is the inheritance of the more elderly."

FOOTNOTE 2:

Anslinger, Harry J., and Oursler, W. C.: *The Murderers* (New York: Farrar, Strauss & Cudahy, 1961), p. 38.

"As the Marijuana situation grew worse, I knew action had to be taken to get proper control legislation passed. By 1937, under my direction, the Bureau launched two important steps: First, a legislative plan to seek from congress a new law that would place Marijuana and its distribution directly under federal control. Second, on radio and at major forums, such as that presented annually by the New York Herald Tribune, I told the story of this evil weed of the fields and river beds and roadsides. I wrote articles for magazines; our agents gave hundreds of lectures to parents, educators, social and civic leaders. In network broadcasts I reported on the growing list of crimes, including murder and rape. I described the nature of Marijuana and its close kinship to hashish. I continued to hammer at the facts.

"I believe we did a thorough job, for the public was alerted, and the laws to protect them were passed, both nationally and at the state level."

FOOTNOTE 3:

"Traffic in Opium and Other Dangerous Drugs," Report by the Government of the United States of America for the Year Ended December 31st, 1938, by Hon. H. J. Anslinger, Commissioner of Narcotics, p. 7.

"The Narcotics Section recognizes the great danger of marihuana due to its definite impairment of the mentality and the fact that its continuous use leads direct to the insane asylum."

FOOTNOTE 4:

The Pharmacological Basis of Therapeutics, Goodman and Gillman, 1956 ed., pp. 170–177: "There are no lasting ill effects from the acute use of marihuana, and fatalities have not been known to occur. . . . Careful and complete medical and neuropsychiatric examinations of habitues reveal no pathological conditions or disorders of cerebral functions attributable to the drug. . . . Although habituation occurs, psychic dependence is not as prominent or compelling as in the case of morphine, alcohol, or perhaps even tobacco habituation."

FOOTNOTE 5:

Report of the British East India Hemp Commission, 1893–94, Ch. XIII, pp. 263–264 (Summary of Conclusions regarding effects).

"The Commission has now examined all the evidence before them regarding the effects attributed to hemp drugs. . . . In regard to the physical effects, the Commission have come to the conclusion that the moderate use of hemp drugs is practically attended by no evil results at all. There may be exceptional cases in which, owing to idiosyncracies of constitution, the drugs in even moderate use may be injurious. There is probably nothing the use of which may not possibly be injurious in cases of exceptional intolerance. . . .

"In respect to the alleged mental effects of the drugs, the Commission have come to the conclusion that the moderate use of hemp drugs produces no injurious effects on the mind. . . .

"In regard to the moral effects of the drugs, the Commission are of the opinion that their moderate use produces no moral injury whatever . . . for all practical purposes it may be laid down that there is little or no connection between the use of hemp drugs and crime.

"Viewing the subject generally, it may be added that the moderate use of these drugs is the rule, and that the excessive use is comparatively exceptional."

FOOTNOTE 6:

Panama Canal Zone Governor's Committee, April–December, 1925 (*The Military Surgeon,* Journal of the Association of Military Surgeons of the United States, November, 1933, p. 274).

"After an investigation extending from April 1 to December 1925, the Committee reached the following conclusions: There is no evidence that marihuana as grown here is a 'habit-forming' drug in the sense in which the term is applied to alcohol, opium, cocaine, etc., or that it has any appreciably deleterious influence on the individual using it."

FOOTNOTE 7:

Proceedings, White House Conference on Narcotic and Drug Abuse, September, 1962, State Department Auditorium, Washington, D.C., p. 266: "It is the opinion of the Panel that the hazards of Marijuana per se have been exaggerated and that long criminal sentences imposed on an occasional user or possessor of the drug are in poor social perspective. Although Marijuana has long held the reputation of inciting individuals to commit sexual offenses and other antisocial acts, the evidence is inadequate to substantiate this. Tolerance and physical dependence do not develop and withdrawal does not produce an abstinence syndrome."

James H. Fox, Ph.D., Director, Bureau of Drug Abuse Control, Food and Drug Administration: Statement August 24, 1966, before National Student Association Subcommittee on Drugs and the Campus. NSA Convention, Urbana, Illinois; Quoted Champaign *News—Gazette* August 25, 1966.

"My studies have led me to essentially the same conclusion as Mr. Ginsberg's. I think we can now say that marijuana does not lead to degeneration, does not affect the brain cells, is not habit-forming, and does not lead to heroin addiction. I would say that there may very well be some modification in government attitudes towards marijuana."

The Marihuana Problem in the City of New York, by the Mayor's Committee on Marihuana: The Sociological Study, Intro. by Dudley D. Schoenfeld, M.D. Reprinted in *The Marihuana Papers.* Bobbs-Merrill, New York, 1966.

"Conclusions"

7. The practice of smoking marihuana does not lead to addiction in the medical sense of the word.
9. The use of marihuana does not lead to morphine or heroin or cocaine addiction, and no effort is made to create a market for these narcotics by stimulating the practice of marihuana smoking.
10. Marihuana is not the determining factor in the commission of major crimes.
13. The publicity concerning the catastrophic effects of marihuana smoking in New York City is unfounded."

Ibid.: Intellectual Functioning, Florence Halpern, MA

"Conclusions"

6. Indulgence in marihuana does not appear to result in mental deterioration."

Ibid.: Addiction and Tolerance

"The evidence available then—the absence of any compelling urge to use the drug, the absence of any distressing abstinence symptoms, the statements that no increase in dosage is required to repeat the desired effect in users—justifies the conclusion that neither true addiction nor tolerance is found in marihuana users. The continuation and the frequency of usage of marihuana, as in the case of many other habit-forming substances, depend on the easily controlled desires for its pleasurable effects."

Ibid. Summary by George B. Wallace, M.D., Chairman

"From the study as a whole, it is concluded that marihuana is not a drug of addiction, comparable to morphine, and that if tolerance is acquired, this is of very limited degree. Furthermore those who have been smoking marihuana for a period of years showed no mental or physical deterioration which may be attributed to the drug.

No evidence was found of an acquired tolerance for the drug.

The sensations desired are pleasurable ones—a feeling of contentment, inner satisfaction, free play of imagination. Once this stage is reached, the experienced user realizes that with further smoking the pleasurable sensations will be changed to unpleasant ones, and so takes care to avoid this."

☐ ☐ ☐

The use of recreational drugs provides a good example of the various goings on that take place when a counter-institution is about to achieve a place in the institutional order. As more and more people smoke marijuana, and legitimate it to themselves and others, tolerance for the habit grows as well as the clamor of opposition. The institutional order does not change quickly, but it does change to reflect the practices of the people within it. When socialites, lawyers, judges, newspaper editors, television commentators, politicians, folk heroes, and possibly a quarter of the generation born after the Second World War all smoke marijuana there is a lot of culture created, a lot of links with other institutions, and a lot of pressure to legitimate it and drop the penalties against it. Strong law enforcement and fearsome penalties work to contain counter-institutions so long as they are unorganized and powerless, but laws against things that increasing numbers of people find enjoyable become unenforceable and create strong counter-pressures. It is simply impossible to lock up half of the population, or even ten percent of the population for very long. There are not enough guards to go around. The frightening vista of change appears before conventional people and they chant magic formulas to exorcise this growing evil—prohibitive laws didn't stop the counter-institution so they pass more prohibitive laws, formal social control approached its enforcement capacity so the capacity is increased. Deviation amplifying feedback will increase the intensity of the conflict, especially between generations, until a "cease-fire" is the only response left. The danger of any individual being caught declines as the counter-institution grows. The magic ritual of legal exorcism soothes and comforts its actors, but it is a response to the unmanageable, the last effort before compromise. When the tide comes in sand castles are washed away.

How do we determine when a counter-institution is approaching legit-imacy? Almost every counter-institution creates the belief among its followers that it will soon be legitimate, that society is going to change in its direction, and that the members are the avant-garde of the new order. These beliefs are part of the support of the members' biographi-cal legitimations, the beliefs that allow them to hold up their heads. We can't take these assertions at face value; they are not really pre-dictions but hopes, and we must find some way of foreseeing change without being taken in by the propaganda of the counter-institution or the institutional order. Two indicators would seem to be useful.

First is the ratio of people who participate in the counter-institution to the people in the institutional order. A bad habit might be 1 out of 10,000. A prostitute might be 1 out of 500. A marijuana smoker may be one out of ten. A homosexual may be one out of six. Numbers alone can be misleading, however. Most boys commit delinquent acts, but this does not mean that delinquency will become legitimate. Numbers are important only if the ideology is convincing, because together they make for social power.

Second is the social location within the institutional order occupied by the people who are spreading or accepting the legitimations of the counter-institution. When legitimate newspapers recommend relaxing the penalties against a counter-institution they breach the mutual de-fense pact. Newspapers are important reality-defining agents and when the counter-institution gains their support reality change may be on the way. When "recognized" authorities with first-class "credentials" (that is, they have made it and are recognized in the institutional order, they can't be suspected of being frivolous or outsiders) call for a reevaluation of policy toward a counter-institution, this indicates that either theoreticians or legitimate institutions, or both, have been won over in debate—the mutual defense pact is further flawed.

Finally, when powerful men with institutional or moral followings, call for a reevaluation of policy, reality is changing. Dropping the laws against marijuana and homosexuality will only be the next step in the reality changes that are already taking place.

□ □ □

When a counter-institution becomes powerful enough to force its legitimacy to be recognized it becomes part of the institutional order, part of a "new" social reality in which future generations will grow up, live, and believe. Over time it will come to be recognized by one segment of society after another as one of the ways in which things are done. The man on the street will come to consider it "natural" that people should follow such an institution. He may even find it hard to believe that it was once outlawed.

Many of the conventional institutions around us were counter-institutions in the recent past. As they gradually became legitimate, as they gradually moved into the institutional order, the conflict around them decreased. They gradually worked their way out from legal controls, gradually overcame the hostilities directed at them, gradually began to appear in a different light in history books, and finally came to be considered natural, necessary, and worthwhile, perhaps even indispensable by most conventional people.

CREATION
OF A NEW
SOCIAL REALITY

To illustrate the creation of a new social reality it is only necessary to examine briefly the history of an institution that moved from being a "criminal conspiracy" to being one of the key institutions in the institutional order: the trade union. In Britain before 1825, in the popular mind, the price of labor was determined by the laws of supply and demand, as with any other commodity. Interference with the free workings of the market, it was believed, reduced efficiency and consequently the wealth of the nation. Following this belief it was argued that no obstacles should be placed between an employer and an employee when they were making a wage bargain. Trade unions, consequently, were believed to cause dangerous economic friction by hindering the self-adjusting processes of the market, and were considered to be illegally acting in "restraint of trade." So trade unions were made illegal by the Combination Laws, which prohibited freedom of association for employees who had united to defend their common interests. Not only was a combination of employees a breach of the Combination Laws but it was also considered a criminal conspiracy in that the unionists "conspired" to breach a statute. The reality flaw which the unionists experienced was that they were treated as economic equals to their employers in the philosophy of the marketplace, but experientially the employer was far, far more powerful than the individual working man. Their combination in order to fight on a more equal footing was outlawed; trade unions were a counter-institution. Public opinion gradually changed, and in 1825 legislation was passed which allowed collective bargaining to raise wages or shorten hours, but denied the right to strike. A union involved in any dispute over arbitrary dismissal or the limitation of overtime was still considered to be acting in restraint of trade, and was liable to criminal action.

This British law applied in Canada until the passage of the Canadian Trade Unions Act in 1872 which allowed the right to strike to a registered trade union. Even under this statute a properly registered union might find itself open to criminal action for conspiring to molest the employer or for interfering with his right to carry on business. It was not until 1939 that a law was passed in Canada that prohibited discrimination by an employer on account of union activity. Until this law was passed an employer could refuse to employ, or could dismiss a worker, simply because he was a member of a trade union. The passage of this 1939 law brought the recognition that as a matter of public policy, trade unions were legitimate and employers could not use overt acts of intimidation, threats, or conspiracy to keep their employees from belonging to one. Although the legislative history in the United States is somewhat different, the same transition from counter-institution to legitimate institution took place. Trade unions have now given up much of their radical past, much of their concern for social justice, and have become a part of the institutional order whose major activity is getting "more" for their members. Labor colleges have been founded, labor leaders are consulted before important pieces of legislation are offered, and being a member of a union is a respectable activity.

In the process of becoming legitimate trade unions first won de facto (in fact) recognition of their right to collective bargaining, long before they won de jure (by right) recognition. A similar pattern appears to be common to many institutions as they become legitimate. The behavior pattern grows, more and more people follow it, its *internal* legitimations are convincing, and the institutional order adjusts somewhat to it. "In fact" the institution operates as if it were legitimate, although it is still defined as illegitimate by law or by the values of the symbolic universe. The gaining of legitimacy "by right" requires that the institution produce plausible *external* legitimations that, combined with its social power and the generation of public and institutional support, become sufficient to force a redefinition of the institution legally and symbolically.

A counter-institution that has a fair amount of de facto legitimacy, which is relatively immune to prosecution, though unlikely to become completely legitimate, is the Cosa Nostra; it grew out of the old Sicilian Mafias. Its strength lies in its power to enforce secrecy, and in its strong internal bonds; its weakness is its inability to produce plausible external legitimations for its activities. The Cosa Nostra extends throughout the United States and Canada. If various reports are to be believed, it obtains its revenues through gambling, prostitution, loan-sharking, financial manipulations such as false bankruptcies, and when times are tight enough to make the risk worthwhile, through the importation of heroin. The myth of the Cosa Nostra makes it seem almost a second government—in fact it is probably more like a feudal principality operating within a modern bureaucratic state. The Cosa Nostra is the underside of the institutional order—whatever is made illegitimate and therefore profitable is the Cosa Nostra's bread and butter. Theoretically the Cosa Nostra would be fairly easy to eliminate, or at least to force out of illegitimate activities. All it would require is for legitimate agencies to supply the services the Cosa Nostra now supplies: cheap heroin, high risk loans, legal prostitutes, legal bookmaking. As a practical matter, however, it seems that people would rather deal with the Cosa Nostra than disconfirm their values by making their dealings legal. Thus the Cosa Nostra serves the curious purpose of allowing abstract morality to survive by supplying what it forbids. In Kentucky it is often rumored that bootleggers discreetly contribute money to fundamentalist ministers who wish to prohibit the legal sale of liquor in their towns by local option elections. The payoff is that Kentucky towns are known to "vote dry, and drink wet," which provides a nice profit for the bootlegger. Abstract morality made into rules whose systematic violation by the public provides an open field for criminals to exploit at little risk is the basic support for both the Cosa Nostra and the small town bootlegger.

As an all-purpose criminal organization the Cosa Nostra almost automatically excludes itself from de jure legitimacy, because it will take up almost anything that is illegitimate and profitable. But it is a large and powerful organization backed with a myth that makes people take it seriously, and it has a large measure of de facto legitimacy, causing other institutions to comply with it. For example, a large stock market swindle went on for a long period because the Wall Street brokers thought that the businessman had Mafia backing, and they were willing to advance money against Mafia resources. The joke was that he didn't have Mafia backing and they all lost. From Wall Street to the people who lease the Cosa Nostra their computers, from the Swiss banks that take hot money to the companies that lease the racing wires, from dishonest union officials to building inspectors who take payoffs, the institutions of the institutional order cooperate with the Cosa Nostra without regard to its legitimacy. They treat it as if it were in fact legitimate, and in so doing *bestow* de facto legitimacy upon it. The fact that the Federal Bureau of Investigation has made only trivial efforts to control the Cosa Nostra might even indicate that they had reached some accommodation with it. A Justice Department Task force designed to work *around* the F.B.I. has produced a number of indictments, so the Cosa Nostra's de facto legitimacy is not entirely unchallenged.

In the following adaptation Robert T. Anderson traces the development of the Cosa Nostra into a complex bureaucracy. Note well that though it has organization buttressed by its internal legitimacy, wide scope and a great deal of power, it has lost the one element of external legitimation that it had when it was a pseudogovernment in Sicily—protection of its territory against other strong men.

☐ ☐ ☐

27

FROM MAFIA TO COSA NOSTRA

ROBERT T. ANDERSON

Sicily has known centuries of inept and corrupt governments that have always seemed unconcerned about the enormous gap between the very rich minority and the incredibly poor majority. Whether from disinterest or from simple incapacity, governments have failed to maintain public order. Under these circumstances, local strong men beyond reach of the government, or in collusion with it, have repeatedly grouped together to seek out their own interests. They have formed, in effect, little extra-legal principalities. A code of conduct, the code of *omertà,* justified and supported these unofficial regimes by linking compliance with a fabric of tradition that may be characterized as chivalrous. By this code, an "honorable" Sicilian maintained unbreakable silence concerning all illegal activities. [*The code of omertà was a value in the symbolic universe.*] To correct abuse, he might resort to feud and vendetta. But never would he avail himself of a governmental agency. Sanctioned both by hoary tradition and the threat of brutal reprisal, this code in support of strong men was obeyed by the whole populace. The private domains thus established are old. After the 1860's they became known as "Mafias." [*Mafias have long historical roots; they have been an institution long enough to be legitimated by tradition.*]

As an institution, the Mafia was originally at home in peasant communities as well as in pre-industrial towns and cities. (Sicilian peasants are notable for urban rather than village residence.) The Mafia built upon traditional forms of social interaction common to all Sicilians. Its functions were appropriate to face-to-face communities. Mafias persist and adapt in contemporary Sicily, which, to some extent, is industrializing and urbanizing. Mafias also took root in the United States, where industrialization and urbanization have created a new kind of society, and here, too, they have persisted and adapted. But can a pre-industrial peasant institution survive unchanged in an urban, industrial milieu? May we not anticipate major modifications of structure and function under such circumstances? The available evidence on secret organizations, though regrettably incomplete, inconsistent and inaccurate, suggests an affirmative answer. The Mafia has bureaucratized.

.　　.　　.

Adapted from Robert T. Anderson, "From Mafia to Cosa Nostra," *American Journal of Sociology,* Vol. 71, No. 3, November 1965, 302–310. Reprinted by permission of the author and the University of Chicago Press, publisher.

Because models of rational-legal organization are almost universally known, and because modern states provide the possibility of regulating organizations by law, bureaucratization rarely occurs now by simple evolution. The Mafia is one of the few exceptions. Because it is secret and illegal, it cannot reorganize by reconstituting itself as a rational-legal organization. [*It would have to be a legitimate institution to be "rational-legal."*] Yet it has changed as it has grown in size and shifted to an urban environment. Analysis of this change assumes unusual importance, because the Mafia is a significant force in modern life and because, as a rare contemporary example of the reorganization of a traditional type of association without recourse to legal sanctions, it provides a basis for comparison with potential other examples. [*"Legal" sanctions belong to the institutional order.*] Much of the present controversy about the Mafia, particularly about whether such an organization exists in the United States, is the result of confusing a modern, bureaucratic organization with the traditional institution from which it evolved.

THE TRADITIONAL MAFIA

A Mafia is not necessarily predatory. It provides law and order where the official government fails or is malfeasant. It collects assessments within its territory much as a legal government supports itself. [*One of the main legitimations of any government is defense of its institutions against outsiders. When the Mafia took this role it had this legitimacy.*] While citizens everywhere often complain about taxation, these Mafia exactions have been defended as reasonable payment for peace. The underlying principle of Mafia rule is that it protects the community from all other strong men in return for regularized tribute.

To illustrate, the Grisafi band of the Agrigento countryside, led by a young, very large man called "Little Mark" (Marcuzzo Grisafi) formed a stable, though illicit, government that oversaw every event in his area for a dozen years (1904–1916). An excellent marksman, he was able by his strength and with the aid of four to eight gunmen to guarantee freedom from roving bandit and village sneak alike.

On a larger scale, between approximately 1895 and 1924, a group of eleven villages in the Madonie Mountains were also ruled by a Mafia. The head and his assistants had a private police force of as many as 130 armed men. A heavy tax resembling official annual taxes was imposed upon all landowners. As with the Grisafi band, this Mafia was not a roving body of terrorists. Their leaders, at least, were well-established citizens, landowners, and farmers. [*That is, they were leaders of legitimate institutions, and their Mafia had the legitimacy of government because it provided government services, at least in part.*] While they might mount up as a body to enforce their tax collections, they stayed for the most part in their homes or on their farms. They assumed supervision of all aspects of local life, including agricultural and economic activities, family relations, and public administration. As elsewhere, the will of the Mafia was the law. The head, in fact, was known locally as the "prefect" (*"U Prefetto"*).

Although not necessarily predatory, Mafias seem always to be so, despotisms possessed of absolute local power. Many in the band or collaborating with it may find it a welcome and necessary institution in an otherwise lawless land. But multitudes suffer gross injustice at its hands. [*True, historically, for most forms of government.*] No one dares offend the Mafia chief's sense of what is right. The lines between tax and extortion, between peace enforcement and murder, blur under absolutism. Many would claim that the Agrigento and Madonie *mafiosi* were mostly involved in blackmail, robbery, and murder. An over-all inventory of Mafia activities leaves no doubt that it is a criminal institution, serving the interests of its membership at the expense of the larger population.

In organizational terms, the Mafia is a social group that combines the advantages of family solidarity with the membership flexibility of a voluntary association.

The most enduring and significant social bond in Sicily is that of the family. Its cohesiveness is reinforced by a strong tendency to village endogamy. Only along the coast, where communication was easier, was it common to marry outside of the locality. The tendency to family endogamy further included some cross-cousin marriage. Family bonds are not necessarily closely affectionate ones, but the tie has been the strongest social relationship known. It is the basic organizational group both economically and socially, functioning as a unit of production as well as of consumption. [*Thus the institutions of family are important for the institutions of labor and territory in this institutional order.*]

Family ties often bind members of the Mafia together. The Mafia of the Madonie included two sets of brothers, as did the core membership of the Grisafi group. Not only are members of the Mafia frequently concealed and aided by their families, but their relatives commonly speculate on their activities and profit from them so that a clear line cannot be drawn between the criminal band on the one hand and the circle of kinsmen on the other. [*The overlap of these institutions strengthens the counter-institution.*]

Family ties have a certain utility for organizing social action. Brothers are accustomed to work together. They possess a complex network of mutual rights and obligations to cement their partnership. The father-son and uncle-nephew relationships, equally enduring and diffuse, possess in addition a well-established leader-follower relationship. Cousins and nephews may be part of the intimate family, and it has been suggested that the children of brothers are especially close as indicated by their designations as *fratelli-cugini* (brother-cousins) or *fratelli-carnale* (brothers of the flesh). [*These kinship ties make mutual trust a matter of family loyalty as well as collusion.*]

The family has one major drawback as a functioning group: its membership is relatively inflexible. Typically, family members vary in interests, capabilities, and temperaments. While this may be of little consequence for running a farm, it can constitute a serious handicap for the successful operation of a gang. Some offspring may be completely devoid of criminal capacity, while good potential *mafiosi* may belong to other families. To a certain degree this drawback is countered by the extension of ties through marriage. But often a desirable working alliance cannot be arranged through a suitable wedding.

Throughout Europe a technique is available for the artificial extension of kinship ties. The technique is that of fictive or ritual kinship. Godparenthood, child adoption, and blood brotherhood make it possible to extend kin ties with ease. These fictive bonds are especially notable for the establishment of kinlike dyadic relationships. Larger social groups have not commonly been formed in this way in Europe except as brotherhoods, the latter with variable, sometimes minimal, success. The Mafia constitutes an unusual social unit of this general type in that the fictive bond is that of godparenthood, elsewhere used for allying individuals, but only rarely for forming groups. [*The symbolic incorporation of a fellow conspirator into a family network creates complex rather than singular loyalties. A person is less likely to betray his partners in a crime if by so doing he betrays his entire family.*]

The godparenthood tie has had a variable history in Europe. In the Scandinavian countries it is a momentary thing, with few implications for future interaction. But in the Mediterranean area, and especially in Sicily, it is usually taken very seriously. An indissoluble lifetime bond, it is often claimed to be equal or even superior to the bond of true kinship. While the godparenthood *(comparatico)* union may cross class lines to link the high and the low in a powerful but formal relationship, it is more often a tie of friends, affective in an overt way that contrasts with the lesser open affection of the domestic family. Above all, the relationship is characterized by mutual trust. [*Without mutual trust a counter-institution is unlikely to grow or be able to develop beyond a coordination of instrumental activities. Remember heroin addicts.*]

Sicilians in general, then, live with greatest security and ease in the atmosphere of the family with its fictive extensions. The Mafia is a common-interest group whose members are recruited for their special interests in and talents for the maintenance of a predatory satrapy. As noted above, this tie of shared interest often originates within a kinship parameter. When it does not, a kinlike tie is applied by the practice of becoming co-godparents. Although the Mafia *setta* (cell) may or may not be characterized by other structural features, it always builds upon real and fictive kinship.

The Mafia of nineteenth-century Sicily practiced a formal rite of initiation into the fictive-kin relationship. Joseph Valachi underwent the same rite in 1930 in New York. In addition to the "baptism of blood," the chief at the first opportunity normally arranges to become the baptismal godfather of the tyro's newborn child. Lacking that opportunity, he establishes a comparable tie in one of the numerous other *comparatico* relationships. The members among themselves are equally active, so that the passing years see a member more and more bound to the group by such ties. [*The new member becomes involved in institutionalized relationships within the kinship group that monopolize his life. He cannot have outside ties that would divide his loyalties.*]

Ritual ties seem to function in part as a temporizing device. Although efficacious in themselves, they are usually the basis for the later arrangement of marriages between sons and daughters, and thus ultimately for the establishment of affinal and consanguineous bonds. The resultant group is therefore very fluid. It utilizes to the utmost its potentialities for bringing in originally unrelated individuals. Yet it possesses the organizational advantages of a lasting body of kin.

Mafia family culture supports membership flexibility additionally by providing for the withdrawal of born members. The criminal family passes on Mafia tradition just as the farming family passes on farming traditions. Boys are taught requisite skills and attitudes. Girls are brought up to be inconspicuous, loyal, and above all silent. The problems of in-family recruitment are not greatly different from those of non-criminal groups. Just as a son without agricultural propensities or the chance to inherit land leaves the countryside to take up a trade or profession, the Mafia son lacking criminal interests or talents takes up a different profession. Indeed, sometimes Mafia family pride comes to focus upon a son who has left the fold to distinguish himself as a physician or professor. But while such an individual might not himself take up an illegal occupation, he is trained never to repudiate it for his kindred. In the Amoroso family, who controlled Porta Montalto near Palermo for many years in the nineteenth century, Gaspare Amoroso, a young cousin of the chief, degraded himself by joining the police force *(carabiniere)*. When the youth was discharged and returned to his family home, the Amoroso leaders removed this dishonor by having him killed in cold blood. [*Undivided loyalties mean that any betrayal is total.*]

The headship of a Mafia is well defined. Referred to as *capo* ("head") or *capo-mafia* ("Mafia head"), and addressed honorifically as *don,* the chief is clearly identified as the man in charge. Succession to this post, however, is not a matter of clear-cut procedure. In come cases family considerations may result in the replacement of a *capo* by his son or nephew. Commonly, an heir apparent, who may or may not be related consanguineously, is chosen on an essentially pragmatic basis and succeeds by co-optation. Generally, promotion is by intrigue and strength. It must be won by the most powerful and ruthless candidate with or without the blessing of family designation or co-optation. Only the *capo,* in any case, is formally recognized. The appointment of secondary leaders and ranking within the membership are informal.

· · ·

BUREAUCRATIZATION OF THE MAFIA

Though still seriously underdeveloped, Sicily seems poised for industrialization with its concomitant changes. To the extent that change has already occurred, the Mafia has adapted and expanded its techniques of exploitation. Claire Sterling writes of the intensification of urban activities: "Today there is not only a Mafia of the *feudo* (agriculture) but also Mafias of truck gardens, wholesale fruit and vegetable markets, water supply, meat, fishing fleets, flowers, funerals, beer, *carrozze* (hacks), garages, and construction. Indeed, there is hardly a businessman in western Sicily who doesn't pay for the Mafia's 'protection' in the form of *'u pizzu.'* "

Mafia formal organization seems at a turning point. The Mafia so far has remained essentially a hodgepodge of independent local units confined to the western part of the island, although cells have been established outside of Sicily. Co-operation among localities in Sicily has an old history. The more successful *capi* have at times established hegemony over wider areas. But it appears that large-scale groupings could not endure in an underdeveloped milieu with notoriously poor communication systems. Modernization, however, is breaking down this local isolation. The scale of operations is expanding. The face-to-face, family-like group in which relationships on the whole are diffuse, affective, and particularistic is changing into a bureaucratic organization.

· · ·

One may observe further bureaucratization of the Mafia in the United States. Mafias were first established in America in the latter part of the nineteenth century. During the prohibition era they proliferated and prospered. Throughout this period these groups continued to function essentially like the small traditional Mafia of western Sicily. [*Prohibition created a reality flaw of immense proportions almost overnight. Probably a majority of adults in the United States suddenly found one of their institutions or habits illegal. There were no counter-institutions to take care of this new reality flaw, so preexisting criminal groups, such as the Mafia, filled the vacuum and prospered immensely.*]

Recent decades in the United States have witnessed acceleration of all aspects of modernization. Here, if anywhere, the forces of urbanization impinge upon group life. But while American criminals have always been quick to capitalize upon technological advances, no significant organizational innovation occurred until the repeal of prohibition in 1932, an event that abruptly ended much of the lucrative business of the underworld. [*When money is pouring in there is no need to tamper with organization. When times are hard one must be more efficient.*] Small face-to-face associations gave way over subsequent decades to the formation of regional, national, and international combines, a change in which American *mafiosi* participated.

As always, information is incomplete and conflicting. Bureaucratization, however, seems to have increased significantly beyond that even of bureaucratized Sicilian groups. Specialization, generally undeveloped in Sicily, became prominent. Personnel now regularly specialize as professional gunmen, runners, executives, or adepts in other particular operations. Departmentalization was introduced and now includes an organizational breakdown into subgroups such as narcotics operations; gambling; the rackets; prostitution; and an enforcement department, the infamous Murder, Inc., with its more recent descendants. [*Such diversification and specialization is necessary to counteract formal social control carried out both locally and nationally. This institutional structure has a great deal of stability and it exists in an antagonistic-symbiosis with the institutional order; they conflict, but the Mafia serves needs that the institutional order cannot without undermining its values, and the institutional order produces the reality flaws that allow the Mafia to exist.*]

The hierarchy of authority has developed beyond that of bureaucratized Sicilian Mafias. Bill Davidson* describes a highly elaborated hierarchy of the Chicago Cosa Nostra, which he compares to the authority structure of a large business corporation. He points to the equivalent of a three-man board of directors, a president of the corporation, and four vice-presidents in charge of operations. He also notes a breakdown into three geographical areas, each headed by a district manager. District managers have executive assistants, who in turn have aides. Finally, at the lowest level are the so-called soldiers. National councils

---

* Bill Davidson," How the Mob Controls Chicago," *Saturday Evening Post*, November 9, 1963, pp. 22–25.

of the more important *capi* apparently meet from time to time to set up territories, co-ordinate tangential activities, and adjudicate disputes. They serve to minimize internecine strife rather than to administer co-operative undertakings. The problem of succession has still not been solved. The Valachi hearings revealed an equally complex hierarchy for the state of New York.

A written system of rules has not developed, although custom has changed. Modern *mafiosi* avoid the use of force as much as possible, and thus differ strikingly from old Sicilian practice. [*Having lost the legitimacy of being the effective government of an area, force has become more problematic. It is also more dangerous because the institutional order reacts more strongly to force than to criminal business operations, which are based on exchange and fill needs.*] The old *"mustachios"* are being replaced by dapper gentlemen clothed in conservative business suits. But as a criminal organization, the Mafia cannot risk systematizing its rules in written statutes.

A major element of bureaucratization is the further development of impartiality. Mafiosi now freely collaborate on all levels with non-Sicilians and non-Italians. The Chicago association includes non-Italians from its "board of directors" down. In these relationships, consanguineous and affinal ties are normally absent and co-godparenthood absent or insignificant. Familistic organization, the structural characteristic that made for the combination of organizational flexibility with group stability in the traditional associations of Sicily—and that goes far to explain the success of Mafias there—apparently proved inadaptive in urban America. When it became desirable and necessary to collaborate with individuals of different criminal traditions, it sufficed to rely for group cohesion on the possibility of force and a business-like awareness of the profits to be derived from co-operation. Family and ritual ties still function among Sicilian-American criminals to foster co-operation and mutual support within cliques, but pragmatic considerations rather than familistic Mafia loyalties now largely determine organizational arrangements. [*This looser organization is still adequate for self-defense against the somewhat fragmented formal social control applied against the Cosa Nostra. An army does not need to be as tight-knit as a guerrilla band, because it has defense in depth and organization.*]

CONCLUSION

The Mafia as a traditional type of formal organization has disappeared in America. Modern criminals refer to its successor as *Cosa Nostra*, "Our Thing." The Cosa Nostra is a lineal descendant of the Mafia, but it is a different kind of organization. Its goals are much broader as it exploits modern cities and an industrialized nation. The real and fictive kinship ties of the old Mafia still operate among fellow Sicilians and Italians, but these ties now coexist with bureaucratic ones. The Cosa Nostra operates above all in new and different terms. This new type of organization includes elaboration of the hierarchy of authority; the specialization and departmentalization of activities; new and more pragmatic, but still unwritten, rules; and a more developed impartiality. In America, the traditional Mafia has evolved into a relatively complex organization which perpetuates selected features of the older peasant organization but subordinates them to the requirements of a bureaucracy.

☐ ☐ ☐

The Cosa Nostra illustrates an important theoretical point: *power is not enough.* In terms of men, economic power, organization, and control it is probably the most powerful counter-institution organization in North America. It has a large measure of de facto legitimacy; but in its present form it is not going to attain de jure legitimacy and symbolic integration into the institutional order. As a counter-institution it lives on reality flaws, but because it is exploitative and not organized by the people who suffer from the flaws, the integration of any of its services into the institutional order will simply diminish it rather than make it more legitimate.

Good legitimations without power or organization are also not enough. Think of the immense number of "good ideas" around for better ways to organize government services, for better ways of dealing with divorce, with abortion, with race relations, and our polluted environment. These ideas may be terribly legitimate, almost everyone may agree that they are "good ideas," but nothing happens. The inertia of the regularized transactions within the institutional order is rooted in the everyday lives and assumptions of many people and institutions. Without the development of a counter-institution with organization and a power base to press against the inertia, the "good ideas" die in committee.

It is instructive to watch the way in which university governments respond to "good ideas" in times of calm and in times of crisis. When ideas are simply proposed through normal channels they go from committee to committee, they are tabled, dismissed as impractical or low priority. It may take two years to introduce a new course, by which time the instructor who wanted to teach it has left. The idea may be so discussed, passed around, influenced by all the present institutional transactions, and modified by so many special interests that if it ever does see the light of day its proposer may not recognize the transmogrified gargoyle it has become. When the "good idea" is backed up by a sit-in or some similar demonstration of power, committees meet quickly, funds are found, decisions are made, some reasonable or unreasonable compromise is offered, and what ordinarily takes years is accomplished in days. The greater the inertia the greater the force needed to overcome it. I have oversimplified the processes involved to make my point. There may be many outcomes in addition to or instead of the "good idea" being implemented. Counterforce, repression, polarization, trivialization, mystification, tokenism, and perfidy may also occur in a power conflict. But whether the conflict is overt or not *good legitimations are not enough, either.* To hope to have any success in altering the nature of the institutional order permanently and to have the alteration accepted as permanent there must be a combination of power and legitimacy.

A third element that makes the acceptance of a new institution more likely is largely out of the hands of the people involved: the overall climate of opinion in the institutional order. At some times there is much questioning of the status quo even by those who benefit from it, at other times there is a great deal of complacency. When there is widespread doubt about the ultimate efficacy of current institutions in any sector of society, counter-institutions have more of a chance for gaining a hearing and perhaps legitimacy. In the crisis of doubts about the capitalist system that went along with the great depression, labor unions finally became legitimate de jure, and part of the institutional order. The current and growing crisis in the institution of the nuclear family allows a more favorable hearing for homosexuals, communal families, women's liberation, divorce law reform, abortion law reform, trial marriages, and a host of other counter-institutions. The point is not that these counter-institutions could not get a hearing when the nuclear family was dominant, but the hearing probably wouldn't be as sympathetic. When many people are personally affected by the failures of a dying institution, or a sickly institution, their confidence is undermined and they are willing to listen to alternatives. Their reaction may be to affirm their flagging faith by repressing alternatives. They may blame the problems of the institution on the alternatives that have grown up. Or, for the counter-institutions with sufficient support, power, and legitimations, they may grant more legitimacy. The factors that caused the crisis in the legitimate institution may be quite different from, or only somewhat related to, the reality flaws that caused the counter-institutions to grow; the growth of the counter-institution may have accelerated the disintegration of the legitimate institution; many patterns are possible. The important factor is that a crisis in a legitimate institution weakens its ability to fight against other legitimate and counter-institutions that would replace it, because it is then no longer unquestionably right and beneficial.

Assuming that a counter-institution has some special social power, some popular support (these are necessary conditions for obtaining even a partial de facto legitimacy), let us look at the factors that go into the creation of legitimations intended to gain de jure legitimacy. The creation and transmission of counter-institutional legitimations may be carried on by individuals or by groups or organizations. The legitimations that are created must be acceptable and plausible to three categories of others: theoreticians who pass judgment on the "correctness" of the idea within their organizations of the symbolic universe; powerful men who lead institutions, and/or collections of powerful men who form a power elite; finally, the concerned public.

Each of these three audiences needs to have its own questions answered; successful legitimation will answer all three. Although there are exceptions, the *individual* who is legitimating a counter-institution probably is not too effective in reaching the concerned public; his natural targets are theoreticians and institutional leaders. *Groups or organizations* are probably least successful with theoreticians and most successful with the general public and leaders. Groups alone have the resources required by mass public media public relations efforts, and often groups alone can muster a sufficient display of power to be impressive to important men.

The questions that powerful men ask revolve around the impact that the legitimation of a counter-institution would have on their own institutions, on their positions of power and influence, and on the institutional order. They must be convinced that it is in their interests to vote or act in a certain way, that it is in the social interest for them to do so, and only secondarily are their personal feelings important. As the Anti-Saloon League put it when lobbying for prohibition, it is better to have a drunkard who will vote right, than to have a saint who will vote wrong. Thus it is often not necessary to convert a politician to labor, or homosexuality, or marijuana, but only to convince him that his support for their legitimation will be useful to him and to society. An important factor in converting powerful men is to give *them* plausible legitimations for use in explaining their positions to their own publics or institutions. "Face" is extremely important and a counter-institution that seeks to gain support of these men must find ways to keep them from losing it.

For example, if one wishes to impress legislators that marijuana could be beneficial, it is pointless to argue scientific theories or to speak of the religious experiences that people have on drugs. Far more to the point is the argument that a marijuana producing and marketing industry will provide a cash crop for disadvantaged farmers, employment for many in manufacturing marijuana cigarettes, and income and profit to many retailers. It would provide employment and funds to many people who might remember the government gratefully, especially if the government, through its agriculture department, helped them get started. It might also be useful to point out that the movement toward legalization is essentially world-wide and that the first country that has an entire industry producing a high quality marijuana cigarette will be in a very favorable competitive position with regard to foreign trade and balance of payments, as it becomes legal in other countries. The tax revenues from ordinary business taxes would increase, and additional tax revenues could be collected on marijuana.

It could also be pointed out that available statistics indicate that probably a majority of urban youth are at least favorable toward marijuana whether or not they use it, and for demographic reasons, the low birth rate in the depression thirties and the high birth rate after the Second World War, these urban youth are going to hold the electoral balance of power in many urban areas in the next election.

Other social problems and social institutions with which a politician might be concerned are the diversion of police court and penal resources into an ever increasing and apparently hopeless fight against the spread of marijuana; resources that could be used to better protect persons and property against "serious" crimes such as homicide, forcible rape, robbery, assault, larceny, and auto theft. Many, many social resources are expended on the disasters caused by alcohol, and if marijuana gradually replaced alcohol these funds could be expended elsewhere. For example, drunk arrests are the largest single category of arrests for most metropolitan police departments, alcoholics constitute one of the largest categories of admissions to psychiatric wards, hospital care for the physical damage done by alcohol is often an expense to the public. The revenues lost on the sale of alcohol could be regained by a tax on marijuana, and some of the proceeds could be put aside to deal with any problems which did arise from the use of marijuana. The cost of controlling public events might also be lower. Large crowds of marijuana smokers seem to produce little aggression, while alcohol drinking crowds almost always produce fights.

A politician might also be concerned that the larger the portion of the population engaged in "criminal" activity the less cooperation and respect the police will have, and the more society will be polarized into warring factions. At an age when they are first experiencing society as young adults, a large minority today find themselves outlawed, and this cannot help but to shape their future attitudes toward laws and many social institutions. Deviation amplifying feedback processes initiated by the criminalization of a large portion of the population might develop in a number of ways.

A powerful businessman might be interested in the economic opportunities marijuana provides either directly or indirectly. Many businessmen are already benefiting from psychedelic clothing styles and psychedelic advertisements derived from drug culture. A man who leads an institution needs to hear of these possible benefits because he often hears about the possible problems. In order to be truly convincing these arguments should be backed by careful research and should be presented by other powerful men within the institutional order. For example, if a banker in a farming area writes to his representative about the benefits to his region of the development of a marijuana crop the representative is far more likely to be impressed than if a street person tells him. A government is far more likely to be impressed if a judge or a prison warden says that priorities need to be reallocated than if a professor says so.

Contacting and mobilizing these institutional leaders is a job much more suited to a group than to an individual. An individual may have the ideas, but in order to propagandize them to many differently located institutional leaders some organization is required.

In the following adaptation Donald Webster Cory and John P. LeRoy discuss the formation and tactics of a counter-institutional "spokes-group" that is attempting to present the case for homosexuals to powerful men and the general public. Since it was written homosexuals have become much better organized and are now occasionally using pressure tactics, such as picket lines against stores that discriminate against homosexuals. Test cases have been won in courts, and homosexuality has been partially legalized in several countries for consenting adults in private. Many of the problems and tactics mentioned by Cory and LeRoy are in some degree common to any counter-institutional spokes-group.

□ □ □

28
THE HOMOSEXUAL IN HIS OWN BEHALF
DONALD WEBSTER CORY AND JOHN P. LeROY

In the first publication of one of the present writers, *The Homosexual in America,* the thesis was advanced that the invert is a member of a minority group, differing from ethnic and other minorities essentially in that his status as a minority group is unrecognized. Today, more than a decade later, the lack of recognition is disappearing. As a manifestation of the new recognition, and as a result of it, a feeling of group identification has grown among these people; a feeling that they are not the sinners but the sinned against. Homosexuals have discovered themselves and have launched a struggle for the rights guaranteed to all citizens of a free democratic society. [*That is, the "minority group" legitimation has done its job and legitimacy is just a few years away.*]

Against a background of hostility and oppression, the first beginnings of an idealistic leadership have begun to emerge. Small secret underground groups formed, which have found friends and allies and with trepidation have shed their secrecy. Soon a small public voice became faintly audible, and then the voice began to increase in volume. With diminishing secrecy, several distinct groups and societies have found their way on the American scene, fighting a legal, social, and political battle in order to help win public acceptance for the invert and his way of life. [*In other words, the homophile spokes-group for the homosexual counter-institution began as an underground, waged "guerrilla warfare" with the institutional order, and has now engaged in several battles, some of which it has won.*]

In the United States, abortive attempts in this direction had been made in the 1920's, only to be suppressed by the police and members of other groups. [*Formal and relational social control wiped out the first attempt to start a spokes-group for the homosexual counter-institution.*] Now the Mattachine Society, One, Inc., and the Daughters of Bilitis, have been formed to help accomplish these ends. The Mattachine Society and One, Inc., have members of both sexes, but with most emphasis on the problems of the male homosexual, while the Daughters of Bilitis operates exclusively on behalf of the Lesbian.

.   .   .

Adapted from Donald Webster Cory and John P. LeRoy, "The Homosexual in His Own Behalf," in *The Homosexual and His Society* (New York: Citadel Press, 1963), pp. 240–250. Reprinted with permission.

In the mid-fifties, the new prosperity of the postwar era, despite a few minor recessions, was beginning to take root. With this new prosperity, greater ease of transportation, communication, and vocational mobility had made it possible for people to have more casual experiences with each other. The growth of urbanization provided anonymity to the few who would dare to organize on behalf of deviant groups.

Homosexuality came to be included among these practices, and as knowledge of its prevalence in post-Kinsey America spread, so did increased communication regarding it. In such an atmosphere, it became possible for the voice of the homosexual to make itself heard and to find receptive listeners among the more concerned, enlightened, and sophisticated elements of society.

Perhaps society is only defending itself more insidiously in making itself take on the appearance of a listener when before it had turned its head the other way, or punished anyone who whispered what it considered unpleasant to talk about. But if society can be said to be on the defensive, then it must follow that the forces of the homosexual minority are consolidating for the exploration and exploitation of that defense. In such a struggle, the vital weapon is access to the means of public communication, and in the course of but a decade or so, the homosexuals—organized and unorganized—together with their friends and defenders, have achieved a foothold here where practically none existed before. [*The development of external communications.*] Objective articles have been written in mass circulation magazines; columnists and editorial writers have devoted space to it; plays and movies have appeared in which the homosexual has been depicted more and more as he is, rather than in the role of the stereotyped image, which is now becoming *passé*. A superficial, though somewhat accurate, semi-sensationalized account of gay life has made the best-seller list; a panel of homosexuals themselves have been permitted to talk freely about themselves and their condition in a spontaneous fashion over a small listener-sponsored FM radio station; TV panel discussions now allow the subject to be mentioned and, at times, discussed with some degree of intelligent candor; an hour-long documentary devoted entirely to the subject has been favorably received in several cities. Most important of all, in one state, Illinois, it is no longer a crime for two adults of the same sex to have sexual relations in private by mutual consent. [*This is partial* de jure *legitimacy.*] In the motion picture *The Victim,* the title does not refer to the innocent or the seduced, but to the deviate man. Sympathy pervades discussions of the subject.

All this and much more has occurred since the mid-fifties. At this writing, an exceedingly courageous group of Mattachine members in Washington, D.C., is contacting key officials in all branches of government in order to further remove legal restrictions against those practicing homosexuality. [*Propagandizing the power elite.*] These people are today banned from government employment and other privileges as undesirables and security risks. Two members of Congress have responded favorably to the plea for a hearing.

The main difference in the social climate, however, is reflected in the organized groups, generally known today as the homophile movement.

The purposes of the organizations are several. First, there is the formidable task of gaining official recognition for the plight of the homosexual in the form of less hostility, elimination of criminal status, expunging prejudice, and finding greater acceptance. [*Winning the debate and having the troops withdrawn.*] The second—closely related to the first—involves helping the homosexual to overcome his problems and better adjust to himself and society under the realistic conditions in which he must function, even while the struggle intensifies to alter these conditions. [*Soften the consequences of the reality flaw until it is corrected.*] The third involves helping to initiate and promote intelligent, enlightened, and unprejudiced research, providing subjects for study wherever indicated and suggesting (out of inner experience and subjective participation) possible areas and methods of study. [*Help to create scientifically legitimate data to use to convert theoreticians and others.*]

A fourth by-product of these three objectives is to provide better places for people to meet each other, so they can make contacts and form friendships under conditions which they themselves consider personally and socially acceptable. This latter objective is not officially stated, and the leadership of the organizations are loath to admit its existence, but it is undeniable, and is very far from being reprehensible, in our view. Socializing, in many instances, may become an end in itself; there have been social discussion groups, coffee klatches, picnics, and other forms of entertainment. Some of these functions have been useful in helping to raise funds, but otherwise they do not in themselves contribute significantly toward helping the homophile organizations achieve their other and openly proclaimed objectives. [*The fact that homosexuals meet each other through homophile groups and enact their counter-institution with one another is important in solidifying the new identity and self-concept through interpersonal affirmation and the creation of internal communication institutions.*]

The manner in which these organizations have functioned has been flexible and varied. In order to help mitigate the official disapproval of homosexuality and improve its legal status, they have held public discussion forums and meetings, and like other groups seeking upward mobility, have gone to the cities' best hotels and assembly halls. In

New York such a group has been accepted as an organization that meets in Freedom House. Many fearful persons have discovered, to their surprise, that such meetings are not illegal, provided that decorum is observed. Noted psychologists, psychiatrists, lawyers, judges, social workers, writers, clergymen and legislators have spoken before homosexually sponsored audiences in an atmosphere of free discussion. In many cases, panel discussions, with audience participation, have taken place. [*These were important gains but they have been far surpassed. This now seems dated because homosexuals are on the street picketing stores that discriminate in San Francisco and fighting back against the police in New York.*]

New "little magazines" have arisen in the United States, sponsored by several of the organizations, containing articles, stories, poetry, editorials, comment, and correspondence, of varying and uneven quality. *One* Magazine, perhaps the best known, has been directed primarily toward the homosexual himself. It has been quite militant in its orientation. The significance of the change taking place in American society is emphasized when it is realized that this little journal is distributed on the newsstands of many large cities, has several thousand subscribers, and its right to publish was upheld by the Supreme Court of the United States. A generation ago, who would have dared bring such a case before the court? Where could a lawyer have been obtained? And could the Court have possibly ruled in its favor? [*The institutional order is rapidly losing its image of totality. Mobility and communications have undercut traditional beliefs and practices everywhere in the world.*]

The *Mattachine Review* features many reprints of articles that have appeared elsewhere on subjects of interest to its readers. The *Review* has included some fiction and poetry and a few original non-fiction articles and commentary. *The Ladder,* the organ of the Daughters of Bilitis, is probably the only Lesbian magazine in the world, but in France, Germany, and other European countries, men have for years been issuing small literary journals similar to *One.*

Finally, many of the local organizations, among which the more influential are the Mattachine groups of New York and San Francisco, distribute newsletters and similar publications, often multigraphed or mimeographed, containing newsworthy information, reviews, critiques, and other material. [*Institutionalized internal communications.*]

The combined readership and circulation lists number into the thousands—an indication that the fear of exposure is beginning to diminish in American life. But not only are the homosexuals reading these magazines; numerous professional people and libraries have been receiving them. For the professional, they help provide some insight into the mind of the articulate invert, his values, and his way of life. [*Giving theoreticians knowledge of the counter-institution that they did not have before.*]

Circulation of the newsletters and magazines being quite limited, the great bulk of publicity about the existence of homophile organizations —as they are usually called, somewhat euphemistically—has been, of necessity, by word of mouth. [*The pattern of gay bar contacts common among some homosexuals facilitates word-of-mouth communication.*] From these, news of the organizations and their activities has spread. The existence of such organizations has now been reported in the press, with meetings sometimes being advertised. Books and magazines have also made mention of them—first the scandal sheets, later the more respectable periodicals. Surprise, shock, and amazement have often greeted non-members, homosexuals and heterosexuals alike, at discovering that such organizations can and do function. [*The sense of "surprise, shock, and amazement" is a consequence of the exclusion of homosexuality from social reality.*]

These organizations, several of which are incorporated, are found in many of the large cities of the United States. They try to help the homosexual to come to grips with himself and the hostile society, by means of group discussions, which at their best have at least the cathartic effect of group therapy, provide a free-from-fear atmosphere for discussion and an opportunity for social mingling on what these people consider a respectable basis. Some of the leaders of these groups make themselves available as lay counselors or give referrals to competent professionals, thus seeking to be of aid in helping homosexuals in distress overcome some of their problems. Contacts with lawyers, psychiatrists, and clinics are maintained, while sometimes liaisons with sympathetic employers, agencies and school officials have helped locate a job or college for men who have been in difficulty. But unfortunately, the social reality has its ugly impact when the question is almost invariably asked: "Is he obvious?" [*The "obvious" members of counter-institutions have formal and relational social control used against them.*]

·   ·   ·

Most of the members of the homophile organizations are drawn from middle-class backgrounds, and incorporate middle-class values and ethics into their organizations. Robert's *Rules of Order* are adhered to in business meetings. Propriety—sometimes exaggerated super-propriety—is the rule. In order to win acceptance among middle-class heterosexuals, they must be as much like them as possible. [*Fighting on one front at a time, not fighting the battles of other counter-institutions.*] There are few radicals, beatniks, or other off-beats in evidence. The members act more like middle-class people than they do like homosexuals, though they feel a certain amount of security in the fact that this is *their* group; they are not the rejected and the outsiders. And heterosexuals who attend these meetings sometimes make their form of sexuality known by bringing along a girl friend.

Fear is the major obstacle to group development. [*Socialized self-control as a barrier to affiliation.*] Many feel that their name and address on a mailing list is a sure means of letting any law-enforcement official know about their predilections, with all the imaginary and real consequences. The organizations pledge anonymity, at the same time assuring the prospective member that it is not illegal to belong to such a movement, nor does it identify a person with the group, any more than belonging to an association opposed to capital punishment makes one a murderer. Yet, the fear of receiving homosexual literature through the mail, or the possibility, however remote, of being discovered is considered enough. However, many of these same people do not mind going to gay hangouts, where the chances of being discovered are even greater.

Another obstacle is apathy. Many inverts have found their way of life so familiar that the thought of changing conditions, even for the better, is alien to their personalities. [*The limitation caused by segmental involvement is probably less relevant to homosexuality than to most counter-institutions.*] Their own sheltered world, furtive as it may be, is the world they want, because it is familiar to them and because they fear the thought of having to adjust to something strange. They thrive on public rejection. Others believe that the idea of protest organizations is fine, but not for them, because life is as fulfilling or as rewarding as they expect it to be. They claim to have little need or desire for direct benefit from such amelioration. Finally, there are the guilt-ridden. They actually believe that protest organizations are not worthwhile, that no good is likely to come of them, that homosexuality *should* be condemned. Self-pity, a feeling of helplessness, of being caught involuntarily in a trap, is mingled with their otherwise negative attitude. [*These are people who have not broken free of the social definition of reality in spite of the fact that it contradicts and condemns their own experience.*]

Yet, in spite of all these difficulties, and many more disabling influences both inside and outside the organizations, the homophile movement is growing. The number of dedicated people will, for a variety of reasons, remain small, but the organizations are probably here to stay, and they have gained, in a short time, a surprising amount of acceptance and respectability. But whether or not these organizations function efficiently, they do function, and their objectives are gradually beginning to be realized.

The increased social tolerance of sexual variations is becoming manifest. The period after the Second World War was marked in

America and elsewhere by a vociferous struggle for minority rights. The reaction against persecution in Germany, the struggle of the integrationists in the United States, the rise of colonial peoples the world over—all these brought to the world a new awareness of the position of minority groups. Although the agitation was concerned with racial and religious and ethnic group rights, the dynamics of the message had to affect the homosexual. An awareness of the propriety of his struggle took root in only a few, but the soil had been prepared for the homophile movement.

The general relaxation of the American puritan attitude toward all things sexual, coinciding with this pro-minority orientation of a few of the most advanced social thinkers, proved to be a successful combination in which the homophile movement would not merely gain adherents, but would gain considerable social respectability. The operation of the homophile organizations will serve to increase the public acceptance even more, though it may not always appear to be significant. Yet, their existence is proof of the fact that a group of sexual variants, when conditions are hostile, can and do solidify as an articulate minority to insist upon its rights. [*While it is hard to measure organizational effectiveness, homophile organizations are probably speeding social change.*] In a democracy, where free interchange of opinion is essential, this is inherently a step in the direction of progress and freedom for *all* citizens.

☐ ☐ ☐

A spokes-group can propagandize the general public with the legitimations that will allow powerful men to grant either de facto or de jure legitimacy. By arguing that the laws are unfair and that their counter-institution is in fact not bad but a valuable addition to the institutional order they can prepare the public for a change in their legal or theoretical status.

The third important target for conversion is the theoreticians of the society. A counter-institution can win de facto legitimacy without a plausible theoretical legitimation but theoreticians are very important in the granting of de jure legitimacy. In a very basic sense the theoreticians of a society determine what is *right* for the society. The theoreticians work within the framework of the symbolic universe and they must be convinced within the framework of that universe that an institution has been wrongly conceived of in the past, and that it does fit within the framework of the values that ultimately legitimate their society. Before institutional leaders can make decisions they must take into account public expectations and the theoretical climate. When a leader postpones a decision, saying "we need more research," it may be a delaying tactic to wait for public opinion to catch up, or for theoretical opinion to coalesce.

In our complex society it is probably incorrect to speak of a theoretical legitimation except as a kind of shorthand. We have many theoreticians who will become involved in any issue, sometimes even theoreticians working within different symbolic universes. For example, as marijuana becomes legitimate many different kinds of "scientists" will become involved in rendering it acceptable or fighting its acceptability, many kinds of "philosophers" and "theologians" will also come to be involved, each in their own framework, each with their special questions. Among scientists concerned are psychiatrists, neural specialists, internists, psychologists, sociologists, economists, public health physicians, and child specialists. Each with his own concerns, each grounded in his own scientific theoretical tradition. Each counter-institution becoming legitimate makes a different pattern of theoreticians relevant, and different kinds of legitimations relevant.

There is, of course, a social organization among theoreticians; some are more famous, some have the ear of the President, some are on the payrolls of organizations that will be affected positively or negatively (physicians who work for cigarette firms are dubious about smoking causing lung cancer).

A "complete" theoretical legitimation has to answer all the questions which these theoreticians raise. The psychiatrist will want to be convinced that marijuana does not negatively affect social functioning, the neural specialist that it does not damage the brain, the internist that the smoke doesn't cause cancer, the psychologist that it doesn't slow reactions, the sociologist that it doesn't cause interpersonal tensions, the economist that it won't disturb the economy, the public health physician that it won't constitute a general health hazard, the child specialist that it won't interrupt normal development. And that is only a sample of the questions that have to be answered in order to get a wholesale endorsement by "science." In point of fact there is probably no substance that we consume, no activity that we engage in, no idea that we believe in, that would gain the unanimous endorsement of "scientific" theoreticians. The battle is likely to rage for a long time, but a number of obvious questions have to appear to be answered before it can be said that there is a theoretical legitimation for a counter-institution. Questions such as, within current theory does it seem beneficial or harmful? If all the theoreticians think that it is harmful it is unlikely to become legitimate, if most of them think it is beneficial or at least not positively harmful, this is a powerful stimulus to legitimation. Sociologists may also have to speculate on its effects on the society as a whole, on social values, though this is not their exclusive province.

Battles among theoreticians are interesting to watch, though most of us only get a partial view since we are not able to read the arcane literature in many scientific fields.

In the following adaptation by Howard S. Becker we can see one of the theoretical battles that is taking place over marijuana. There has long existed the idea, supported by certain medical and psychiatric literature, that marijuana produces a "psychosis" in the smoker. Obviously if some substance makes people mentally ill and dangerous this unpredictable substance is not going to be made a legitimate part of the institutional order; it would violate a great many of our scientific and humanitarian values to allow a dangerous substance into general use, something like giving children real flame-throwers. What Becker does is to examine how the "psychosis" concept came into being and why it is not a scientifically legitimate description of the reality of drug behavior. By so doing he undercuts a crucial argument of antimarijuana and anti-LSD theoreticians and implicitly suggests that the inference based on this scientifically faulty base is worthless. In other words, if marijuana and LSD do not cause "psychosis," then this is not a reason to consider them dangerous.

29

HISTORY, CULTURE AND SUBJECTIVE EXPERIENCE
An Exploration of the Social Bases of Drug-Induced Experiences

HOWARD S. BECKER

THE SUBJECTIVE EFFECTS OF DRUGS

The physiological effects of drugs can be ascertained by standard techniques of physiological and pharmacological research. Scientists measure and have explanations for the actions of many drugs on such observable indices as the heart and respiratory rates, the level of various chemicals in the blood, and the secretion of enzymes and hormones. In contrast, the subjective changes produced by a drug can be ascertained only by asking the subject, in one way or another, how he feels. (To be sure, one can measure the drug's effect on certain measures of psychological functioning—the ability to perform some standardized task, such as placing pegs in a board or remembering nonsense syllables—but this does not tell us what the drug experience is like.)

We take medically prescribed drugs because we believe they will cure or control a disease from which we are suffering; the subjective effects they produce are either ignored or defined as noxious side effects. But some people take some drugs precisely because they want to experience these subjective effects; they take them, to put it colloquially, because they want to get "high." These recreationally used drugs have become the focus of sociological research because the goal of an artificially induced change in consciousness seems to many immoral, and those who so believe have been able to transform their belief into law. Drug users thus come to sociological attention as lawbreakers, and the problems typically investigated have to do with explaining their lawbreaking.

Nevertheless, some sociologists, anthropologists and social psychologists have investigated the problem of drug-induced subjective experience in its own right. Taking their findings together, the following conclusions seem justified. First, many drugs, including those used to produce changes in subjective experience, have a great variety of effects and the user may single out many of them, one of them, or none of them as definite experiences he is undergoing. He may be

Adapted from Howard S. Becker, "History, Culture and Subjective Experience: An Exploration of the Social Bases of Drug-Induced Experiences," *Journal of Health and Social Behavior*, Vol. 8, No. 3, September, 1967, pp. 163–176. Reprinted with permission of the author and The American Sociological Association.

totally unaware of some of the drug's effects, even when they are physiologically gross, although in general the grosser the effects the harder they are to ignore. When he does perceive the effects, he may not attribute them to drug use but dismiss them as due to some other cause, such as fatigue or a cold. Marihuana users, for example, may not even be aware of the drug's effects when they first use it, even though it is obvious to others that they are experiencing them.

Second, and in consequence, the effects of the same drug may be experienced quite differently by different people or by the same people at different times. Even if physiologically observable effects are substantially the same in all members of the species, individuals can vary widely in those to which they choose to pay attention. Thus, Aberle remarks on the quite different experiences Indians and experimental subjects have with peyote and Blum reports a wide variety of experiences with LSD, depending on the circumstances under which it was taken.

Third, since recreational users take drugs in order to achieve some subjective state not ordinarily available to them, it follows that they will expect and be most likely to experience those effects which produce a deviation from conventional perceptions and interpretations of internal and external experience. Thus, distortions in perception of time and space and shifts in judgments of the importance and meaning of ordinary events constitute the most common reported effects.

Fourth, any of a great variety of effects may be singled out by the user as desirable or pleasurable, as the effects for which he has taken the drug. Even effects which seem to the uninitiated to be uncomfortable, unpleasant or frightening—perceptual distortions or visual and auditory hallucinations—can be defined by users as a goal to be sought.

Fifth, how a person experiences the effects of a drug depends greatly on the way others define those effects for him. The total effect of a drug is likely to be a melange of differing physical and psychological sensations. If others whom the user believes to be knowledgeable single out certain effects as characteristic and dismiss others, he is likely to notice those they single out as characteristic of his own experience. If they define certain effects as transitory, he is likely to believe that those effects will go away. All this supposes, of course, that the definition offered the user can be validated in his own experience, that something contained in the drug-induced melange of sensations corresponds to it.

Such a conception of the character of the drug experience has its roots, obviously, in Mead's theory of the self and the relation of objects to the self.* In that theory, objects (including the self) have meaning for

* George Herbert Mead, *Mind, Self and Society,* Chicago: University of Chicago Press, 1934.

the person only as he imputes that meaning to them in the course of his interaction with them. The meaning is not given in the object, but is lodged there as the person acquires a conception of the kind of action that can be taken with, toward, by and for it. Meanings arise in the course of social interaction, deriving their character from the con- sensus participants develop about the object in question. [*This is part of the social construction of reality.*] The findings of research on the character of drug-induced experience are therefore predictable from Mead's theory.

DRUG PSYCHOSES

The scientific literature and, even more, the popular press frequently state that recreational drug use produces a psychosis. The nature of "psychosis" is seldom defined, as though it were intuitively clear. Writers usually seem to mean a mental disturbance of some unspecified kind, involving auditory and visual hallucinations, an inability to control one's stream of thought, and a tendency to engage in socially inappro- priate behavior, either because one has lost the sense that it is inappro- priate or because one cannot stop oneself. In addition, and perhaps most important, psychosis is thought to be a state that will last long beyond the specific event that provoked it. However it occurred, it is thought to mark a more-or-less permanent change in the psyche and this, after all, is why we usually think of it as such a bad thing. Over- indulgence in alcohol produces many of the symptoms cited but this frightens no one because we understand that they will soon go away.

Verified reports of drug-induced psychoses are scarcer than one might think. Nevertheless, let us assume that these reports have not been fabricated, but represent an interpretation by the reporter of some- thing that really happened. In the light of the findings just cited, what kind of event can we imagine to have occurred that might have been interpreted as a "psychotic" episode? (I use the word "imagine" advisedly, for the available case reports usually do not furnish suffi- cient material to allow us to do more than imagine what might have happened.)

The most likely sequence of events is this. The inexperienced user has certain unusual subjective experiences, which he may or may not attribute to having taken the drug. He may find his perception of space distorted, so that he has difficulty climbing a flight of stairs. He may find his train of thought so confused that he is unable to carry on a normal conversation and hears himself making totally inappropriate remarks. He may see or hear things in a way that he suspects is quite different from the way others see and hear them.

Whether or not he attributes what is happening to the drug, the experiences are likely to be upsetting. One of the ways we know that we are normal human beings is that our perceptual world, on the evidence available to us, seems to be pretty much the same as other people's. We see and hear the same things, make the same kind of sense out of them and, where perceptions differ, can explain the difference by a difference in situation or perspective. We may take for granted that the inexperienced drug user, though he wanted to get "high," did not expect an experience so radical as to call into question that common sense of assumptions.

In any society whose culture contains notions of sanity and insanity, the person who finds his subjective state altered in the way described may think he has become insane. We learn at a young age that a person who "acts funny," "sees things," "hears things," or has other bizarre and unusual experiences may have become "crazy," "nuts," "loony" or a host of other synonyms. When a drug user identifies some of these untoward events occurring in his own experience, he may decide that he merits one of those titles—that he has lost his grip on reality, his control of himself, and has in fact "gone crazy." The interpretation implies the corollary that the change is irreversible or, at least, that things are not going to be changed back very easily. The drug experience, perhaps originally intended as a momentary entertainment, now looms as a momentous event which will disrupt one's life, possibly permanently. Faced with this conclusion, the person develops a full-blown anxiety attack, but it is anxiety caused by his reaction to the drug experience rather than a direct consequence of drug use itself. (In this connection, it is interesting that, in the published reports of LSD psychoses, acute anxiety attacks appear as the largest category of untoward reactions.)

It is perhaps easier to grasp what this must feel like if we imagine that, having taken several social drinks at a party, we were suddenly to see varicolored snakes peering out at us from behind the furniture. We would instantly recognize this as a sign of delirium tremens, and would no doubt become severely anxious at the prospect of having developed such a serious mental illness. Some such panic is likely to grip the recreational user of drugs who interprets his experiences as a sign of insanity.

Though I have put the argument with respect to the inexperienced user, long-time users of recreational drugs sometimes have similar experiences. They may experiment with a higher dosage than they are used to and experience effects unlike anything they have known before. This can easily occur when using drugs purchased in the illicit market, where quality may vary greatly, so that the user inadvertently gets more than he can handle.

The scientific literature does not report any verified cases of people acting on their distorted perceptions so as to harm themselves and others, but such cases have been reported in the press. Press reports of drug-related events are very unreliable, but it may be that users have, for instance, stepped out of a second story window, deluded by the drug into thinking it only a few feet to the ground. If such cases have occurred, they too may be interpreted as examples of psychosis, but a different mechanism than the one just discussed would be involved. The person, presumably, would have failed to make the necessary correction for the drug-induced distortion, a correction, however, that experienced users assert can be made. Thus, a novice marihuana user will find it difficult to drive while "high," but experienced users have no difficulty. Similarly, novices find it difficult to manage their relations with people who are not also under the influence of drugs, but experienced users can control their thinking and actions so as to behave appropriately. Although it is commonly assumed that a person under the influence of LSD must avoid ordinary social situations for 12 or more hours, I have been told of at least one user who takes the drug and then goes to work; she explained that once you learn "how to handle it" (i.e., make the necessary corrections for distortions caused by the drug) there is no problem.

In short, the most likely interpretation we can make of the drug-induced psychoses reported is that they are either severe anxiety reactions to an event interpreted and experienced as insanity, or failures by the user to correct, in carrying out some ordinary action, for the perceptual distortions caused by the drug. If the interpretation is correct, then untoward mental effects produced by drugs depend in some part on its physiological action, but to a much larger degree find their origin in the definitions and conceptions the user applies to that action. These can vary with the individual's personal makeup, a possibility psychiatrists are most alive to, or with the groups he participates in, the trail I shall pursue here.

THE INFLUENCE OF DRUG-USING CULTURES

While there are no reliable figures, it is obvious that a very large number of people use recreational drugs, primarily marihuana and LSD. From the previous analysis one might suppose that, therefore, a great many people would have disquieting symptoms and, given the ubiquity in our society of the concept of insanity, that many would decide they had gone crazy and thus have a drug-induced anxiety attack. But very few such reactions occur. Although there must be more than are reported in the professional literature, it is unlikely that drugs have this effect in any large number of cases. If they did there would necessarily be many more verified accounts than are presently available. Since the psychotic reaction stems from a definition of the drug-induced experience, the explanation of this paradox must lie in the availability of competing definitions of the subjective states produced by drugs.

Competing definitions come to the user from other users who, to his knowledge, have had sufficient experience with the drug to speak with authority. He knows that the drug does not produce permanent disabling damage in all cases, for he can see that these other users do not suffer from it. The question, of course, remains whether it may not produce damage in some cases and whether his is one of them, no matter how rare.

When someone experiences disturbing effects, other users typically assure him that the change in his subjective experience is neither rare nor dangerous. They have seen similar reactions before, and may even have experienced them themselves with no lasting harm. In any event, they have some folk knowledge about how to handle the problem.

They may, for instance, know of an antidote for the frightening effects; thus, marihuana users, confronted with someone who has gotten "too high," encourage him to eat, an apparently effective countermeasure. They talk reassuringly about their own experiences, "normalizing" the frightening symptom by treating it, matter-of-factly, as temporary. They maintain surveillance over the affected person, preventing any physically or socially dangerous activity. They may, for instance, keep him from driving or making a public display that will bring him to the attention of the police or others who would disapprove of his drug use. They show him how to allow for the perceptual distortion the drug causes and teach him how to manage interaction with nonusers.

They redefine the experience he is having as desirable rather than frightening, as the end for which the drug is taken. What they tell him carries conviction, because he can see that it is not some idiosyncratic belief but is instead culturally shared. It is what "everyone" who uses the drug knows. In all these ways, experienced users prevent the episode from having lasting effects and reassure the novice that whatever he feels will come to a timely and harmless end. [*This is the "how-to-do-it" knowledge of the counter-institution of behavior.*]

The anxious novice thus has an alternative to defining his experience as "going crazy." He may redefine the event immediately or, having been watched over by others throughout the anxiety attack, decide that it was not so bad after all and not fear its reoccurrence. He "learns" that his original definition was "incorrect" and that the alternative offered by other users more nearly describes what he has experienced. [*The individual adopts the knowledge from the counter-institution in preference to the knowledge provided in social reality, because it fits his experience better.*]

Available knowledge does not tell us how often this mechanism comes into play or how effective it is in preventing untoward psychological reactions; no research has been addressed to this point. In the case of marihuana, at least, the paucity of reported cases of permanent damage coupled with the undoubted increase in use suggest that it may be an effective mechanism.

For such a mechanism to operate, a number of conditions must be met. First, the drug must not produce, quite apart from the user's interpretations, permanent damage to the mind. No amount of social redefinition can undo the damage done by toxic alcohols, or the effects of a lethal dose of an opiate or barbiturate. This analysis, therefore, does not apply to drugs known to have such effects.

Second, users of the drug must share a set of understandings—a culture—which includes, in addition to material on how to obtain and ingest the drug, definitions of the typical effects, the typical course of the experience, the permanence of the effects, and a description of methods for dealing with someone who suffers an anxiety attack because of drug use or attempts to act on the basis of distorted perceptions. Users should have available to them, largely through face-to-face participation with other users but possibly in such other ways as reading as well, the definitions contained in that culture, which they can apply in place of the common-sense definitions available to the inexperienced man on the street.

Third, the drug should ordinarily be used in group settings, where other users can present the definitions of the drug-using culture to the person whose inner experience is so unusual as to provoke use of the common-sense category of insanity. Drugs for which technology and custom promote group use should produce a lower incidence of "psychotic episodes." [*The drug culture and legitimations are best transmitted in face-to-face communications (internal communications). Culture provides biographical legitimations that make status legitimate: "You're not crazy, you're high." Being crazy is something to worry about, a stigma; being high, however, is something one achieves.*]

The last two conditions suggest, as is the case, that marihuana, surrounded by an elaborate culture and ordinarily used in group settings, should produce few "psychotic" episodes. At the same time, they suggest the prediction that drugs which have not spawned a culture and are ordinarily used in private, such as barbiturates, will produce more such episodes. I suggest possible research along these lines below.

NON-USER INTERPRETATIONS

A user suffering from drug-induced anxiety may also come into contact with non-users who will offer him definitions, depending on their own perspectives and experiences, that may validate the diagnosis of "going crazy" and thus prolong the episode, possibly producing relatively permanent disability. These non-users include family members and police, but most important among them are psychiatrists and psychiatrically oriented physicians. (Remember that when we speak of reported cases of psychosis, the report is ordinarily made by a physician, though police may also use the term in reporting a case to the press.)

. . .

Physicians, confronted with a case of drug-induced anxiety and lacking specific knowledge of its character or proper treatment, rely on a kind of generalized diagnosis. They reason that people probably do not use drugs unless they are suffering from a severe underlying personality disturbance; that use of the drug may allow repressed conflicts to come into the open where they will prove unmanageable; that the drug in this way provokes a true psychosis; and, therefore, that the patient confronting them is psychotic. Furthermore, even though the effects of the drug wear off, the psychosis may not, for the repressed psychological problems it has brought to the surface may not recede as it is metabolized and excreted from the body. [*This is the definition of reality legitimated as a "scientific" one in social reality.*]

Given such a diagnosis, the physician knows what to do. He hospitalizes the patient for observation and prepares, where possible, for long-term therapy designed to repair the damage done to the psychic defenses or to deal with the conflict unmasked by the drug. Both hospitalization and therapy are likely to reinforce the definition of the drug experience as insanity, for in both the patient will be required to "understand" that he is mentally ill as a precondition for return to the world.

The physician then, does *not* treat the anxiety attack as a localized phenomenon, to be treated in a symptomatic way, but as an outbreak of a serious disease heretofore hidden. He may thus prolong the serious effects beyond the time they might have lasted had the user instead come into contact with other users. This analysis, of course, is frankly speculative; what is required is study of the way physicians treat cases of the kind described and, especially, comparative study of the effects of treatment of drug-induced anxiety attacks by physicians and by drug users.

. . .

AN HISTORICAL DIMENSION

Consider the following sequence of possible events, which may be regarded as a natural history of the assimilation of an intoxicating drug by a society. Someone in the society discovers, rediscovers or invents a drug which has the properties described earlier. The ability of the drug to alter subjective experience in desirable ways becomes known to increasing numbers of people, and the drug itself simultaneously becomes available, along with the information needed to make its use effective. Use increases, but users do not have a sufficient amount of experience with the drug to form a stable conception of it as an object. They do not know what it can do to the mind, have no firm idea of the variety of effects it can produce, and are not sure how permanent or dangerous the effects are. They do not know if the effect can be controlled or how. No drug-using culture exists, and there is thus no authoritative alternative with which to counter the possible definition, when and if it comes to mind, of the drug experience as madness. "Psychotic episodes" occur frequently.

But individuals accumulate experience with the drug and communicate their experiences to one another. Consensus develops about the drug's subjective effects, their duration, proper dosages, predictable dangers and how they may be avoided; all these points become matters of common knowledge, validated by their acceptance in a world of users. A culture exists. When a user experiences bewildering or frightening effects, he has available to him an authoritative alternative to the lay notion that he has gone mad. Every time he uses cultural conceptions to interpret drug experiences and control his response to them, he strengthens his belief that the culture is indeed a reliable source of knowledge. "Psychotic episodes" occur less frequently in proportion to the growth of the culture to cover the range of possible effects and its spread to a greater proportion of users. Novice users, to whom the effects are most unfamiliar and who therefore might be expected to suffer most from drug-induced anxiety, learn the culture from older users in casual conversation and in more serious teaching sessions and are thus protected from the dangers of "panicking" or "flipping out."

The incidence of "psychoses," then, is a function of the stage of development of a drug-using culture. Individual experience varies with historical stages and the kinds of cultural and social organization associated with them.

Is this model a useful guide to reality? The only drug for which there is sufficient evidence to attempt an evaluation is marihuana; even there the evidence is equivocal, but it is consistent with the model. On this interpretation, the early history of marihuana use in the United States should be marked by reports of marihuana-induced psychoses. In the absence of a fully formed drug-using culture, some users would experience disquieting symptoms and have no alternative to the idea that they were losing their minds. They would turn up at psychiatric facilities in acute states of anxiety and doctors, eliciting a history of marihuana use, would interpret the episode as a psychotic breakdown. When, however, the culture reached full flower and spread throughout the user population, the number of psychoses should have dropped even though (as a variety of evidence suggests) the numbers of users increased greatly. Using the definitions made available by the culture, users who had unexpectedly severe symptoms could interpret them in such a way as to reduce or control anxiety and would thus no longer come to the attention of those likely to report them as cases of psychosis.

Marihuana first came into use in the United States in the 1920's and early '30's, and all reports of psychosis associated with its use date from approximately that period. A search of both *Psychological Abstracts* and the *Cumulative Index Medicus* (and its predecessors, the *Current List of Medical Literature* and the *Quarterly Index Medicus*) revealed no cases after 1940. The disappearance of reports of psychosis thus fits the model. It is, of course, a shaky index, for it depends as much on the reporting habits of physicians as on the true incidence of cases, but it is the only thing available.

. . .

The evidence cited is extremely scanty. We do not know the role of elements of the drug-using culture in any of these cases or whether the decrease in incidence is a true one. But we are not likely to do any better and, in the absence of conflicting evidence, it seems justified to take the model as an accurate representation of the history of marihuana use in the United States.

. . .

LSD

We cannot predict the history of LSD by direct analogy to the history of marihuana, for a number of important conditions may vary. We must first ask whether the drug has, apart from the definitions users impose on their experience, any demonstrated causal relation to psychosis. There is a great deal of controversy on the point, and any reading of the evidence must be tentative. My own opinion is that LSD has essentially the same characteristics as those described in the first part of this paper; its effects may be more powerful than those of other drugs that have been studied, but they too are subject to differing interpretations by users, so that the mechanisms I have described can come into play.

The cases reported in the literature are, like those reported for marihuana, mostly panic reactions to the drug experience, occasioned by the user's interpretation that he has lost his mind, or further disturbance among people already quite disturbed. There are no cases of permanent derangement directly traceable to the drug, with one puzzling exception (puzzling to those who report it as well as to me). In a few cases the visual and auditory distortions produced by the drug reoccur weeks or months after it was last ingested; this sometimes produces severe upset among those who experience it. Observers are at a loss to explain the phenomenon, except for Rosenthal, who proposes that the drug may have a specific effect on the nerve pathways involved in vision;* but this theory, should it prove correct, is a long way from dealing with questions of possible psychosis. [*Possibly the user has simply learned a new mode of perception, as Ginsberg suggested was possible with marijuana. An unnoticed or sublimal stimulus may reactivate the perceptual mode as in the déjà vu experience. The upset that is experienced when such a flashback takes place is probably a consequence of the intrusion of a perceptual mode learned in a state of non-ordinary reality into the taken-for-granted reality of everyday life. Anything we learned to see once we can see again—it is only when it is unusual or unexpected that it becomes upsetting.*]

The whole question is confused by the extraordinary assertions about the effects of LSD made by both proponents and opponents of its use. Both sides agree that it has a very strong effect on the mind, disagreeing only as to whether this powerful effect is benign or malignant. Leary, for example, argues that we must "go out of our minds in order to use our heads," and that this can be accomplished by using LSD. Opponents agree that it can drive you out of your mind, but do not share Leary's view that this is a desirable goal. In any case, we need not accept the premise simply because both parties to the controversy do.

Let us assume then, in the absence of more definitive evidence, that the drug does not in itself produce lasting derangement, that such psychotic episodes as are now reported are largely a result of panic at the possible meaning of the experience, that users who "freak out" do so because they fear they have permanently damaged their minds. Is there an LSD-using culture? In what stage of development is it? Are the reported episodes of psychosis congruent with what our model would predict, given that stage of development?

Here again my discussion must be speculative, for no serious study of this culture is yet available. It appears likely, however, that such a culture is in an early stage of development. Several conceptions of the drug and its possible effects exist, but no stable consensus has

* S. H. Rosenthal, "Persistant Hallucinosis Following Repeated Administration of Hallucinogenic Drugs," *American Journal of Psychiatry*, 121, 1964, pp. 238–244.

arisen. Radio, television and the popular press present a variety of interpretations, many of them contradictory. There is widespread disagree-
ment, even among users, about possible dangers. Some certainly
believe that use (or injudicious use) can lead to severe mental difficulty.

At the same time, my preliminary inquiries and observations hinted
at the development (or at least the beginnings) of a culture similar to
that surrounding marihuana use. Users with some experience discuss
their symptoms and translate from one idiosyncratic description into
another, developing a common conception of effects as they talk. The
notion that a "bad trip" can be brought to a speedy conclusion by taking thorazine by mouth (or, when immediate action is required, intra-
venously) has spread. Users are also beginning to develop a set of
safeguards against committing irrational acts while under the drug's
influence. Many feel, for instance, that one should take one's "trip" in
the company of experienced users who are not under the drug's influence at the time; they will be able to see you through bad times and
restrain you when necessary. A conception of the appropriate dose is
rapidly becoming common knowledge. Users understand that they may
have to "sit up with" people who have panicked as a result of the drug's
effects, and they talk of techniques that have proved useful in this
enterprise. All this suggests that a common conception of the drug is
developing which will eventually see it defined as pleasurable and desirable, with possible untoward effects that can however be controlled.

Insofar as this emergent culture spreads so that most or all users
share the belief that LSD does not cause insanity, and the other understandings just listed, the incidence of "psychoses" should drop mark-
edly or disappear. Just as with marihuana, the interpretation of the
experience as one likely to produce madness will disappear and, having
other definitions available to use in coping with the experience, users
will treat the experience as self-limiting and not as a cause for panic.

The technology of LSD use, however, has features which will work
in the opposite direction. In the first place, it is very easily taken;
one need learn no special technique (as one must with marihuana) to
produce the characteristic effect, for a sugar cube can be swallowed
without instruction. This means that anyone who gets hold of the drug
can take it in a setting where there are no experienced users around
to redefine frightening effects and "normalize" them. He may also have
acquired the drug without acquiring any of the presently developing
cultural understandings so that, when frightening effects occur, he is
left with nothing but current lay conceptions as plausible definitions.
In this connection, it is important that a large amount of the published
material by journalists and literary men places heavy emphasis on the
dangers of psychosis. It is also important that various medical facilities
have become alerted to the possibility of patients (particularly college

students and teenagers) coming in with LSD-induced psychoses. All these factors will tend to increase the incidence of "psychotic episodes," perhaps sufficiently to offset the dampening effect of the developing culture.

. . .

As an LSD-using culture develops, the proportion of those exposed who interpret their experience as one of insanity will decrease. But people may use the drug without being indoctrinated with the new cultural definitions, either because of the ease with which the drug can be taken or because it has been given to them without their knowledge, in which case the number of episodes will rise. The actual figure will be a vector made up of these several components.

NOTE ON THE OPIATES

The opiate drugs present an interesting paradox. In the drugs we have been considering, the development of a drug-using culture causes a decrease in rates of morbidity associated with drug use, for greater knowledge of the true character of the drug's effects lessens the likelihood that users will respond to those effects with uncontrolled anxiety. In the case of opiates, however, the greater one's knowledge of the drug's effects, the more likely it is that one will suffer its worst effect, addiction. As Lindesmith has shown, one can only be addicted when he experiences physiological withdrawal symptoms, recognizes them as due to a need for drugs, and relieves them by taking another dose. The crucial step of recognition is most likely to occur when the user participates in a culture in which the signs of withdrawal are interpreted for what they are. When a person is ignorant of the nature of withdrawal sickness, and has some other cause to which he can attribute his discomfort (such as a medical problem), he may misinterpret the symptoms and thus escape addiction, as some of Lindesmith's cases demonstrate.

This example makes clear how important the actual physiology of the drug response is in the model I have developed. The culture contains interpretations of the drug experience, but these must be congruent with the drug's actual effects. Where the effects are varied and ambiguous, as with marihuana and LSD, a great variety of interpretations is possible. Where the effects are clear and unmistakable, as with opiates, the culture is limited in the possible interpretations it can provide. Where the cultural interpretation is so constrained, and the effect to be interpreted leads, in its most likely interpretation, to morbidity, the spread of a drug-using culture will increase morbidity rates.

☐ ☐ ☐

Disputes among theoreticians over the nature or effects of a counter-institution are many-sided, with many isolated battles. Many theories turn out to be irrelevant, many theorists are astonished to find themselves in the controversy at all, and others intentionally provoke it. Even agreement on the basic rules of evidence is hard to come by with many complex descriptions of complex events bypassing one another. Even when some facts or interpretations are agreed upon they may be valued quite differently by different sides.

The work of theoreticians is called into the battle to win over powerful men and the general public, but it is called upon by interested parties, often selectively, always within their own structure of values. Suppose, for example, that it were "scientifically proven" that the use of marijuana allowed for freer sexual expression. This would be interpreted by its opponents as a destroyer of inhibition and a spur to promiscuity, and by its proponents as a removal of hang-ups and an opening of the self to the world. Suppose that the use of marijuana were proven to lead to new perceptions. Opponents would argue that it was an escape from "reality" by which they mean old forms of perception, while proponents would argue, as Ginsberg did, that it would lead to new forms of artistic expression and understanding. Since we do not live in Inca society where the Inca decided what was true and everyone who wished to live believed it was true also, we will always be faced with many truths, and ultimately there is no way of deciding among them. Thus the theoreticians, be they scientists, philosophers, or priests, attempt to establish what is a fact or what is an effect, each within his own essentially arbitrary structures of rules of evidence. Their efforts are then interpreted within the values that have been generated by conflicting life styles by individuals and groups with ulterior motives. Out of this collage of theories and values relatively simple propaganda lines are developed by the counter-institution's spokes-group and by the concerned legitimate institutions.

These relatively simple propaganda lines serve as the theoretical legitimations for and against the counter-institution in the ultimate battle to redefine social reality. These theoretical legitimations will be used to convince institutional leaders and the general population that the counter-institution should become legitimate, or more legitimate.

The several processes of gaining de facto legitimacy, de jure legitimacy, and altering social reality are all proceeding more or less simultaneously. In most cases it would be a mistake to separate out these three as distinct and isolated processes. Although they may be seen to have different ends, different natures, different social processes, they reflect back and forth on one another, magnifying or reducing the speed of each other. They could all be seen as a set of interactive subprocesses of the process of reality adjustment. The fact that an institution has de facto legitimacy does not automatically lead to de jure legitimacy, or to its acceptance as an element of social reality. In 1954 the United States Supreme Court conferred de jure legitimacy on the institution of racially-integrated education, which has still not achieved de facto legitimacy in many parts of the South. The alteration of social reality depends to a large extent on having achieved legitimacy, but alterations often start long before a counter-institution has either kind of legitimacy, and continue long after.

How much and what part of a counter-institution becomes legitimate is a matter of debate. In the process in which the counter-institution builds itself up, undergoing deviation amplifying feedback processes, generating its own understandings about many related issues, developing organizational forms, making alliances with other institutions, generating a recruiting ideology, and keeping up hope among adherents, what may have been a fairly simple pattern of behavior has taken on a load of baggage, ideas, appendages that fan out in many directions. A counter-institution may be closely tied with other counter-institutions, the followers of both may support one another, they may see the collection as part of a wave, as part of an entirely new social order. What happens when legitimacy is granted to the "central program" of one counter-institution? The answer depends on the position of the viewer. From the point of view of the institutional order, and of those whose only involvement in the counter-institution has been enacting it, a victory has been won; it is now a legitimate institution. From the point of view of the allies, and of those who saw the counter-institution as part of a wave, for those whose participation is more broadly ideological, the process of co-optation has begun. The labor movement had many radical ideas for restructuring society; it often allied with other underdogs in their fights; many people participated in the movement because they thought it was going to lead to the downfall of the capitalist system and equality and justice for all working men. In the process of becoming a legitimate institution it limited its goals, purged Communists from its ranks, developed an interest in the continuance of the capitalist system, and became considerably less interested in the fights of other underdogs. Many building trade unions excluded blacks, and the involvement in fighting for human rights slowly shifted from participation in the fight to buying full-page advertisements in popular magazines to indicate how concerned they were with human rights. The right to bargain collectively, the right of unions to organize and to strike effectively without unfair pressure, became legitimate both de facto and de jure, and as these practices were legitimately enacted they restructured social reality and brought great improvements to the economic status of the unionized workingman.

As homosexuality becomes legitimate it seems it will leave behind many homosexuals in illegitimate activity. Where it is being legalized it is being restricted to consenting adults in private. Many young hustlers, and many men without a private place they can use for lovemaking, many turkish baths and many gay bars with glory holes, are still going to be counter-institutional. When marijuana becomes legalized many related drugs and many parts of the drug culture will probably be left behind. There will probably be age restrictions, and a breakdown of the distinctive habits and practices associated with group smoking.

Thus the institution is changed as it becomes legitimate—it does not alter the structure of institutions as much as its proponents hoped it would and fought for; it also does not alter the pattern of institutions as much as its opponents feared that it would. Only a limited and essentially unthreatening part of the institution becomes legitimate.

In a way we could look at the granting of de jure legitimacy as the final act of social control of the institutional order. By granting legitimacy to the "central program" of the counter-institution the major reality flaw that motivated it is removed, and most participants are happy to become legitimate. The leaders and allies who hoped for larger changes are left without a power base, with more marginal legitimations, and often with factional conflicts. By selectively legitimating counter-institutions the institutional order modifies itself but retains its continuity. If it steadfastly refuses to adapt the results may be, finally, a revolution as various counter-institutions and their power bases coalesce and begin challenging the basic ordering of the institutional order. The Townsend movement for old age pensions was effectively emasculated by the enactment of Social Security legislation. The suffragettes who sought basic changes in the status of women were stopped in their tracks when women were granted the right to vote; their other programs are only now being taken up.

Whether we see the granting of legitimacy to a counter-institution as a radical or conservative step, the fact is that it is a step in the alteration of social reality. It grants a formal, legal, or authorized status to the institution. In itself this status is powerful, because the institution takes on some of the status of its legitimator. Now the institution is legal, or orthodox, and it may well gain a number of new followers since its symbolic stigma has been removed.

The institution that grants legitimacy does so by tying the action to some principle or value relevant to its symbolic universe. Courts may speak of freedom of choice, equality or the constitution, legislators may invoke God-given rights, or natural rights, the church may reinterpret a revelation or miracle, or it may make one to order as the Mormons will have to in order to admit blacks to their ministry. The Chinese Communist party may legitimate changes by conferring upon them the titles "correct practice" or "correct analysis." Mao's method for the resolution of "non-antagonistic contradictions," that is, conflicts that do not challenge the continuity of *his* institutional order, is essentially the same as that adopted in North American society. He sums it up succinctly: "unity, struggle, unity." It is important to note, however, that this social control process is only applied to counter-institutions that can find their legitimations within the Marxian symbolic universe, and can lay claim to a "scientific" (in the Marxian sense) analysis. Antagonistic contradictions are dealt with in other ways. It should be interesting to see what changes had to take place before a contradiction could move from "antagonistic" to "non-antagonistic," so that it could be accommodated within the system. The processes of internal change and social control in communist countries follow essentially the same pattern found in Western society.

In our complex institutional order there may be a number of different institutions that grant de jure legitimacy, so it may not come all at once. It is analogous to the differences between coming of age in a tribal society and in North America. In a tribal society the boys may be taken away for a period of time and taught magic and the practices of manhood. When they come back they are men by right, and everyone treats them as men from that point on. In our society a boy becomes a man, according to the movie theaters and airlines, when he is twelve, a man according to his religion when he is thirteen or fourteen, a man according to the driving laws when he is sixteen, a man for criminal actions when he is eighteen, for civil actions when he is twenty-one, and in an important sense when he takes his first job and stops being a student, which may be at twenty-two or thirty, or thirty-five for people in some professions. In addition to his own biological manhood, in other words, he is de facto or de jure considered to have become a man on no fewer than six different occasions as he grew up. A counter-institution may gain legitimacy in a similar fashion, being legitimated by one institution after another, with some abstaining from making the step. So "science" may provide legitimacy for a counter-institution, while the church does not. The courts may grant de jure legitimacy and government agencies may refuse to recognize the decision. This means that the very presence or absence of de jure legitimacy may be a matter of question since it doesn't come in a blinding flash but as a discrete series of acts. Looked at in historical perspective, however, it is generally possible to find a critical act that essentially made an institution legitimate, such as the decision in Canada in 1939 that forbade discrimination against employees on the basis of their union activity.

Social reality, however, is a lived and shared understanding about the nature of the world. A decision by one group of men, no matter how legitimate, does not automatically alter the minds, living patterns, and institutions of all men. Many of the opponents of the counter institution will still be opposed and ready to fight it however they can many will still consider it evil or degraded and not to be allowed withir their town or house if they can help it. Legitimacy can even be lost prohibition became law and was then repealed, primarily because it dic not change everyday activities and the realities they supported.

The process that changes the reality of the society comes about when the new institution progressively establishes links and transactions with other institutions in the institutional order. Labor, for example, became instrumental in agitating for construction of highways and in so doing joined with bankers, contractors, and politicians for mutual benefit. Time after time the new institution is found to be part of a cooperative effort with other legitimate institutions. The leaders interact and get to know one another as partners rather than as enemies. Gradually the dependence of institutions on one another grows in an increasingly complex set of exchanges, and the new institution comes to be seen as necessary and useful to the stable operation of the other institutions. Having a good union contract is now seen as useful protection against wildcat strikes.

As marijuana becomes part of the institutional structure many people will find that their economic well being, and that of their family, has come to depend on the industry. Others may find that it is the common denominator of sociability in their set of friends. They would no more think of having a party without something to smoke than a drinker would now think of having a party without some alcohol to drink. Others will find that they are taking a few friendly puffs to cement business deals (already common among dealers), to make an afternoon's drive more enjoyable, to relax after a hard day at the office, or to prepare for a dull assembly line job. People smoking joints on the street will be a commonplace (as they already are in San Francisco), employers may forbid their employees to do up while serving customers, but wink at washroom smoking. People will give others cartons of joints at Christmas, families will get high together to watch movies on television. New Skid Rows will appear and Krishna people will play Salvation Army. Professionals will develop techniques and programs for dealing with old heads, mental hospitals will open drug wards to take care of the people who have problems with it, and gradually close their alcoholic wards. People with family problems will start blaming them on smoking rather than drinking. New art forms will become popular and the sale of color television sets will increase. In short, as its use becomes an everyday routine in one social world after another, as other institutions come to depend on it, as it plays a part in many habits, reciprocal typifications, and institutions it will become an unquestioned part of social reality.

The acceptance of a new institution may be partial for a long period, there are still places where the sale of alcohol is prohibited. In general, urban areas with their reduced relational social controls have adopted new institutions much more quickly than have rural areas; total adoption of an institution is not a necessary condition for its acceptance as an element of social reality, few institutions are totally accepted and followed. The critical point in acceptance for a new institution comes when the man in the street does not notice its enactment as being anything unusual.

From a distinct and isolated institution carried by a distinctive group or subculture it gradually fans out to become some of the threads in the fabric of understandings that we encounter as taken for granted reality in our daily lives. All institutions are somewhat problematic, most are open to question by some people; the existence of an institution in the institutional order does not guarantee that it will be followed unquestioningly. At some point, however, the new institution will fade into the background of consciousness for most people as they come to worry about a war, or some new counter-institution that appears fearsomely on the horizon. For the child growing up, or for the immigrant just arriving, the reality they encounter is composed of many institutions and values, and the "new" institution does not stand out particularly from the background of the other institutions of the society. If they ask about it, the average member of the society will be able to tell them how to do it, why it is done, and how it fits in with everything else in society. It is a part of the ongoing social reality—unquestioned, routine, and a basis for actions.

Thus, over time, through conflict, victory, and assimilation, the nature of social reality has been altered a small bit. As one counter-institution after another undergoes this process, social reality continuously changes while seeming to the average participant to be continuous and unchanging.

From our naïve and subjective points of view as actors in the world, the myriads of different institutions that we encounter every day seem stable unless we change them by moving ourselves or by making other conscious choices. A change or alteration in one institution seems to affect us little if at all. After all, the vast majority of our understandings are the same from one day to the next, and even changes may approach us slowly and indirectly. Our conception of social reality is as a monolithic external facticity. It objectively surrounds us, grows, is maintained, and is reified into absolute truth; this keeps us from realizing that it is an ever-changing human product—which we can change.

☐ ☐ ☐

□ □ □

To this point we have dealt with *the* institutional order and *the* social construction of reality as if there were but one institutional order and but one construction of reality. Although this has been necessary in order to examine the ways in which social reality changes, it actually oversimplifies the situation in a complex society. While it is proper to speak of a predominant social reality, we should realize that there can also be *other* realities, carried and sustained by subgroups within the population. There are also the realities of other societies that have grown in their own historical matrix and correspond to ours only roughly.

In a society that divides its work along sex lines and has few areas of occupational specialization, the life experience of each person is so similar that the creation of an alternate reality is most unlikely. In such a primitive society there will be *an* institutional order and *a* symbolic universe. But as a society becomes more complex, individuals and groups become involved in many diverse occupational and leisure

CHANGING REALITIES

activities. Subgroups can form within the population who see the world somewhat differently from the majority in their society. These different experiences and constructions of social reality may be minor variations well contained within the overarching legitimations of the symbolic universe, or they may be radical variants that challenge the entire structure and legitimacy of the predominant social reality. Every occupational specialty develops certain distinct ways in which its members view the world around them. Certain facts will be taken to be of the utmost importance by members of an occupational group; the same facts will seem trivial to outsiders. Medical doctors develop a set of values around the problems of their profession and their economic status. Professors become involved in the social world of their specialties and come to value the world around them from their distinctive viewpoint. Hockey players do likewise. Old maids develop views about sex and men that reflect their unmarried status. People living in particular regions of the country share a reality among themselves that may seem quite strange to an outsider. These are all more or less "normal" variations of social reality which are recognized as being within the same symbolic universe. Sometimes these "normal" variations of reality conflict—for example, southern and northern views on race—and people who hold to one view become categorized as "deviants" by those who hold the other.

In most cases the individual learns the special reality accents of a subgroup through the normal processes of occupational, regional, and sexual socialization. For example, when a student goes to graduate school he begins to find that the "interesting" people he meets share his course of study. Through contacts with professors in his discipline, other students, attending annual meetings of his profession, being rewarded by good grades for making "appropriate" distinctions, and working on the "important" problems of the discipline, he gradually focuses his interest in the world around him within the frame of reference of his occupation. The boundaries between disciplines are jealously guarded, and the perspectives, languages, and critical facts become mutually incomprehensible. Studies of interdisciplinary research projects often find that the various specialists literally do not understand each other, though they maintain a polite façade of seeming agreement. Troublesome as these misunderstandings may be, they are not generally considered to be "deviance," but a price one pays for living in a complex society.

But other realities, also available, are considered "deviant." These other realities constitute a basic challenge to the organization of the subjective and objective world legitimated by the symbolic universe. For the people who live within these alternate realities, the entire structure of the symbolic universe is error, evil, or a form of barbarism.

They have an absolute faith in their values and their view of the world. In other words they have, to a greater or lesser extent, *their own* symbolic universe, and there are few correspondences between universes.

The people who live in conventional reality view those in alternate realities as "nuts," "kooks," "anarchists," and "insane." They think of them as living in error, in evil, or in barbarism: in short, total "deviants."

There is little debate and much misunderstanding between realities because the very most basic assumptions about the world are not shared. How, for example, could there be understanding between a person living in the conventional more or less scientific world and a person who has organized his entire life around the anticipation that the second coming of Jesus Christ and the destruction of the world was going to happen in one year, three months, and five days? How can there be understanding between a middle-class housewife and a person who believes that Western imperialism will destroy itself from historical necessity? How can there be understanding between a person who has organized his entire life according to invariable, eternally true moral principles laid down by God and a hippie who sees abstract morality as a dangerous hang-up?

The believer in alternate realities is most generally viewed as a heretic. I have always liked a definition of heretic quoted by Samuel Johnson in his dictionary because it seems to catch succinctly the way in which alternate realities are viewed. Heretics are: "...any persons willfully and contentiously obstinate in fundamental errors." In other words, a person who voluntarily and with complete conviction holds beliefs that violate the values of the symbolic universe.

Although it is not a statistically common occurrence, a person can reorganize his entire subjective reality, his evaluation of himself, his past, and the world around him, and can "convert" from one reality to another. Although his physical body is the same, and the physical universe is the same, his entire set of assumptions, even about his body and the physical universe, can be altered.

To illustrate the process involved in changing realities as outlined by Berger and Luckmann I am going to examine the process of becoming "hip" in the contemporary North American scene. The "hip" reality involves a near total reorganization of the assumptive world in which we live. Though one could make a more total break by, say, becoming a Buddhist monk, I think that the processes of conversion can be illustrated by reference to this fairly common alternate reality.

The distance that one has to travel to become hip varies greatly with age and residence. For many of the readers of this book the distance will be very short, if they are not already there. A young person, living in a city on the east or west coast, will find hip people and communities close at hand. A young person living in the Midwest will not find such a complete environment. An older person, no matter where he is, will find more difficulty in becoming hip, but especially so in the Midwest. It is possible to chart the location and distance between conventional and hip realities and, of course, to suggest that conversion is easier the more one is in contact with others who already live within the hip reality.

Most individuals in a society are spared contact with alternate realities. They may hear about them, read about them, talk about them, but know no one who lives in them. Particularly for people who have had little contact with the hip reality, I would like to illustrate some of the ways in which it differs from conventional reality, both in its values and in the institutions enacted by those within it.

In the following adaptation Jerry Simmons and Barry Winograd explore the values of the hip reality. They illustrate the ways in which the "philosophy" or the "ideology" of the "happenings" can be seen as an emerging reality.

☐ ☐ ☐

30

THE HANG-LOOSE ETHIC

J. L. SIMMONS AND BARRY WINOGRAD

The emerging ethic is hang-loose in a number of senses, but, its deep-running feature is that things once taken for granted as God-given or American Constitution-given—those basic premises about the world and the way it works—are no longer taken for granted or given automatic allegiance. [*The basic assumptions of conventional reality are being questioned.*]

In other words, many Americans are hanging a bit loose from traditional Americana.

This new ethos is still in the process of forming and emerging; the adherents themselves are mostly unaware of the credo they are participating in making and are already living by. For instance, if you went up to many of the likely young people about town and said, "Say, are you an adherent of the hang-loose ethic?," many of them would look at you oddly and wonder what the hell you were talking about. [*Emerging realities are often uncodified until they have faced conflict and dissent, which causes them to define their boundaries. Most people live naïvely within their reality, and this may also be true for alternate realities.*]

. . .

At first glance, it might seem as if the hang-loose ethic is the absence of any morality, that it rejects every ideology, that the followers have no rudder and no star except the swift gratification of all impulses. At a second glance it appears only as a bewildering melange of scenes in various locales. But upon closer examination, one can see that it does embody some values and some guiding principles which, although still ill-formed and vaguely expressed, shape the attitudes and actions of the followers. [*The first glance is from the perspective of conventional reality, the second glance is closer, and the values are finally seen from within.*]

. . .

When we search for the "philosophy" which is the common denominator running through the variety of happenings—the implicit code of values pushing those involved toward some things and away from other things—some of the characteristics of this yet crystallizing view can be discerned.

One of the fundamental characteristics of the hang-loose ethic is that it is *irreverent*. It repudiates, or at least questions, such cornerstones of conventional society as Christianity, "my country right or wrong," the sanctity of marriage and premarital chastity, civil obedience, the accumulation of wealth, the right and even competence of parents, the schools, and the government to head and make decisions for everyone —in sum, the Establishment. This irreverence is probably what most arouses the ire and condemnation of the populace. Not only are the mainstream institutions and values violated, but their very legitimacy is challenged and this has heaped insult upon moral injury in the eyes of the rank and file. [*The values of the symbolic universe and the institutions of the institutional order are seen as arbitrary from the point of view of hip reality.*]

Sin, as the violation of sacred beliefs and practices, is nothing new and most of us have had at least a few shamefully delightful adventures somewhere along the way. But what is qualitatively new is that the very truth and moral validity of so many notions and practices, long cherished in our country, are being challenged. When caught by parents or authorities, youths are no longer hanging their heads in shame. Instead, they are asserting the rightness, at least for themselves, of what they're doing. And they are asking what right do their elders have to put them down? [*If conventional reality lacks legitimacy then its right to attempt control is also without legitimacy.*]

And not infrequently the irreverence takes a form which goes beyond this openly aggressive challenging. An increasing number of happeners have reached a level of disrespect so thoroughgoing that they don't even bother to "push their cause." Not only have they dropped their defensive posture, but their own assertiveness has become quiet, even urbane, in its detachment and indifference toward the "other morality." This withdrawal has aroused some of the greatest resentment and opposition since it is perhaps the gravest affront to an established ethic not to be taken seriously. To be defied is one thing; to be simply ignored and dismissed out of hand is something else. The spread of this more fullblown irreverence testifies to the fact that a good many happeners are managing to set up a life that is relatively independent of conventional society. [*If one lives completely in an alternate reality it is not necessary to defend it all the time. No complete reality takes any other reality seriously.*]

Another basic aspect of the hang-loose ethic is a diffuse and pervasive *humanism* which puts great store upon the value of human beings and human life. Adherents don't necessarily proclaim the rationality of men or their inherent "goodness," but they do claim that people are precious and that their full development is perhaps the most worth-while of all things.

Killing is a heinous violation of this ethos and so is any action which puts others down, except under extreme circumstances. The most approved method of defense and retaliation is to turn one's oppressors onto the good life they're condemning and to help them resolve hang-ups which prevent this from happening. If this fails, one may attempt to "blow their minds," to shock their preconceptions and prejudices in some way and hence force them to open their eyes, to re-evaluate, and hopefully to grow. The happeners refuse under most circumstances to employ the weapons of their adversaries because they feel that by so doing they would merely become like them. Instead, they try to trans-form their adversaries into fellows. The only really endorsed aggression is to try and force your enemies to become your friends. Only in extreme cases is putting down—the main strategy of the Establishment —even partly acceptable.

.   .   .

Another basic aspect of the hang-loose ethic is the pursuit of *experience* both as a thing in itself and as a means of learning and growing. The idea is that a great variety and depth of experience is beneficial and not at all harmful as long as you can handle it. This entails a heightened attention to the present ongoing moment and far less concern with the past or future. It also involves a mistrust of dogmas and principles which tend to obscure the richness of life. For this reason, they also often reject the categorizing and generalizing which is so rampant in our educational system.

.   .   .

This courting of raw experience is what gives many people the impression that those participating in the happenings are without any morals whatsoever; that they are selfishly pursuing swift gratification of their impulses. And it is true that the unabashed seeking of expe-riences will frequently lead the seeker to violate what other people consider proper. But such judgments are one-sided. Although they see that swingers are breaking standards, they entirely miss the point that swingers are following another, different set of standards; so that argu-ments between the camps are in reality debates between conflicting ideologies [*realities*].

As part and parcel of the importance placed on directly experiencing oneself and the world, we find that *spontaneity,* the ability to groove with whatever is currently happening, is a highly valued personal trait.

Spontaneity enables the person to give himself up to the existential here and now without dragging along poses and hangups and without playing investment games in hopes of possible future returns. The purest example of spontaneity is the jazz musician as he stands up and blows a cascade of swinging sounds.

Another facet of the hang-loose ethic is an untutored and unpretentious *tolerance.* Do whatever you want to as long as you don't step on other people while doing it.

．　　．　　．

The swingers, when you come down to it, are anarchists in the fullest sense. They chafe at virtually all restrictions because they see most every restriction that modern man has devised as a limitation on directions people can travel and grow. They feel that the irony of contemporary society is that the very restrictions necessary to curb an immature populace prevent that same populace from becoming mature enough to live without restrictions, just as a girdle weakens the muscles it supports.

．　　．　　．

But they are not pro-Communist either, although sympathetic toward revolutionaries in under-developed countries. They see Communism as at least as odious and repressive as the societies of the West and probably a good deal more so.

The hang-loose people are not joiners; indeed this is one of their defining attributes. They tend to shy away from any kind of conventional ideologies or fanaticisms, seeing them as unfree compulsions and obsessions rather than noble dedications. They regard those who are too intensely and doggedly involved in even such highly approved causes as integration and peace, a little askance and happeners will sometimes describe their own past involvements in these movements as something of a psychological hangup. [*They participate, of course, in institutions of their own creation, but the flavor is different because the entire value scheme is different.*]

The villains in the hang-loose view are people and social forces which put other people down and hang them up, which teach people to be stolid and dignified rather than swinging, self-righteous and moralistic rather than responsible, dutiful rather than devoted. Those who, for the sake of some ideology, will set fire to other people's kids; who, for the sake of some ideology, will slap their own children into becoming something less than they might have been. The villains are those who pass their own hangups onto those around them and thus propagate a sickness, "for your own good."

□ □ □

The extent to which a person participates in the hip reality and lives by the "hang-loose" ethic is obviously variable. Some may live conventional lives but experiment with drugs. Others may believe in sexual freedom but accept the constraints of the work-a-day world. Still others may live entirely within a hip community, rejecting planning, punctuality, career orientation, the rationality of convention reality, concern for the future, and any emphasis on success. They may be involved in communal families rejecting all of the institutions of marriage. They may think of private property as a form of theft. They may think of drugs as recreation, institution, or a method for regulating their attitude toward life—taking whatever, to go a little bit up, a little bit down, a little to the right, a little to the left, as the need or desire arises. They may reject the conventional concept of "intelligence" as measured by "IQ" tests and take pride that their scores have dropped. They may read only underground newspapers, listen only to underground radio, work only at hip occupations, or treat straight occupations in a highly irreverent way—like the hip postman who could deliver a day's mail in two hours because he split his job up with all the members of his commune. He may see astrology or the I-Ching as a useful way of ordering his life, rather than taking vocational aptitude tests for the same purpose. In short, the hip reality has all the accoutrements of any social reality, a set of assumptions about the world, and a society in which they are enacted and taken as real.

Since the boundaries of hip reality are not tightly drawn a person may move part way in and then return to conventionality. The further they move in, however, the more difficult becomes a return. In discussing this process with a number of hip people I get the feeling that few have become completely hip and then returned. Some may have stopped using drugs, others may have taken over their parents' business, but aside from these changes they have retained their identification with the reality. It is too soon to say whether this perception will continue to be valid, but it appears now more likely for a person to go from being conventional to being hip than vice versa.

Our basic question, and the question of all conversion is: what is the process of giving up an entire reality to take up another? What causes a young person, or, more critically because of the greater distance, an older person who has been socialized by conventional society, to reject its most basic values for others? From the point of view of conventional reality every conversion points to a failure of socialization—the individual was not closely enough tied to the reality to keep him from rejecting it. Unsuccessful socialization may occur when primary socialization is handled by significant others, who themselves hold to discrepant realities leaving the child confused—parents, peer groups, schools, nurses—anyone who teaches the child. Since hip reality is already established, unsuccessful socialization into conventional reality may be matched by successful socialization into the hip reality. A young person who finds rejection or indifference from parents and school, for almost any reason, may find acceptance within the hip reality. An older person whose socialization was successful is protected against the seduction of another reality, but even here the protection may break down under certain circumstances.

Every reality that hopes to convert people has "lines" into the other reality—beneficial institutions from one reality that can be taken up by a person functioning in another without causing him much trepidation. The worlds of occult have astrology that conventional people often read in their newspapers; these can form a bond to the world of the occult reality. The Book of Revelations in the Bible can also be used as a common talking point with Christians. The Communist Party used to seek common causes and united fronts to gain access to conventional people. Christian missionaries may build and staff schools or hospitals in primitive villages to lure the natives into the fold. Hip reality has many lines into the conventional world: the popularity of various forms of rock music; psychedelic art, which has become a staple in advertising and fashion; freer sexuality, which brings people into contact with one another; entire sections of towns full of "head" shops; radio stations in some cities; underground newspapers sold on the streets; and, of course, the expanding use of drugs.

Probably *the* most important element in any conversion is strong emotional attachment to someone in the new reality. Emotional attachments only happen among people who can meet one another, thus the importance of the lines into the conventional world. This strong attachment is very similar to the emotional attachment that leads a child through primary socialization; it is someone or some group that he finds rewarding and seeks to be like.

A second necessary element in conversion is that there be a large enough group living within the reality to make it work. The group must have enough interlocking institutions and legitimations, enough control over territory, sexuality and labor so that a person *can* live within the new reality. This may be accomplished by withdrawing to a sectarian retreat if the group is small, or by other forms of physical or psychological isolation if the group is larger. In other words, a reality must have a society of sorts, its own institutional order that is complete enough so that a person can migrate to it from conventional reality.

The potential convert is introduced to this society, has it explained to him, is guided into it, by the significant others whom he likes or loves, who met him through one of the lines to the conventional world. Not all alternate realities are equally successful in converting new believers. At one extreme is the Doomsday cult studied by John Lofland,[1] which was terribly unsuccessful in converting new adherents for a variety of reasons. Hip reality is probably at the other extreme: wildly successful.

An older person who eventually becomes part of hip reality probably had some dissatisfactions with his conventional life. His marriage may have broken down, his job may have been tedious, he may have gotten so far into debt and possessions that he is revolted or desperate. It is probably also likely that he enjoyed at least some of the things younger people did, or that he had some contact with younger people as friends. In other words he is very unlikely to convert if he is living entirely in the middle-aged world—he simply has no contacts and no way to develop them. A younger person may have moved into contact with hip reality through his peer and friendship groups while participating in any of the things that hip people do.

Forming an emotional bond is fairly easy in the open hip world. The potential convert, who usually doesn't think of himself as this, meets a boy, girl, or group that he enjoys being with. His being with them becomes something of a routine. Since this person or group lives within the new reality the potential convert is gradually introduced to new values, new ideas, new activities as he interacts with them. If he has no similar strong attachment to a person or group living in conventional reality his interaction may come to be quite intense within the new reality. This process may be gradual or sudden, making one or two friends and seeing them more and more often, or total immersion by running away from home. The individual reaches a point where he can see that the new reality might fit him.

In religious conversions a great deal is made of the 'conversion experience" where the individual suddenly finds God, or the second Christ, or whatever. But conversion experiences soon disappear if the individual cannot begin living them. Year after year revivals tour the country, and year after year the same people come forward to accept Christ on Wednesday only to "backslide" Saturday night. Christ may have been within them but they went back to living in their same old community. Since hip reality is still so loose there is not one point at which a blinding flash of light marks a conversion. There are, however, a number of conversion markers that a person might display. One revolves around the clothes that the convert wears. When he appears

---

[1] John Lofland, *Doomsday Cult: A Study of Conversion, Proselytization and Maintenance of Faith* (Englewood Cliffs, N.J.: Prentice-Hall, Inc., 1966).

in public in hip clothes he is stating a new identity and asking to be treated differently. When he keeps on growing his hair or beard after the "final ultimatum" of his parents, principal, or employer, he is asserting his new identity. When he buys his first lid of marijuana so that he can repay those who have turned him on he is signaling a change in his subjective reality. When he or she can manage a sexual encounter with another person without feeling compelled to protest undying love and suggest marriage, there has been a change.

One of the elements of conversion experience is being able to see the world in a new way, and to a certain extent the first marijuana high that a person experiences can perform this function. As noted previously, marijuana is almost always smoked in a group context, in a small circle of friends, very often the group that guides the convert into the new reality. He may have smoked and conversed with the group several times, each time building up knowledge and questions about the hip reality, and when he finally does feel the high the group will explain it to him. Feeling the high is also a validation of the other things they have told him. He will probably enjoy it, so he finds it beneficial in itself. As he continues to converse and feel his own reactions he suddenly feels that he really understands what the people around him are saying—for the first time. Whether or not the experience he has with his high turns out to be a conversion experience depends largely upon what the group does, how they interpret it, what they connect it with. If they suggest that it is a gas to see "Yellow Submarine" high and take him out to watch it he may discover a whole new world of visual perceptions. If they listen to music he may "really" hear it for the first time. If the group sits around silently, each involved in his own thoughts, the convert may not get much out of it. It is because of the alteration in perceptions taking place within the context of hip reality that the first few marijuana highs may constitute something *like* a religious "conversion experience."

To mark one's entrance into the hip world in any of the ways mentioned previously, even to have a sudden flash when high, may be necessary for converting to hip reality, but it is far from sufficient. Many people have these experiences, run into something or some group they don't find rewarding, or that they find threatening, and go back to conventionality little the worse for wear. In order to become a convert a person must live the reality; it has to become his world. He must be able to be involved in a community of hip people in such a way that its values and institutions become his.

This new hip world must gradually displace all other worlds he lives in, especially the world of conventionality from which he is migrating. At first he and his hip friends may be together only when he is able to take time from his job, home, wife, school, tavern. As he becomes more involved he spends more and more time in the hip world replacing one by one the institutional involvements he has with the conventional world. If he was not finding much reward in the conventional world to begin with he may already be alienated from a number of institutions. He or she may leave home, parents, or spouse, and move into the hip community either as friend, lover, temporary resident in a crash pad, or member of a communal family. This move breaks many of the informal and formal controls that legitimate institutions had over him, and frees him for further participation in the hip world. Hip people rarely "date" one another. They drop over, run into each other, go for walks in the park, meet each other at rock dances or on the street. The pattern of interaction is much more fluid, because it presupposes that the individual does not have many institutionalized arrangements for his time. He may become involved in the projects his friends are working on, making things to sell, dealing drugs, organizing or attending happenings. He may find a job in a "head shop" or as an assistant in a light show. He might even retain his job in the conventional world because it is expedient, but he will probably modify his motivation for having it. Instead of working to get ahead, to buy a house, to succeed, he is working to make money to travel, to contribute to his commune, to buy drugs. Given the explosive expansion of the drug market in the sixties, a great many new converts found they could make enough money to live on—$60 to $100 a month—by doing small-scale dealing to their straighter friends. The hip community's weakest institutions are in the area of labor, getting sustenance from the environment. It can be done, but nowhere as easily as in the conventional world.

The hip convert finds himself increasingly segregated from contact with the straight world. Because he may be carrying drugs, or because he may be high much of the time, he tends to avoid taxing dealings with conventional institutions. Because his hair is long and he is not working or going to school he may not visit home much. Because his clothes are unconventional he may avoid or be excluded from many restaurants. He comes to define the conventional world as a drag, a place where one occasionally has to go to get something but at the risk of bodily harm and psychic damage. He not only develops these attitudes on his own but picks them up from others in his group. Importantly, he comes to think of the police as the *last* people to call when in need of help, and his attitudes toward the police come to resemble those of Blacks and other ghetto residents. Most people who have converted to being hip started out with fairly positive attitudes toward the police, reflections of their primarily middle-class background. But the more obviously hip a person becomes, the more the police pay attention. Time after time I have seen attitudes toward the police do a flip-flop after the individual has been rudely spread-eagled against the wall and searched; ticketed and searched for jay-walking; stopped and searched for minor vehicle defects; not to mention being clubbed, tear-gassed, or shot. As a friend of mine in Berkeley commented, "I'm afraid to go out at night. The streets are unsafe. They are full of police." Hip reality is, of course, strengthened by this segregation from conventional reality no matter what its source.

People living in the hip reality see relations with the conventional world as dangerous. Of particular danger to the reality as a whole, and to the convert's subjective reality, are relationships with the old significant others from the conventional world. People who knew the convert in childhood are not likely to take his new reality seriously. They say, "my, you look filthy, why don't you cut your hair?" They invoke old family institutions and aspirations: "come with us on the picnic," "we so wanted you to finish college." To walk into the family home with everything in its place, with thousands of memories, with hundreds of familiar institutions, with the reality left behind radiating from every familiar object and person, is a frontal blow to the convert's new reality. In addition to memories and admonitions there may also be temptations. "I'll hand over the family business to you if you'll come back to work in it long enough to get to know the ropes." "George Brown was asking about you yesterday, he needs somebody in his public relations department and he thought you might like to try the job." "I'll change my will if you'll come home and stop doing those things." "Why don't you move into this room in the basement, you can come and go as you like, have your own phone, but we'd just like you to live at home."

Other territories in the conventional world may be dangerous because there is someone there who is in love with the convert and would like to marry him and of course get a house, and of course get a job, and of course get a haircut, and of course stop using drugs, and of course entertain the boss at dinner, and of course join the golf club. Although hip reality is not old enough, nor are its members, to tell what inducements will eventually cause reconversions, none of the ones mentioned seem to be making much headway at the moment.

"The visit home" is often the occasion for strategic briefing of the convert by his friends. They point out the dangers, mock the temptations, provide him with excuses for leaving home, and tell him how glad they'll be to see him back. Each of these procedures immunizes the convert's sense of self-esteem against the guilt-producing mechanisms of parents. Should the convert show signs of being tempted, his friends may treat him to a full-scale analysis of the situation and himself from the point of view of hip reality. This therapeutic analysis provides much the same sort of social control for hip reality that the heart-to-heart talk and visit to the priest or psychiatrist does for conventional reality. All realities provide therapy to induce potential migrants to return to the fold, but the therapy provided for a convert in a somewhat marginal reality when he may be quite tempted by conventional reality is extremely intense.

The primary force maintaining subjective reality is the information and affirmation both contained and understood in conversations. Not only what is said, but what is not said affirms the reality of everyday life shared by the group. When the convert moves from conventional reality to hip reality his partners in conversation change, the significant topics of conversation change, even the language itself changes. Though occasionally the same event might be discussed, each discussion will affirm its own reality, and the "correct" subjective reality for the respective participants. Thus, in conventional reality one might "talk about the sit-in at the college," while in hip reality one "raps about the pig administrators." In conventional reality it's a "Negro riot," in hip it's "urban guerrilla warfare." In conventional, drugs are an "escape from reality," in hip they are "part of reality." In conventional it's "the government, the schools, business, the club, the police, liberals and conservatives, law and order, morality, propriety, freedom, justice, investment, marriage, home ownership, and chastity," in hip it's "the system." In conventional it's "filthy commie degenerates," or "alienated youth we've failed," in hip it's "light shows and sunsets, dancing and friends, love and help, rip-offs and bummers, his thing and our thing, the way it is." Each reality makes some distinctions, overlooks others, values some things, rejects others. Each reality contains a total perspective on the world built into the language used in everyday conversations. To use either language comfortably implies that one's view of the world fits the distinctions made in the conversation. Thus conversations with significant others within a reality tend to support and elaborate the subjective reality and sense of identity of the participant. Speaking fluently the languages of two realities in conflict with one another signals a corresponding split in the speaker's subjective realities.

When a person changes realities he acquires a problem in biographical legitimation. His dilemma is simple: in his old reality many of his actions were bad; according to his new reality, perhaps his entire life style was bad. The dilemma is actually more complex if he changes within the same symbolic universe from one subreality to another; he cannot totally reject his past and he must selectively reinterpret it, give more emphasis to some events and less to others. When he converts from one reality to another he can reject his entire past as being inspired by ignorance of the truth, or the evil system. If the truth could be found between realities I suspect that not every religious convert led such a life of sin before he found the truth, and many hip people probably enjoyed some aspects of the system.

For converts to hip reality their conventional past is a matter of little discussion. A fairly universal way of thinking about it was expressed by Bob Dylan: "I was so much older then, I'm younger than that now." Since part of the value structure of hip reality is an orientation to an unstructured present there does not seem to be much motivation for providing biographical legitimations for the conversion process. A hip person wishes to be taken for what he concretely *is* now, and how he got there and where he might be going are generally considered to be slightly improper questions indicative of conventional thinking. That this disinterest in the maintenance of a logical biography is not shared by most other converts from one reality to another is illustrated by the central role given it by communist and religious converts.

What is generated in hip reality, however, is a perspective on the system and the significant others formerly around the convert. The system and the people in it are generally viewed as unfree, routine, dull, and curiously locked into conventional perspectives. It is not so much that there is evil within the system, though there is that too, but rather that there is a seemingly mindless repetition of ritual activity that seems to have little point or effect. The actors are zombies playing out their roles of teacher, parent, businessman, official, moving by rules and regulations and closed to human vision. This collection of sleepwalkers sometimes gets things done but more often leaves irrational loose ends that create chaos and impede their own efforts. This perspective on conventional reality is well summed up by a little sign that has been appearing in hip territory:

> **THE SYSTEM
> DOESN'T WORK**

When hip and conventional people come into contact they are speaking their separate languages, and though they might understand one another's words there is little convergence on meanings. Since neither understands the "sense" of what the other is saying no dialogue takes place. It is always interesting to watch two people each construct an argument that seems totally convincing to themselves, then find that the other is not only not convinced but didn't even understand it. The dialogue becomes transformed into statements of position. After the statement of positions there can be a mutual withdrawal in recognition of the stalemate, recourse to shouting or to physical violence.

These parallel monologues come to no resolution between strangers. The convert's old significant others, however, can reject his monologue as "crazy talk" and assert their rights and his obligations within the structure of the reality they once shared. Prophets rarely sway those who can remember them "back when . . ."

I have tried to illustrate the mechanisms involved in converting from one reality to another by examining the process of becoming hip. As I indicated, the conversion from conventional to hip reality involves more subjective alterations than changes between subrealities within the same symbolic universe, and fewer changes than conversion to a totally alien reality and universe. As a consequence there are elements in this conversion process that differ from the more and less extreme processes. One of the most important of these differences is the extent to which "conversion" is a consciously organized and staffed operation. Hip people are not *assigned* the task of making friends and converting them; rather they fall into the job. Similarly potential converts do not see it as a hard road requiring torturous self-examination; they too fall into the process.

When one symbolic universe or reality sets out to consciously convert those who believe in another the process of conversion itself becomes institutionalized, rationalized, funded, and administered. Such an organized conversion process needs a steady input of potential converts, and it often does not await their seeking it out. Coercion by one means or another may be used to bring the potential converts into the process, rejection of the old reality may have to be stimulated by artificial means, the potential convert may have to be forcibly kept in the "therapeutic" milieu, a paid interrogator or persuader may take the place of the friend or lover.

In the following adaptation Jerome Frank summarizes the elements of the process of organized conversion. His focus is somewhat broader than ours has been to this point because he includes the "therapeutic" procedures used to revitalize faith in an old reality as well as the procedures used for converting a person to an alternate reality. His focus is logical since an essentially similar procedure is used in both cases and it is only our focus on alternating realities which has inhibited discussion of the psychiatric procedures used to attempt to revitalize faith in conventional reality.

31
PERSUASION AND HEALING
A Comparative Study of Psychotherapy

JEROME D. FRANK

As thought reform, revivalist religion, miracle cures, and religious healing in primitive societies have important common features that will be
found to bear on psychotherapy, a brief recapitulation of these characteristics may be in order at this point. Since the English language lacks
a common word for invalid, penitent, and prisoner on the one hand
and shaman, evangelist, and interrogator on the other, the first categories will be referred to as sufferers and the second as persuaders.
The sufferer's distress has a large emotional component, produced by
environmental or bodily stresses, internal conflicts and confusion, and
a sense of estrangement or isolation from his usual sources of group
support. He tends to be fearful and despairing and to be hungry for
supportive human contacts. [*The sufferer is not receiving the benefits
of his symbolic universe, a sense of identity and certainty in his actions.*]
    The persuader and his group represent a comprehensive and perva-
sive world view, which incorporates supremely powerful suprapersonal
forces [*alternate symbolic universe*].
    That communism identifies these forces with the Party, while reli-
gions regard them as supernatural is relatively unimportant for the
purpose of this discussion. The world view is infallible and cannot be
shaken by the sufferer's failure to change or improve. [*The symbolic
universe is believed to be ultimately legitimate; it is the sufferer who
needs changing.*] The suprapersonal powers are contingently benevo-
lent in that the sufferer may succeed in obtaining their favor if he
shows the right attitude. In return for submitting himself completely to
them he is offered the hope of surcease from suffering, resolution of
conflicts, absolution of guilt, and warm acceptance, or re-acceptance,
by the group. The persuader is the point of interaction between the
sufferer, his immediate group, and the suprapersonal powers. He guides
the group's activities and embodies, transmits, interprets, and to some
extent controls the suprapersonal forces. [*The persuader makes the universe plausible for the person he wishes to "rescue." He and the
group enact the reality to make it real for the sufferer.*] As a result the
sufferer perceives him as possessing power over his welfare.

The means by which changes in the sufferer are brought about include a particular type of relationship and some sort of systematic activity or ritual. The essence of the relationship is that the persuader invests great effort to bring about changes in the sufferer's bodily state or attitudes that he regards as beneficial. The systematic activity characteristically involves means of emotional arousal, often to the point of exhaustion. This may be highly unpleasant, but it occurs in a context of hope and potential support from the persuader and group.

The activity requires the participation of the sufferer, persuader, and group and frequently is highly repetitive. The sufferer may be required to review his past life in more or less detail, with emphasis on occasions when he may have fallen short of the behavior required by the world view, thus mobilizing guilt, which can only be expiated by confession and penance. This serves to detach him from his former patterns of behavior and social intercourse and facilitates his acceptance by the group representing the ideology to which he becomes converted.

If the process succeeds, the sufferer experiences a sense of relief, peace, and often joy. His sense of identity is restored and his feeling of self-worth enhanced. His confusion and conflicts have diminished or been resolved. He is clear about himself and his world view and feels himself to be in harmony with his old group, or with a new one representing the new world view, and with the universe. Life regains its meaning or becomes more meaningful. He is able to function effectively again as a significant member of a group which, by its acceptance, helps to consolidate the changes he has undergone. [*His subjective reality becomes congruent with the objective reality of the group.*]

□ □ □

This discussion of the organized conversion process completes our examination of the ways in which people come to change realities. The realities which people convert are not all of the same extensiveness; some have quite limited social substruction, while others dominate complete societies. Some realities must exist within others, while others are isolated and independent. In the next chapter we will discuss the difference these factors make for the individual and for the success of the alternate reality.

□ □ □

□ □ □

Flying saucerians live in two realities at once. In their daily round of activities they rely upon the scientific laws of physics; they carry out normal transactions in legitimate institutions relying upon conventional reality. When they meet together the laws of gravity and inertia dissolve, the dead speak, auras glow, and Jesus Christ becomes a saucer pilot. Flying saucerians have a part-time alternate reality. Their everyday lives are enlivened by the possibility of interpreting a seemingly commonplace event as the workings of the space brothers, and in their alternate reality the space brothers affect their lives, and all of our lives. ·

Over a period of several years I attended a great many meetings of a flying saucer club, observing and recording what went on, and talking with the members. Their alternate reality derives its ultimate legitimacy from the space brothers, a superrace whose visible manifestation is the flying saucers that they pilot. Their conception of the universe is basically a mythology of science. Prometheus brought fire to

twelve

OF SAUCERS
AND CHRISTIANS

the Greeks, the space brothers will bring peace, the beginning of the "new age," and a society in which the people who understand the message of the saucers will be the elect.

Flying saucers are a central symbol of the new-age reality, but not the only symbol. Saucers are useful; they are "unexplained" by science, and many people believe in them. Not all the groups that have formed around flying saucers are new-age groups. Some people who study flying saucers call them Unidentified Flying Objects, and think they *may* come from other planets. New-age people consider them "identified" flying objects, and both interplanetary and spiritual. People who fall into neither of these categories believe in flying saucers because they have seen something in the sky or have read something about them.

The name *flying saucer'* was coined by Kenneth Arnold in June 1947, to identify something he had seen while flying his airplane near Mount Rainier. The gleaming disks appeared to him to be twenty or twenty-five miles away, about the size of a cargo plane, and moving at 1,200 miles an hour, which was half again faster than any man had flown at that time. Arnold's observation was widely and skeptically reviewed in the press. This attention served as a catalyst for many people to start seeing and reporting things in the sky. Many physical phenomena can cause lights to appear in the sky. These were interpreted, after Arnold's report, as flying saucers.

The U.S. Army Air Force began an inquiry that it soon closed on July 3, 1947, citing possible meteorological explanations for the saucers, and denying that they were some new kind of missile. Three days later there had been so many sightings from all over the United States that a new inquiry was ordered. For nine days in July 1947, flying saucers were a sensation. The *New York Times* had front-page articles on saucers for four of these nine days, a good indication of their presumed importance.

Sightings of saucers continued to be reported at a rate of one to two hundred a year through 1951. In May 1950, the American Institute of Public Opinion asked on its regular poll, "What do you think these flying saucers are?" of a national sample of Americans. Ninety-four percent of the respondents claimed to have heard of saucers, a demonstration that the name was widely diffused, and people had a number of speculations about their nature. A third answered that they didn't know what they were, a fifth thought they were some military device, one out of twenty thought they might have come from another planet, the rest gave various answers. In 1950 there was a high degree of

---

[1] The books and articles upon which this chapter is based are listed in the bibliographies on flying saucers and the Christian Karen.

public awareness, but no predominant orientation. The Government asserted, in 1951, that the reliable sightings were 100-foot plastic balloons used in cosmic ray research.

On April 7, 1952, *Life* magazine printed an article that suggested that the saucers came from other planets. At the time there were "war jitters" over the Korean War. It was also the beginning of the "silly season" for the newspapers, the early summer period when there seems to be little "real" news and almost any hoax will get a wide play. Whether stimulated by *Life,* the war, the silly season, or more flying saucers, saucer sightings began to multiply daily. By the end of 1952 over 1,500 sightings had been reported. Scientists did not provide a plausible explanation, but a number of other people tried.

During 1953 and 1954 authors of ten different books claimed to have experienced personal contact with the pilots of flying saucers, and in some cases had been given rides in the saucers. These books were widely read, particularly by people previously interested in the occult, and flying saucers became a central and unifying symbol connected with many occult beliefs. The authors of these books may be looked upon as the innovating theoreticians, the prophets, of the new-age reality. They have a new understanding of the cosmos that they spread.

Through various published sources and personal interviews I have attempted to ascertain the background of the people who claimed to have contacted men from space. Frequently contactees, as they are called, use titles such as "Doctor," "Reverend," and "Professor." I was unable to find that any of them had graduated from college, with the exception of one from an unaccredited Bible college. I found a few had graduated from high school, and the majority had finished grade school and perhaps a year or two of high school. The titles and degrees they use are either self-granted, or granted by new-age institutions run by others within the reality.

The contactees' occupations were congruent with their education. One was an electrician, another a painter and decorator, another held a "minor technical job," another ran an emergency airport in the desert, another was a night watchman, and yet another was an evangelist.

Depending on which contactee one reads or talks with, a variable picture of the space brothers emerges. On the average the space brothers look human, though they are morally and scientifically advanced beyond earthmen, and they have some superhuman attributes. They live on Saturn, Mars, and Venus in an earthlike but utopian civilization. Both the men and the women wear long hair and flowing robes in some accounts, and short hair and snappy uniforms in other accounts. Their space ships (flying saucers) run on gravity or magnetism. Their purpose in coming to earth and contacting the people they did was to warn the men of earth about the dangers of nuclear war, and the dangers of technology outrunning social science. They also brought a "new" rule for moral conduct, roughly "do unto others as you would have them do unto you." Among the saucer pilots are various "ascended masters" from earth, men who had graduated into the heavenly hierarchy or who had come from other planets to live among men and teach them. Jesus Christ, who came from either Venus or Saturn (the point is in dispute), was one of the more famous ascended masters, and is still piloting his saucer.

Since flying saucers are not ordinary material devices they can not only travel in space but also through various levels of the spirit world, astral levels as they are called. In some accounts the spirits of the dead can talk to the still living through flying saucers moving on their astral level. The flying saucer gradually came to unite many different mysteries as the revelation progressively unfolded: mysterious happenings in the sky, the promise of a moral civilization, a life after death, and a paradise on earth, if men would only follow the message.

This revelation is broad enough to legitimate many activities. Since the space brothers often commented on earthly institutions, praising some, condemning others, an incipient legitimation for an entire institutional order was also created.

But very few new-age institutions have arisen, and those that have are mostly devoted to spreading the word rather than institutionalizing new-age realities in labor, sex, territory, or communications. As a result, no matter how strongly one believes in the new-age reality it is necessary to participate in the conventional institutional order for the necessities of life. New-age people are aware of the discrepancy between their reality and the reality of those they have to deal with in mundane affairs, and they generally adopt a policy of silence. They feel that "unbelievers" are inclined to scoff and are very difficult to enlighten, so in most cases they remain quiet rather than pressing their point.

A fairly usual interaction between a new-age individual and a conventional individual involves the opening of a few conversational possibilities as tentative lines. The new-age person might drop some reference to saucers, to space people, or to some occult wisdom into the conversation. If the other person scoffs they generally do not pursue the matter further. If the other person makes polite but noncommittal noises they may follow up by explaining more about what they first mentioned or by suggesting another occult line of conversation. This is still tentative, and until they are fairly convinced that they are speaking with an "open-minded" person they tend not to press their points. Should they encounter a sympathetic listener who encourages them to continue and nods his assent, they will begin speaking from and thinking within new-age reality. All realities must be protected from the intrusion of other realities, all realities are precarious. This must be particularly true for a reality generated within a limited social circle, a reality without a functioning institutional order, which must exist surrounded by a contradictory reality. The social problem of maintaining such a fragile "deviant" (from the conventional point of view) reality is ever present and requires immense effort and care. From their experience with disbelievers new-age people have learned caution. Time after time they go through a cycle that starts with an increasing confidence in their message, the perception of a sympathetic outside audience, an explanation of their reality to this audience, and dejection and confusion when the message is not understood, rudely or patronizingly received, or cognitively rejected. The maintenance of faith requires immersion in their own reality and isolation from conventional reality.

The reality maintaining environments are very few. Sometimes new-age people meet their other new-age friends and spend a few hours in conversation in the jointly understood world of assumptions that they share. Mostly, however, reality maintenance goes on within meetings of new-age groups. There are a number of groups that could be considered to be part of the new-age reality. Each group has a somewhat distinct central focus, but there is a great deal of overlap. Thus one group might be primarily interested in astrology, another in magical healing, another in occult knowledge, another in occult religion, another in spiritualism, and another in flying saucers. Of all these groups the most central to new-age reality is the flying saucer group, because all of the other groups are welcome within it. In many ways the development of a cohesive new-age reality depended upon the emergence of flying saucer groups and their open door policy. Although many of the new-age groups have been in existence far longer than flying saucer clubs, they each tended to be isolated from one another. An individual might join one such group, remain for a time and go on to another group to learn what they had to say, thus picking up several distinct parts of the new-age reality, but as separate and distinct areas of knowledge. The flying saucer clubs welcomed speakers from all of these groups, and welcomed people to attend their meetings. As a result the common stock of knowledge grew and became more varied. Ideas that had been separate began to be linked together. There had been, for example, groups that were interested in the lost continent of Mu, that began to speak of flying saucers as the Lemurians' mode of interplanetary travel. Likewise, groups interested in the spiritual world began to see flying saucers as a partially spiritual phenomenon. Through such joinings of traditions and ideas, a complex set of beliefs began to be generated that encompassed many previously isolated traditions. While this complex set of beliefs does not logically integrate all of the different traditions, it forms a centralizing focus and legitimation for new-age reality.

The flying saucer clubs grew out of the first wave of books claiming contact with the space brothers. The particular club I joined and attended for several years was organized to discuss these books. The organizer had been a member of a number of religious and occult groups for many years, and she invited the friends she had made in these groups to come to her new club. Her club soon affiliated with a growing chain of similar clubs organized by one of the original contactees. Almost from the beginning there were discussions about space people in the Bible, and other extensions of the flying saucer story. As a matter of fact there is only a certain and limited amount of "meat" in the stories of contacts with the flying saucers. Each group was really only interested in hearing each contactee's story once, and if he wished to be invited back again he would have to have something different to say. The stories that were told of the space brothers' civilization, way of life, and beliefs often linked them up with other occult happenings and traditions, which opened a natural avenue of approach to these other traditions. For example, the fact that A-lan, the space man who contacted the founder of the chain of clubs, said that the space brothers originally came from Lemuria, the civilization of the lost continent of Mu, provided the saucer clubs with a natural reason to invite a guest from one of the groups that specialized in Lemurian "history."

A brief list of some of the ideas that have been presented in flying saucer clubs and conventions can give some idea of the areas of new-age beliefs. The club I studied defined itself as open to any ideas that would help to make a better world, and in fact its boundaries were quite wide. In all the meetings I attended, the only speaker who was given a hard time was a man who claimed to have seen a flying saucer close up, but who rejected the idea that anyone had experienced actual contact with space people. This, of course, is fundamental heresy, and it was treated as such. With this exception the clubs seemed to follow their creed: ". . . to examine all things and subsequently to cling to that which is good. Here follows a collection of some of the ideas presented in one way or another to flying saucer clubs that were part of the chain.

The Lemurian Fellowship produced a newsletter in which they discussed various elements of Lemurian civilization and its applicability to the new age. This knowledge had been kept secret by a small band of survivors of the sinking of Mu in the Pacific 26,000 years ago. The Lemurian Fellowship offered a course of instruction in this knowledge that was fairly extensive, and they often had their members attending flying saucer club meetings, and copies of their literature around.

A somewhat mysterious group called White Star, in southern California, regularly produces and mails to new-age people on its mailing list instructions on self-preparation for the Second Coming of true Christ consciousness. For a time these instructions appeared as a set of commands from a bureaucratic office in the heavenly hierarchy. Apparently a work of complete dedication to the ideals is involved; I have been on their mailing list for seven years and they have never asked for a donation, though they have hinted that money for postage would be useful.

On many occasions astrologers come to flying saucer meetings; occasionally they speak on the astrological significance of world happenings. Most of the members of the club I studied seemed to be well versed in astrology; I suspect it is the major "science" of new-age reality.

The Rosicrucians, who claim long historical roots, often come to saucer club meetings to discuss their course of studies. A number of saucer club members either have been Rosicrucians or are currently following their course. They offer studies in the Development of Personal Magnetism, the Mysteries of Time and Space, and the Human Aura and its Vibratory Effect, among others. Much of Rosicrucian knowledge is a part of the taken-for-granted assumptions of new-age reality.

A number of exotic religions claim followers in the saucer clubs, and representatives often attend club meetings to seek out new members. The ones I noted included Theosophy, Science of Mind, Unity, Yoga, Christian Yoga, Baha'i, and the Doomsday Cult studied by Lofland.

A major belief in new-age reality is in "free energy." "Free energy" is the leftover energy that a perpetual motion machine produces in excess of that required for its own operation. A great many of the visions of the future that are shared in new-age reality depend upon free energy for the motive power to free man from the drudgery of work and from the enslavement of the money system. One of the points of hostile contact with conventional reality comes from the assumption that international cartels know of and are suppressing "free energy" machines to protect their profits.

New-age reality has its own systems of mental and physical healing. Psychic suffering is diagnosed by reading the "aura" or glow surrounding the human body. In certain states of depression the aura is very pale, and good health manifests itself in a shining gold or silver aura. A form of psychoanalysis is provided by readings of the individual's "akashic record," which is the imprint of the individual's mind through all of its previous incarnations on the universal mind. Knowing his history through all of his incarnations helps the individual to guide his life in his present incarnation.

Physical disease also has its own therapeutic procedures. Rejuvenation of the body may be obtained by a walk through a healing temple constructed without a single piece of metal. Reductions of age of ten to twenty years can be expected when one's magnetism has been realigned by such a walk. Diseases such as cancer are treated by a complex system of colored lights, but the therapeutic legitimation of this practice is not known to me.

The healing professions are another area of conflict with conventional reality, and a great deal of distaste is reserved for organized medicine, which calls new-age procedures "quackery," and for the psychiatric ideology of the community mental health movement, which is seen as a major weapon of conventional reality to be used against the new-age followers. The idea that they may be carted off to a hospital and kept there against their will until they accept conventional reality is quite frightening and explains much of their opposition to the community mental health programs that allow for speedy commitment.

Another aspect of new-age reality involves close attention to the foods taken into the body. Health foods, vegetarian diets, organically grown foods without poisonous pesticides, are seen as being necessary to maintain the body and mind in top condition.

No particular set of political ideas predominates in new-age reality, though there is generalized hostility toward the money system, banks, Communism, organized medicine, organized religion, and "bad people." New-age people are generally in support of peace, guaranteed incomes, and lower taxes. A number of different political philosophies have been presented at one time or another by people attempting to gain followers. It has been my observation that these were generally met with polite but massive disinterest. In the new age, government will follow the plans of the ascended masters and space brothers and the mundane politics of today are more of a distraction than a way to further changes. As the brothers said, "Your politics and your money are the darkest blot upon your earth."

I have really only touched upon the complexities of new-age reality, and I have had to omit many aspects that I heard about at one time or another but was unable to follow up. New-age reality is very complex, and not very systematized. As with any reality, the individual's objective reality is made up of certain parts that he has experienced and heard of, not the totality of the elements in the reality.

Just as hip reality is centered on the young, new-age reality is centered on the old. In the course of twelve meetings, both club meetings and meetings to hear contactees and healers, I kept a record of the attendance by age and sex. By my observation 4.5 percent of the audience were men under 30, 3 percent were women under 30, 8.5 percent were men between 30 and 50, 7.8 percent were women between 30 and 50, 14.2 percent were men over fifty, and 62 percent of the average audience were women over 50 years old. At every meeting an absolute majority of the audience was composed of women over 50 years old.

Their average age appears to be about 65. Clearly new-age reality has a special appeal for older women.

Most of the members seem to be widowed or single, some few couples come to meetings, and some are married to nonbelievers. The latter particularly must have a hard time maintaining their subjective reality.

The socioeconomic status of the members appears to be low. Many are living on Social Security, and from appearances most came from working-class families.

The formal education of the members is very limited. I met a number of ladies who had not finished grammar school. A high school graduate was rare. As a consequence they did not have the conceptual tools to build up "knowledge" as we think of it in conventional reality, systematizing, ordering, comparing, and analyzing what they had read. But they built up knowledge in new-age reality, because they read, studied, and attended lectures constantly. It is difficult to convey the way in which new-age knowledge is built up, but I suppose that the idea of examining all things and clinging to the good can convey part of it. From the perspective of conventional reality their knowledge seems disorganized, fragmented, and contradictory, but they don't use the same rules.

It seems to me that a person who is old, female, alone in the world, poor, and uneducated has very little to gain from believing in conventional reality. She is defined as useless, incompetent, and essentially worthless. She has few tools to cope with the complexities of twentieth-century urban life. New-age reality offers her an alternative way of putting the world together, a way which gives her hope, self-esteem, and a feeling of being worthwhile. New-age reality is a precarious vision, surrounded as it is by conventional reality, unsupported by new-age institutions, but a precarious vision may be better than none at all.

A part-time reality may solve the specific problems of the group that carries it but it is unlikely to become a predominant reality for a society. There simply must be a network of institutions that function within the values to provide support at all points in the daily round of activities for the reality to be complete.

The development of a complete, full-time reality that offers a basic challenge to the predominant reality of a society is often a long-term affair. In the following section I will explore the history of the establishment of such a "deviant" reality in Burma.

CHRISTIANITY AS AN ALTERNATE REALITY

Christianity established itself in Burma as an alternate reality to the Buddhist-Burmese reality by converting an important portion of the Karen to Christianity, and by building a Christian-Karen institutional order. The Karen are a distinct ethnic group, which probably has lived in Burma for more than a thousand years. Before the advent of the British with their legalistic ethic, the Burmese subjected the Karen to various forms of exploitation. The effect of Burmese oppression is clearly evident from the reports of the first Europeans to enter Burma, who noted that the Karen were shy, oppressed jungle dwellers, who lived in fear of their Burmese or Talaing rulers.

In addition to the services the Karen were called upon to perform, which could be looked upon as a form of taxation or tribute that benefited themselves as well as the Burmese, they also were exploited in the course of prosecuting a feud between the Burmese and the Talaing. Both sides in the feud seemed to feel that the Karen were a ready and convenient source of materials and supplies for their sides. As a consequence, most of the Karen tried to keep out of harm's way by hiding in the hills or swamps.

After years of this sporadic exploitation the Karen endured the forages and taxation with a dull indifference. They were very thoroughly cowed. They could not even fight back except with local raids on poorly defended villages or with assaults on stray Burmese found in outlying districts or in the jungle.

In an institutional order where gradations of social rank were most important and widely accepted, the lowest, most despised Burmese citizen felt himself to be superior to the Karen. The very words used by the Burmese to name the Karen are terms of opprobriation. They were variously called "wild cattle of the hills," or "wild men," and the Buddhist Bishop of Toungoo suggested that the word Karen is derived from a word meaning "dirty feeders," or "people of inferior caste." The Burmese had little information about the Karen because they thought them little removed from beasts and did not bother to inquire into their customs, habits, or life style. The dominant Burmese element regarded the Karen in unconcealed contempt.

This thorough subjection of the Karen is recorded in their mythology, their folklore, and the ditties of their children. It was a part of their reality. The Burmese, especially the Buddhist *Pongyi* (monk), was someone to fear. A Karen could not speak up in the presence of a Burmese to voice his hatred; it would have led to severe punishment. But the Karen children playing in their village sang: "The 'pongyi' with close shaven head, miserably hungry,/went to eat his food on the ridge./The unpoisoned arrow falls and pierces his head." The song loses something in translation, but it is clear that the Buddhist monk was an object of terror for the Karen children. A Karen proverb from the year 1827 illustrates the self-pitying and frustrating nature of existence under Burmese domination: "We are the eggs, other races are rocks; the egg fell on the rock and was broken; the rock fell on the egg and it was broken." This fear and hatred even appears as part of the demonology of the Karen. An entire class of particularly evil demons that prey on the spirits of the sick is expected to appear in the form of giants, goblins, or Buddhist *Pongyis*. Their subjection had burned itself into the subconscious dreams and imaginings of the Karen people.

The Karen and the Burmese moved in entirely different social worlds, without a common culture. There was conflict between the animist Karen and the Buddhist Burmese, but the Karen were so thoroughly controlled that their reality was entirely discredited.

The coming of the British ended this. In three wars, in 1824–26, 1852, and 1885, the British captured all of Burma. They outlawed slavery and brought British-style justice to Burmese and Karen alike; both were subject to British rule. The Burmese found that rule distasteful, but it gave the Karen an opportunity. They now had equality before the law, a chance for education and social advancement.

The problem for the Karen was to achieve self-respect and social equality. Christianity offered itself as the answer. Christianity had the status of being the religion of the conqueror, and the Karen presumed its adoption would lead to acceptance by the British. Embracing Christianity was all but unthinkable to the Buddhist Burmese, who had a sophisticated theology, but the Karen had little to lose. The Christians also provided institutional structures: among other activities they ran the schools, which were open to Karen. If a Karen wished to become educated he became a Christian.

A myth had long existed among the Karen that led them to hope for deliverance from the Burmese when the white foreigner came with his book. Another Karen myth seems to duplicate Genesis, though every symbolic universe has an explanation for creation, and at a symbolic level there cannot be many different myths. These were discovered— sifted is a better word in the case of the Genesis myth—by Christian missionaries working through Christian Burmese translators. The possibility for motivated interpretation of ambiguities is obvious. Nonetheless the impact of the Bible on the Karen was great. When it was presented, some bowed down and worshipped, others wept, and some kissed it. They felt that they had been permitted to witness the "return" of their lost book, and immediately believed that with its power they would no longer be a despised group.

The Reverend Adoniam Judson, from the American Baptist Foreign Mission Society, taught Ko Tha Byu, a Karen, to read the Bible. In 1828 Ko Tha Byu set out for Karen villages in the hills to spread the Gospel.

According to all sources Ko Tha Byu was an ideal choice for an initial convert. He was single-minded in his pursuit of future converts, using the only appeal of Christianity that he apparently understood: justification by faith. He shortly earned for himself the title of the Karen

Apostle; he was instrumental in over a thousand conversions to Christianity among the Karen.

Ko Tha Byu was a charismatic leader, but one of such a limited repertoire that he soon exhausted the patience of his audiences and had to move on. The movement prospered so well with the help of Ko Tha Byu that it came to the attention of the Burmese authorities, who forbade him to come to Rangoon.

For the Burmese, "Buddhist" and "Burmese" are almost the same words, inseparable parts of their symbolic universe. If a Burmese took up Christianity he would be called a "foreigner" by his fellow Burmese, very much as an American who takes up Communism is likely to be told to "go back to Russia/China where you belong." One of the reasons for the cohesion of Buddhism and Burmese identities was that the national civilization, the institutional order, was held together by the Buddhist *Sangha,* an assembly or order of monks, which was the only thing the Burmese, the Arakanese, the Talaings, and the Shan had in common. Much of the Burmese Court opposition to the Christian missionaries was due to the feeling that attempting to convert a Burmese was tantamount to challenging his allegiance to the King. Since the Karen were not thought of as being more than wild men, no serious governmental opposition was raised to missionary work among them, at first. As might be expected, the leading Abbots of Buddhist monasteries, being theoreticians, were more open-minded to Christianity than were politicians and government officials.

The Burmese reaction to the success of the Christian reality was at first conciliatory, but later, after a royal order to exterminate the white people and their religion, Christian Karen were seized and beaten, mothers separated from their children and raped. A minister and his congregation were captured, the congregation ransomed, but the minister, adhering to his faith, was tortured, disemboweled, and shot. The Burmese Viceroy of Rangoon threatened to shoot instantly the first Karen whom he should find capable of reading.

Many a Karen must have wondered, when a Christian minister first came to his village, whether or not to convert. There were many appeals, not the least of which was novelty. But there were also many drawbacks. When a person is converted to an alternate reality he is likely to break up his home life and institutionalized relations with his friends and neighbors. According to some observers Christianity caused a disruption of village life that was sometimes quite violent. Except in the rare case of mass conversion, the individual is required to abandon, even turn on, his entire old life and begin learning new habits and patterns of institutions. It is a serious step to take, and one not taken without some thought.

For the Karen who *could* convert, one who had the opportunity and was not dependent on a non-Christian, there were a number of benefits.

At the institutional level conversion made available education, medicine, and some contact with the ruling class. These institutions of behavior provided benefits in and of themselves quite apart from their symbolic value. These were new vistas which had been opened by the British occupation and the Christian missionaries. Important as these were, the value of a new reality, a new world view that went along with Christianity, was quite appealing.

The new reality Christianity offered the Karen was one where the fact of being a Karen was something to take pride in, not something to hate; it offered a distinctiveness that any Karen could achieve. Not simply a transformation of the traditional structure of Burmese on top and Karen inferior into Burmese inferior and Karen on top, the reality offered by the missionaries and Karen Christian ministers added entirely new dimensions to the relations with the Burmese. The Karen Christian had a pride of community, a pride of accomplishment, a sense of historic mission, even a feeling of being the elect of God; a reality with the Karen at the center; a transvaluation.

The provision of a coherent world view in which self-respect was possible cut short the deviation amplifying feedback process of repression, self-hatred, and resentment that drove some Karen into apathy and others into "passing" as Burmese. It was now thought possible to accomplish something, to gain respect from Burmese and British alike. The Christian reality provided a new alternative to the insolvable problem of the old order, the symbolic and institutional subjection that had driven the whole ethnic group into apathy. No reworking of the animistic and mythological religion, no change of its emphasis, could get rid of the fact that it was considered "beneath contempt" and as the religion of "wild cattle" by the Burmese. As long as a continuity of culture remained, the genuineness of any new parts would ring false in the ears of those who had experienced the old order. A complete break with tradition provided the answer.

An example of the difference of outlook that this new reality caused is the reaction of the Karen to persecution. Before Christianity, there was retreat. After some segments of the Karen population converted, and were involved with Christian institutions, there was militant counterattack and martyrdom. The sense of self-esteem legitimated by the Christian symbolic universe produced a "confident" Karen. He was confident that he had the God of Israel at his back and that all must fall before him. He was confident that he could lead his people against the hated Burmese. He was confident that he would never have to *shiko* (worship) a Burmese again. He lost his sense of inferiority.

It is interesting to note that at the same time the American Baptist Foreign Mission Society was turning the Karen into revolutionaries, the American Baptist Home Mission Society was preaching servility to American slaves. Christians would not attack their own institutional order but they would create revolutionaries in a foreign one.

In order for the Karen to gain the benefits of Christianity he had to give up his attachment to parts of his culture, and possibly to his family. If a Karen did not attend the feast that was given to drive off demons from a sick relative, as Christian Karen did not, he was thought to desire the death of the relative, calamity for the family and disaster for its members. Changing realities produces deep psychological conflicts, one reason few people change. Other pre-Christian institutions were also dropped. Karen boys used to carry harps constantly and play on any occasion, but with the adoption of Christianity most of the old songs and tunes were put aside for Christian hymns. The old life had to be put entirely behind them. These hard decisions kept many from converting, and made those that did convert more dedicated.

The person who became a Christian probably had to be a little more alienated, or a little more motivated than the person who did not. Since the Baptists would only allow adult Baptism most conversions must have involved weighing the various alternatives. Conversion was not an easy experience; it required burning the bridges back to the old culture, and this meant that the converts belonged completely to the institutions of the Christian Karen. Once having made the decision to convert, the individual tied his fate to that of Christianity among the Karen. This had great importance in the effect of Christianity on the entire Karen ethnic group. The fact that a Christian would find it in his own interest to protect and defend Christianity made him "deployable"—he could be assigned to do things for the cause. The existence of deployable personnel at both the ministerial and lay levels turned Christian-Karen institutions from voluntary associations into managerial structures, articulated organizations, and sometimes into what Philip Selznick called "organizational weapons."

CHRISTIAN SUBVERSION

The American Baptist Mission to the Karen provided individuals and scattered tribes with their first continuous contact with the other tribes of Karen in Burma. Before the Baptists there was no institutionalized communication, no internal communications network. Through the institution of yearly conferences of all the Baptist churches the Karen leaders from different communities got to know one another, and began to develop a national consciousness, a consciousness of a Karen-

Christian reality spanning the entire nation. When a village failed to send a representative to the yearly meeting pastors were dispatched to inform them of the proceedings. This regular communications structure immensely increased the limits of effective communications, creating for the first time a *Karen* social reality instead of isolated Karen villages. The communications structure followed that of the Baptist church, and tended to emphasize the roles of people who were important within it.

The Karen minister was often the only link his village had with the larger body of Karen. The minister went to conferences and brought back news, not only church news, but gossip about incidents, plans, and events that he learned at the conference. This monopoly on information, along with other factors, made the minister an important man in the village for both Christians and non-Christians. Due to his eminence, he was often called upon to settle disputes over land or property, giving him a certain measure of independent political leadership not directly related to his Christian ministry. This power tended to increase the prestige of both the minister and Christianity in the local community. In times of crisis the Karen looked to their ministers and missionaries for protection and leadership, increasing the span of the alternate reality.

The effect of training a Christian ministerial corps of Karen was to provide a tested and true cadre, the nucleus of an organization much more powerful than its numbers would indicate. With a dedicated cadre, the less involved could be brought into disciplined soldiering when necessary. The process of turning members into agents is clearly recognized in aggressive missionary activity. A Karen-Christian minister could be sent to organize (convert) a village; he could be used as a messenger; he could even be expected to die for the cause. In addition to the ministers the Christian lay people who had been trained in Christian schools provided a large supply of trained, dedicated agents, completely reared within the reality. They could be counted upon to take positions of leadership should the necessity arise. Thus the provision of a two level leadership net that reached into every Karen village with a minister allowed quick response to threats and a quick mobilization of the non-Christian Karen. Even the lay Christian had prestige and substance because of his education, and the villagers would often follow him if the necessity arose.

The first step toward mobilization of the mass, and toward unification of the entire ethnic group, was the formation, in 1881, of the Karen National Association. All the districts in which Karen lived were represented. A few non-Christians attended, but all the leaders were Christians. The Karen National Association was a political organization that used the clannish spirit of the Karens in order to bridge the gap between various language groups and between Christians and non-Christians.

It proposed to cooperate with the British, to promote the social and economic advancement of the Karens as a whole through education and self-help, and to fight off any future attempts at Burmese domination. This establishment of a territorial base helped the Christian reality to gain leadership and control of the Karen, especially in fighting off the Burmese.

The policy succeeded admirably. When danger presented itself in the aftermath of the third Anglo-Burmese war of December 1885, in the form of marauding bands of Burmese who burned Karen villages under the leadership of politically minded Buddhist monks, the Karen villagers rallied around the Christian and missionary leadership. The Christian organization took control of all the Karen and provided leadership for them. The willingness of the Karen to fight was aided by the definition of the conflict as a holy war, which is common when established realities clash. Dr. Vinton, American Baptist Missionary in Rangoon wrote from the battlefield on February 28, 1886, as quoted by J. F. Cady in *A History of Modern Burma:*

> The Karens universally interpret [*the presence of monks on the battlefield*] as God's sign that Buddhism is to be destroyed forever. They say that the challenge of Thebaw [*the "cause" of the Anglo-Burmese war*] could be answered by the British government, but the challenge of the fighting poongyees can only be taken up fitly by the Karens under their own missionaries . . . I have never seen the Karens so anxious for a fight. This is . . . welding the Karens into a nation. . . . The heathen Karens to a man are brigading themselves under the Christians. This whole thing is doing good for the Karen. This will put virility into our Christianity.

Later, on May 15, 1886, he wrote:

> Tribes that once were constantly fighting each other now stood side by side. From a loose aggregation of clans, we shall weld them into a nation yet. . . . When the danger is over, the Karen will be as soundly hated as ever by the officials. [*But*] the Karen will not *shiko* [*act of worship*] if he can help it, and will not . . . [*accept*] those who enforce servility.

It would be well to note that whatever the intentions of the Christian missionaries they were leading a segment of an ethnic minority in subversive action against the majority of their society. They were killing Burmese in a conflict of realities.

The Christian-British symbolic universe welded the Karen into a cohesive national group and protected its place in the British-dominated institutional order of Burmese society until Burmese independence in

1948. When Burma gained its freedom the Karen immediately started a full-scale military rebellion that lasted for several years. This rebellion was called the "Baptist Rebellion" because Karen Baptist constituted most of the leadership. Conflict between the Christian Karen and the Buddhist Burmese still continues to break out on occasion.

The Christian Karen got their reality by importation, the new-age reality is an internal creation. New-age reality participation is segmental and part-time, Christian Karen participation was total and possibly full time. New-age organization is weak, Christian Karen was strong. These are some of the factors that determine whether a "deviant" reality will succeed in establishing a hegemony over a society or will remain a collection of people who have "strange" ideas. In the next chapter we will examine the elements necessary for a self-sustaining reality.

□ □ □
Each of the realities we have examined to this point has had some sort of obvious flaw. Hip reality has an incomplete institutional base. New-age reality has practically no institutional base at all. Christianity in Burma was mostly limited to the Karen, and dependent on the British. These flaws did not keep the realities from being attacked as "deviancies" but they did preclude them from becoming dominant and redefining adherence to conventional reality as deviant. In order to have a chance to force such a redefinition, a reality must at the very least be able to sustain itself and to grow.

To be self-sustaining, a reality must have a comprehensive system of legitimations that covers all aspects of the symbolic world in which its adherents live, an explanation of its own origin, its own necessity, and its "purpose." It must explain the lives of its adherents, by providing them with both ordered biographies and a system of concepts that explains their psychology. It must legitimate the institutions of behavior that are enacted by its

SELF-
SUSTAINING
REALITIES

adherents, decide upon precedences among them, and explain them in a manner plausible within the reality.

A reality must be supported and bolstered by the enactment of the institutions contained within it. The institutions must form a complete institutional order so that an individual can satisfy all of his needs without having to encounter another reality. It must have institutions to socialize the young in the important dimensions of the reality, and institutions that can socialize converts to the reality. Finally, it must have institutions that can provide "therapy" for those who doubt the reality, and those who would migrate to another.

A reality must maintain its boundaries by theoretical distinctions that are both theoretical and popularly understood. It must maintain its boundaries by physical or territorial segregation from other realities. It must not be overly penetrated by communications from other realities. Finally, it may have to defend its boundaries by force.

Can such a reality be consciously created?

In the following adaptation LeRoi Jones suggests that it can, working with the black institutions of North America.

32

THE NEED FOR A CULTURAL BASE TO CIVIL RITES & BPOWER MOOMENTS

LeROI JONES

The civilrighter is usually an american, otherwise he would know, if he is colored, that that concept is meaningless fantasy. Slaves have no civil rights. On the other hand, even integration is into the mobile butcher shop of the devil's mind. To be an american one must be a murderer. A white murderer of colored people. Anywhere on the planet. The colored people, negroes, who *are* Americans, and there are plenty, are only colored on their skin. They are white murderers of colored people. Themselves were the first to be murdered by them; in order to qualify. [*In other words white American reality is intrinsically anti-black, and a black man living within it becomes anti-black.*]

The blackpower seeker, if connected to civilrights mooment can be bourgeois meaning. He wants the same civilrights/power white people have. He wants to be a capitalist, a live-gooder, and a deathfreak. In whatever order. There is the difference Frantz Fanon implies in *BlkSkn-WhiteMask.* Black Bourgeoisie can be white or black. The difference is critical only if Black Black Bourgeoisie can be used for good, possibly. White ones are examples of shadow worship, and are deathfreaks and American. [*Blacks involved in white reality are useless.*]

Black Power cannot mean ONLY a black sheriff in the sovereign state of Alabama. But that is a start, a road, a conceptualizing on heavier bizness. Black Power, the power to control our lives ourselves. All of our lives. Our laws. Our culture. Our children. Their lives. Our total consciousness, black oriented. [*A comprehensive black reality.*] We do not speak of the need to live in peace or universal humanity, since we are peaceful humanists seeking the spiritual resolution of the world. The unity of all men will come with the evolution of the species that recognizes the need for such. The black man does. The black man is a spirit worshiper as well. The religious-science and scientific-religion is the black man's special evolutional province. He will reorder the world, as he finds his own rightful place in it. The world will be reordered by the black man's finding such place. Such place is, itself, the reordering. [*Black reality will take its place as a predominant reality in the world.*] Black Power. Power of the majority is what is meant. The actual majority in the world of colored people.

Census
Black People Black People Black People
Yellow People Yellow People Yellow People
Brown People Brown People Brown
Red People Red People Red People
Poor People Poor People Poor People Poor
People Poor People Poor People Poor People

. . . .
& others.

Bourgeois black power seeks mostly to get in on what's going down now. The implication of murderermembership is clear. Of course the form of Bourgeois black people can be harnessed for heavier ends. The control by black people for their own benefit CAN BE set up similar to bourgeois black power, but if the ends are actually to be realized, you are talking again about nationalism, nationalization. Finally the only black power that can exist is that established by black nationalism. We want power to control our lives, as separate from what americans, white and white oriented people, want to do with their lives. That simple. We ain't with yuall. Otherwise you are talking tricknology and lieconjuring. Black power cannot exist WITHIN white power. One or the other. There can only be one or the other. They might exist side by side as separate entities, but never in the same space. Never. They are mutually exclusive. [*A self-sustaining reality must be independent, it cannot be a sub-reality.*]

"Might exist," because that is theoretically possible, except the devils never want to tolerate any power but their own. [*Conventional reality excludes other realities.*] In such cases they want to destroy what is not them. However, the power of the majority on the planet will exist, this is an evolutional fact. [*The emergence of a black reality is legitimated as an evolutional, historical necessity.*] The adjustment, what the world must go through because of this, is current events.

The socio-political workers for black power must realize this last fact. That the black and white can never come to exist as equals within the same space. Side by side perhaps, if the devils are cool, but the definition of devil is something uncool.

This means that any agitation within the same space for Black Power is for control of the space you *can* control called part of the society, but in reality in black enclaves, cities, land, black people are usually already in control in terms of population. Further control must be nationalization, separation. Black power cannot exist except as itself, power, to order, to control, to legalize, to define. There are wars going on now to stop black power, whether in Sinai, Vietnam, Angola, or Newark, New Jersey. [*In black reality all colored-white conflicts are defined as being similar.*] The difference is that in Newark, New Jersey, many colored people do not even *know* they are in this war (tho they might realize, on whatever level of consciousness, that they are losing).

Black power is nationalization. Absolute control of resources beneficial to a national group. It cannot come to exist in areas of white control. Neither Harlem nor Hough nor Watts &c. are really America. They are controlled by America . . . this is the sickness. Black power is the cure for this sickness. But it must be the alternative to what already exists, i.e., white power. And to be an actual alternative it must be complete. [*Black reality must be in complete control of black institutions.*]

Black power cannot be complete unless it is the total reflection of black people. Black power must be spiritually, emotionally, and historically in tune with black people, as well as serving their economic and political ends. To be absolutely in tune, the seekers of black power must know what it is they seek. They must know what is this power-culture alternative through which they bring to focus the world's energies. They must have an understanding and grounding in the cultural consciousness of the nation they seek to bring to power. And this is what is being done, bringing to power a nation that has been weak and despised for 400 years.

That is, to provide the alternative, the new, the needed strength for this nation, they must proceed by utilizing the complete cultural consciousness of this black nation's people. We should not cry black power unless we know what that signifies. We must know full well what it is we are replacing white power with, in all its implications. We are replacing not only a white sheriff, for the values that sheriff carries with him are, in fact, an extension of the white culture. *That black sheriff had better be an extension of black culture, or there is NoChange!* (In the sense that Edward Brooke, so-called Negro Senator from Massachusetts, as a representative of white culture, could never signify in any sense, Black Power. He is, for all intents and purposes, a white man.)

There are people who might cry BlackPower, who are representatives, extensions of white culture. So-called BlackPower advocates who are mozartfreaks or Rolling Stones, or hypnotized by Joyce or Hemingway or Frank Sinatra, are representatives, extensions, of white culture, and can never therefore signify black power. Black power, as black, must be, is in reality, the total realization of that nation's existence on this planet from the year one until this moment. [*The totality of black experience must be contained within black reality.*] All these experiences which have been this lost nation's must be brought to bear upon all its righteous workings; especially for Power. (And with Power will come Freedom.) Black Power first to be Black. It is better, in America, to be white. So we leave America, or we never even go there. (It could be twelve miles from New York City (or two miles) and it would be the black nation you found yourself in. That's where yourself was, all the time.)

The very failure of the civil rights and blackpower organizations (collecting memberships on strictly socio-political grounds) to draw more membership is due to the fact that these organizations make very little reference to the totality of black culture. The reason Mr. Muhammad's Nation of Islam has had such success gathering black people from the grass roots is that Mr. Muhammad offers a program that reflects a totality of black consciousness. Islam is a form of spirit worship (a moral guide) as well as a socio-economic and political program. Religion as the total definer of the world. (This is as old as the world, and finally will be the only Renewal possible for any of us to submit to the Scientific-Religious reordering of the world, through black eyes and black minds.) It must be a culture, a way of feeling, way of living and being, that is black, and, yes, finally, more admirable.

Hence, the socio-political must be wedded to the cultural. The socio-political must be a righteous extension of the cultural, as it is, legitimately, with National groups. The american negro's culture, as it is, is a diphthong with the distortions of the master's hand always in back or front ground, not real but absolutely concrete and there; . . . the culture, the deepest black and the theoretical . . . socio-politico (and art &c.) must be wedded. A culturally aware black politics would use all the symbols of the culture, all the keys and images out of the black past, out of the black present, to gather the people to it, and energize itself with their strivings at conscious blackness. The Wedding . . . the conscious-unconscious. [*A complete reality unites the conscious and the unconscious in a comprehensive explanation.*] The politics and the art and the religion all must be black. The social system. The entirety of the projection. Black Power must mean black people with a past clear back to the beginning of the planet, channeling the roaring energies of black to revive black power. [*A complete reality encompasses all history, explaining and interpreting it.*] If you can dig it???. Not to discover it now . . . but to revive. Our actual renaissance (Like the devils pulled themselves out of their "dark ages" by re-embracing the "classics," or Classicism: what they could see as the strengths and beauties of a certain kind of "pure" European (whiteness). And with that went to the source! Eastern Thought . . . black african-middle eastern, also the re-embracing of the Far East via Marco Polo, &c., like *Trade*.)

So that no man can be "cultured" without being *consciously* Black. Which is what we're talking about all the time, in any Rising (Evolutional) Pitch. *Consciousness*. [*Everyday life explained and interpreted through black reality*.]

The Civil Righters are not talking about exchanging a culture. They are, no matter what moves they make, layin' in the same place, making out. Black Power, as an actuality, will only exist in a Black-oriented, Black-controlled space. It is White Culture that rules us with White Guns. Our only freedom will be in bringing a Black Culture to Power. We Cannot Do This Unless We Are Cultured. That is, Consciously Black. (The Consciousness of Black Consciousness must know & Show itself as well.)

The erection of large schools teaching Black Consciousness. Wherever there are Black People in America. [*Children must be socialized in black reality.*] This should be one definite earnest commitment of any Black Power group. Even the rundown schools full of black children deep in the ghettos are white schools. The children are taught to value white things more than themselves. All of them are white-controlled, and the quality of education suffers because white people want the quality of our education to suffer, otherwise something else would be the case. We will have no quality education for our children until we administer it ourselves. You *must* know this!

There is no black power without blackness conscious of itself. "Negro History" is not what we must mean, but the absolute reordering of our Education Systems. In other words the philosophy of blackness, the true consciousness of our world, is what is to be taught. The understanding of the world as felt and analyzed by men and women of soul. [*Blacks defining their own reality in their own terms.*]

The Black Student Union of San Francisco State College has started moving toward a "Black Studies Program" at that school. A Black Studies Program on departmental status at the school, where students could spend all of their time recreating our black past, and understanding, and creating the new strong black nation we must all swear to bring into existence.

The black power groups must help to create the consciousness of who we black people are, and then we will be driven to take power, and be faithful to our energies as black people with black minds and hearts, quite a *different* people from the species that now rules us.

Afro-American History, African History, Realistic World History, Eastern Philosophies-Religion, Islam-Arabic-African Religion and Languages, Black Art-past and contemporary, The Evolving Patterns of the Colored World, Black Psychology, Revolutionary Consciousness, Socio-Political Evolution of Afro-Americans, Africans, Colored Peoples, War, The Placement of the New Culture, Eastern Science, Black Science, Community Workshops (How To) in Black Power, Business and Economics: Keep to a new black world, given the strengths our studies into times of the black man's power will build for us. Black Studies is to make us cultured, i.e., consciously black.

The so-called Negro Colleges ought to be the first to be forced into Blackness. [*Black colleges now function within white reality.*] The consciousness of the self, without which no righteous progress is possible. Instead the Negro Colleges are "freak factories," places where black children are turned into white-oriented schizophrenic freaks of a dying society. But many of the students have already shown that they are not willing to be misused by the whiteminds of their puppet professors.

A cultural base, a black base, is the completeness the black power movement must have. We must understand that we are *Replacing* a dying culture, and we must be prepared to do this, and be absolutely conscious of what we are replacing it with.

We are sons and daughters of the most ancient societies on this planet. The reordering of the world that we are moving toward cannot come unless we are completely aware of this fact, and we are prepared to make use of it in our day-to-day struggle with the devil.

E.G.: Black Art—The recreation of our lives, as black . . . to inspire, educate, delight and move black people.

It is easier to get people into a consciousness of black power, what it is, by emotional example than through dialectical lecture. Black people seeing the recreation of their lives are struck by what is wrong or missing in them.

Programmatic application of what is learned through black art is centrally the black power movement's commitment.

The teaching of colored people's languages, including the ones we speak automatically, moves the student's mind to other psychological horizons. European language carries the bias of its inventors & users. *You must be* anti-black, speaking in their language, except by violent effort. [*Recall the differences in the languages of hip and conventional reality.*] The masses of black people, for instance, have never spoken the European's languages. Or let me say, they have never spoken them to such degree that the complete bias of that "competence" would dull their natural turning. [*Black reality can be built upon existing black languages. Perfection in English is automatically dangerous.*]

The teaching of Black History (African and African-American) would put our people absolutely in touch with themselves as a nation, and with the reality of their situation. You want them to move to take power, they must know how they can deserve this power. [*There must be an historical legitimation.*]

Black Power must be a program of Consciousness. The consciousness to Act. (Maulana Ron Karenga and the US group in Los Angeles work very successfully at making black consciousness cultural and of course socio-political.) It should all be one thing. Blackness.

Voting nor picketing nor for that matter fighting in the streets means anything unless it is proposed by a black consciousness for the aggrandizement and security of the Black culture and Black people. Each of our "acts of liberation" must involve the liberation of the Black man in every way imaginable.

Black Power movements not grounded in Black culture cannot move beyond the boundaries of Western thought. The paramount value of Western thought is the security and expansion of Western culture. Black Power is inimical to Western culture as it has manifested itself within black and colored majority areas anywhere on this planet. Western culture is and has been destructive to Colored People all over the world. No movement shaped or contained by Western culture will ever benefit Black people. Black power must be the actual force and beauty and wisdom of Blackness . . . reordering the world.

□ □ □

The creation of a black reality would signal massive changes in the North American institutional order. Blacks (and Indians) have successively been considered nonhuman, subhuman, and human-but-retarded in the North American reality. These views have successively legitimated their slavery, segregation, and inferior social position within the institutional order. First Christianity *excluded* the black and the Indian from the human race and allowed whites in complete Christian faith to enslave the black and exterminate the Indian. If God could not admire the lazy Indian and black, how could God's faithful do other than follow His footsteps? When Christianity allowed that blacks and Indians could be converted to Christianity, white reality shifted to the philosophical assumption that white superiority over the colored races was a law of nature. Thus blacks and Indians were *included* in the human race, and in the institutional order, in an inherently inferior position. It was the natural order of *things* that the white man could not violate. With the spread of scientific thinking the black's inherent inferiority is legitimated as biologically determined. Intelligence tests, standardized in white reality on white subjects, very scientific, demonstrate that blacks have lower "Intelligence quotients" than whites. This "scientific" finding legitimates the black's inferior social position. Since a black man cannot live entirely within the white reality that rejects him, no matter how much he might desire to do so, it is hardly surprising that he should not do as well on tests built on the assumptions of white reality. Social science is a part of the reality that generates it, and the standards it assumes to be universal are only valid within the terms of its own reality. Should a black reality be established, and should its social scientists devise a test of "intelligence," however defined, whites will be "inherently" and just as "scientifically" inferior.

Since the institutional order of North American society considers black institutions as "culturally deprived" there is little chance of a black reality consolidating within white reality. Since the institutional order is intimately tied to and partially dependent upon blacks and black institutions, the idea of black separation brings forth visions of massive readjustments and chaos. The National Advisory Commission on Civil Disorders concluded that American society was rapidly moving toward two societies, one black, one white, separate and unequal. Their recommendations for massive programs to bring blacks into the institutional order as equals, have been largely ignored.

The problem of creating a black reality in North America is almost completely the opposite of the problem of creating a new age or even hip reality. The institutional base already exists, but structures of legitimation must be articulated and communicated. This is the core of LeRoi Jones's suggestions for black art as a means for reaching and communicating with black groups.

COUNTERATTACKS FROM CONVENTIONAL REALITY

There are four basic methods that realities use to protect themselves against the threat of alternate realities: therapy, nihilization, segregation, and extermination.

Therapy is used on individuals who show threats of migrating to an alternate reality. Although there are specialists in therapy who use the sophisticated techniques of psychiatry, religion, or witchcraft, there are far more lay therapists who have a notion of what the potential migrant is doing, and some ritual procedures to make him "face reality." The objective of these procedures is to provide the individual with reasons, legitimations, and motivations for "returning to reality." The hip person might be told that he has a low reality orientation, that if he continues he will be unable to get a job, procreate "normal" children, and get ahead in the world. The black may be told that equality is the only way, and that black separation is just black racism. The new-age person may be told to give up her "hallucinations" and to stop acting crazy. Whether or not the therapy works depends on a great many variables.

Nihilization involves explaining the alternate reality within terms of the conventional reality. Here too there are specialists, Marxians who explain bourgeois motivations, psychiatrists who talk of identity crises in adolescence, and so forth. Lay explanations, however, are probably more influential in protecting the subjective reality of the conventional people. Thus the hip person is explained as "just interested in easy sex." A black who promotes black reality is explained as a "troublemaker." The Karen is dismissed as a "wild man." The new-age person is considered to be a "kook" who ought to be in a mental institution. Blacks and Indians could be enslaved because they are "known" not to be descended from Adam and therefore could not be human. The process of nihilization is designed to protect the nihilators' reality rather than to convert or convince those in the alternate reality, though it is sometimes used for this purpose also.

Segregation of realities also keeps people from being tempted to migrate. It might take the form of physical segregation (beyond our boundaries live the barbarians), or conceptual segregation (it is all right for Karens to be Christians because they are just wild men, but no Burmese should be tempted).

If these conceptual tactics show or promise little success and the balance of power is favorable, the alternate reality may be exterminated. Hitler attempted a "final solution" to the Jewish problem. Pope Innocent III and the Inquisition exterminated the Albigensian "heresy" in the thirteenth century by killing the adherents. "Counterrevolutionaries" are often executed. Whether blacks and hip people will be next is still an open question; other solutions are also possible.

All of these techniques have been used against people and groups defined as "deviant" because of their adherence to an alternate reality.

REALITY CONFLICTS

Three different forms of conflict between self-sustaining realities can be distinguished. There are many similarities, and some differences, between the tactics used in all three.

The *first* form of conflict is a long-term historical change in the entire symbolic universe that ultimately involves a complete transformation in the entire legitimation structure of the universe. The conflict in Western society between religion and science is a good example of this form of transformation. Over a period of five hundred years the conceptions of almost every human activity were transformed from religious ones to scientific ones. Institutional structures changed in the process, as did subjective realities. The conception of the universe changed from one in which the earth stood still to one in which space was curved. The conception of man has changed from a person of essentially divine soul to one of unconscious tendencies; he is now thought to have evolved from lower animals rather than having been created in a day. Each of these changes involved conflicts between the religiously based reality and the scientifically based reality. The scientific view of man was heretical at first, and the religious view of man is now considered archaic.

The *second* form of conflict is between distinct, mature realities. Deviance is not much involved in such conflicts, except as a representative of one reality is found within another. In the cold war, a Communist is considered deviant in North America, and a capitalist or bourgeoisie is considered deviant (counterrevolutionary, reactionary) in a Communist country. Such conflicts are most likely to be resolved by segregation of the realities, or by extermination of one or the other. When the Spanish priests came to the Yucatan they collected and burned all the Mayan books, destroying their civilization. In North America the Indians were segregated on reservations.

The *third* form of conflict comes about when a revolution brings forth an entirely new social reality. The process of rebuilding the reality accents for an entire society may involve therapy, nihilation, segregation, and extermination. The most vivid examples of such transformation are probably China and Cuba.

Within each form, conflict takes place on every level, theoretical, institutional, and subjective. The objective is the establishment of a new reality of everyday life, or the maintenance of an old reality of everyday life. Whatever reality is established will define some individuals as having bad habits, some patterns of behavior as counter-institutions, and all other realities as anathema.

☐ ☐ ☐

□ □ □
SUMMARY
Peter Berger and Thomas Luckmann's theoretical exposition, *The Social Construction of Reality,* outlined the way in which habitualized activity on the part of individuals comes to be jointly considered as both real and external to the particular individuals involved. In essence, their argument is simple. Human beings make habits out of their routine activities in order to reduce the number of choices they have to make. Almost any activity that is done repeatedly will become habitualized and capable of being carried out without much conscious thought. This leaves the mind free to give conscious thought to the problematic aspects of the environment. The fact that action is habituated allows others to make reasonable predictions about our future course, wherein they can assume that we are "doing again" the same thing we "did before" without having to watch us complete the entire act. When two or more actors make this sort of assumption, each about the other, they may be said to have reciprocally typified the

RETROSPECT AND PROSPECT

ongoing activity. This is a constant social process. We make these reciprocal typifications with all of the people with whom we are engaged in various coordinated activities. Further we make them about "types" of people, assuming that policemen will act like policemen, professors like professors, and students like students. We both create our own reciprocal typifications and fall into patterns of reciprocal typifications that have been established by others before us.

When some pattern of coordinated activity is passed on to recruits or to children it becomes a social object, an "institution" of behavior. In the process of being passed on, it becomes more rigid and less open to change. Some institutions of behavior have been so generally applicable that they are assumed by the people involved to be the only proper way of gaining some particular goal; they have become the predominant institutions for the given society. These predominant institutions are often centered around the coordinations involved in labor, sex, territory, and communication.

As a social institution develops from a habit to a reciprocal typification, then to a recruiting institution, and finally to a predominant institution that all of the people of the society "should" follow, it requires increasingly abstract levels of legitimation to make it subjectively plausible to the people involved, and acceptable as a form of behavior to other people not directly involved. A personal, private habit may not need to be explained even to one's self. If it does need to be explained all that will be necessary is an explanation of how to do it. Generally, unless it is a habit that is socially considered a bad one, the question of why it is done will not be raised at all. Why one takes a certain route rather than another route to work in the morning, for example, is rarely called into question.

In order for a reciprocal typification to take place with a consequent coordination of activities it is necessary that both parties, or all parties involved, understand the answer to the question "how to do it"; it is possible that they then will begin to answer the question "why" do it. And when this coordination of activity comes to be passed on to an outsider, either a new recruit or a child, the same "how" information and "why" justification must be passed on to them. And it is possible that an even higher level of explanation at a theoretical level will be used to explain why it fits in with all the other things that people think are proper to do. At this level of explanation one might, for example, explain some pattern of economic activity as legitimate because it fits in with "free enterprise" or "socialism," depending on the country in which one is explaining it. When an institution becomes predominant within a society, when formal instruction is required in the institution for "all" or for "all appropriate members of the society," it is necessary that there be simplified explanations of how it's done and why it's done;

it is necessary that it be intellectually fit into the total pattern of the culture so that this question can be answered, and so that it is possible to link the institution to the cosmos. At this level of explanation, economic institutions are explained by patterns of historical necessity, by the laws of nature, or by the laws of God, depending on the time and place where the explanation is required.

These institutions and their legitimations encompass the everyday life of the individual. He is both involved in institutions and convinced by their legitimations that he is following a proper path, one that is moral, customary, and legal. Indeed, the pattern of institutions and legitimations structures his social reality and creates social control over his own activity. The institutions in which the individual is directly involved can potentially benefit him, and he follows the patterns of institutional behavior required because this is the only way in which he *can* get the benefit of the institution. He receives acceptance, survival, friendship, love, and emotional support from others who coordinate their activities with him, as long as he follows the institution properly. If he does not follow it properly he will be ostracized, hated, or excluded from activities. Because he has long participated in these institutions and he has followed a progression of institutions from early childhood —each of which was successively legitimated to him within terms of a larger theory accepted in that society at that time—he has come to take into himself the controls of various social institutions. He has internalized these controls in such a way that his ego leads him to feeling good, proud, and satisfied when he does things in the proper institutionalized way, and leads him to feel guilt, shame, doubt, and uncertainty when he violates the rules.

Furthermore, the predominant institutions of a society, those that are presumed to be required paths for all appropriate members of the society to follow, are equipped with formal social controls to coerce those recalcitrant members of society who might not otherwise follow them into doing so. These formal controls are effected by "legally" authorized agents such as the police, mental hospitals, social workers, administrators, and psychiatrists, and in general are directed only at those who do not follow the proper institutions of behavior. Agents of formal control rarely reward people for doing what is expected. Instead, through fines, imprisonment, death, therapy, treatment, or excommunication, they punish people who have not followed the correct path. These three levels of social control: *relational control* from the coparticipants in institutions, *self-control,* which is an internalized regulation from past, present, and anticipated future coordinations and institutionalizations, and the *formal controls* that have been abstracted through social processes, constitute both the foundations and the defenses of socially constructed reality.

Habits, coordinations, and institutions, however, grow up from specific people involved in specific coordinations with specific others for specific ends in specific contexts. Each institution is not necessarily coordinated with each other institution, nor do they all fit into a master plan. While the institutions seem to hang together—because we have a certain amount of knowledge about our society we have legitimated the pattern of institutions in which we participate—there is no necessary or logical reason why one institution should be coordinated peacefully with another. (There will, of course, be historical reasons why a certain pattern of institutions has arisen within a society.) Neither is there any reason why the particular collections of institutions that are predominant in one society should be as they are and not something else. This being the case, it is entirely possible that people will form new institutions of behavior that accord better with their positions in life but that are not accepted within the institutional order of society. Institutions that fall outside of the institutional order of society fall also outside of the socially defended reality of society, and consequently are seen by social participants as being evil, demonic, unscientific, or antinatural, which one again depending upon their own ultimate legitimation of social reality. Berger and Luckmann have pointed to four historically-used mechanisms for the defense of the entire institutional order. These systems of thought, which they call "symbolic universes," have been grounded successively on mythology, theology, philosophy, and science.

A symbolic universe organizes the totality of knowledge within a social structure, providing explanations for everything, if one goes to a sufficiently abstract level of explanation. It orders phases of individuals' biography, keeps subjective identity straight, makes death a legitimate part of life, legitimates the institutional order, sets the limits of social reality, even decides who will be considered people and who will not; it orders history and the future in a meaningful logical totality, integrates all discrete institutional realities, and defends the social sense of reality from chaos. Just as there can be counter-institutions of behavior, which are not legitimated within the institutional order, there can also be alternate realities, which legitimate and define alternate institutional patterns.

In the article by Norton E. Long, the creation of social order within a local community was seen as the outcome of contentions among many different local institutions that cooperated and fought with one another, each for their own particular ends, but with a resulting overall ordering and governance of the community activities. Long makes a number of points that can aid understanding of some basic dimensions in the ordering of institutions within a community. He suggests that the order of the territory is an outcome of many historical processes, not of planning; that the goals and strategies that men spend most of their lives working for, and with, come mostly from the particular institutions of behavior they follow, not from general consensus on general values. Further, there are diverse institutions within an area interacting with one another, and their interaction governs the nature of the community, not in the formal sense of government as an institution, but as an organizer and regulator of all the possibilities for activity that exist in the community. Long suggests that these institutions do not necessarily form a single, comprehensive, organized group; there may be many practical and theoretical bases of organization, each of which would include a different collection of institutions. Consequently there is probably no single group of people that organizes everybody and directs everything (though there may be a relatively powerful elite who often decides issues). He suggests that most individual behavior in institutions comes from following the expectations of the institutions. People sometimes switch from one institution to another and are involved in several institutions at the same time, so that their behavior in one often affects their behavior in others. This links the institutions together and causes them to reciprocally influence one another. Any distinct multiinstitutional activity within a community will be affected by the transactions and bargains of each of the institutions involved. As an example, the construction of a highway is the outcome of contention and cooperation between a professional highway engineering institution, a departmental bureaucracy, a set of contending politicians seeking to use the highways for political capital, and patronage; bankers concerned with bonds, taxes, and the effect of highway real estate, newspaper men interested in headlines, scoops, and the effect of the highway on paper circulation; contractors eager to make money by building roads; churchmen concerned with the effect of highways on their parishes and on the fortunes of the contractors who support their churchly ambitions; labor leaders interested in union contracts and their status as community influentials with a right to be consulted; and civic leaders who must justify the contribution of their bureaus of municipal research or chambers of commerce.

A complicated pattern of pushing and hauling creates the patterns of activity that become the social reality of the particular community. Since these institutions within a community interact with one another, not once but repeatedly, they develop patterns of expectations, patterns of coordination, patterns of routinization, that lead to an overall stability. Thus, the meshing of institutions brings about the overall institutional order that keeps people fed, housed, clothed, married, divorced, and in touch with one another through communications.

It is this complicated pattern of institutional arrangements, cooperations, and understandings, into which a person is inducted as he grows up within society. Institutions that fit into the established pattern of institutional interaction are considered legitimate because they are part of the ongoing social process seen as a theoretical whole, as understood by the people who live in it. Other institutions such as bank robbing, prostitution, homosexuality, and the use of drugs, at one time or another have not fit into the pattern of institutions that have been established within a territory. They are seen as either individual or social lapses, breaks away from the social expectations created by the routine institutions, and legitimations of customary patterns of social behavior.

Thus social reality is a complex understanding of what is correct and proper, arising from repeated patterns of activity, social institutions, and the customary explanations for these patterns of activity, legitimations. Social reality generally accords with majority activities in most areas of behavior and explanations; but because social reality is an abstraction from many different independent patterns of institutions, and many different kinds of explanations, it very often leaves out other behavior, other explanations, that some people have found to be more suitable for them than the predominant pattern within a society.

Since social reality is of necessity abstracted from the many diverse patterns of ongoing human experience, there will often be social realities that are not congruent with subjective realities. This occurs when the real life styles and conditions of some people (engaged in certain activities or positions in society) do not correspond to the social ideals of the predominant social order. A "reality flaw" is this incongruence between socially constructed reality and the subjective reality of an individual. Ideally, subjective realities reflect social realities because they are derived from them. But given the complexity of experience, the complexity of the abstraction of social realities, the complexity of the transmission of realities through socialization by parents (who themselves exist in different places in the social structure), there will be a great many people who, in one area or another, experience or potentially experience, a flaw in social reality.

Historically, the conflict between socially constructed reality and individual reality has been examined from the point of view of social reality. Taking the social facts of Durkheim as the beginning point, and examining the situations in which individuals will be forced into deviant behavior through disjunctions between their experience and the social reality that they had been led to expect, has been a long tradition in sociology. Durkheim's theory of anomic suicide pointed to this discontinuity of experiences in economic booms, or crashes, when a married person became divorced, or when a long-term decline in moral or political controls would lead to a long-term rise in anomie. Robert Merton later elaborated Durkheim's analysis in his 1938 paper on social structure and anomie. Merton identified "cultural goals" and "institutionalized means" as the two basic elements of the social structure and pointed out that various forms of relationships between cultural goals and institutionalized means could lead to anomic individuals, and various adaptive forms of deviant behavior. Merton's analysis was more sophisticated than Durkheim's, identifying as he did the sources of reality flaws for individuals. But Merton, as well as Durkheim, accepted the totalitarian claims of the symbolic universe and adopted the perspective of social reality to analyze individual conflicts with social reality. Merton's logical schema produced four types of individual adaptations: conformity, innovation, ritualism, and retreatism. His fifth type, rebellion, constituted a residual category for his theory. In it a person could reject cultural goals and institutionalized means while accepting different cultural goals and different institutionalized means. It is necessary to elaborate Merton's argument even further in order to take into account the existence of multiple realities. A first, somewhat piecemeal step toward elaboration of Merton's analysis was taken by Richard Cloward when he suggested that in addition to legitimate institutions, there could also be illegitimate institutions. A person might fail to achieve cultural goals, both legitimately *and* illegitimately, thus becoming a "double failure."

Actually, it seems clear that in order to deal in a deductive way with disjunctions between individual experience and socially constructed reality, it is necessary to use four different independent variables instead of the single variable that Durkheim used, the two variables that Merton used (with a residual category), or the three variables Cloward used. In order to deal with the possible combinations logically and completely, one must consider the symbolic universe and its goals and values, and the legitimate institutions with their proper way of doing things, as well as the possibility of an alternate reality and the possibility of counter-institutions (institutions not legitimated within the institutional order). Using these four independent variables, a sixteen-fold typology may be constructed that more clearly lays out the dimensions of conflict between social reality and individual experience, still from the point of view of social reality.

Deductive theorizing of this nature, however, produces many difficulties, not the least of which is that it is a rather circuitous way of describing social life. Since the theory itself is an abstraction, and the cross-classification of abstractions produces more minute abstractions, there may be little relation between the logical types and the distribution of actual conflicts between the individual and social reality as they are found within any particular society. A methodologist would say that there are a great many logically possible, but empirically empty, cells in such an analysis.

Another way of looking at reality flaws is to examine them from the point of view of subjective reality: to look at the knowledge a person has of the world, and the ways in which his knowledge fits, or does not fit, into the knowledge that social reality says he should have of the world. By taking the commonsense knowledge of the individual actor as a beginning point, it is possible to study the ways in which he elaborates his knowledge, in which he joins together with others who have similar conflicts with society, and the ways in which he can sometimes change the nature of socially constructed reality.

Every individual has thousands of habits, from the tunes he whistles under his breath to the routes he takes in driving around town, in the way he holds his cigarette, to the kinds of hashish he prefers, the way he smiles, the way he reads his newspapers. Habits may be quite individual—always wearing a leather wrist strap, or quite general—smoking cigarettes. Habits are not themselves institutions of behavior because they are individual, but many habits form the basis of institutions—such as offering cigarettes around—and ultimately all institutions of behavior depend on certain habits and were long ago created from them. Since habits are performed by individuals and yet fall into very broad cultural patterns, it is entirely possible that one will have some habits that other people will characterize as bad or as wrong, or a habit one learned incorrectly that is usually characterized as being wrong or bad—not congruent with the accepted pattern of habitual behavior. The reaction of other people varies greatly with the habit concerned. Predictably, since they are individual and not patterned, many bad habits are considered to be examples of mental illness. Sometimes bad habits are profoundly disturbing to people who are conventionally inclined. Having a bad habit may cause an individual to be so treated by others that it ultimately becomes an important or even crucial part of his life. Habits may be picked up in many ways, as an adaptive response to an impossible situation in a family, an adaptive response to ongoing life problems, or a simple failure to learn the proper process of socialization.

Jay Haley, and others who have been concerned with the double-bind pattern of communications as a factor in schizophrenia, have pointed out the way in which a person begins to habitually not communicate in order to respond to a situation in which every communication they might legitimately make is blocked. As the child learns schizophrenic communication patterns (bad habits of communication), in order to adapt to the communication structure within his family he progressively incapacitates himself for dealing with the larger reality that defines "proper" communications. Since schizophrenia comes from a reality flaw within an individual family, and the adaptation to it is likewise individual, it isolates the individual from others, not only from those who communicate properly but also from other schizophrenics. While a number of people with different patterns of communications may be lumped together analytically and be called schizophrenics, they probably derive their bad habits of communications from a number of different sources. The fact that a schizophrenic cannot communicate with others means that his behavior will stay at the level of habit. He cannot form coordinations and reciprocal typifications with others in order to elaborate his pattern of communication into a more general pattern.

Another bad habit that does not develop into a social institution, is the practice of dressing in the clothes of the opposite sex. With transvestites, as well as with schizophrenics, there are elements of the habit that make institutionalization unlikely. First, the transvestite adopts his behavior in retreat from others. Second, there is no necessity for having a partner or another person with whom reciprocal typification could be made. Third, the transvestite feels he cannot talk about his behavior openly without some negative response. As a consequence the organizations of transvestites that do exist are not institutionalizations of transvestism but groups where mutual emotional support and defence may be found. Transvestism itself remains a "bad habit."

People may also practice bad habits through failure to learn good habits, as defined within their society. In John Blazer's study of married virgins most of the women seem to suffer from a simple lack of proper sexual information on which good sexual habits could be founded. A bad habit may not break any particular social rule but may be a general inability to meaningfully participate in any social institutions, or counter-institutions. Increasingly, as Stewart Wolf suggested, medical research focusing on the role of the brain in cardiac death has found it related to social alienation and social isolation, which may be considered as bad habits of interaction. For the "retreatist" the experience–social reality conflict is a completely overwhelming one. The definitions of the situation that he accepts keep him from making any adaptations other than withdrawal from sociability and possibly lead to voluntary death through vagal stimulation and myocardial infarction.

The social reaction to bad habits has been well summed up by Thomas Scheff's theory of mental illness, and Walter Buckley's formalization of it. In this theoretical analysis Scheff and Buckley point out the way in which breaking of residual rules leads to the individual being processed through a social system characterized by deviation amplifying feedback, until he assumes a stable role as a career deviant.

Bad habits are thus individual responses to conflicts between subjective and socially constructed realities; these responses, categorized and typified as deviant behavior, often aggravate the conflict between subjective reality and social reality.

If a person's pattern of behavior is not inherently asocial, or does not cause difficulties in communication, he may very well desire to meet other people who share his habits, his thoughts, his special view of social reality. Edwin Lemert pointed out that stutterers, although they have many similar problems and are able to identify one another, do not have the possibility of forming effective groups because of their handicap in communication.

Albert Cohen noted the way in which people with similar experience in social reality conflicts may tentatively feel one another out. He suggests that each person opens conversational possibilities, sticks his neck out a little bit, and if the other person responds appropriately, will stick it out further. He suggests further that a joint cultural product (a reciprocal typification in our terms) may emerge, one which has elements intended by neither party: in other words, an emergent counter-institution.

At this level of reciprocal typification, legitimations are not highly structured. They tend to be more or less *social excuses* for doing something that is prohibited within social reality. Gresham Sykes and David Matza suggested that delinquent boys neutralize others' criticism of their behavior through a number of common social excuses, such as the denial of responsibility, the denial of injury, the denial of the victim, condemnation of the condemners, and an appeal to higher loyalties.

While the creation of new and emergent counter-institutions is of theoretical interest, most people in fact fall into ongoing counter-institutions of behavior when they have a subjective reality–social reality conflict. Edwin Sutherland's theory of differential association indicates that the person's social location will frequently be important in determining what patterns of institutions and counter-institutions he is likely to learn. In addition, as Marie-Anne LeGrand has shown, "Rounders" learn and pick up counter-institutions of behavior as they sample among a great many available, in a process very much like choosing a career at the university level.

Many counter-institutions of behavior have a fairly complex technology to be mastered, such as all of the paraphernalia associated with learning to smoke marijuana. Other counter-institutions have formal periods of apprenticeships, as James Bryan illustrated in his article on prostitution.

In short, a person may either create a new counter-institution when his experience and his subjective reality diverge from social reality, or he may join like-minded fellows who have already established such a counter-institution of behavior.

After a counter-institution has been established there are a number of factors that cause it to grow and thrive or that keep it stabilized at some lower level where its recruits and its attritions approximately balance one another. For example, the bottle gang on Skid Row is an almost universal institution among Skid Row men but not one that is likely to sweep the country; this is because the conditions of reality conflict that create the bottle gang are isolated and only applicable to men who live on Skid Row. For people not simultaneously homeless and destitute, there are few reasons for joining a bottle gang.

Another limitation on the growth of a counter-institution may come from its irreversible physical effects. Heroin addiction, for example, begins with a normal process of institutional recruitment but ends with the addicts in antagonistic cooperation with one another, in retreat both from their fellow addicts and society as a whole. This limits the growth of the institution as a functioning pattern of behavior.

Given the pervasive normalcy of everyday reality, and the fact that recruitment to counter-institutions proceeds generally by small increments, the actor is often subjectively unaware of the distance he has traveled until he reconstructs his biography to take account of his new illegitimate activities through an act of retrospective consciousness. In this reconstruction process he, and the others involved, will often create the beginnings of legitimations to explain not only how to go about the behavior, but also why the pattern of behavior is chosen. Within a counter-institution group the discussions and talk that takes place often create legitimations and methods for countering the negative social definition of their behavior.

Counter-institutions are cognitively protected by the creation of legitimations, and they grow more and more stable by other normal processes of institutional defense. For example Sherri Cavan illustrated the way in which homosexuals protect their home territory bar against outsiders by embarrassing heterosexuals when they wander in.

An additional complication may come when counter-institutions are part of legitimate institutions within the institutional order. Many studies conducted by the *Reader's Digest,* The Better Business Bureau, and others, have illustrated that the chance of being cheated while having an appliance or an automobile repaired is very high and that many seemingly legitimate institutions practice routine thievery against their customers.

Informal social controls, both self-controls and relational controls, which are created within legitimate institutions, keep most people conventional most of the time. Counter-institutions, however, create their own controls, which encourage and sustain deviance. Which set of controls is more effective depends on many elements in the situation in which they contend.

Social reality is protected against counter-institutions of behavior through formal social control: official or legal action taken by legitimate institutions against variant forms of institutionalization.

On occasion, as Becker noted, the stimulus for formal social control comes from a moral crusader, an individual who feels that the counter-institution is completely wrong and crusades to have a law passed against it or to increase the law enforcement against it. In other cases Dickson suggested that social reality is "protected" by the organized response of bureaucratic enforcement groups that serve their own needs for institutional survival by criminalizing sections of the environment and thus providing work for themselves.

However a rule is formulated to defend social reality from counter-institutions, its enforcement is a matter of institutionalized activity and may be carried out with a great deal of vigor or as one activity among many.

In many cases, those who violate social reality by being involved in counter-institutions of behavior, are routinely punitively processed, thereby keeping up the work norms of the institutions which do the processing but not producing any significant change in their behavior. In most cases, formal social control is ineffective in halting already institutionalized behavior. Self-controls and relational controls derived from social reality prevent bad habits and counter-institutions if they can be prevented, but what cannot be prevented is then harassed by formal social controls.

The response of the counter-institution to the pressures exerted by relational control and formal social control may be either unorganized or organized. In general, if the followers of the counter-institution do not also form a social group, and if they cannot establish internal communications with one another (in order to create new and better legitimations for their behavior and organized ways of responding to social pressure), they will remain isolated and "managed" by formal social control. McDonald and Copeland noted that prostitution is managed and fragmented by the amount of enforcement that is used against it; though it is never completely eliminated it never takes over as the predominant mode of sexual relationships in a society. It bounces back and forth between the reality flaws that create it and the formal control that contains it. On occasion, even an unorganized group may, through its violent actions, transmit a message regarding its distress to the members of the institutional order. Such is the case with riots in the black ghettos in the United States.

If a counter-institution has generated sufficient legitimations internally so that it can define a part of reality for its participants, members of the institutional order may attempt to negate this definition, this reality. These attempts, through relational and formal controls, are likely to fail because the participants have found their own reality construction a reliable guide to the world around them. Young people do not believe the narcotics bureau's propaganda about marijuana leading to heroin because they can see that it does not. The process of deviation amplifying feedback as exemplified by labeling theory in deviance, is one example of the way in which an individual or a group may become more confirmed in delinquency when labeled as delinquent by the institutional order. This process of labeling has been explored by John Kitsuse, Kai Erikson, and Howard Becker.

The group that is being attacked by the institutional order has some advantages over the individual who is being similarly attacked, because the group members can reinforce one another's definition of reality. The fact that social groups close their ranks and forget their internal differences when they are faced with a hostile environment or an outside enemy has been repeatedly noted by anthropologists. This process may also be termed "deviation amplifying feedback," as noted by Paul Wender. Deviation amplifying feedback processes have often been seen in the escalation of violence between the police and residents of the black ghettos in the United States.

The defense of a counter-institution and its definition of social reality against the socially constructed reality of the institutional order is both physical and theoretical. The knowledge of the members of the group is organized into theoretical legitimations for their behavior that are intended to deflect the criticism of the institutional order. For example, Cory suggests that homosexuals have been taking the position that they are a minority group and should be treated as a minority group rather than as sexual deviants.

Similarly, marijuana smokers such as Allen Ginsberg have created complex theoretical legitimations for their behavioral institution, which take into account all of the criticisms leveled at it by the institutional order. As more and more people smoke marijuana and legitimate it to themselves and to others, tolerance for the habit grows as well as the clamor of opposition. The institutional order does not change quickly, but it does eventually change to reflect the practices, both habits and institutions, of the people within it. When socialites, lawyers, judges, newspaper editors, television commentators, politicians, folk heroes, and possibly a quarter of the generation born after the Second World War all smoke marijuana, there is created a very strong counter-definition of reality.

When a counter-institution is followed by a large enough portion of the members of society, when they have collectively created legitimations that define reality for themselves acceptably, and that are at least *plausible* to those who are opposed to them, and when the followers of the counter-institution occupy social locations of prestige, importance, or power, the counter-institution stands a very good chance of forcing a redefinition of social reality for the society as a whole.

When a counter-institution becomes powerful enough to force formal sanctions against it to be withdrawn, and when enough people are following it so that informal sanctions likewise have been withdrawn, it has achieved a place in the institutional order of the particular society. A classic example of this is the progress of the labor movement from being a radical and anarchistic illegal organization into a pillar of respectability in North American society. Numerous contemporary examples might come from the spreading legitimacy and acceptance of marijuana smoking and of homosexuality as parts of the institutional order of American society. Before a counter-institution is completely accepted it must have theoretical legitimations that fit it into the prevailing pattern, and it must have practical and everyday legitimations that will make it acceptable to a large number of people within the society. The process of changing social reality through the integration of counter-institutions into the institutional order is one that takes many years and is seldom totally finished—there will be many members of the institutional order who have been isolated from the legitimating communications. Rural areas may be slower to accept social changes than urban areas. People functioning within a religious context, for example, may be unprepared to accept homosexuality as moral behavior even though it has scientific or philosophical legitimations.

Social reality construction thus is a process that continues constantly, a process that is falsified by looking at reality as an invariant social fact. Socially constructed reality is a social fact, external to the individual, external to groups in society, but it is also constantly in the process of change as new groups and individuals spread their new realities.

In complex societies the possibility of alternate realities arises. There are, of course, realities appropriate to occupational subgroups within a society, but those are generally considered legitimate variants of the reality legitimated by the overarching values of the symbolic universe. In addition there are other realities in which the entire cosmos is evaluated upon different assumptions. These realities are considered deviant. Those who believe in them are considered heretics.

Simmons and Winograd illustrated the values of an emerging hip reality, which is not yet complete. Some of its values are widespread, others are only held by people who live entirely within the reality. Conversion from conventional to hip reality may be stimulated by unsuccessful socialization. The various "lines" that one reality extends into others provide a means of gaining access to converts. Hip reality has many lines into conventional reality: music, art, sexuality, underground newspapers, drugs, and hip communities. Each of these "lines" facilitates making an emotional attachment between someone within the reality and someone else outside. Hip reality has, in certain areas of the country, an institutional base that allows a potential convert to migrate from the conventional world entirely to the hip world. This institutional base means that an individual can carry out all of his activities within an environment that supports and confirms the reality. The "conversion experience" that a person might have, perhaps when smoking marijuana, is insufficient for a complete conversion. The convert must live the new reality, segregating himself from the conventional world.

Conventional reality offers temptations to lure the convert back, but in most cases these are anticipated and countered by his significant others in hip reality. The convert's linguistic structure undergoes a change that reflects his socialization to the new values. Although converts to other alternate realities find it necessary to reinterpret their biographies, the general lack of interest in the past manifested in hip reality makes such reinterpretations somewhat unnecessary. A view of people living in conventional reality as "unfree" does grow, however, along with a general feeling that "The system doesn't work." Since their languages are different, hip and conventional people often talk to one another in parallel monologues and do not reach agreements.

Alternate realities that are older, better organized, and more total than hip reality often have recourse to formal means of therapy or conversion. Jerome Frank noted the similarities between thought reform, revivalist religion, miracle cures, and religious healing. All are organized techniques to convert or return an individual to the point where his subjective reality is congruent with an alternate or conventional social reality.

People who believe that the space brothers have come in flying saucers to instruct and protect man live in a part-time alternate reality. Though new-age reality is intellectually complex, it exists without any significant degree of institutional substruction. A believer thus only finds his reality confirmed on selected occasions, rather than every day in every way.

New-age reality appeals primarily to older people, ladies, who seem to be not very well off, and undereducated, for participation in modern society. It offers them a meaningful existence in which they can feel worthwhile. Conventional reality assigns poor, uneducated old ladies to the refuse pile, and gives them few things to be proud of.

A full-time alternate reality with complete institutional substruction was created by the Christian missionaries to the Karen in Burma. The missionaries converted the Karen, at first without Buddhist dissent, later in the face of it. A number of Karen myths allowed Christianity easy access, and the fact that it was the religion of the British ruling class and provided education and other services allowed it to spread quickly.

The process of conversion to an alternate full-time reality required converts to break their ties to their old ways, and often to become hostile even to members of their families. When they converted they belonged completely to Christianity and they became deployable agents who could be assigned to help convert others, or to fight against the Burmese when the need arose.

Christianity provided an organizational structure for bringing together the scattered Karen tribes. It provided continuous communications. It provided two levels of leadership in Karen villages: the minister and the lay Christians. When bands of Burmese, under the leadership of politically minded Buddhist monks, began burning Karen villages, the Karen banded together under Christian and missionary leadership and fought back.

Although they received their alternate reality by importation, its foundations were well laid, and conflict between the Christian Karen and the Buddhist Burmese still breaks out on occasion.

A truly self-sustaining reality must have a complete explanation for everything in the lives of its adherents. It must contain a complete institutional order. It must be able to protect its boundaries both theoretically and physically. LeRoi Jones suggested the ways in which such a reality could be constructed for North American blacks: rediscovering black history, and building upon the institutions that blacks already have. The religious, philosophical, and "scientific" legitimations for black inferiority that have been created in white conventional reality indicate that blacks must establish their own reality or face continued subjection.

The four basic methods that realities use when in conflict with one another are: therapy, nihilization, segregation, and extermination. All of these techniques are used in conflict between self-sustaining realities, though in different mixtures depending on whether the conflict is a long-term evolutional one, a conflict between distinct mature realities, or one brought forth by revolution.

Any reality will define some individuals as deviant because they have "bad habits," some behavior patterns as counter-institutions, and all alternate realities as fundamental error.

WHAT NOW?

It seems to me that the perspective that this book represents opens a number of relevant questions that need investigation.

How, for example, do individuals wind up with their own distinctive subjective realities? To what extent are subjective realities shared with larger aggregates of individuals—families, groups, organizations, and total societies? Can we find some way of describing the relationship between the individual's knowledge and the social knowledge around him? Perhaps the analysis of autobiographies would be the most productive way of approaching this problem. Where people have not written their autobiographies they can be helped to do so. The biographies of the rich and powerful are easy to find, but biographies of the ordinary individual are rare. We need to know more about the realities of the ordinary individual, and the institutions of behavior he follows.

Is it any longer fruitful to study social deviance? The name of our enterprise often colors our perspective. Perhaps what we should be looking at is the "politics of subreality conflicts." What I have variously called conventional reality, and the realities of the institutional order are also subrealities that only seem to us to be "reality" if we live within it. If we were to study the politics of subreality conflict we might be able to see the processes involved without giving our automatic assent to one or the other party to the conflict.

If it is impossible to stand above the conflict perhaps it would be useful to look at the conflict inside out. I think it would be interesting to see a sociologist study the legitimate institutional order and symbolic universe as a "deviant" system, perhaps from the perspective of hip reality. Only by making the conventional seem incongruous can we free ourselves of our cultural blinders.

The concept of "reality flaws" needs more specification. How do people become aware of them? What are the ways in which people cope with conflicts between their subjective reality and social reality besides becoming "deviant"? What reality flaws affect individuals, what reality flaws affect collections of individuals, what reality flaws affect groups?

A very interesting area of research would involve participant observation of an organization that was attempting to make a counter-institution legitimate. What are the strategies? What are the tactics? How do such organizations arise? Alternatively one might study the opposition to legitimating a counter-institution. Whose interests are served by keeping some behavior illegitimate? How are these interests related to the strategies and tactics adopted? What are the legitimations adopted? I suspect that such conflicts will become much more frequent in the near future as many counter-institutions are on the road to legitimacy and conservatives feel assaulted from all sides.

A related question would be the role of power in establishing and maintaining predominant institutions, and the role of power in defining and redefining social reality. Who has power? How is it used? What are the relationships between power and legitimacy?

A number of questions might be raised about the purpose of formal social control. Is social control used to keep people from hurting others, to enforce a particular conception of reality, or to maintain someone's status quo? An analysis of social control might start with finding out who actually *has* it used against them and comparing this with the people it *might* be used against.

Another interesting area of study might be the routes that a new element of social reality follows as it spreads through the population. Who accepts it first? Who accepts it later? Who never accepts it? Various studies of the diffusion of information and invention might provide models for analyzing the acceptance of the legitimacy of a former counter-institution.

Finally, and possibly most important, what are the social bases from which alternate realities spring? Marx answered that relationship to the means of production was central. But what of relations to kinship structures, to territories, to communications? Given a collection of people who potentially could create an alternate reality, what leads them to do so, or not to do so?

These are some of the questions I would like to see answered.

☐ ☐ ☐

BIBLIOGRAPHY OF GENERAL AND THEORETICAL WORKS ON DEVIANCE

These bibliographies have been organized to aid the student who is doing his own research on deviance. The first bibliography contains references to works on deviance in general and works that emphasize theoretical concerns. The twenty subject bibliographies that follow the first bibliography are selected lists of works on particular subjects.

Arnold, T.W. 1935. *The Symbols of Government.* New Haven: Yale University Press.

Becker, E. 1962. *The Birth and Death of Meaning.* New York: The Macmillan Company.

―――――. 1964. *The Revolution in Psychiatry.* New York: The Macmillan Company.

―――――. 1968. *The Structure of Evil: An Essay on the Unification of the Science of Man.* New York: George Braziller, Inc.

Becker, H.S., ed. 1964. *The Other Side.* New York: The Macmillan Company.

―――――. 1963. *Outsiders: Studies in the Sociology of Deviance.* New York: The Macmillan Company.

―――――. 1967. "Whose Side Are We On?" *Social Problems* 14:239–247.

―――――. "Notes on the Concept of Commitment." *American Journal of Sociology* 64:32–40.

Berger, P. L., and T. Luckmann. 1966. *The Social Construction of Reality: A Treatise in the Sociology of Knowledge.* New York: Doubleday & Company, Inc.

Bordua, D. J. 1967. "Recent Trends: Deviant Behavior and Social Control." *The Annals of the American Academy of Political and Social Science* 369:149–163.

Brown, C. 1965. *Manchild in the Promised Land.* New York: The Macmillan Company.

Buckley, W. 1967. *Sociology and Modern Systems Theory.* Englewood Cliffs, N.J.: Prentice-Hall.

Buckner, H.T. 1965. "A Theory of Rumor Transmission." *Public Opinion Quarterly* 29:54–70.

―――――. 1970. "Transformations of Reality in the Legal Process." *Social Research* 37:88–101.

Burgess, R.L., and R.L. Akers. 1966. "A Differential Association-Reinforcement Theory of Criminal Behavior." *Social Problems* 14:128–147.

Chambliss, W.J. 1964. "A Sociological Analysis of the Law of Vagrancy." *Social Problems* 12:67–77.

Clinard, M. B. 1968. *Sociology of Deviant Behavior.* 3rd ed. New York: Holt, Rinehart and Winston, Inc.

Cohen, A.K. 1966. *Deviance and Control.* Englewood Cliffs, N.J.: Prentice-Hall, Inc.

_____. 1959. "The Study of Disorganization and Deviant Behavior." In *Sociology Today.* Edited by R.K. Merton, L. Broom and L.S. Cottrell. New York: Basic Books, Inc., pp. 461–484.

Coser, L.A. 1962. "Some Functions of Deviant Behavior and Normative Flexibility." *American Journal of Sociology* 68:172–181.

Cressey, D.R. 1955. "Changing Criminals: The Application of the Theory of Differential Association." *American Journal of Sociology* 61:116–120.

_____. 1965. "Social Psychological Foundations for Using Criminals in the Rehabilitation of Criminals." *Journal of Research in Crime and Delinquency* 2:49–59.

_____. 1962. "Role Theory, Differential Association and Compulsive Crimes." In *Human Behavior and Social Processes.* Edited by A. Rose. Boston: Houghton Mifflin Company, pp. 443–467.

Cronon, E.D. 1955. *Black Moses: The Story of Marcus Garvey and the Universal Negro Improvement Association.* Madison: University of Wisconsin Press.

Davis, F. 1961. "Deviance Disavowal: The Management of Strained Interaction." *Social Problems* 9:120–132.

Dentler, R.A., and K.T. Erikson. 1959. "The Functions of Deviance in Groups." *Social Problems* 7:98–107.

Deutsch, R. M. 1961. *The Nuts Among the Berries.* New York: Ballantine Books, Inc.

Douglas, J. D. 1967. *The Social Meanings of Suicide.* Princeton, N.J.: Princeton University Press.

_____. 1969. "The General Theoretical Implications of the Sociology of Deviance." In *Theoretical Sociology: Perspectives and Developments.* Edited by J.C. McKinney and E.A. Tirakian. New York: Appleton-Century-Crofts.

Dynes, R., and F.L. Quarantelli. 1968. "What Looting in Civil Disturbances Really Means." *Trans*-Action, pp. 9–14.

Elliott, M., and F.E. Merrill. 1934. *Social Disorganization.* New York: Harper & Row, Publishers.

Erikson, K.T. 1967. "A Comment on Disguised Observation in Sociology." *Social Problems* 14:366–373.

————. 1962. "Notes on the Sociology of Deviance." *Social Problems* 9:307–314.

————. 1966. *Wayward Puritans: A Study in the Sociology of Deviance.* New York: John Wiley & Sons, Inc.

Festinger, Leon *et al.* 1956. *When Prophecy Fails: A Social & Psychological Study of a Modern Group That Predicted the Destruction of the World.* New York: Torch Books, Harper & Row, Publishers.

Garfinkel, H. 1956. "Conditions of Successful Degradation Ceremonies." *American Journal of Sociology* 61:420–424.

Gibbs. J. P. 1966. "Conceptions of Deviant Behavior: New and Old." *Pacific Sociological Review* 9:9–14.

Goffman, E. 1961. *Encounters: Two Studies in the Sociology of Interaction.* Indianapolis, Ind.: The Bobbs-Merrill Co., Inc.

————. 1959. *The Presentation of Self in Everyday Life.* New York: Doubleday and Company, Inc.

————. 1963. *Stigma: Notes on the Management of Spoiled Identity.* Englewood Cliffs, N.J.: Prentice-Hall, Inc.

Gusfield, J. R. 1957. "The Problem of Generations in an Organizational Structure." *Social Forces* 35:323–330.

Hewitt, J. P. 1970. *Social Stratification and Deviant Behavior.* New York: Random House, Inc.

Horowitz, I. L., and M. Leibowitz. 1968. "Social Deviance and Political Marginality: Toward a Redefinition of the Relation Between Sociology and Politics." *Social Problems* 15:280–296.

Horton, J. 1966. "Order and Conflict Theories of Social Problems as Competing Ideologies." *American Journal of Sociology* 71:701–713.

Jacobs, J. 1963. *The Death and Life of Great American Cities.* New York: Vintage Books.

Jones, LeRoi. 1968. "The Need For a Cultural Base to Civil Rites & Bpower Mooments." In *The Black Power Revolt.* Edited by Floyd B. Barbour. Boston: Porter Sargent, Publisher.

Keniston, K. 1965. *The Uncommitted.* New York: Harcourt, Brace & World, Inc.

Kinch, J. 1963. "A Formalized Theory of the Self Concept." *American Journal of Sociology* 68:481–486.

Kitsuse, J. I. 1962. "Societal Reaction to Deviant Behavior: Problems of Theory and Method." *Social Problems* 9:247–256.

Lea, H. C. 1961. *The Inquisition of the Middle Ages.* New York: Citadel Press.

Lemert, E. M. 1948. "Some Aspects of a General Theory of Sociopathic Behavior." *Proceedings of the Pacific Sociological Society* 16:23–29.

————. 1967. *Human Deviance, Social Problems and Social Control.* Englewood Cliffs, N.J.: Prentice-Hall, Inc.

————. 1951. *Social Pathology.* New York: McGraw-Hill Book Company.

Lofland, J. 1969. *Deviance and Identity.* Englewood Cliffs, N.J.: Prentice-Hall, Inc.

Long, N.E. 1958. "The Local Community As an Ecology of Games." *American Journal of Sociology* 64:251–261.

Malcolm X (with the assistance of Alex Haley). 1966. *The Autobiography of Malcolm X.* New York: Grove Press, Inc.

Maruyama, M. 1963. "The Second Cybernetics: Deviation-Amplifying Mutual Causative Processes." *American Scientist* 51:164–179.

Matza, D. 1961. "Subterranean Traditions of Youth." *The Annals of the American Academy of Political and Social Science* 328:102–118.

————. 1969. *Becoming Deviant.* Englewood Cliffs, N.J.: Prentice-Hall, Inc.

McLuhan, M. 1966. *Understanding Media.* New York: Signet.

Merton, R., and R. Nisbet. 1962. *Contemporary Social Problems.* New York: Harcourt, Brace & World.

Messinger, S.L. 1955. "Organizational Transformation: A Case Study of a Declining Social Movement." *American Sociological Review* 20:3–10.

Mills, C.W. 1963. "The Big City: Private Troubles and Public Issues." In *Power, Politics and People: The Collected Essays of C. Wright Mills.* Edited by I. L. Horowitz. New York: Ballantine Books, pp. 395–402.

Mills, C.W. 1942. "The Professional Ideology of Social Pathologists." *American Journal of Sociology* 49:165–180.

————. 1940. "Situated Actions and Vocabularies of Motive." *American Sociological Review* 5:904–913.

————. 1950. *The Sociological Imagination.* New York: Oxford University Press, Inc.

Nettler, G. 1961. "Good Men, Bad Men, and the Perception of Reality." *Sociometry* 24:279–294.

Polsky, N. 1967. *Hustlers, Beats, and Others.* Chicago: Aldine Publishing Company.

Reynolds, F. 1967. *Freewheelin Frank: Secretary of The Angels, As Told to Michael McClure.* New York: Grove Press.

Roszak, Theodore. 1969. *The Making of a Counter Culture.* Garden City, N.Y.: Anchor Books, Doubleday & Company, Inc.

Rubington, E. and M.S. Weinberg, eds. 1968. *Deviance: The Interactionist Perspective.* New York: The Macmillan Company.

Sagarin, E. 1969. *Odd Man In: Societies of Deviants in America.* Chicago: Quadrangle Books.

Schutz, A. *Collected Papers.* The Hague: Martinus Mijhoff, vol. 1 (2nd ed.) 1967; vol. 2, 1964; vol. 3, 1966.

————. 1967. *The Phenomenology of the Social World.* Northwestern University Press.

Schur, E. 1965. *Crimes Without Victims.* Englewood Cliffs, N.J.: Prentice-Hall, Inc.

Sellin, T. 1938. *Culture Conflict and Crime.* New York: Social Science Research Council, Bulletin 41.

Selznick, P. 1951. "Institutional Vulnerability in Mass Society." *American Journal of Sociology* 56:320–331.

————. 1960. *The Organizational Weapon, A Study of Bolshevik Strategy and Tactics.* New York: The Macmillan Company.

Silberman, C. E. 1964. *Crisis in Black and White.* New York: Vintage Books.

Simmons, J. L. 1964. "On Maintaining Deviant Belief Systems." *Social Problems* 11:250–256.

Simmons, J. L. and B. Winograd, 1966. *it's happening.* Santa Barbara: Marc-Laird.

Smelser, N. J. 1963. *Collective Behavior.* New York: The Macmillan Company.

Stark, R. 1963. "On the Incompatibility of Religion and Science." *Journal for the Scientific Study of Religion* 3:3–20.

Sutherland, E. H., and D. R. Cressey. 1966. *Principles of Criminology.* 7th ed. Philadelphia: J. B. Lippincott Company.

Sykes, G. M., and D. Matza. 1957. "Techniques of Neutralization: A Theory of Delinquency." *American Sociological Review* 22:664–670.

Thompson, H. S. 1967. *Hell's Angels.* New York: Ballantine Books.

Weber, M. 1946. *From Max Weber: Essays in Sociology.* Translated by H. H. Gerth and C. W. Mills. New York: Oxford University Press, Inc.

Weisstein, N. 1969. "Kinder, Küche, Kirche as Scientific Law: Psychology constructs the female." *Motive* 29:78–85.

Wender, P. H. 1968. "Vicious and Virtuous Circles: The Role of Deviation Amplifying Feedback in the Origin and Perpetuation of Behavior." *Psychiatry* 31:309–324.

Wilkins, L. T. 1965. *Social Deviance.* Englewood Cliffs, N.J.: Prentice-Hall, Inc.

Wolf, S. 1967. "The End of the Rope: The Role of the Brain in Cardiac Death." *The Canadian Medical Association Journal* 97:1022–1025.

ANOMIE

Clinard, M. B., ed. 1964. *Anomie and Deviant Behavior: A Discussion and Critique.* New York: The Macmillan Company.

Cloward, R. A. 1959. "Illegitimate Means, Anomie, and Deviant Behavior." *American Sociological Review* 24:164–176.

Cloward, R.A., and L.E. Ohlin. 1960. *Delinquency and Opportunity.* New York: The Macmillan Company.

Durkheim, E. 1951. *Suicide.* New York: The Macmillan Company.

Merton, R. K. 1957. *Social Theory and Social Structure.* New York: The Macmillan Company.

BAD HABITS OF INTERACTION

Blazer, J.A. 1964. "Married Virgins: A Study of Unconsummated Marriages." *Journal of Marriage and the Family* 26:213–214.

Cameron, N. 1943. "The Paranoid Pseudo-Community." *American Journal of Sociology* 49:32–38.

_____. 1959. "The Paranoid Pseudo-Community Revisited." *American Journal of Sociology* 65:52–58.

Dohrenwend, B.P., and E. Chin–Shong. 1967. "Social Status and Attitudes Toward Psychological Disorder: The Problem of Tolerance of Deviance." *American Sociological Review* 32:417–433.

Eaton, J.W. in collaboration with R.J. Weil. 1955. *Culture and Mental Disorders: A Comparative Study of Hutterites and Other Populations.* New York: The Macmillan Company.

Edgerton, R.B. 1967. *The Cloak of Competence: Stigma in the Lives of the Mentally Retarded.* Berkeley and Los Angeles: University of California Press.

Foucault, M. 1967. *Madness and Civilization: A History of Insanity in the Age of Reason.* New York: New American Library.

Friedman, L.J. 1962. *Virgin Wives: A Study of Unconsummated Marriages.* Springfield, Ill.: Charles C. Thomas, Publisher.

Haley, J. 1959. "The Family of the Schizophrenic: A Model System." *The Journal of Nervous and Mental Disease* 129:357–374.

Hollingshead, A.B., and R.C. Redlich. 1958. *Social Class and Mental Illness: A Community Study.* New York: John Wiley & Sons Inc.

Lemert, E.M. 1962. "Paranoia and the Dynamics of Exclusion." *Sociometry* 25:2–20.

Lorber, J. 1967. "Deviance as Performance: The Case of Illness." *Social Problems* 14:302–310.

Phillips, D.L. 1963. "Rejection: A Possible Consequence of Seeking Help for Mental Disorders." *American Sociological Review* 28:963–972.

Rokeach, M. 1964. *The Three Christs of Ypsilanti.* New York: Alfred A. Knopf, Inc.

Scheff, T.J. 1963. "The Role of the Mentally Ill and the Dynamics of Mental Disorder: A Research Framework." *Sociometry* 26:436–453.

_____. 1963. *Being Mentally Ill.* Chicago: Aldine Publishing Company.

_____, ed. 1967. *Mental Illness and Social Processes.* New York: Harper & Row, Publishers.

_____, with the assistance of D.M. Culver. 1964. "The Societal Reaction to Deviance: Ascriptive Elements in the Psychiatric Screening of Mental Patients in a Midwestern State." *Social Problems* 11:401–413.

Szasz, T.S. 1961. *The Myth of Mental Illness.* New York: Hoeber-Harper Books.

_____. 1970. *The Manufacture of Madness: A Comparative Study of the Inquisition and the Mental Health Movement.* New York: Harper & Row, Publishers.

Weinberg, S.K., ed. 1967. *The Sociology of Mental Disorders: Analyses and Readings in Psychiatric Sociology.* Chicago: Aldine Publishing Company.

CHRISTIAN KAREN

Brohm, J.F. 1952. "The Function of Basic Religious Roles in Burmese Culture." (Unpublished M.A. thesis, Cornell University).

Buckner, H.T. 1964. The Christian Karen in *Deviant-Group Organizations.* (Unpublished M.A. thesis, University of California).

Cady, J.F.A. 1958. *History of Modern Burma.* Ithaca, N.Y.: Cornell University Press.

Christian, J.L. 1942. *Modern Burma.* Berkeley and Los Angeles: University of California Press.

Mason, Rev. F. 1843. *The Karen Apostle: or Memoir of Ko Thah-Byu.* Boston: Gould, Kendall and Lincoln.

McMahon, Lt. Col. A.R. 1876. *The Karens of the Golden Chersonese.* London: Harison.

Truxton, A.S. 1958. "The Integration of the Karen Peoples of Burma and Thailand into their Respective National Cultures: A Study in the Dynamics of Cultural Contact." (Unpublished M.A. thesis, Cornell University).

CRIME

Amir, M. 1967. "Patterns of Forcible Rape." In *Criminal Behavior Systems: A Typology*. Edited by M. Clinard and R. Quinney. New York: Holt, Rinehart and Winston, Inc., pp. 60–75.

Anderson, R. T. 1965. "From Mafia to Cosa Nostra." *American Journal of Sociology* 71:302–310.

Bell, D. 1953. "Crime as an American Way of Life." *Antioch Review* 8:131–153.

Cameron, M. O. 1964. *The Booster and the Snitch: Department Store Shoplifting.* New York: The Macmillan Company.

Clinard, M.B., and R. Quinney, eds. 1967. *Criminal Behavior Systems: A Typology.* New York: Holt, Rinehart and Winston, Inc.

Gasser, R. L. 1955. "The Confidence World as a Criminal Behavior System." (Unpublished Ph.D. dissertation, American University).

Genet, J. 1949. *The Thief's Journal.* New York: Bantam Books, Inc.

Gibbons, D. C. 1968. *Society, Crime and Criminal Careers.* Englewood Cliffs, N.J.: Prentice-Hall, Inc.

Lemert, E. M. 1958. "The Behavior of the Systematic Check Forger." *Social Problems* 6:141–149.

_____. 1953. "An Isolation and Closure Theory of Naïve Check Forgery." *Journal of Criminal Law, Criminology and Police Science* 44:296–307.

Maurer, D. W. 1962. *The Big Con.* New York: Signet.

Quinney, R. 1970. *The Social Reality of Crime.* Boston: Little, Brown and Company.

Roebuck, J. B. and M. L. Cadwallader. 1961. "The Negro Armed Robber As a Criminal Type: The Construction and Application of a Typology." *Pacific Sociological Review* 4:21–26.

Sutherland, E. H. 1937. *The Professional Thief.* Chicago: University of Chicago Press.

Taft, D.R., and R.W. England, Jr. 1964. *Criminology.* 4th ed. New York: The Macmillan Company.

Tannenbaum, F. 1938. *Crime and the Community.* Boston: Ginn and Company.

Tyler, G. 1967. *Organized Crime in America.* Ann Arbor, Michigan: Ann Arbor Paperbacks.

CRUSADES

Bittner, E. 1963. "Radicalism and the Organization of Radical Movements." *American Sociological Review* 28:928–940.

Dickson, D. T. 1968. "Bureaucracy and Morality: An Organizational Perspective on a Moral Crusade." *Social Problems* 16:143–156.

Gusfield, J. R. 1967. "Moral Passage: The Symbolic Process in Public Designation of Deviance." *Social Problems* 15:175–188.

_____. 1957. "The Problem of Generations in an Organizational Structure." *Social Forces* 35:323–330.

_____. 1956. "Social Structure and Moral Reform: A Study of the Woman's Christian Temperance Union." *American Journal of Sociology* 59:221–232.

Keniston, K. 1968. *Young Radicals: Notes on Committed Youth.* New York: Harvest Books.

Klapp, O. E. 1969. *Collective Search for Identity.* New York: Holt, Rinehart and Winston, Inc.

Messinger, S. L. 1955. "Organizational Transformation: A Case Study of a Declining Social Movement." *American Sociological Review* 20:3–10.

Sutherland, E. H. 1950. "The Diffusion of Sexual Psychopath Laws." *American Journal of Sociology* 56:142–148.

Toch, H. 1965. *The Social Psychology of Social Movements.* Indianapolis, Ind.: Bobbs-Merrill Co., Inc.

DELINQUENCY

Bordua, D. J. 1961. "Delinquent Subcultures: Sociological Interpretations of Gang Delinquency." *The Annals of the American Academy of Political and Social Science* 338:119–136.

Briar, S., and I. Piliavin. 1965. "Delinquency, Situational Inducements and Commitment to Conformity." *Social Problems* 13:35–45.

Cloward, R. A. 1960. *Delinquency and Opportunity: A Theory of Delinquent Gangs.* New York: The Macmillan Company.

Cohen, A. K. 1955. *Delinquent Boys.* New York: The Macmillan Company.

Cohen, A. K., and J. F. Short, Jr. 1958. "Research in Delinquent Subcultures." *Journal of Social Issues* 14:20–37.

Dinitz, S., F. R. Scarpitti and W. C. Reckless. 1962. "Delinquency Vulnerability: A Cross Group and Longitudinal Analysis." *American Sociological Review* 27:515–517.

Downes, D. M. 1966. *The Delinquent Solution: A Study in Subcultural Theory.* New York: The Macmillan Company.

Erickson, M., and L. T. Empey. 1963. "Court Records: Undetected Delinquency and Decision Making." *Journal of Criminal Law, Criminology and Police Science* 54:456–469.

Harris, D.B. 1968. "On Differential Stigmatization for Predelinquents." *Social Problems* 15:507–508.

Kobrin, S. 1951. "The Conflict of Values in Delinquency Areas." *American Sociological Review* 16:653–661.

Lemert, E.M. 1967. "The Juvenile Court—Quest and Realities," in the "President's Commission on Law Enforcement and Administration of Justice," *Task Force Report: Juvenile Delinquency and Youth Crime.* Washington, D.C.: U.S. Government Printing Office.

Matza, D. 1964. *Delinquency and Drift.* New York: John Wiley & Sons, Inc.

————, and G.M. Sykes. 1961. "Delinquency and Subterranean Values." *American Sociological Review* 26:712–719.

Meyer, H., and E. Borgotta. 1965. *Girls at Vocational High.* New York: Russell Sage Foundation.

Reckless, W.C., S. Dinitz and B. Kay. 1957. "The Self Concept in Potential Delinquency and Potential Nondelinquency." *American Sociological Review* 22:566–570.

Rosenberg, B., and H. Silverstein. 1969. *The Varieties of Delinquent Experience.* Waltham, Mass.: Blaisdell Publishing Company.

Sellin, T., and M.E. Wolfgang, eds. 1969. *Delinquency: Selected Studies.* New York: John Wiley & Sons, Inc.

Shaw, C.H. 1931. *The Natural History of a Delinquent Career.* Chicago: University of Chicago Press.

Short, J.F., and F.I. Nye. 1958. "Extent of Unrecorded Delinquency." *Journal of Criminal Law, Criminology and Police Science* 49:296–302.

————, and F.L. Strodtbeck. 1965. *Group Process and Gang Delinquency.* Chicago: University of Chicago Press.

————. 1963. "The Response of Gang Leaders to Status Threats." *American Journal of Sociology* 67:571–579.

Sykes, G., and D. Matza. 1957. "Techniques of Neutralization: A Theory of Delinquency." *American Sociological Review* 22:664–670.

Thrasher, F. 1927. *The Gang.* Chicago: University of Chicago Press.

Wade, A.L. 1967. "Social Processes in the Act of Juvenile Vandalism," in *Criminal Behavior Systems: A Typology.* M.B. Clinard and R. Quinney, eds. New York: Holt, Rinehart & Winston, Inc., pp. 94–109.

Werthman, C., and I. Piliavin. 1967. "Gang Members and the Police," in *The Police: Six Sociological Essays.* D. Bordua, ed. New York: John Wiley & Sons, Inc., pp. 56–98.

Vaz, E.W., ed. 1967. *Middle-Class Juvenile Delinquency.* New York: Harper & Row, Publishers.

DRUGS

Aberle, D. F. 1966. *The Peyote Religion Among the Navaho.* Chicago: Aldine Publishing Company.

Abramson, H. A., ed. 1966. *The Use of LSD in Psychotherapy and Alcoholism.* Indianapolis, Ind.: The Bobbs-Merrill Co., Inc.

Becker, H. S. 1967. "History, Culture and Subjective Experience: An Exploration of the Social Bases of Drug-Induced Experiences." *Journal of Health & Social Behavior* 8:163–176.

Blum, R. and associates. 1964. *Utopiates: The Use and Users of LSD 25.* New York: Atherton Press.

Castenada, C. 1969. *The Teachings of Don Juan: A Yaqui Way of Knowledge.* New York: Ballantine Books.

Ditman, K. 1968. "The Use of LSD in the Treatment of the Alcoholic," in *Alcoholism: Behavioral Research, Therapeutic Approaches.* R. Fox, ed. New York: Springer Publishing Company, Inc., Chap. 23.

Gellman, I. P. 1964. *The Sober Alcoholic.* New Haven, Conn.: College & University Press.

Ginsberg, A. 1966. "The Great Marijuana Hoax." *The Atlantic Monthly,* November issue.

Gusfield, J. R. 1963. *Symbolic Crusade: Status Politics and the American Temperance Movement.* Urbana, Ill.: University of Illinois Press.

Hoffer, A. 1965. "D-Lysergic Acid Diethylamide (LSD): a Review of Its Present Status." *Clinical Pharmacology and Therapeutics* 6:183–255.

Jellinek, E. M. 1952. "Phases of Alcohol Addiction." *Quarterly Journal of Studies on Alcohol,* 13:673–684.

Suchman, E. A. 1968. "The 'Hang-Loose' Ethic and the Spirit of Drug Use." *Journal of Health and Social Behavior* 9:146–155.

FLYING SAUCERS

Adamski, G. 1955. *Inside the Space Ships.* New York: Abelard-Schuman, Inc.

Allingham, C. 1955. *Flying Saucers from Mars.* New York: British Book Centre.

Angelucci, O. M. 1955. *The Secret of the Saucers.* Amherst, Wisconsin: Amherst Press.

Bethurum, T. 1954. *Aboard a Flying Saucer.* Los Angeles: DeVorss & Company.

Buckner, H. T. 1966. "Flying Saucers Are for People." *Trans*-Action.

Dohrman, H. T. 1958. *California Cult: The Story of "Mankind United."* Boston: Beacon Press.

Fry, D. W. 1954. *Alan's Message to the Men of Earth.* Los Angeles: New Age Publishing Company.

_____. 1954. *The White Sands Incident.* Los Angeles: New Age Publishing Company.

Heard, G. 1950. *Is Another World Watching?* New York: Harper & Row, Publishers.

Jessup, M. K. 1957. *The Expanding Case for the UFO.* New York: The Citadel Press.

Jung, C. G. 1959. *Flying Saucers, A Modern Myth of Things Seen in the Skies.* Translated by R. F. C. Hull. New York: Harcourt, Brace & World, Inc.

Keyhoe, D. 1953. *Flying Saucers from Outer Space.* New York: Permabooks.

_____. 1950. *The Flying Saucers Are Real.* New York: Fawcett Publications, Inc.

Kraspedon, D. 1960. *My Contact with Flying Saucers.* Clarksburg, W. Va.: Saucerian Books.

Leslie, D., and G. Adamski. 1954. *Flying Saucers Have Landed. New York:* British Book Centre.

Lorenzen, C. E. 1962. *The Great Flying Saucer Hoax.* New York: William-Frederick Press, for the Aerial Phenomena Research Organization of Tucson, Arizona.

Menzel, D. H. 1953. *Flying Saucers.* Cambridge: Harvard University Press.

Nebel, Long John. 1961. *The Way Out World.* Englewood Cliffs, N.J.: Prentice-Hall, Inc.

Reeve, B. and H. 1957. *Flying Saucer Pilgrimage.* Amherst, Wisconsin: Amherst Press.

Scully, F. 1950. *Behind the Flying Saucers.* New York: Holt, Rinehart and Winston.

Taoker, Lt. Col. L. J. 1960. *Flying Saucers and the U.S. Air Force.* Princeton, N.J.: D. Van Nostrand Company, Inc.

Van Tassel, G. W. 1952. *I Rode a Flying Saucer.* Los Angeles: New Age Publishing Company.

Vegan, P. 1961. *Telah Speaks.* Lemon Grove, California: Telah Press.

Wilkins, H. T. 1954. *Flying Saucers on the Attack.* New York: The Citadel Press.

Williamson, G. H. and A. C. Bailey. 1954. *The Saucers Speak.* Los Angeles: New Age Publishing Company.

HOMOSEXUALITY

Cavan, S. 1963. "Interaction in Home Territories." *Berkeley Journal of Sociology* 8:17–32.

Cory, D. W. 1960. *The Homosexual in America.* 2nd ed. New York: Castle Books.

Hauser, R. 1962. *The Homosexual Society.* London: The Bodley Head.

Kinsey, A. C. *et al.* 1948. *Sexual Behavior in the Human Male.* Philadelphia: W. B. Saunders Company.

—————. 1953. *Sexual Behavior in the Human Female.* Philadelphia: W. B. Saunders Company.

Leznoff, M., and W. A. Westley. 1956. "The Homosexual Community." *Social Problems* 3:257–263.

Simon, W., and J. H. Gagnon. 1967. "The Lesbians: A Preliminary Overview," in *Sexual Deviance.* J. H. Gagnon and W. Simon, with the assistance of D. E. Carns, eds. New York: Harper & Row, Publishers, pp. 247–282.

Ward, D. A., and G. Kassebaum. 1964. "Homosexuality: A Mode of Adaptation in a Prison for Women." *Social Problems* 12:159–177.

INFORMAL SOCIAL CONTROL

Becker, H. S. 1962. "Marihuana Use and Social Control," in *Human Behavior and Social Processes.* Edited by Arnold Rose. Boston: Houghton Mifflin Company, pp. 589–607.

Goffman, E. 1969. "The Insanity of Place." *Psychiatry* 32:357–388.

Reiss, A. J., Jr. 1951. "Delinquency as the Failure of Personal and Social Controls." *American Sociological Review* 16:196–207.

Shibutani, T. 1962. "Reference Groups and Social Control," in *Human Behavior and Social Processes.* Edited by Arnold Rose. Boston: Houghton Mifflin Company, pp. 128–147.

Simmons, J. L., with the assistance of H. Chambers. 1965. "Public Stereotypes of Deviants." *Social Problems* 13:223–232.

MENTAL HOSPITALS

Belknap, I. 1956. *Human Problems of a State Mental Hospital.* New York: McGraw-Hill Book Company.

Goffman, E. 1961. *Asylums.* New York: Doubleday and Company, Inc.

Kesey, K. 1962. *One Flew Over the Cuckoo's Nest.* New York: Signet.

Miller, D. 1967. "Retrospective Analysis of Posthospital Mental Patients' Worlds." *Journal of Health and Social Behavior* 8:136–140.

————, and M. Schwartz. 1966. "County Lunacy Commission Hearings: Some Observations of Commitments to a State Mental Hospital." *Social Problems* 14:26–35.

Scheff, T. J. 1964. "Social Conditions for Rationality: How Urban and Rural Courts Deal with the Mentally Ill." *American Behavioral Scientist* 7:21–27.

Sommer, R. 1959. "Patients Who Grow Old in a Mental Hospital." *Geriatrics* 14:581–590.

Stanton, A. H., and M. S. Schwartz. 1954. *The Mental Hospital.* New York: Basic Books.

Steinfeld, G. J. 1970. "Parallels Between the Pathological Family and the Mental Hospital: A Search for a Process." *Psychiatry* 33:36–55.

NONVERBAL COMMUNICATION

Birdwhistell, Ray. 1952. *Introduction to Kinesics.* Mimeographed. Louisville, Ky.: University of Louisville.

Critchley, M. 1939. *The Language of Gesture.* London & New York: Edward Arnold, Longmans Green.

Efron, D. 1941. *Gesture and Environment.* New York: King's Crown Press.

Goffman, E. 1956. "The Nature of Deference and Demeanor." *American Anthropologist* 58:473–502.

————. 1963. *Behavior in Public Places.* New York: The Macmillan Company.

————. 1967. *Interaction Ritual.* New York: Doubleday & Company, Inc.

Hall, E. T. 1959. *The Silent Language.* Garden City, New York: Doubleday & Co.

————. 1966. *The Hidden Dimension.* Garden City, New York: Doubleday & Co.

Krout, M. H. 1935. "Autistic Gestures." *Psychological Monograph* 46, no. 208.

LaBarre, W. 1947. "The Cultural Basis of Emotions and Gestures." *Journal of Personality* 16:49–68.

Maranon, G. 1950. "The Psychology of Gesture." *Journal of Nervous and Mental Diseases* 112:469–497.

Paget, R. A. S. 1937. "Gesture Language." *Nature,* London, 39.

Weiss, P. 1943. "The Social Character of Gestures." *Philosophical Review* 52:182–186.

OPIATES

Akers, R. L., R. L. Burgess and W. T. Johnson. 1968. "Opiate Use, Addiction and Relapse." *Social Problems* 15:459–469.

Chein, I., D. L. Gerard, R. S. Lee, E. Rosenfeld. 1964. *The Road to H: Narcotics, Delinquency, and Social Policy.* New York: Basic Books, Inc.

Feldman, H. W. 1968. "Ideological Supports to Becoming and Remaining a Heroin Addict." *Journal of Health and Social Behavior* 9:131–139.

Hughes, H. M., ed. 1961. *The Fantastic Lodge.* Boston: Houghton Mifflin Company.

Lindesmith, A. R. 1968, *Addiction and Opiates.* Chicago: Aldine Publishing Company.

_____. 1965. *The Addict and the Law.* Bloomington: Indiana University Press.

Ray, M. 1961. "The Cycle of Abstinence and Relapse Among Heroin Addicts." *Social Problems* 9:132–140.

Volkman, R., and D. R. Cressey. 1963. "Differential Association and the Rehabilitation of Drug Addicts." *American Journal of Sociology* 69:129–142.

Winick, C. 1961. "Physician Narcotic Addicts." *Social Problems* 9:174–186.

THE POLICE

Banton, M. 1964. *The Policeman in the Community.* New York: Basic Books, Inc.

Bittner, E. 1967. "Police Discretion in Emergency Apprehension of Mentally Ill Persons." *Social Problems* 14:3, pp. 278–292.

Buckner, H. T. 1967. *The Police.* Unpublished Ph.D. dissertation, University of California at Berkeley.

_____. 1970. "Transformations of Reality in the Legal Process." *Social Research* 37:88–101.

Harney, M. L., and J. C. Cross. 1962. *The Informer in Law Enforcement.* Springfield, Ill.: Charles C. Thomas, Publisher.

Lafave, W. R. 1965. *Arrest: The Decision to Take a Suspect into Custody.* Boston: Little, Brown & Company.

Mulbar, H. 1951. *Interrogation.* Springfield, Ill.: Charles C. Thomas, Publisher.

Piliavin, I., and S. Briar. 1964. "Police Encounters with Juveniles." *American Journal of Sociology* 70:206–214.

Schwartz, R. D., and J. H. Skolnick. 1962. "Two Studies of Legal Stigma." *Social Problems* 10:133–142.

Silver, A. 1967. "The Demand for Order in Civil Society: A Review of Some Themes in the History of Urban Crime, Police, and Riot," in *The Police: Six Sociological Essays.* Edited by D. Bordua. New York: John Wiley & Sons, Inc., pp. 1–24.

Skolnick, J. H. 1966. *Justice Without Trial.* New York: John Wiley & Sons, Inc.

_____, and J. R. Woodworth. 1967. "Bureaucracy, Information and Social

Control: A Study of a Morals Detail," in *The Police: Six Sociological Essays.* Edited by D. Bordua. New York: John Wiley & Sons, Inc., pp. 99–136.

Sudnow, D. 1965. "Normal Crimes: Sociological Features of the Penal Code in a Public Defender Office." *Social Problems* 12:255–276.

Westley, W. A. 1951. *The Police: A Sociological Study of Law, Custom and Morality.* Unpublished Ph.D. dissertation, University of Chicago.

───────. 1953. "Violence and the Police." *American Journal of Sociology* 59:34–41.

Wilson, O. W. 1963. *Police Administration.* New York: McGraw Hill Book Company.

PRISONS

Clemmer, D. 1958. *The Prison Community.* New York: Holt, Rinehart & Winston, Inc.

Cressey, D. R., ed. 1961. *The Prison: Studies in Institutional Organization and Change.* New York: Holt, Rinehart & Winston, Inc.

Garabedian, P. G. 1963. "Social Roles and the Process of Socialization in the Prison Community." *Social Problems* 11:139–152.

Glaser, D. 1964. *The Effectiveness of a Prison and Parole System.* Indianapolis, Ind.: The Bobbs-Merrill Co., Inc.

Sykes, G. M. 1965. *The Society of Captives: A Study of a Maximum Security Prison.* New York: Atheneum.

Ward, D. A., and G. Kassebaum. 1965. *Women's Prison: Sex and Social Structure.* Chicago: Aldine Publishing Company.

PROSTITUTION

Bryan, J. H. 1965. "Apprenticeships in Prostitution." *Social Problems* 12:287–297.

───────. 1966. "Occupational Ideologies and Individual Attitudes of Call Girls." *Social Problems* 13:441–450.

Davis, K. 1962. "Prostitution," In *Contemporary Social Problems.* Edited by R. Merton and R. Nisbit. New York: Harcourt, Brace and World, Inc.

Gagnon, J. H. and W. Simon, eds. 1967. *Sexual Deviance.* New York: Harper & Row, Publishers.

Greenwald, H. 1958. *The Call Girl.* New York: Ballantine Books.

Hirschi, T. 1962. "The Professional Prostitute." *Berkeley Journal of Sociology* 7:33–49.

Maurer, D. 1939. "Prostitutes and Criminal Argots." *American Journal of Sociology* 44:546–560.

McManus, V. 1960. *Not for Love.* New York: Dell Publishing Company, Inc.

Rolph, C. H., ed. 1955. *Women of the Streets.* London: Seeker and Warburg.

Winick, C. 1962. "Prostitutes' Clients' Perception of the Prostitute and Themselves." *International Journal of Social Psychiatry* 8:289–297.

Wolfenden Report, The. 1964. Report of the Committee on Homosexual Offenses and Prostitution. New York: Lancer Books.

SKID ROW

Anderson, N. 1961. *The Hobo: The Sociology of the Homeless Man.* Chicago: University of Chicago Press.

Peterson, W. J., and M. A. Maxwell. 1958. "The Skid Row Wino." *Social Problems* 5:308–316.

Rooney, F. 1961. "Group Processes Among Skid Row Winos: A Re-evaluation of the Undersocialization Hypothesis." *Quarterly Journal of Studies on Alcohol* 22:444–460.

Straus, R. and R. G. McCarthy. 1951. "Non-addictive Pathological Drinking Patterns of Homeless Men." *Quarterly Journal of Studies on Alcohol* 12:601–611.

Suttles, G. D. 1968. *The Social Order of the Slum.* Chicago: University of Chicago Press.

Wallace, S. E. 1965. *Skid Row as a Way of Life.* Totowa, N.J.: Bedminster Press, Inc.

THOUGHT REFORM AND CONVERSION

Catton, W. R., Jr. 1957. "What Kind of People Does a Religious Cult Attract?" *American Sociological Review* 22:561–566.

Empey, L. T., and J. Rabow. 1961. "The Provo Experiment in Delinquency Rehabilitation." *American Sociological Review* 25:679–695.

Frank, J. D. 1961. *Persuasion and Healing: A Comparative Study of Psychotherapy.* Baltimore, Md.: The Johns Hopkins Press.

Harris, S. 1953. *Father Divine, Holy Husband.* New York: Doubleday and Company, Inc.

Kiev, A., ed. 1964. *Magic, Faith and Healing.* New York: The Macmillan Company.

LaBarre, W. 1962. *They Shall Take Up Serpents.* Minneapolis: University of Minnesota Press.

Lifton, R. J. 1963. *Thought Reform and the Psychology of Totalism: A Study of "Brainwashing" in China.* New York: W. W. Norton & Company, Inc.

Lofland, J. 1966. *Doomsday Cult: A Study of Conversion, Proselytization and Maintenance of Faith.* Englewood Cliffs, N.J.: Prentice-Hall, Inc.

————, and R. Stark. 1965. "Becoming a World-Saver: A Theory of Conversion to a Deviant Perspective." *American Sociological Review* 30:862–875.

Sargant, W. 1957. *Battle for the Mind.* London: William Heinemann Ltd.

Schein, E. H. 1961. *Coercive Persuasion.* New York: W. W. Norton & Company, Inc.

————. 1956. "The Chinese Indoctrination Program for Prisoners of War." *Psychiatry* 19:149–172.

Schein, E. H. 1957. "Reaction Patterns to Severe, Chronic Stress in American Army Prisoners of War of the Chinese." *Journal of Social Issues* 13:21–30.

Yablonsky, L. 1965. *The Tunnel Back: Synanon.* New York: The Macmillan Company.

TRANSVESTISM

Benjamin, H. 1966. *The Transsexual Phenomenon.* New York: The Julian Press.

————. 1954. "Transsexualism and Transvestism as Psycho-somatic and Somato-psychic Syndromes." *American Journal of Psychotherapy* VIII.

Brown, D. G. 1961. "Transvestism and Sex-Role Inversion," *The Encyclopedia of Sexual Behavior.* Edited by A. Ellis and A. Abarbanel. New York: Hawthorne Books, Inc.

Buckner, H. T. 1970. "The Transvestic Career Path." *Psychiatry* 33:381–389.

Gebhard, P. H., J. H. Gagnon, W. B. Pomeroy, and C. V. Christenson. 1965. *Sex Offenders: An Analysis of Types.* New York: Harper & Row, Publishers.

Hirschfeld, M., M.D. 1948. *Sexual Anomalies.* New York: Emerson Books, Inc.

Kinsey, A. C., W. B. Pomeroy, and C. C. Martin. 1953. *Sexual Behavior in the Human Female.* Philadelphia: W. B. Saunders Company.

Kraft-Ebbing, R. von. 1922. *Psychopathia Sexualis.* Brooklyn, N.Y.: Physicians & Surgeons Book Co.

WHITE-COLLAR CRIME

Cressey, D. R. 1950. "The Criminal Violation of Financial Trust." *American Sociological Review* 15:738–743.

————. 1953. *Other People's Money*. New York: The Macmillan Company.

Geis, G., ed. 1968. *White-Collar Criminal: The Offender in Business and the Professions*. New York: Atherton Press.

————. 1967. "White Collar Crime: The Heavy Electrical Equipment Antitrust Cases of 1961." In *Criminal Behavior Systems: A Typology*. Edited by M. B. Clinard and R. Quinney. New York: Holt, Rinehart & Winston, Inc., pp. 139–151.

Sutherland, E. H. 1949. *White-Collar Crime*. New York: Holt, Rinehart & Winston, Inc.

————. 1940. "White-Collar Criminality." *American Sociological Review* 5:1-12.

index